WITHDRAWN
AUGUSTANA COLLEGE
LIBRARY

Love in a Green Shade

Love in a Green Shade

IDYLLIC ROMANCES
ANCIENT TO MODERN

❧ ❧

RICHARD F. HARDIN

University of Nebraska Press, Lincoln and London

Acknowledgment for
the use of previously published
material appears on page x.
© 2000 by the University of Nebraska
Press. All rights reserved. Manufactured
in the United States of America. ∞
Library of Congress Cataloging-in-Publi-
cation Data. Hardin, Richard F. Love in a
green shade : idyllic romances ancient to
modern / Richard F. Hardin. p. cm.
Includes bibliographical references and
index. ISBN 0-8032-2394-3 (cloth: alk. paper) 1. Pastoral literature—History and
criticism. 2. Love stories—History and
criticism. 3. Romances—History and criticism. 4. Literature—Greek influences.
5. Country life in literature. 6. Longus.
Daphnis and Chloe. 7. Love in literature.
8. Longus—Influence. I. Title.
PN56.P3H37 2000
809′.93321734—dc21
99-36931
CIP

For Virginia

CONTENTS

	List of Illustrations	viii
	Preface	ix
1	Idyllic Romance	1
2	Renaissance Rediscoveries	25
3	Wit and Innocence	52
4	Paul, Virginie, and George	79
5	Ladies of Maine	107
6	Spanish Idylls	135
7	British Naturists	161
8	Innocence and Radical Innocence	192
9	Points of Departure	215
	Notes	243
	Works Cited	261
	Index	275

ILLUSTRATIONS

Daphnis and Chloe Embrace 82
Daphnis and Chloe Sitting under an Oak Embracing 83

PREFACE

Although no previous book exists concerning the influence of *Daphnis and Chloe* in literature, such is not the case with my parallel subject, the genre of idyllic or pastoral romance. Besides the many treatments of pastoral in Renaissance studies, several welcome books on the Victorian idyllic tradition have appeared. An interest in locale predominates in W. J. Keith's *Regions of the Imagination: The Development of British Rural Fiction*, a work that examines a body of fiction from which imaginary "pastoral" regions are excluded. Shelagh Hunter's *Victorian Idyllic Fiction: Pastoral Strategies*—strongly influenced by William Empson's idea of the complex in the simple—is valuable for its treatment of George Sand's influence and the "village sketch" tradition. In *Idyllic Realism from Mary Russell Mitford to Hardy*, P. D. Edwards analyzes a tradition of "realistic idyll" that "not merely turns potential tragedy and heroic passion into comedy but implicitly denies the existence of the tragedy and heroic passion, whether in art or in life" (3). In a more general discussion, pastoral narrative—especially *Daphnis and Chloe*—profitably occupies the last two chapters of Paul Alpers's *What Is Pastoral?*

For my understanding of *Daphnis and Chloe*'s reception history, I owe great debts to Giles Barber's absorbing bibliographical study, "*Daphnis and Chloe*": *The Markets and Metamorphoses of an Unknown Bestseller*, and to Maria Ferrini's *Bibliografia di Longo, "Dafni e Cloe."* I also use certain lists of works that evidence Longus's influence in literature and other forms of art from the past two centuries, the fullest inventory being the "Nachleben" appendix to Otto Schönberger's edition, *Hirtengeschichten von Daphnis und Chloe*. Margaret Anne Doody's *The True Story of the Novel* has focused long-needed attention on the Greek romance backgrounds of the "novel"; I am indebted, as she is, to David Konstan for drawing attention to the "sexual symmetry" in all those Greek narratives, which are so different from the male- or female-centered early modern romances and novels.

My method of citation and documentation varies according to the kinds of works that I cover. I use Paul Turner's Penguin translation of *Daphnis and Chloe* for all quotations except in cases where I find it helpful to give my own literal translation, and for those, I provide the Greek in brackets. The parenthetical citations refer to book and chapter numbers in Turner, which are the same as those in the Greek text of Longus that I use, Michael D. Reeve's Teubner edition. With longer prose works that exist in several editions, I provide both chapter and page numbers in the parenthetical citations. Translations from foreign languages are mine, unless otherwise indicated.

Supporting this project, the University of Kansas provided me with a research grant, a sabbatical leave, and a paid leave to study Greek. The Hall Center for the Humanities helped with travel funds. Michael Shaw and Jean Valk were splendid teachers, tolerant of someone who wanted more Greek in order to read an author like Longus rather than (or at least before) the Bible or Homer. Vernon Chamberlin taught me a great deal about Spanish literature; my chapter on Spain builds on our jointly authored "Pepita Jiménez and the Romance Tradition," *Anales Galdosianos* 25 (1990): 69–75. I thank the editors of this journal for allowing me to use part of this article in chapter 6. Along the way I have received helpful advice and information from my Kansas colleagues Robert Anderson, David Bergeron, Al Habegger, Rob Melton, Alan Pasco, Elizabeth Schultz, and Chester Sullivan. I also valued the comments of Robert Evans of Auburn University and the help I received from the staffs of the British Library and the Cambridge University Library and especially from Rob Melton and the staffs of the University of Kansas libraries. Many scholars and critics have aided my understanding, but I am particularly indebted to Northrop Frye's *The Secular Scripture: A Study of the Structure of Romance*, a fact that will be obvious in my many citations of his name.

Love in a Green Shade

Idyllic Romance

THE LITERARY TRADITION

Love stories take place in every kind of setting, but stories of love in nature belong to a special class. When young people fall in love in the country, when they discover themselves and their humanity in a selfless passion, their story is often called an idyll. I wish to explore a history of this kind of story, which I call "idyllic romance." At the same time, I wish to trace the original, or earliest survivor, of the species—*Daphnis and Chloe*—as it leaves its tracks through literature from the Renaissance to the twentieth century.

The term "idyllic romance" skirts the overlapping and much trampled territory of "pastoral"—and with reason. First, idyllic romance involves marriage, of little interest to Theocritus and Virgil, the models for most theories of pastoral. Idyllic romance, moreover, has drawn a vast readership, both serious and casual, in the English language. A recent investigator, Giles Barber, calls *Daphnis and Chloe* "an unknown best seller," tracing its continuous publication in English and other languages. Derivations like *The Tempest*, *Paul et Virginie*, and *O Pioneers!* show the endurance of the idyllic romance; million-plus sellers such as Henry De Vere Stacpoole's *The Blue Lagoon*, Louis Hémon's *Maria Chapdelaine*, and Harold Bell Wright's *Shepherd of the Hills* show the form's wide appeal. Someone with ambition who wants to make some money should, right now, be writing a novel in which two young lovers discover themselves in nature.

Nature's usual uneventfulness, of course, will do little for the plot. Shakespeare's Touchstone knew the limitations of country life: "In respect that it is solitary, I like it very well; but in respect that it is private, it is a very vile life. Now in respect it is in the fields, it pleaseth me well; but in respect it is not in the court, it is tedious" (AYL 3.2.15–18). If this is so, then Sarah Orne Jewett's *A Marsh Island* and Willa Cather's *O Pioneers!* are conceived in tedium. Cather's Alexandra, on resuming her friendship with Carl, tells him, "You have lived where things move so fast, and everything is slow here. . . . Our lives are like the years, all made up of weather and crops and cows" (121). What I am calling idyllic romance shares this placidness with nature—a quality that, like total darkness, modern people can experience only with deliberate effort. Characters grow but in a scarcely perceptible process, the way the land around them changes through the seasons. *Daphnis and Chloe* is the supreme instance of a story of beginnings spun out from the still center of the seasonal cycles that organize it.

Often in this kind of story, boy does not even meet girl, since they know each other already. How can so simple a formula produce such successful books? The question insinuates a premise not to be granted, the priority of conflict, of plot, in fiction. "I can't write plots," Willa Cather once said. "Sometimes I wish I could, but we have to do with what we have. I don't see life in terms of action. Persons like me who see it in terms of thought and imagery would best keep away from suspense. It's design they want, not conflict" (Mary Ellen Chase, "Portraits" 512). Thought, imagery, design—these chief constituents of most idyllic narratives explain why their style so often tends toward the lyric and meditative.

In the half-century before Cather, idyllicism sometimes reacted against the exciting, violent popular fiction in vogue. The narrator of Harriet Beecher Stowe's *The Pearl of Orr's Island* pauses to admit that the Maine islanders' dutiful, God-fearing way of life "is no great recommendation to a world gaping for sensation and calling for something stimulating" (9). A drunken public rages for the "stimulants" of mass-market fiction. Stowe's preface to the periodical version of this novel says, "our characters have no strange and wonderful adventures of outward life, and the changes that occur to them and the history they make is that of the inner life, that 'cometh not with observation'" (Fields and C. E. Stowe 287). Stowe understands keenly the trap of false idyllicism for those seeking the inner life through nature. It is revealing that she was the first (says the OED) to use the word "idyllic," which appears in her antislavery novel *Dred: A Tale of the Great Dismal Swamp* (1856).

In chapter 29, "The Troubadour," a southern gentleman remarks to a southern lady, Anne Clayton, "But how perfectly cool and inviting you look. Really, quite idyllic!" (Dred 407). It is a calculated coinage. A few pages earlier, sensible Anne hears flighty Nina recall: "When I was a child, I remember there was an old torn translation of a book called Gesner's Idyls, that used to lie about the house; and I used to read in it most charming little stories about handsome shepherds, dressed in white, playing on silver and ivory flutes; and shepherdesses, with azure mantles and flowing hair; and people living on such delightful things as cool curds and milk and grapes and strawberries and peaches; and there was no labor, and no trouble, and no dirt, and no care" (402). Even as Nina speaks, a black slave waits to clean up after her. Stowe implies that the idealism typified in the eighteenth-century prose-poems of the Swiss Salomon Gessner falsifies human actualities. Such Arcadianism seems to belong to a time before the social crisis that preoccupies Wordsworth's generation, before European humanity supposedly lost authentic nature.

A writer who anticipates Stowe's movement from political to pastoral fiction—whose admiring review of *Uncle Tom's Cabin*, in fact, guaranteed Stowe's European reputation—is George Sand. Her rustic novels aim at restoring tranquillity after the political turmoil of 1848, just as Stowe, in her *Pearl* of 1861 hopes to provide solace in the midst of her own country's woe. Sand retains the classical comic vision of rustic life, however, in contrast with the melancholy sentiment of Bernardin de Saint-Pierre, Stowe, and most later authors. Nowadays some critics dismiss Sand's idyllic romances, in particular *François le Champi* and *La Petite Fadette*, as *too* happy—safe schoolroom reading, without the dangerous ideology of her more substantial novels (see Dickenson 150). Yet in the preface to *La Petite Fadette*, a novel that began serialization in December 1848, Sand describes idyllic writing as in itself a political act: "In times when evil comes from men's misunderstanding and hating each other, the mission of the artist is to celebrate sweetness, confidence, and friendship, and thus to remind hardened or discouraged men, that pure morals, tender sentiments, and pristine justice still exist, or can exist in this world. . . . Better a story to put little children to sleep without fear and suffering, than the spectacle of real evils augmented and darkened still more by the colors of fiction" (16).[1] Abjuring "the colors of fiction" Sand recalls Stowe on the "stimulating." With her love affairs and unconventional behavior, Sand may seem light years away from Stowe's moral universe, but in a furious time she shares Stowe's aim of administering rest-therapy to a public desperately needing "sweetness, confidence, and friendship."

In Germany a generation before Sand, the "idyllic" acquired new status with Schiller's famous discussion in *Naive and Sentimental Poetry*. Although he does not precisely define it, Schiller uses the term to refer to literature concerned with human innocence in the state of nature: Theocritus but also *Paradise Lost* and, by extension, what I am calling idyllic romance. Schiller assigns idylls to "sentimental" rather than "naive" poets—two types who differ in their perspective on humanity's relation to nature. As Julias A. Elias explains it in his introduction to Schiller's essays, the naive poet (Homer or Shakespeare), with an apparently unreflecting spontaneity, "*is* nature"; the sentimental poet "*seeks* nature"—the "ideal unity" of nature —"because it is lacking in himself" (25).[2] The idyll is the characteristic form of sentimental poets; it aims to hold in suspension the ideal and the actual, nature and culture.

As a contrast Schiller poses the other two forms of the sentimental: elegy, where nature is lost and the ideal is unattainable; and satire, where nature is alienated and the ideal is opposed to the actual. If Schiller scarcely mentions the Renaissance, when both pastoral and Longus were rediscovered and assimilated into the literary culture as never before, it may be because, despite all that period's Virgilian pastoral, the difficult balance of the "idyll" is rarely maintained during that age. Only at the end of the period does Schiller find his great exemplar, *Paradise Lost*, "the most beautiful idyll known to me of the sentimental type. Here nature is noble, spiritual, at once full of range and depth, the highest meaning of humanity clothed in the most graceful form" (*Naive* 152).

To *Paradise Lost* Schiller might have added Shakespeare's romances. These adapt idyllic stories that confront what he calls the "opposition between actuality and the ideal" (153). True, he thinks of Shakespeare as a naive poet whose oneness with nature makes his heart unknowable (107), but he was perhaps too greatly influenced by the myth of Shakespeare the "untutored genius" to think otherwise. Especially when illuminated by an acquaintance with *Daphnis and Chloe*, these late plays also seem preoccupied with the idyllic elements of nature, the feminine, and innocence.

When Sand's admirer Matthew Arnold describes her great theme as "the sentiment of the ideal life, which is none other than man's normal life as we shall some day know it" (240), he sounds as if he has been reading Schiller. This impossible-sounding reconciliation of the normal and ideal, Schiller's "actual and ideal," constitutes one goal of idyllic romance, which exists in a place, Edenic or just natural, where the ideal *is* the normal. One of the most sentimental writers in Schiller's sense is W. H. Hudson, who in his studies of nature is capable of both mysticism and scientific rigor. Hudson writes in *The Purple Land* that happiness "was with us once and ours, but we despised it, for it was only the old common happiness which Nature gives to all her children" (261). His *Green Mansions* both recovers nature and, in elegiac fashion, ponders its loss.

Thomas Hardy assumes the disappearance of "common happiness" in his best-known novels, but he anchors the early and less-discussed *Under the Greenwood Tree* on precisely this quality. Then comes *Far from the Madding Crowd*, which P. D. Edwards calls the first major English novel of its century to "tip the balance between English idyllicism and French realism decisively towards French realism" (148). The term "French realism" is adequate to literary history, but is *Under the Greenwood Tree* less "real" than *Far from the Madding Crowd* or *Tess*? Real people, like the actual shepherd whom Hudson portrays in *A Shepherd's Life*, can live idyllic lives without great tragedy or personal bitterness.

In the interviews that shape Hudson's book, an old shepherd does not hide the cruelties accompanying real English pastoral life. Unfeeling masters exploit workers, even children; kangaroo-court justice hangs men "maddened by want" for stealing sheep (218). Yet this real shepherd, knowing the pains of the life, can look back on his ninety years with joy: "I don't say that I want to have my life again, because 'twould be sinful. We must take what is sent. But if 'twas offered to me and I was to choose my work, I'd say, Give me my Wiltsheer Downs again and let me be a shepherd there all my life long" (332). The speaker seems never to have experienced the starvation and injustice known to some other Wiltshire rustics, perhaps because he has a touch of the divine *tychê* of Longus's shepherds.

John J. Winkler—having found that the love-leading-to-marriage story first entered the West with the Greek romances—concedes that it is "one particularly fine fantasy, which life sometimes resembles" ("Invention" 24). When life does resemble so neat and pleasant a story, practicing novelists tend to stay away. Arnold Weinstein has declared that "the novel is the ideal genre to depict failed marriages" (42). "There are so few complacent relationships between lovers on any level," says Thomas McGuane, "and if there were, they'd be inappropriate for fiction. Fiction is not about stability" (15).

Unstable lives seldom join the ideal to the normal, but there is a literature, even a fiction, of stability.

Sand, her reputation now justifiably being saved from predatory biography and masculine condescension alike, deserves her fame in part because she recognized, in Julian Barnes's words, "as opposing, irreconcilable forces in art the search for 'la vérité idéale' and the study of 'la réalité positive.'" Barnes goes on to say that "these polarities were exemplified for her by *The Vicar of Wakefield* on the one side and *Les Liaisons dangereuses* on the other. In our own century we prefer Laclos to Goldsmith, but what is that the result of? Intellectual argument, the proven nature of the world, changing literary taste?" (12). The two novels mentioned constitute alternative possibilities that humanity had better always keep in view. Idyllic fiction looks toward the ideal, but it is no less lifelike for that.

Hardy must have deplored the reductive, otiose version of rural life propagated in some idyllic fiction. Had he read, in Marmontel's "Shepherdess of the Alps" or Harold Bell Wright's *Shepherd of the Hills*, that any inexperienced transient can take care of sheep, Hardy might have pointed to the example of Gabriel Oak, saving Bathsheba's bloated herd in *Far from the Madding Crowd*. Oak belongs to georgic, not pastoral, fiction: hard life-in-nature, not soft. In the storm scene in chapter 37, when Gabriel and Bathsheba work together to save the harvested sheaves, we see the effect of combining the theme of love with the georgic: "love's old dream of combining moral responsibility and the stunning force of the erotic" (Polhemus 240). The georgic, a category that Schiller neglects, revels in the human struggle with nature, while the idyll makes work part of the landscape, of the cycle of life in nature. When Daphnis has trouble with his animals, when they fall into a wolf pit, the work of saving them becomes the occasion for a love scene. Georgic novelists such as Knut Hamsun in *Growth of the Soil*, or Patrick White in *The Tree of Man*, or the North Carolina writer John Ehle in *The Land Breakers* celebrate the post-Edenic curse, even showing a certain contempt for those who seek to keep one foot in Eden.

Also countering the idyllic sensibility, besides the tragic and georgic versions of nature, is the historical moment of naturalism ("French realism") exemplified in Emile Zola's *La Faute de l'abbé Mouret* and *La Joie de vivre*, or in *La madre Naturaleza* by his demidisciple Emilia Pardo Bazán. Here are battles without victory. If Northrop Frye is right to claim that the novel parodies romance (39), nowhere is this relationship more evident than in the literary naturalists' subversion of idyllic benevolent nature. Naturalism of the Zola-Dreiser-Gissing sort furthered the modern belief in a nature seething with destructive forces and competing species. But this viewpoint may exaggerate the situation even more than its opposite. Joseph Meeker has urged that the proper study of mankind in nature requires comedy: "Evolution itself is a gigantic comic drama, not the bloody tragic spectacle imagined by the sentimental humanists of early Darwinism" (33).

With considerable support in recent science, Stephan Lackner's *Peaceable Nature* has worked to dislodge from the modern imagination the image of nature "red in tooth and claw." Lackner's evidence suggests, for one thing, that "only 5 percent of all animals are killed by other animals," not counting those killed by humans (12). Winged insects had the air to themselves for two hundred million years without predators, and "as far as diversification, stamina, and morphological progress are concerned, the insects did very well without being selectively eaten" (11). Even mating depends more on aesthetics than aggression: Grant's gazelles joust for the attention of females but never fight to the death (44). Television cannot sustain an audience with peaceable nature, so "filmmakers select combat, hunting, devouring of prey and compress these into a short time period, thereby falsifying the animal life they purport to present" (47). Still craving "stimulation," humans project their own destructive fantasies onto a mostly harmless natural world. If a true naturalism or realism would seem to require something more like idyllic than violent nature, then one might wish the image of human nature could be formed on this model.

When idyllic romances lack the expected happy ending, it is not always because of nature's cruelty. Hudson's Rima, one with nature even in death, falls victim to human ignorance and rage. The incestuous brother and sister of *La madre Naturaleza* violate society's norms because society has paid them no mind, has left them to the only mother they know. In a way, this novel is more about a society caught up in its own mythology than about a fall from innocence. Mary Ellen Chase's orphaned heroine in *Uplands* moves through loss and misfortune to complete a self-discovery that began with love. Again, her unhappiness is tied to human indifference that would mythologize her as a "fallen woman" needing a man's "salvation."

Several of these texts, including those by Hudson, Chase, and Pardo

Bazán, are unsettled by what de Rougemont calls "the inescapable conflict in the West between passion and marriage" (8). "Romance feeds on obstacles," writes the French moralist, "short excitations, and partings; marriage, on the contrary, is made up of wont, daily propinquity, growing accustomed to each other" (292). Yet romance-passion thrives not just in the atmosphere of stimulants. In *Paul et Virginie*, written in imitation of *Daphnis and Chloe*, the heroine, about to reunite with and marry the hero, drowns at sea rather than remove her heavy clothes and let her future husband see her naked. Nothing could be further from Longus's casual pagan sense of the body. Who told Virginie she would be naked? The secretiveness of romantic passion in a vexed civilization encumbers with artifice what is natural in love. Sand wrote one of her novels in response to her little son's plea for a story without love, so anguished was he after she read him *Paul et Virginie* (preface to *Les Maîtres mosaïstes*). The heroine of *Maria Chapdelaine* gets one chance at passionate fulfillment, and when that slips by, she determines her marriage purely on duty.

Almost all these stories, like *Daphnis and Chloe*, center on a couple, not a single character. More recent literature has countered the long vogue of male-centered struggles against nature with two or three decades of fiction —including popular romance (Radford 5)—about female-only self-discovery or self-loss in nature. But the 1900s are not the century of the couple and may even signal "the end of the novel of love." A recent study of love in literature concludes, "In the modern period a desire to fuse with a beloved did not disappear, but it was increasingly interpreted as an illusion, a failure, or a projection of oneself" (Kern 289).[3]

Psychology often claims that such fusion, or "participation mystique," must be transcended if the woman is to obtain "the destiny of separation that is consciousness" (Neumann 85). Yet romantic love exists in almost all cultures (as Jankowiak's collection of essays in *Romantic Passion* amply demonstrates)—a fact leading to the conclusion that "the sense of merging, the overcoming of existential loneliness [is] the core experience of passionate love, and surely its healthiest intoxicant" (Collins and Gregor 82). Feminist thought sometimes repudiates the quest for oneness as a purely masculine desire for "refusion with the mother." Therefore, so the theory goes, "men love and fall in love romantically, women sensibly and rationally"; moreover, "developmentally, men do not become as emotionally important to women as women do to men" (Chodorow 194, 197–98). Against this counterintuitive viewpoint, an anthropologist (quoting Simenon's definition of love as "being two in one") insists that "falling in love is an act of imagination" so that "to love 'for a reason' is not to love at all" (Lindholm 57, 66). The great love stories may not all be masculine fantasies.

Whether or not people ever fall in love "sensibly and rationally," support for the counterintuitive view exists in differences between idyllic romances by men and by women. With male authors, if the happy ending in marriage (occurring in Longus, Juan Valera, or Yukio Mishima) is impossible, the effect is likely to be devastating, as it is in Bernardin, Hudson, and Jeffers. By contrast, Jewett, Cather, and Chase show women able to bear loss more resignedly. As of this moment no one on earth can say whether men and women can love in the same way and, if they cannot, whether the difference is constitutional or conditioned.

After reading hundreds of love letters for her collection *The Book of Love*, Cathy N. Davidson confesses: "The more letters I read, the less I was able to generalize about female versus male ways of loving or expressing that love" (15). Carolyn Heilbrun validates a certain kind of fusion or oneness in her concept of "androgyny," allowing for male and female characteristics shared across the sexual divide. This "spirit of reconciliation between the sexes" entails "a full range of experience open to individuals who may, as women, be aggressive, as men, tender" (Heilbrun x). George Sand's rustic love stories work toward such reconciliation, as both men and women find their way to a transgendered humanity through the beloved.

Yet traces remain of the dual-protagonist idyllic romance in contemporary literature amid the prevalence of the strongly defined individual's love story. Instances are the horridly written yet popular *The Bridges of Madison County*, or John Updike's *Brazil*, or Ursula Le Guin's *The Beginning Place*. Le Guin's couple, the products of broken families and miserable homes, represent, in a fantasy setting, a return to natural beginnings. As in the first idylls, their return also marks a withdrawal into an inner landscape of imagination.

The canon of idyllic romance is not as well established as that of pastoral poetry. I exclude stories of initiation in nature with exclusively male or female protagonists; I also discount what I earlier called georgic fiction. Another close cousin to idyllic romance can be termed *pastourelle*, after the medieval French narrative type in which an aristocrat wanders abroad in the country and loves or seduces a country maid. In the Renaissance, for reasons yet to be seen, idyllic romance needs a pastourelle cover, as in Shakespeare's *The Winter's Tale* and in Spanish pastoral romances. A familiar modern variant of pastourelle is the "return to paradise" story (Melville's *Typee*, for instance) or that of the city-dweller falling in love during a country holiday (Wharton's *Summer*). Some of my examples are pastourelles played off against idylls in love triangles, such as Jewett's *Marsh Island* or Pardo Bazán's *La madre Naturaleza*, where an outsider interrupts a rustic romance. Some echoes seem less reverberating than others. Rumer Godden's *A Breath of Air* and Cyril Hume's screenplay *Forbidden Planet* foreground too exclusively, for my purposes, the utopian aspect of their source, Shakespeare's *Tempest*. Mishima's Longus-inspired *Sound of Waves*, however, touches all the right chords. Rather flat echoes such as Gessner's *Idylls* (of Longus) and Allan Ramsay's *Gentle Shepherd* (of *The Winter's Tale*) deserve mention but have perhaps lost much of their audience.

"Popular" fiction sometimes mingles here with its more reputable kindred. Stacpoole, prolific and prosperous in the earlier twentieth century, especially with his *Blue Lagoon* books, deserves to be seen in good company. Less so, perhaps, Harold Bell Wright, speaking to a segment of American readers who may still thrive. Besides making Wright a rich man, *The Shepherd of the Hills* has helped support a thriving Ozark tourist trade. Louis Hémon did not live to enjoy the profits from *Maria Chapdelaine*, but this book, too, mingles idyllicism with the cherished social mythology of its readership. Finally, echoes sound in many less-known authors: I have found especially appealing narratives by Mary Ellen Chase, Ramón Pérez de Ayala, and Jo-Ann Mapson. Hardly well known in modern fiction, they belong to the vast legion of good writers over the past century whom fame has kissed but not embraced.

THE FIRST IDYLLIC ROMANCE: *DAPHNIS AND CHLOE*

Romance *Daphnis and Chloe* certainly is, but it makes odd company with the other "Greek romances" of the first centuries AD. Unlike Heliodorus's *Ethiopian Story* it has a tight narrative structure and, most noticeably, foregrounds the operation of nature rather than luck, or tychê, in the plot. Most of the incidents lack adventure compared with the frequent sensational episodes of the other romances. The unidentified Longus, probably a rhetorician of the period known as the Second Sophistic, reveals a crafted style, wide literary learning, and an unusually sophisticated, self-conscious narrative technique.

He is especially conscious of his pastoralism. Manuscripts of Longus announce the beginning of the "pastorals" or "things of herdsmen," the *Poimenikôn*—a word the author applies to the names he gives his main characters, names that are *poimenika* (1.3, 6). Longus enjoys reminding readers they are in a fictional world, as when Pan, scolding the general who leads the army against Daphnis's people, says in effect that the general should behave more properly because he is in a love story: "you've stolen herds of oxen and goats and sheep that are under my care, you've dragged away from the altar a girl whom Love has chosen to make a story about" (2.27).

Because romance easily accommodates allegory, the heavily allusive, mythic quality of this story has led people to read it as a coded initiation text of a mystery religion, a discourse for and accessible only to initiates.[4] When Colin Still and others made the same case for *The Tempest* as an allegory of initiation, they unconsciously exposed the links between Shakespeare's play and the Greek romance.[5] To discuss *Daphnis and Chloe* as literature, we need not pick sides in the mystery religion controversy, except to say that it reads quite well as a love story. In a way, the painting viewed in the prologue, foretelling the story to come, answers the question of intention when Longus says it attracts both *iketai*, suppliants, and *theatai*, viewers (as in a theater); some may read it as allegory, some as love story.

An absorbing piece of archeology has proposed roots for this story in Sumerian texts such as "Dumuzi's Dream," a narrative poem in which the shepherd Dumuzi is pursued by demons. The motif of the sacred marriage and Philetas's sermon on love's power also may hark back to Sumerian literature (Anderson 6–14, 222–23). These origins suggest that, even if Longus is not consciously writing an allegory, his story may well be doing so—belonging to the same narrative family as the Genesis story of Adam and Eve. Such primal stories share with *Daphnis and Chloe* a fundamental interest in human nature at large in a natural world charged with supernatural power.

Longus knew Theocritus's idylls and must have been a confirmed disciple. Scholars find in the Daphnis-Dorcon singing contest a "mosaic of reminiscences" from the *Idylls*, which also contains names like Daphnis, Cleariste, and Philetas—the last, a sage counselor in both Longus and Theocritus (see G. Rohde and Bowie). Theocritus's poems came to be called *eidyllia*, either "little poems" or, more traditionally, "little pictures." In the minds of later idyll-writers the picture etymology requires foregrounding the visual element and has shaped readers' expectations for centuries. Longus has the Theocritean picturesqueness, of course, from his very first page: the description of a picture containing his story leads at once to a little picture of Mytilene. His prose may not be Theocritus's verse, but it has a crafted, lyric quality, with symmetry of phrasing, wordplay, and assonance.[6]

The artifice of the prose enhances the spontaneous joy in life that *Daphnis and Chloe* communicates even in translation. One of many amusing ironies occurs when the warring enemies in book 3 cancel their campaigns because "they find peace more profitable" (3.2). Pan's intervention has determined the outcome, of course, but human self-interest and common sense help. A cheerful confidence governs the feeling for the seasons and cycles of life. Like characters in a comedy, the lovers return at the end to their community to live happy lives as they, their foster and true parents—even the parasite, repenting his sexual predatoriness toward Daphnis—all join for the concluding feast. One thinks of the ending of Plautus's *Rudens*, where the characters welcome even the pimp Labrax in to supper. The ending foresees that despite their new wealth and new families, the pastoral lovers will always return to their rural haunts. With the discovery that the children's death-tokens have become birth-tokens, death itself recedes from the picture. Every genre mixes illusions with its truth, and the illusion of the idyllic romance conjures up a godlike continuity in stasis.

The grape harvesting scene at the beginning of book 2, anticipating many idyllic paintings and poems, sets human action in rhythm with the seasons. During later summer, literally "fruit time" [tês opôras], the narrator describes the panorama of human harvest-work viewing all the participants collectively: "Some were getting wine-presses ready, some were cleaning out wine jars, and some were weaving baskets. One man was busy with a small reaping-hook for cutting bunches of grapes, another with a stone for squeezing the juice out of the bunches, and another with a dry willow-shoot that had been pounded to shreds to provide torchlight by which the must could be drawn off during the night" (2.1). Like the picture of shepherds and foundlings in the prologue, this composition shifts from action to action, from groups to individuals ("some" to "one"), from time to time (day to night). In the next book when winter sets in, pastoral inactivity seems to freeze the lovers' passions until Daphnis manages his visit. With spring, while the goats and sheep take their "erotic leaps" [erôtikôtera pêdêmata], the young men go about "swollen" [sphrigôntes] with erections (3.13). The next "fruit time" comes with book 4 and the story's final harvest.

The schematic seasonal structure, a pronounced feature of many succeeding idyllic romances—*The Winter's Tale, Under the Greenwood Tree,* and *Luna de miel,* for example—represents but one kind of natural sympathy in the narrative. The romances also tell us that it is human nature to imitate nature. Both Daphnis's and Chloe's foster fathers, on discovering the infants, decide to care for them because of the care-giving animals' example. As the babies grow, they learn by imitating the animals, singing with the birds, dancing with the gamboling lambs (1.9). Philetas's pipes imitate the sounds of cattle, sheep, and goats (2.36).

Rustic characters, by the same token, often behave like animals. Villagers descend on the abusive Methymnean youths "like starlings or jackdaws" (2.17). Lycaenion lives up to her name, "she-wolf" [lykaina]; the predatory Dorcon waits to ambush Chloe in a wolf skin; Chloe swears that if she is not true to Daphnis, he should kill her "like a wolf" (2.39). When a sheepdog grabs Dryas's meat from the table, the herdsman "did what another dog would have done—dashed off in pursuit" (3.7). Lampis tramples the garden "like a pig" (4.7). Philetas's son Tityrus walks like a capering kid and runs like a fawn (2.32–33). The young couple, provided with natural rather than human models for conduct, receive an "education through nature from below," as Georg Rohde has put it (40). Yet at the same time the divine tutelage of the nymphs, Pan, Eros, and Dionysos also brings guidance from "above." In fact, nature and the divine are so intermingled here that "above and below" seem to lose all definition.

An animal vitality of feeling and a childlike spontaneity set Daphnis apart from "heroes" of other ancient modes of literature, particularly the epic. When Longus reemerges in the Renaissance, such qualities are either not appreciated or culturally invisible, to judge from the more conventional virtues of Renaissance swains. Daphnis attracts Chloe when he bathes in front of her, and yet he seems not entirely heroic to look at. In the "beauty contest" before Chloe, Dorcon lists his rival's shortcomings: he is short, beardless, "dark as a wolf," goat-smelly, and poor (1.16). Daphnis himself denies only the "smelly" part. Nor is emotional control Daphnis's forte. Helpless at Chloe's abduction, weeping over her loss, he faints with joy on seeing her return (2.30). Even at the end, if Chloe sheds tears when she thinks newly rich Daphnis will forget her, he himself weeps when he fears that Lampis has raped her. Such faintheartedness, not uncommon in Greek romance heroes, ill suits their counterparts in early modern romances.

Daphnis's character draws more from traditions of comedy than heroic literature. Active and resourceful, even when battered and frustrated, Daphnis combines traits of both the crafty slave and the young lover of new comedy.[7] His little speeches of consternation—when he worries about the effects of love or his chances of marrying Chloe—resemble the "whatever shall I do?" speeches of several Roman comic characters (the young wastrel in *Mostellaria* when he hears his father has returned; Aeschinus in his soliloquy in *Adelphoe*; Pamphilus at his wits' end over an unwanted marriage in *Andria*). Consider Daphnis's self-dialogue as he plans a winter visit to Chloe, trying to "invent some excuse," asking himself "what would be the most plausible thing to say" to her parents (3.6). Both Longus and the comic playwrights use such moments for suspense but also for sympathy and fellow-feeling in the audience, who will share memories of such social tight spots. This kind of "hero" cannot distance himself from us with conventional heroics. In Renaissance romance, when his type is replaced by a nobler sort of man, this effect of fellow-feeling diminishes. By the nineteenth century (though not in Sand, Hardy, and Valera) idyllic romances often lose utterly these original links with comedy, inclining toward the morose.

Since heroines are usually heard of but not seen in new comedy, Chloe's origins may lie elsewhere, partly in the long-suffering but adaptable women of other romances. Although younger than Daphnis, Chloe is more sensitive and thus is the first to feel love stirring in the scene where she washes Daphnis's back (1.13)—a scene that elicits the first love-complaint in the story ("There is something wrong with me these days, but I don't know what it is"). Chloe's foster father discovers her as an infant in the cave of the nymphs, a setting abundant with female symbolism—the nymphs' statues, the womblike cave, "hollow inside and rounded outside" (1.4), with grass growing thick and soft at the entrance. Chloe's aura of the transcendent feminine, particularly in her special relation with the nymphs, lends a measure of support to the claims for allegory.

During her capture Daphnis dreams that these goddesses try to console him, saying, "Chloe is a greater care to us than to you" [Chloês gar hêmin mallon ê soi melei] (2.23). In more distinctive ways, however, she resembles Daphnis, with his lively energy and a similar resourcefulness—for example, in saving Daphnis from the wolf pit by lowering to him her "breast band" (so Turner, 1.12, injecting an erotic foreshadowing, though *tainian* could mean "headband"). She is as eager as Daphnis to learn about lovemaking and contributes equally to their study sessions: "But Daphnis, haven't *you* noticed that the rams and the he-goats do it standing up, and the ewes and the she-goats have it done to them standing up?" (3.14). In fact, she complements and resembles Daphnis in so many ways that the identification or fusion of the two lovers seems a central point of the story.

This mutuality in love, so crucial to the meaning of this story, sets the Greek romances apart from other literature of love in antiquity. *Daphnis and Chloe* tells of two lovers' initiation together, not apart. Even Winkler, a critic who thinks Chloe is being introduced to the painful laws of a "phallocentric" society (*Constraints* 117), admits that "what is truly remarkable about *D&C* [*sic*] is the sensitive portrayal of the lovers' equality, confirmed by their later indifference to city living even when they are entitled to indulge in its freedoms" (114–15).[8] David Konstan makes a strong case for this "sexual symmetry" in the Greek romances: "What is especially surprising to the reader of the modern romantic novel is the extent to which the actions and reactions of the hero and heroine in the Greek novel are alike. Both tend to be represented as victims, both give way to tears, lamentations, and despair, sometimes in language that is all but identical" (54). Most readers seem to find the mutuality or symmetry principle especially evident in Longus's story, where "the lovers become mirror images of each other" (Montague 241). This was the one feature of the idyllic romance that Renaissance imitators, informed by their own cultural prejudices, seemed least able to imitate.

Beginning with the circumstances of abandonment and discovery, Longus frequently shows the two characters undergoing the same tychê, or fortune. As children they tend flocks together, sharing their daily lunch; they both learn to play the syrinx: "Altogether, you would have been more likely to see the sheep or goats separated from one another than Chloe separated from Daphnis" (1.10). Their foster fathers both dream the same dream on the same night about Eros's plans for the children. Both lovers suffer "much the same" [paraplêsia] from love (1.12). In a symbol of this mutual feeling, Chloe puts on Daphnis's clothes while he bathes (1.24)—(the scholar Keith McMahon tells me that lovers similarly don each other's clothes in eighteenth-century Chinese romances). After Eros says he will one day bring the two together as one [eis hen synagogô], they depart separately but have the same thoughts as they utter parallel love complaints in the first-person plural: "People who are in love feel pain, and so do we" (2.8). Each undergoes capture, then is mourned by the other. The first time they lie together kissing, they look "as if they had been tied together" (2.11).

With Lycaenion comes a first-time break in the lovers' closeness, since Daphnis must afterward keep the great secret from Chloe. But Lycaenion, not Daphnis, is the sexual exploiter here. Naive in his seduction, delighted at the outcome, Daphnis shudders like a proper suitor when the city woman suggests that he do this with Chloe where no one can hear her scream with pain (3.19). The she-wolf Lycaenion typifies animal hit-and-run love in nature, while Daphnis, exercising restraint out of consideration for Chloe, shows a different kind of love. Just outside the protection of the nymphs lies a cold world of selfish, indiscriminate appetite, the same world that abandoned Daphnis and Chloe in their infancy.

Yet humans belong to nature also. The Echo myth (3.23) deals with the imitativeness and interplay among different orders of being, one of many instances of humans, gods, or animals imitating each other. Longus uses "echo" in several crucial contexts: Chloe answers Daphnis like an echo when he swears he is not deceiving her (3.11); Philetas praises Echo because she used to repeat his calls for Amaryllis (2.7). Hints of two Pan stories, of Echo and Syrinx, appear in one phrase when Dorcon, about to die, tells how his cattle have learned to follow the "panpipe's echo" [êcho syriggos]. Later Echo's mangled parts, lying hidden in the earth, continue to sing, to "imitate" [mimeitai] sounds of men, gods, musical instruments, and wild beasts. The singing parts "even imitate Pan when he plays his pipe," and Pan goes running over the hills trying to discover who is echoing him. Had this story stopped with Pan's revenge, it would constitute a mere caution against unresponsiveness to Eros. The remainder celebrates a spiritual beauty transcending death in nature. Music, beginning as an echo or imitation of natural sounds, elevates and perfects nature just as human art does in the gardens of Philetas or Dionysophanes.

Daphnis and Chloe combines the human, animal, and divine in an intricate network of correspondences; similarly, male and female become one—a theme widely dispersed in the ancient world, from Genesis to the fable told by Aristophanes in Plato's *Symposium*. The Sanskrit phrase *eko bhu* is said to mean both "become one" and "be married" (Huxley 110). If there is a mystery-religion allegory in this narrative, it surely refers in part to this theme of fusion. Earlier, Roman love elegy identified love with mere desire and appetite (Lindholm 58). Contemporary with Longus, however, Christianity incorporated the Genesis concept of two-as-one (see Mark 10.6–8), securing in the West the view that, by joining male and female, marriage aims, in Mircea Eliade's words, to "integrate internally the complete human image, that is to say the divine and original image" (102). The reasons for Longus's "unclassical" attitude toward love have been located in the historical moment of his romance, the age of Hellenistic and Roman culture when, Eliade continues, "a cultural force not unlike that of sensibility in the eighteenth century, was pacifying and softening the erotic relations of the sexes" (102).

A French scholar, Paul Veyne, similarly concludes that there occurred during the first century AD, "un grand événement ignoré," a transformation of "relations sexuelles et conjugales" (quoted in Hagstrum 118) independent of Christianity but identical to the future Christian marriage ethic (Hagstrum 94).[9] For the most part, before the period of the Greek romances, "the coincidence of eros and *gamos* was not a privileged norm, not an important and sought-after ideal"—a fact that lends support to the view that romance itself is "a resident alien in Greek culture" hailing from the Near East (Winkler "Invention" 29, 35). Aristide Maillol's images of Daphnis and Chloe duplicate the lovers' facial features as if to recognize their oneness (see pp.82–83).

The isolation of woman and man makes Longus's story not quite a "novel" as the term is now used. The characters seem to exist in a social vacuum; as Bruce MacQueen observes, they alone are Arcadian, while the other characters are typical rustics (162). The cast contains other youths, such as the rivals Dorcon and Lampis and the nameless males who admire

Chloe and go about "swollen" in the springtime. But no boy or girl friends appear, no society of adolescents who in the usual course of things would have settled all the couple's questions about lovemaking. Longus establishes early that the foster parents give his couple special treatment because of their seemingly high birth: they enjoy better food and an education in letters. Yet this does not fully explain the absence of playmates, confidantes, and other young couples who populate the novels of Sand, Hardy, and Mishima. The answer must lie in these works' concentration upon the couple alone, while the two young lovers retain some of the solitude of their mythic antecedents. The resulting thinness of social texture helps give the story its often-noted fairy-tale quality.

The nature of the couple's love resists easy explanation, however, if only because *eros* and *amor* are such elusive terms in antiquity. Daphnis and Chloe experience not just the fugitive, painful love of Sappho and Propertius, though that is included. They have never heard the word *eros* before they meet Philetas. Chloe swears to "love" Daphnis both alive and dead, but uses the verb *stergô* (2.39), which means "to have a natural affection for," as for a mother or brother. The brother-sister relationship (they grow up as constant companions despite having different families) clings to the idyllic romance long afterward (*Cymbeline, Paul et Virginie, The Pearl of Orr's Island, La madre Naturaleza, The Blue Lagoon, Luna de miel, Le Blé en herbe*). Just as no one can read the names of the nymphs on their statues (1.8) and people know the goddesses only as sensory images, so the lovers do not know what their feeling is called (1.13, 15) or the name of the "disease" love brings (1.18). As in Eden, innocence is ignorance, but the defect lies in not knowing words rather than in not knowing right and wrong. Such defective innocence does more than anything else to distance the reader from the characters. The narrator's sophisticated slant intrudes as a constant reminder, sustaining this distance to the end.

ECHOES

Some idyllic romances follow Longus directly; others follow texts that may themselves lie at more than one remove. In Stowe's *Pearl of Orr's Island*, elements of *Daphnis and Chloe* survive through Shakespeare's *Tempest*. A father and daughter watch her husband's ship destroyed at sea. Later the daughter's little girl, now orphaned, discovers an old text of *The Tempest*. It begins to shape her perceptions of herself and her closest friend, raised with her as a brother, a boy who was washed up like Ferdinand in a later storm. The storm itself as an idyllic image begins with Longus, and Shakespeare augments its significance for Stowe (human-induced disorder, nature's providence despite her wrath). Additionally, storms in *Paul et Virginie* may influence Stowe, for the French novel was very well known in her society.

The echo continues. In Jewett's *Country of the Pointed Firs* a long-widowed sea-wife tells the narrator of her standing on a promontory to watch her husband's ship break up in a storm. Jewett greatly loved Stowe's work, especially *Pearl*, which had kindled her first hopes for a literary career. A few pages later, Jewett mentions a boat called the *Miranda*, perhaps thinking of Shakespeare. Still another, earlier resonance: Jewett planned one of her stories as an imitation of Theocritus, whom she greatly admired. She thus follows the poet whom Longus himself imitated, though she could easily have read Longus too. Jewett's younger disciples Cather and Chase acknowledge her mastery, but both had read *The Tempest* and Stowe's *Pearl*, along with the fiction of George Sand, particularly favored by Jewett. While Cather shifts the scene from Jewett's Maine coastland to her own prairie, the Maine-bred Chase, a Minnesota PhD with a strong classical background, introduces Thomas Hardy into the mix—Hardy, the subject of her dissertation, who had read Theocritus and whose *Under the Greenwood Tree* appropriates details that he himself may have found in Longus. Adding to these intertextualities, Chase injects a pastoral character named Colin, like Spenser's figure in book 6 of *The Faerie Queene*. That Colin, first met in *The Shepheardes Calender*, is cast in a story about a foundling named Pastorella, who resembles Chloe.

The family traits of these narratives are visible in their imagery. Heading the inventory of human images or "characters" are the foundlings themselves. The foundling raises questions about identity apart from either nature or nurture, deriving something from both but also remaining simply himself. This self has something divine about it, like the "genius" inherent in ancient ideas of the soul. Nature's helping role is perhaps best described by Wordsworth's "Intimations" ode:

> The homely Nurse [Earth, Nature] doth all she can
> To make her Foster-child, her Inmate Man,
>   Forget the glories he hath known,
> And that imperial palace whence he came.
>
> (lines 82–85)

Each foundling retains a mysterious otherness. Chloe possesses a spiritually charged beauty that draws down Pan's protection; it is traceable neither to her parents (who seem distinguished only by their wealth) nor to her surroundings (other girls grow up in the same circumstances without divine notice). Daphnis is a more loving person than either his biological parent or his rustic foster father. Unlike his brother, who takes city ways for granted, he finds the parasite Gnatho loathsome. His father finds him too expensive to keep in infancy, yet against similar monetary obstacles Daphnis himself manages to win the object of his love.

The remaining characters include the usual landscape rustics but also urban people such as Lycaenion, Gnatho, and the wealthy parents—types imported from comedy who are reminders, sometimes unpleasant, of rusticity's opposite. There is usually a rival like Dorcon, a boorish yet occasionally lovable older youth. The rustic parents, temporary guardians of foundlings on the path to self-discovery, represent the transitoriness of the parent-child relationship. With their cheerfully selfish, cunning-peasant manners, they typify both the good and the bad in country life. The bad is summed up in the surly incivility of Lampis, "pond scum," who destroys the garden when he finds he can't have Chloe. Usually a sage appears, such as the love-wise Philetas with his all-important lecture in book 2: the love-lecture figures prominently in Tasso's *Aminta*, in early French operatic adaptations, and (morbidly) in *Paul et Virginie*. The narrative describes idyllic peace as though by contrast: natural dangers (the oft-mentioned but seldom-seen wolves) complement those in the human order—pirates. Pirates threaten the idyllic world, living on the unpredictable sea, the domain of passion and fortune, and not on the solid, fruitful earth.

As for the setting, the isolation necessary for this kind of love story explains the island locales of *Daphnis and Chloe, The Tempest, Paul et Virginie, Pearl*, and the novels of Jewett, Stacpoole, and Mishima. Akin to the island is the remote community or household in Sand, Hardy, Valera, Pardo Bazán, Cather, Chase, Hudson, Hémon, and Wright. Storms occur at significant moments, disrupting inner human nature or human harmony with external nature, as happens when Pan raises a storm against the Methymneans after they capture Chloe. In imitation of Longus, storm with shipwreck occurs in several Renaissance idyllic texts (*Menaphon, Winter's Tale, Tempest*). There are equally momentous storms in *Paul et Virginie*,

Pearl, Maria Chapdelaine, the Blue Lagoon books, *Uplands,* and *The Sound of Waves.*

Besides islands and storms, readers encounter certain natural features in the landscape: the garden, the singular tree, and the grotto or cave. Gardens since antiquity have called to mind the merging of nature with human art; when a garden is called a *paradeisos,* as in Longus, an allegorical reflex in biblically educated readers must follow, even if historically irrelevant. The cave can be an island within the island world of the romance, often carrying symbolism of the womb. Finally, the land contains pastoral animals that support the major idyllic theme of imitating nature. In Longus these include the sheep and goats, who teach humanity the essential idyllic virtues of peace (proverbial), kindness (in caring for the infants), and the spontaneous joy in their dancing and love-play. Equally important are the animals' roles in the cycle of work, of perfecting nature, so essential to the texture of this story—work that in Longus includes the grape harvests of 2.1 and 4.5.

Besides these images, a characteristic trope of idyllic romances is *ecphrasis,* the description of a work of art, an image of an image, like the painting Longus describes in his prologue. The belief that Theocritus's idylls were "little pictures" may explain not only the presence of pictures but pictorial style in such stories as *Marsh Island, The Country of the Pointed Firs, O Pioneers!,* and *The Shepherd of the Hills.* Sand begins one of her idylls, or *romans champêtres,* by comparing an actual rural scene with one in a Holbein engraving. Hardy subtitled *Under the Greenwood Tree* "A Rural Painting of the Dutch School." A cinerary urn described on the first page of *Green Mansions* effectively contains Hudson's story, just as the painting does that of Longus. Such work is "art" in that it both imitates nature's work and perfects it. Perdita's festive scene in *The Winter's Tale* (4.4) illustrates this principle while discussing it. Defining nature through art, or the country through the city, requires also admitting the complementarity of these opposites. Mytilene, with its canals and white stone bridges, looks more like an island than a city (1.1).

This joining of art and nature may explain the fondness for ecphrasis in Longus and many of his successors. Especially in a romance, as Wendy Steiner has observed, this practice of describing a work of art seems to point to the story itself as the "enlivening of a picture" (51), recording the progress of the story from nature or experience to text. A romance is "not merely the story of love but the story of love perceived" (48); hence the paradigm: the painting in Longus's prologue leads to an "exegesis" or interpretation, which becomes a story (196 n.11).[10]

A feature in the plots of many idyllic romances is the lapse of time, the hidden years, between infancy and adolescence. In Longus the second and main time-phase begins with the identical prophetic dreams of the two foster fathers. The coming of sexual knowledge and love brings the young people rebirth, a new identity, as though they were participants in some ritual initiation into adulthood. It does not take a student of psychoanalysis to recognize that this second birth starts the process of individuation. A notable difference between Longus's foundling-initiation story and that of most twentieth-century writers is the absence of a "fall" into knowledge of evil. This is irrelevant to *Daphnis and Chloe*, though habitual associations may lead some to describe this romance as a fall-from-innocence narrative.

As stories dependent on romance structures, these idylls share motifs familiar in romance of any sort: lost or concealed aristocracy, episodes of captivity, encounters with wild men or savages, prophetic dreams, metamorphoses. The night world or underground of traditional romance shows up in Shakespeare's romances as the domain of evil kings or queens and courtiers. From about 1800 on, the underworld is a somewhat displaced city or court: the France of Virginie's captivity, the count's gaming house in *Pepita Jiménez*, the Marquis of Ulloa's crumbling manor, the mean-spirited town of *O Pioneers!*, the mean-spirited church of *Under the Greenwood Tree*, the slave-owning pseudoaristocratic Florida of *Pearl*. More modern stories depict the underworld as some perversion of the natural: for example, Hudson's devious forest Indians, the similarly threatening islanders in Stacpoole, the menacing arctic winter in *Maria Chapdelaine* that kills the heroine's beloved.

Some points of similarity exist in narrative technique. Most texts are relatively brief, since the couple is the focus and the wedding is the end of the story. The feeling that nature somehow exists in sympathy with humans —John Ruskin's "pathetic fallacy," a theme either assumed or questioned in all these stories—explains a tendency, beginning in Longus, to organize the plot by seasons. The seasonal cycle lies at the heart of *The Winter's Tale* and helps shape the novels of Sand (*Fadette*), Valera, Stowe, Hardy, Jewett, Cather, Pérez de Ayala, and Chase. While the seasons form the *chronos*, the temporal background, of the novel, the critical time, the *kairos*, is that of the second birth into adulthood, the "sexual awakening" of the couple.

Idyllic narrators are often distanced from the idyllic events: consider the frame narrators of Longus, Bernardin, and Hudson. The focal point is dual, not just because these are love stories but because a single lover as center would destabilize the two-as-one theme, the "participation mystique," in most of them. The effect is a wider distribution of human feeling than if centering were restricted to one character. Sympathy extends to all humanity: in *Daphnis and Chloe* the rapacious Gnatho wins understanding, even applause, by the story's end.

THE HISTORY IN BRIEF

Rediscovered in the Renaissance, Longus offered poets new possibilities for romance, breaking with the masculine-centered chivalric-heroic models inherited from earlier centuries. Still, from the sixteenth to the eighteenth century the story is only partially assimilated in a culture that resists the Greek romance's feminism and pagan naturalism. Although during this time, romance frequently puts humanity at odds with nature, both Shakespeare and Milton rise above their culture's prejudices about *natura naturans*, "creating nature."

Yet another way to distance one's text from Longus's naturalism, while retaining his sweetness, is to generalize in the way of Salomon Gessner in the mid–eighteenth century. Schiller found fault with Gessner's shepherds as too ideal, insufficiently actual, yet the *Idylls* captured a feeling for what Samuel Johnson called "just representations of general nature." Introduced into fashionable culture by French literati, among them Diderot, the Swiss prose-poet was celebrated for decades, to be eclipsed only in the aftermath of the French Revolution. In the ensuing period Bernardin de Saint-Pierre's *Paul et Virginie* captured readers with a new story of love in nature. Bernardin's novel heralds the advance of elegiac sentiment in nineteenth-century fiction about nature while also testifying to the new sense of nature that arrived in the later eighteenth century. Of this development one scholar writes, "Quite simply, more people enjoyed [nature] more, and the minority at least was led increasingly to a deep sense of the affinity between man and nature, of a harmony that is psychological, aesthetic, even economic and moral" (Charlton 217).

From the mid–seventeenth century to the French Revolution, the dream of innocence jostles curiously against the enjoyment of wit, a contest apparently settled in favor of innocence during and beyond the vogue of *Paul and Virginie*. I spend most of my remaining pages on the period from the mid–nineteenth to the mid–twentieth century, beginning with George Sand's conscious movement away from sensational fiction to the idyllic mode so favored by Jewett and Cather. The uses of idyllicism as a catharsis for violence are also evident in Yukio Mishima's post–World War II novel of a young couple in a fishing village. This is not to say that postindustrial idyllic romance is merely reactive or escapist. Hardy, Valera (still known in Spain as Longus's translator), and Pérez de Ayala show how the form can reacquire its ironic distancing and still communicate the quality of human life close to peaceable nature. Questioning the "natural" order of aristocracy and male supremacy, Emilia Pardo Bazán seems to counter Valera's optimism in her two dark accounts of mother nature's grim, inexorable processes—*Los pazos de Ulloa* and its sequel, *La madre Naturaleza*.

Pardo Bazán, Valera, and Pérez de Ayala, now unfortunately strangers to American and British readers, provide the enjoyable, wise, and delicately ironic notes of the language that gave us Cervantes, Buñuel, Borges, and García Márquez. Alone among modern idyllic romance authors whom I have read, the Spaniards seem most consistently able to manage the balance Longus obtained between the comedy of courtship and the dream of eternal union.

Renaissance Rediscoveries

LONGUS FOUND

Had Longus been absorbed into the medieval West, his story would probably have taken a shape not unlike Marie de France's "Le Fresne" (The ash tree). In this *lai*, or short narrative poem, a noblewoman has slandered another who gave birth to twins, saying she must have slept with two men. When she herself has twin girls, she orders one infant to be abandoned at a nearby abbey. Found in the branches of an ash tree near the gate, Fresne grows into a beauty and becomes the mistress of a knight named Gurun. Later, yielding to his vassals' pleas that he take a wife, Gurun chooses Fresne's twin sister (no one notices their resemblance). Fresne patiently accepts the decision, even preparing the marriage bed, which she spreads with the coverlet that had enwrapped her when she had been abandoned. Seeing this, the bride's mother recognizes Fresne, confesses all to her husband, and Fresne, now of acceptable rank, replaces her sister as Gurun's bride (the sister soon finds an equal match).

The foundling story joined with a love story, the birth tokens, the resolution of apparent class differences, the image of the tree (the ash in northern Europe carrying much of the symbolism of oak in the Greek Mediterranean)—all invite comparison with *Daphnis and Chloe*. Marie says that the silk coverlet came from Constantinople: did some part of her story also make that voyage? Longus was known in the Byzantine empire well before this time.

As characters, Marie's lovers belong to the world of courtly romance, of *gentilesse*, of eros in conflict with marriage. Fresne's striking beauty and her dignified acceptance of her loss of place show her to be no peasant girl. A tree protects her (the residue of an older folk-motif?), but otherwise her tutors and care-givers are human. Raised entirely within the abbey, she has the church, not nature, to guide her. Marie explicitly contrasts the safety of the abbey's ash tree with the danger of the forest, a sinister setting for Marie's original Breton audience (Saunders 49). A historian of nature writes that "The Breton hagiographical epic, most of which was written after the tenth century . . . , abounds in descriptions of the clearing away of undergrowth and wild forest" (Glacken 311). If not quite the fearful place it had been earlier in northern Europe, nature as experienced in the European forest still held, in Marie's time and long afterward, a sense of mystery less available in the coastal plains and open meadows of Greek romance.

Renaissance romance settings often oddly merge forest with pastoral meadows, attesting to the genre's hybrid Greek-medieval origins. When, beginning in the 1500s and continuing for three centuries, European fiction becomes littered with young shepherds falling in love, uttering love complaints, and living happily or miserably ever after, it is not uncommon to find them grazing sheep in or around the forest: witness Shakespeare's *As You Like It* or Jonson's *Sad Shepherd*. Forget, for the moment, that in many parts of Europe forests were disappearing to become grazing land for sheep.

The differences between Marie and Longus reveal something more—about medieval romance and perhaps even about the civilization of the West. Marie's story, with only one foundling, follows the essential outlines of the pastourelle, a popular medieval lyric type in which a knight encounters a country maid.[1] The decorum of romance for a courtly audience made it unthinkable that both lovers should be rustics. The asymmetrical "pastourelle relationship" persists throughout the Renaissance even after Longus revives the idyllic romance.

The rediscovery of Longus spurred a sixteenth-century vogue for narrative and dramatic pastoral, as distinct from the lyric tradition of Theocritus and Virgil. *Daphnis and Chloe* first saw print in the celebrated French of Jacques Amyot in 1559, a translation that not only remained in demand throughout the ensuing centuries but nourished pastoral-minded authors across Europe. Longus's first Western readers, however, were the Renaissance textual scholars who knew him in manuscript, and who applauded his romance for its sheer delight. Raphael Columbianus, editor of the first printed text, was attracted by "the pleasantness of the subject":

> I recently obtained from the library of Luigi Alamanni, a most distinguished man, very schooled in Greek letters, the pastorals of Longus to

examine. When I had carefully read them and discussed my reading with some quite learned men, this author became so amusing to us, both with his pure and elegant language and the pleasantness of his subject, that (insofar as it was in our ability) we would have deemed ourselves almost criminals if a work of this sort were to waste away any longer in the darkness: especially since I knew it was enthusiastically sought after by men of learning. (prelim. fol. 2–2ᵛ)[2]

Columbianus's amused tone means that he saw the comedy in this romance, though literary fashion would subsume comedy to melancholy in pastoral romances to come.

Of Columbianus himself little is known. Alamanni, the forty-year-old grandson of the famous poet, belonged to the Florentine Academy. Among these "learned men" consulted for this 1598 Florence edition was the illustrious old scholar Fulvio Orsini, who collated Alamanni's manuscript variants in Rome. Another collaborator was Henry Cuff (1563–1601), the Oxford Greek scholar who served with Essex in Spain and Ireland—and went to the block with him in 1601 (Barber 17).

The difference between Greek sexual symmetry and medieval courtly love had already occurred to one Byzantine reader. In a long verse-narrative titled *Drosilla and Charicles*, Nicetas Eugenianos (Nikítas Evyenianós, a contemporary of Marie) imposes many trials on his lovers until they finally come home to wed, escorted by a helpful merchant named Gnathon. Dionysos figures prominently in the story of these mostly Heliodoran lovers. Rustic they are not. In book 6, however, the injured and famished Drosilla stumbles into an Arcadian village (people are well-fed, beautiful, and generous despite their simple ways). Once she recovers, she becomes the unwilling love-object of a country youth, Kallidemos—"beautiful folk." Rejected, he utters a long plea invoking the stories of Hero and Leander, Galataea and the Cyclops, and Daphnis and Chloe:

> The boy Daphnis and Chloe were joined thrice-luckily [triseutuchôs] in marriage; that sweet Daphnis, only a shepherd, not ignorant of the arrows of love, was yet loved, having his fill of love in return, and knowing nothing of the fullness of love; for from his swaddling clothes the child was joined with the maiden Chloe to tend love's flocks. Long ago he was lover of the beautiful Chloe, of that Chloe, artless [aplastou]

maiden, whose glance was fire to the youth, whose words were arrows, unerring darts. The age of gold came before the love-charm; the lover received love in return more fully; not so in the age of iron; the one loved does not wish to love in return. O what word, what deed, what nature rules our loved maidens who strike down the lovesick heart of him who seeks love in return? Can it be that our maidens do not feel desire? They desire, but are filled with deceitful wiles; they love, but wear away their lovers, keep their hearts in suspense. (6.439–60)[3]

Expecting his twelfth-century readers to recognize Longus's story, Eugenianos protests against chivalric romance's usurping of idyllic romance. At the same time, his speaker's rusticity makes his protest comical, like the oafish Cyclops's pining for Galataea. As for Drosilla, she retains her independence in this long adventure, even keeping her true lover at bay until they can be properly married. But she and Charicles, no matter how unique the feeling for nature in this romance (Beaton 73–75), stand apart from nature and natural people.

In the West, aside from a mention of Longus's Eros in Angelo Poliziano's *Miscellanea* (1.2), around 1489, the earliest notable allusion to Longus appears in a painting of Daphnis and Chloe by Giovanni Battista Bertucci, active from 1498 to 1516 (the painting was formerly attributed to Francesco Bianchi Ferrari; see Ingamells 215–17). Knowing more about this shadowy painter would aid us in tracing the prepublication history of Longus in the Renaissance because Bertucci's painting of Daphnis and Chloe reflects a close study of book 1, at least, if not the whole romance.

Bertucci represents the moment when Chloe has fallen asleep in midday, and Daphnis, in the first pangs of erotic love, "began to gaze insatiably at every part of her." He wants to kiss her but restrains himself because "kisses sting one's heart and drive one mad, just like new honey. And if I kiss her I'm afraid I may wake her up" (1.25). A friend has pointed out to me the eloquent gesture of Daphnis's hand: a blessing or a desire to touch? Or are these one and the same? In the upper left, on a hill two men stand beside some cattle—a vignette that depicts an earlier episode (1.9), when the cowherd Dorcon tries to win Chloe's hand from her father. Behind Daphnis's head rises a hill with a cave at the base surmounted by a ruined structure having a partly visible arched entrance.

Undoubtedly this is the nymphs' cave and shrine, which the artist seems to see as two separate places: "There was a cave sacred to the nymphs which consisted of [the relative clause is not in the Greek text] a great rock hollow inside and rounded outside" (1.4). A little later in this paragraph Longus says, "The mouth of the cave [seen as a different cave?] was in the very middle of the rock, and from it water came gushing out and flowed away in a stream; so there was an expanse of very lush meadow in front of the cave, as the moisture made the grass grow thick and soft" (1.4). The meadow, with a stream flowing to a village in the middle distance, appears in the painting, while in the landscape behind Daphnis's head sits an isolated house, perhaps his family's, set apart from the other houses—consistent with the distance Daphnis has to travel for the winter meeting of book 3.

Not until later in the sixteenth century is Longus's literary influence felt—and then in poetry, not romance. In 1555 Henri Estienne published two pastoral poems based on episodes from book 1 of *Daphnis and Chloe*: "Chloris" (the title shepherdess is aroused after seeing Daphnis bathing) and "Rivales" (two shepherds contend for a shepherdess's kiss).[4] Neither Sannazaro's *Arcadia*, with its prolonged melancholy and unrequited love, nor Montemayor's later *Diana*, essentially a Heliodoran romance with Virgilian shepherds, really belongs in the Longus family. But Tasso's *Aminta* (written in 1573), a composite of virtually all previously written pastoral, certainly does, especially in the recollections of Aminta's and Sylvia's childhood innocence. Aminta remembers himself as a boy,

> so young as yet scarse able
> To reach the fruit from the low-hanging boughes
> Of new growne trees.
> (1.2.65–67)

Longus says that the vines in Lesbos grow so low that a baby could reach up and grab a bunch of grapes (2.1).

Tasso's Silvia, daughter of a rich goatherd, is out of Aminta's price range (as Chloe is thought beyond Daphnis's) even though Aminta and Silvia grew up together:

> long alas
> Liv'd I so near her, and then lov'de of her,
> As like two turtles each in other joy'de;

Neere our abodes, and neerer were our hearts;
Well did our yeares agree, better our thoughts;
Together wove we netts t'intrapp the fish
In flouds and sedgy fleetes; together sett
Pitfalls for birds.

(1.2.74–81)

Aminta's pretending (1.2.131) to be stung by a bee on the lip may recall Daphnis's complaint that Chloe's kiss hurts more than a bee sting (1.18—though Achilles Tatius provides a closer parallel). Tasso's Satyr repeats the bee sting image in 2.1., and his lustful lying in wait for Silvia seems to imitate Longus's Dorcon in the wolf skin. Yet Silvia's disdain for Aminta, whose "Curtesie" in saving her life is "full ill repayde" (3.1.105), puts her in a far different world from Lesbos.

This combination—unattainable lady plus yearning for rustic innocence—can be expected when Renaissance poetry enlists *Daphnis and Chloe* or native conventions of verse about country lovers. Several examples of these in Frank Kermode's important anthology require at least mention, some dating to the 1400s. Henryson's "Robyn and Makyne," untouched by Latin and Greek, lets us overhear a fickle shepherdess twist her lover in knots. In "Harpalus's Complaint," an anonymous poem in the 1557 *Songs and Sonnets*, the complaining shepherd (his name from *harpaleos*—"greedy," or "eager"?) weeps his life away because his shepherdess loves Corin and not him. Chivalric romance's love-melancholy has come to dwell with swains. Mythology and disguised aristocracy are nowhere in sight.

Michael Drayton's popular verse tale of Dowsabel (the eighth eclogue in his 1593 collection, later moved to fourth) offers a more complex example of shepherd love. We know that Dowsabel, gathering flowers in the country, is a knight's daughter, but the piping shepherd appears too well dressed to be what he seems. He also looks like another shepherd, Tamburlaine, a sure sign of higher destiny if not rank. The tale ends with Dowsabel's bending her "snow white knee" and kissing the "fond boy":

With that the shepheard whoop'd for joy,
Quoth he, ther's never shepheards boy,
    That ever was so blist.

Ostensibly a woman-dominant pastourelle, the poem seems to end by blowing the shepherd's cover—no mere shepherd's boy could bring this off.

Tasso's play depends on the Virgilian melancholy already present in Sannazaro. The mood persists in Battista Guarini's equally influential *Il pastor fido*, a play that inspires the Jacobean English vogue of tragicomedy. Longus certainly contributed much to Guarini's play, apart from what already exists in *Aminta*. It opens with an old servant's Philetas-like lecture on human and cosmic love, and it ends with marriage and a recognition-scene between father and lost son. In act 4, Silvio meets with the nymph Echo and encounters what he thinks is a shepherd in a wolf's skin. This scene—the shepherd turns out to be Silvio's beloved Dorinda, whom he almost kills with an arrow—retains the symbolism of wolfish passion prominent in *Daphnis and Chloe*: Dorinda's near-death results from Silvio's animal desire, which must be transmuted into the higher love praised in the old servant's lecture.

In addition to its most famous echo, John Fletcher's *Faithful Shepherdess*, Guarini's play had many imitations in England—Lady Mary Wroth's unpublished play "Love's Victorie," for example, and the anonymous Latin play acted at Cambridge in the early 1600s, *Pastor Fidus*. This latter adaptation has all the themes and characters typical of Longus-based Renaissance romance-drama: a rustic who doesn't acknowledge love, an older man's speech on love's cosmic power, a character nearly killed when mistaken for a wolf, an echo song, a lost child's reunion with his parent.

As did pastoral itself, these trappings lasted long. Joseph Boismortier's musical version of *Daphnis and Chloe* in the mid–1700s begins, like Guarini's play, with a soliloquy in praise of love, and when the aged Rousseau set out to compose an opera based on Longus's story, one of his first episodes was old Philetas's song in praise of love. This foregrounding makes what was in Longus a stage of education into a thematic prelude directing the audience's interpretation. Rousseau may not even have known Tasso's and Guarini's role in moving this scene to the front of the story.

The translation of Longus by Annibale Caro can be dated to 1538, though it remained unnoticed until the eighteenth century.[5] Its chief interest is the passage Caro invented (169–76) to substitute for the great lacuna (Daphnis's bath) in book 1. Amyot's translation simply unites the passages before and after the lacuna. Caro describes the character Dorcon as a "cotal tarpagnuolo inframmettente"—an intruding little wild horse of a so-and-so—and as "insomma un cattivo bestiuolo" (172) because of his envy.[6] He invents exuberant descriptions of the pool where Daphnis bathes, of Daphnis cavorting in the water, and of the fusion of aristocratic refinement and pastoral vigor in Daphnis's boyish beauty: "a person who had the delicate features of an aristocrat and the robustness of a shepherd" (172). Just before rejoining Longus's text, after Daphnis has playfully hidden from Chloe, Caro has Chloe fear that her lover may have died. Caro apparently planned to link his addition with the text at this point but never did so. The episode would have required some winding down: the mannerist indulgence of Caro's description clashes with the terse charm of such moments in Longus.

The publication of Jacques Amyot's translation in 1559 creates the seeming anomaly of a major classical text first made available in a translation almost forty years before the first Greek edition, though Ferrini shows that this was not so unusual (7, 20). In France and England, and probably elsewhere in Europe, the growing sixteenth-century mania for pastoral romances took strength from this French version of the ancient text, incomplete and expurgated though the future bishop's translation was. Stylistically Amyot's work became a benchmark of French translation, long praised for its purity and charm. Amyot also translated Plutarch and Heliodorus, but perhaps Longus's sensuality caused him to leave his name off the first title page.

A gathering interest in Longus is indicated in the new editions of 1578 and 1594 (the year after Amyot's death), then 1596 and 1599. It may well be that Amyot's *Amours pastorales*, as he titled it, dealt a major blow to the still-thriving medieval romance tradition (see Lestringant). If so, the revival of pastoral romance, begun by humanists, may be humanism's contribution to the novel's ascendancy after the Renaissance. In pastoral, after all, the different classes can engage in that mingling of voices which Bakhtin says creates the novel. Although Cervantes never wrote a straight chivalric romance, he did labor extensively, to the great mystification of most of us nowadays, on his pastoral romance *La Galatea*—a work that, like other Spanish romances of this period, seems hardly touched by Longus.

Early French uses of Longus-Amyot, following Henri Estienne, include the pastoral collection of Remy Belleau, *La Bergerie* (1565), especially in the extensive revisions made in 1572 (see Lebègue). Belleau expands his "Description des vendanges" (Description of the grape harvest) from about forty lines in 1565 to almost three hundred, changing the title to "Vendangeurs: L'Amour Rustique." The first version simply describes the activities of wine-making—caulking the barrels, rinsing them, harvesting and pressing grapes—a picture resembling Longus's wine harvest at the beginning of book 2. In the 1572 expansion this scene leads to a tale of love between the shepherd Tenot and "la gente Catin, bergere de haut pris" (Tasso's maiden, too, came at a "high price").[7] There follows a passage closely modeled on Longus. An old man tells Tenot about meeting Love in his garden: the winged boy-archer evades him like a young partridge, "perdriau." He claims to be of great age despite his boyish appearance, and he tells how he keeps the garden fresh.

Patriarchalism requires departures from Longus, however. While Philetas addresses both lovers, Belleau's old man speaks only to Tenot, who has cried out against love. The scene ends not with Philetas's revealing the cure for passion (kissing, lying together naked) but with the old man's disclosure that Tenot's father, having heard of his hopes to marry, will endow him with many gifts. "Vendangeurs" transposes a philosophical fable into a tale of benevolent men—lover, father, and sage—arranging a woman's marriage. Love tells the old man: "You know his [Tenot's] father well, Janot the good flutist, and his mother, Janotte. I've made him love Catin his care, and made gentle Catin cherish him too. Go tell his father so he will meet with them and join the two hearts together with a tight bond" (Belleau 235).[8]

Idyllic peace was actually scarce in sixteenth-century France. Two months after the expanded "Vendangeurs" went to press, in August 1572, Belleau's young patron, the third Duke of Guise, on whose estate parts of these poems are set, supported the notorious massacre of St. Bartholomew's Day. The first (original) part of *La Bergerie* ends: "So I spent this beautiful day, and this sweet night. I ask you, if our life were spent in this fashion, managing the days and hours in such pleasures, without offense, without unhappiness, without troubling apprehension, without change of our nature, open and free of avarice, of envy, and of ambition, would we, upon dying, regret having lived so sweetly in this world?" (316).[9] Oblivious to the civil war around him, comfortable in patronage, Belleau's speaker savors the moments passing in a single day. Speaking for all pastoral voices, he shares the same feeling for naturally measured time ("les iours & les heures") flowing smoothly, unbroken by false busy-ness, untroubled by the servile lot of poet and shepherdess alike.

LONGUS ENGLISHED: DAPHNIS WITHOUT TEARS

When the young London stationer Angel Day set out to translate Amyot's French Longus, he also recast the mutual affection and sensual freedom of the Greek lovers. He provided a strong hero, an inconspicuous heroine, even a typically English rural society. As something of a rhetorician, the author of *The English Secretarie*, he enjoyed amplifying all the rhetorically inviting passages, such as love complaints and descriptions of days or seasons. If he omitted some of the choice moments in Longus—the delightful prologue and the concluding scene of the wedding night—it was probably because his printing budget was limited and it was easy to lop off the story's beginning and end. This may also explain why the self-indulgent amplification virtually disappears late in the book. Like other early translators, of course, Day lacks the bath scene in the lacuna of book 1. As Amyot had done, he cut Lycaenion's sex-lesson from book 3—a passage excluded from the French until 1716 (Barber 31). Despite such omissions, Day's *Daphnis and Chloe* is at least double the length of Amyot's.

Yet Day also removes much of the Greek sensuousness that survives in Amyot. When old Philetas ends his lecture on love with "The only remedies are kissing, and embracing, and lying together with naked bodies," Day translates, "I found that kisses gave ease to sighes, liking to longing, and bedding each with other after marriage concluded the some of all our determined affection" (2.7, Day 61). Rewriting Longus, Day strove to accommodate the Elizabethan reader's presumed taste for rhetorical *copia*, so that a nicely turned Greek or French sentence too often becomes a great snarl of English. A comparison of Day and Amyot rightly concludes that "Day makes [Longus's] words undergo a subtle transposition, so as to eliminate from them the spirit of pagan sensuality that inspires them, and to reconcile them with the requirements of Christian morality" (Pruvost 488).[10] Write "patriarchal sentiment" rather than "Christian morality," and the judgment is incontestable.

Day often lets vividness dissolve into vagueness. He omits the stench of the dolphin carcass where Daphnis finds his money: Day's hero inexplicably finds the coins under a bush (3.27, Day 130). While Longus describes the nymphs appearing to Daphnis as "tall and beautiful women . . . , half naked and barefooted, with their hair falling free," Day writes that "their attire" was "altogether Nimphlike, their countenances freight with manifest pleasances," as they "appeared to put forward to his relief many occasions of comfort" (2.23, Day 71). Longus's wit has also been translated away: no tall tale about cows being great swimmers unless the water washes off their hooves, no framing prologue, no moments of ironic self-reference as when the lovers listen to Philetas's stories "as though they had been listening to fiction rather than fact" (2.7, omitted at Day 59). Gone are such psychologically resonant scenes as the moment when the characters, celebrating the harvest, engage in animal-imitative dancing (2.37, omitted at Day 86), or when Chloe puts on Daphnis's clothes while he bathes (1.24, omitted at Day 35).

In the fashion of the times, Day sprinkles his volume with the customary pastoral verse: singing contests, love complaints, panegyric, and moral advice. Just at the point where Lycaenion should be instructing in book 3, some twenty-three pages of prose and verse appear that are separately entitled "The Shepheards Holidaie" and recount the shepherds' yearly feast celebrating their virgin queen, Eliza. At its best, the effect of this section approaches that of the sheep-shearing feast in *The Winter's Tale*, folding an obviously English event into the Greek story. Similar anachronism occurs in the winter episode of book 3. While Longus pictures a modest community of cabins and cottages inhabited by peasants tied to the land, Day sets his story on the grounds of "a goodly Mannour house" (5). His winter scene is one familiar to the English landed gentry and the yeoman farmer:

> The Freesing Boreas called for great fires, which according to ancient hospitalitie of shepheards, was made on a large harth in the midst of their halles, the blasing shewe wherof immediatly after the mornings cocke, invited each one in the cold frostie seasons, to drawe round about it: and there with farre more easie labour then abroade, to dispatch their houshold busines. The hindes and such as tilled and labored the groundes, tooke herein great pleasure, in so much as the bitternesse of the weather, became unto them for the time being, a releasment of their hard endured labour, so that sporting themselves in divers housholde pastimes, they chaunted their countrie tunes, and

divers songes accustomed in their vintages to the honour of Bacchus. (93–94)

Longus's world held no "halles"; no shepherds gathered around a "large harth," and Daphnis and Chloe themselves would have to be seen as "hindes," or laborers (Dorcon says Daphnis is just that, a *penês* [1.16]). The Greek text, with none of that last sentence about chanting country tunes, simply says that the people enjoyed their winter break because they could "have a meal in the morning and sleep late" (3.4).

Maybe sleeping late and eating a big breakfast are pleasures fit only for hindes. Many changes in Day's translation, especially those relating to Daphnis, point up the shepherd's masculinity and his concealed aristocracy. The translator perhaps best reveals his whole aim with the motto on the title page, "Altior fortuna virtus" [Virtue is higher than fortune]: tychê is thus, as in Elizabethan tragedy, a hostile force that can threaten the innate virtue of the best people—though the Roman sense of "manliness" still clings to Day's *virtus* here. Day believes that if a peasant boy is really a blue blood, he will act like one. Parallel with Renaissance self-fashioning runs the aristocratic conviction that God has made some strains of humanity to rule over others.

By contrast, the multiethnic world of the eastern Mediterranean circa AD 200, in many respects a cruel and venal place, tended to judge slavery or wealth a matter of luck, or tychê, and not of essence. The Greek Daphnis can react all too humanly after telling his fellow villagers about his rough treatment by the Methymnians: "Having said this Daphnis burst into tears and made the villagers feel extremely sorry for him" (2.17). Day omits this sentence, as he does a later one where Daphnis cries himself to sleep awaiting Chloe's release from the Methymnians. Similarly he cancels the shepherd's despair over Chloe's possible marriage to another: "This news made Daphnis almost frantic. He sat down and burst into tears, saying that he would die if Chloe stopped grazing her flocks with him" (3.26, omitted at Day 128). A human blend of frailty and resourcefulness makes the original Daphnis appealing. Day's character feels grief, anxiety, and fear but somehow retains his conventional "virtus." Rather than tell the story of *both* Daphnis and Chloe, Day translates Longus's text of mutuality into the story of Daphnis (who marries Chloe) and some shepherds.

Longus's appearance in Robert Greene's *Pandosto*, published the year after Day's adaptation, may mean that Day was Greene's source, but literate Greene would have thought himself capable of reading Amyot. He in fact follows Amyot-Longus more closely than Day does in describing Fawnia's (Chloe's) foster father not as an independent herdsman but as "a poore mercenarie Shepheard . . . , who got his living by other mens flockes" (87). Greene appears reluctant to settle for mere rusticity, however; his romance is only semipastoral. The solitary foundling washes up from the sea—one of many images of Fortune in a story that lingers over the Nature-Fortune opposition more often than either Longus or Shakespeare, in his adaptation of Greene, does. Greene briefly alludes to Pan and the nymphs (99) but leaves them out of the forces at work here. His Fawnia makes a garland (98), having passed over sixteen years (not thirteen, as in Longus and Day) from infancy to sexual awakening (90). But like Shakespeare, Greene follows the pastourelle scenario of a traveling aristocrat meeting a rural beauty. Not until *Paradise Lost* will an English poet situate both lovers in nature.

A year after *Pandosto*, Greene incorporates something of Longus in his less-known romance, *Menaphon*. Again he moderates the Greek story's rusticity. The title character is chief shepherd of the King of Arcadia; the rest of the cast are mostly disguise-wearing aristocrats. A learned but self-centered fool, Menaphon falls in love with Sephestia—who, unknown to him, is the king's daughter, sent into exile by her father's jealous rage. Thinking her husband dead in a shipwreck, she sets up house among the rustics with her uncle and her infant son, whereupon she takes the name Samela. In looks, talent, and virtue her son grows into the superior child of romance tradition—so superior that pirates kidnap him and sell him to the king of Thrace, whose favorite he becomes. Samela's rumored beauty compels her son to visit her island, which inexplicably he does not remember, and after his near-murder by the Arcadian king, the family—lost husband included—are reunited. Menaphon, as a smart but "too aspiring" (92) bumpkin, must return to courting his old shepherdess.

Menaphon, in many respects an idyllic romance told from the rustic rival's viewpoint, surpasses *Pandosto* as fiction in communicating a dramatist's, even a novelist's, sense of social texture. An instance of Greene's ability in this way is the scene of the "merry meeting" when Menaphon introduces Samela to his friends. Greene takes us through the varying reactions to this moment in ways that anticipate George Eliot or Hardy. Samela is so beautiful that the country maids "could not blame *Menaphon* for being over the shooes with such a beautiful creature." When everyone agrees to make Samela mistress of the feast, Menaphon "conceived no small content in the advancing of his mistress," until he notices the other men looking at her, especially Melicertus (her husband, believed dead):

> But amidst all this gazing, he that had seene poore *Menaphon*, how, infected with a jealous furie, he stared each man in the face, fearing their eyes should feede or surfet on his Mistres beautie: if they glaunst, he thought straight they would be rivalls in his loves: if they flatlie lookt, then they were deepely snared in affection; if they once smiled on her, they had receyved some glance from *Samela* that made them so malepart: thus sate poore *Menaphon*, all dinner while, pained with a thousand jealous passions, keeping his teeth garders of his stomach, and his eyes watchmen of his loves. (45–46)

The dinner conversation turns to the question what each guest would choose to become if transformed into some other creature by the anger of the gods. Samela would choose to be a sheep, she says, touching off a string of witty banter that barely conceals the guests' various jealousies:

> *Samela* perceiving these blowes woulde growe to deepe wounds, broke off their talke with this pretty digression. Gentlemen, to ende this strife, I praye you let us heare the opinion of *Doron* [Menaphon's neighbor, also in love with Samela], for all this while neither he nor *Carmela* have uttered one word, but sate as Censers of our pleas; twere necessarie he tolde us how his heart came thus on his halfpenie.
>
> *Doron* hearing *Samela* thus pleasaunt, made presentlie this blunt replie; I was, faire Mistres, in a solempne doubt with my selfe, whether in beeing a sheepe, you would be a Ram or an Ewe?
>
> An Ewe no doubt, quoth *Samela*, for hornes are the heaviest burden that the head can beare.
>
> As *Doron* was readie to replie, came in sodainly to this parley foure or five olde shepheards, who broke off their prattle, that from chat they fel to drinking. (49)

The whole scene allows Greene to develop the comic side to his romance, which largely turns on the incongruous mingling of rustic and princely voices. This pastoral leveling has its down side, however, in the near tragedy of Greene's ending. First the heroine's father (as in *Pandosto*, though not in *The Winter's Tale*) falls passionately in love with her, then her son does likewise. The grotesque, disordering effects of erotic love combine in this romance with the blows of fortune.

Menaphon complements *Pandosto* in that Samela's foundling son, Pleusidippus, is to Daphnis as Fawnia to Chloe. The boy grows up a princely figure among the rustic children (Greene says he leads all the children's games as well). Like Daphnis, Pleusidippus is captured by pirates and is the object of homosexual desire, and his story lapses for some years between his capture as a child and his beginning sexual awareness at age sixteen. Since Elizabethan cultural prejudice seems to disallow a tale of a rural boy and girl both coming of age, Greene's male and female foundlings must inhabit separate tales. In both, however, country people serve as objects of laughter. One of the last poems in *Menaphon*, a mocking love duet between two rustics—"Dorons Eclogue Joyned with Carmelas" (84–86)—features a blazon of Carmela's beauties:

> Thy lippes resemble two Cowcumbers faire,
> Thy teeth like to the tuskes of fattest swine,
> Thy speach is like the thunder in the aire:
> Would God thy toes, thy lips, and all were mine.

This is the pure, boorish rusticity of idyllic romance as represented in Longus's Dorcon and Lampis. When *Menaphon* leaves the country and returns the reader to a renewed court, Menaphon stays behind in banishment. The age demands sifting of the crude from the civilized, of nature from art.

The enlarged distance between rusticity and aristocracy persists in Sir Philip Sidney's *Arcadia* in the rustic love-story of the Third Eclogues—the nearest approach, in a largely Heliodoran romance, to Longus. Sidney's third book tells how the aristocratic lovers Philoclea and Pyrocles consummate their love without marriage. The eclogues draw an obvious contrast between the aristocrats and the conventional love-leading-to-marriage of the shepherds Thyrsis and Kala. Sidney's Thyrsis (Lalus in the *Old Arcadia*), with the fidelity and simplicity of Daphnis, celebrates his wedding feast in these eclogues; his slavish devotion to his bride, his constant gifts and attendance ("all the parish said, never a maid they knew so well waited on"), creates a one-sidedness in the love affair. The shepherds Nico and Pas come forward with songs warning against jealousy and telling how to control one's wife, themes characteristic of Elizabethan marriage literature.

Although Chloe's wedding night brings her unmitigated joy, in Elizabethan Arcadia "the sadder matrons give good counsel to Kala who, poor soul, wept for fear of that she desired" (692). Behind the woman's fear of what she desires lurks the theme, quite alien to Longus, of the woman's "no" meaning "yes." The male lover serves so that he might dominate. Patriarchy requires an ordered seating arrangement at the rural feast, "every one placed according to his age" (691–92)—again the sort of thing Longus never mentions. No eating together, bathing together, or herding together for Thyrsis and Kala. They live in a sunnier world than Pyrocles and Philoclea, but one that is grounded in the same practice of male "service" in courtship leading to female subservience (no quotation marks) in marriage.

Recent cultural studies may have saturated the market with tales of old-time male dominance and patriarchalism, but it seems as if worse revelations are always possible. An early Elizabethan dialogue on the excellence of marriage as "the flower of friendship" looks promising for those seeking evidence for an enlightened view of the relations between the sexes. In marriage, the author seems to say, lies the consummate friendship, the ideal of the friend as another self, the two becoming one. Yet the author can also declare: "In this long, and troublesome journey of matrimonie, the wise man maye not be contented onely with his spouses virginitie, but by little and little must gently procure that he maye also steale away hir private will, and appetite, so that of two bodies there may be made one onelye hart, which she will soone doe, if love raigne in hir" (Tilney 112). In her edition of this text, Valerie Wayne cites a remarkably similar idea from a late Elizabethan clerical treatise on marriage: "The husband ought not to bee satisfied that he hath robd his wife of her virginitie, but that he hath possession and use of her will" (156). The two become one when the wife is absorbed by her husband, when she desires what he desires.

Edmund Spenser's self-contained romance of Calidore and Pastorella, in book 6 of *The Faerie Queene*, again substitutes the knight-hero for the shepherd. No other Renaissance romance plays out more fully the contrast between pastourelle knight and pastoral shepherd-lover. If in pastourelle the knight encounters shepherds, here he becomes one. Calidore's rival Coridon, "the silly shepherds hynd" (6.11.27), inherits Daphnis's cleverness (he escapes the Brigants who kill his fellow rustics) but also his frailties (he cannot save Pastorella), including a readiness to weep. Coridon brings Calidore the news of the Brigants' raid,

> And gushing forth in teares, was so opprest,
> That he no word could speake, but smit his brest,
> And up to heaven his eyes fast streming threw.
> (6.11.28)

Later, finding his stolen sheep, the shepherd "for tender pittie wept" (6.11.37). In simpler days he helped Pastorella drive home her flocks, but he now meets a graver threat than the comic-opera army and pirates of *Daphnis and Chloe*.

Coridon follows Menaphon in the stock role of, in the Tudor sense, "clown"; virtuous action, so central to the proclaimed aims of Tudor poetry, belongs with the aristocrat, not the clown. With Coridon's teary laments we may contrast Sir Calidore's reaction on seeing the sacked, empty village: "half enraged," he "fared like a furious wyld Beare, / Whose whelpes are stolne away, she being otherwhere" (6.11.25). The animal rage of the bear simile derives from Calidore's recent immersion in nature, but it also implies the noble anger, *furor heroicus*, so alien to Longus's essentially comic hero.

Despite her simple upbringing, the foundling Pastorella has never cared for Coridon's love: "Though meane her lot, yet higher did her mind ascend" (6.9.10). This opposition between lot and mind runs all through Renaissance romance, and in book 6 of Spenser's poem the theme of mind over fortune peaks just when the field of imagery moves from romance forest to pastoral meadows. Pastorella's story (which need not have come straight from Longus) "enacts the Neoplatonic idea that the soul is a foundling, an aristocrat long ignorant of its true source" (Berger 241). Pastoral, "the landscape of the mind," signifies the discovery that the sage Meliboe makes when, beaten for ten years "With stormes of fortune" (6.9.31), he sees that "It is the mynd, that maketh good or ill" (6.9.30). Later a personified Fortune, Pastorella's enemy, would have destroyed her had it not been for Calidore. Meliboe can lecture Calidore that the mind triumphs if one bears one's fortune, but what if Fortune does not bear us? For their Arcadianism,

Meliboe and the shepherds will pay with their lives. The well-known ambivalence of Renaissance poets toward pastoral life, the vision of pastoral as preliminary to action, goes far to explain the accommodations required before the European imagination can incorporate Longus into its literature.[11] As hero, Daphnis is an absurdity, an inadequate fiction. Spenser dissociates heroism from rusticity in his Calidore-Coridon antithesis, allowing Pastorella to make the soul's higher choice.

Spenser's idyllic tale resembles Tasso's *Aminta* as a story of the soul's life of love. So much reading of sixteenth-century pastoral has lately dwelt on the social ethos of Elizabethan courtiership that there is a danger of neglecting the corresponding movement of book 6 of *The Faerie Queene*, especially in this episode, "inward toward the mind's center" (Berger 222). This journey has just begun when Calidore interrupts Colin's vision on Mount Acidale—that of the three Graces, "Handmaides of *Venus*, which are wont to haunt / Vpon this hill" (6.10.15). Mount Acidale constitutes the same kind of sacred center for this narrative that Walter Davis finds in *Daphnis and Chloe*: part of a threefold space, encompassing first the internal; then the main arena of the pastoral action; and finally the larger world of cities, courts, and the open sea (Davis and Lanham 33). In Spenser's story the setting abruptly widens to a coastal scene, like that in Longus, when the Brigants try to sell their captives to the slave-traders who regularly "skim those coastes, for bondmen there to buy" (6.11.9).

Colin's Graces invite comparison with Longus's half-naked nymphs in that sacred center of fertility, the cave. In a dream Daphnis sees their statues come to life to console him after Chloe's kidnapping. They are handmaids of Eros and Pan, not Venus, but the nymphs share Spenser's Graces' rural seclusion and, in particular, their associations with the beloved female. For just as Chloe "is a care to" the nymphs (2.23), the dancing Pastorella belongs to the Graces. This is signaled earlier when she appears in a posture that foreshadows (note the word "graced") Colin's heavenly vision:

> Upon a litle hillocke she was placed
> Higher then all the rest, and round about
> Environ'd with a girland, goodly graced,
> Of lovely lasses.
>
> (6.9.8)

Chloe and Pastorella (and, for that matter, other idyllic heroines like Miranda, Perdita, and Virginie) function both as romance heroines and as symbols: each of them is a fourth to the heavenly three, expressing the female principle of great creating nature.[12] The Calidore-Pastorella idyll supports Frye's claim that "in the criticism of romance we are led very quickly from what the individual work says to what the entire convention it belongs to is saying through the work" (60). The entire convention has much to say.

SHAKESPEARE'S ROMANCES

Coincidentally or not, the growing European fashion around 1600 for pastoral romance follows three French editions of Amyot printed during the 1590s, then the first edition of the Greek text at Florence in 1598, and then a parallel Greek text with Latin translation published at Heidelberg in 1601 (as *De Rebus Pastorum, seu, de Castis Daphnidis & Chloes Amoribus Libri Quattuor*). More influential than all these editions, however, was that of Gottfried Jungermann, *Longou Sophistou Poimenikôn* (1605), with parallel Latin again. For one thing, the title page announces the author as "Sophistos" (on what authority is unknown) and thus begins the tradition of Longus as "sophist"—a label with significant implications for his reputation and reception. Jungermann's Latin text was certainly accessible to more readers than the Greek, and with the editor's apparatus it carried an authority that Amyot's French lacked.

For a learned amateur such as Ben Jonson, who owned one copy of the 1598 and two of the Jungermann edition (Evans), the latter would thus have held great significance. By 1605 Jonson was already becoming an arbiter of taste, and the mere fact of his owning three copies of Longus suggests at the very least a current English interest in this newly accessible Greek author. The British Library copy examined by Robert Evans is worth a brief discussion here because it provides some tantalizing glimpses into the way Longus was read after proprietorship of his text passed from Amyot to the German scholar.[13]

On the whole, it looks as if Jonson used Jungermann's Latin translation more than his Greek text. He marked the Latin text more often and, after book 2, marked only the Latin. Jonson seems to have recognized the comic origin of the story, underscoring the humorous scene of Daphnis's trial with Philetas as judge. He marks the sentence on this in the "summarium" of book 2, then the episode itself (2.14). Such moments might have struck him as possible material for a scene in a play or entertainment. The dramatist Jonson also marks set speeches, such as Daphnis's love complaint in 1.18 and Pan's speech to Bryaxis in 2.27.

The learned Jonson of the masque annotations takes special interest in the early descriptions of the nymphs, the material on Pan (2.23–24), and the Echo story (3.23).[14] Someone has erased evidence of Jonson's interest in the Lycaenion episode, including the postcoital conversation. But the playwright appears little interested in the story as a whole. He entirely neglects book 4, except in marking the "summarium," where Daphnis discovers his parentage. Either this is one more instance of Jonson's sporadic reading habits (see McPherson 10–18), or he lost interest when this turned into another of those "lost and found" stories. My own guess is that the story as a whole lacked appeal because of the male-female mutuality. It was a book with philological and mythographic interest, but Jonson, like most of his contemporaries, could not read it with the sympathy of later audiences.

Further evidence of such response among readers exists in the minor characters Daphnis and Cloe of John Fletcher's *The Faithful Shepherdess* (circa 1608), a couple now relegated to satire. As in Shakespeare's *A Midsummer Night's Dream*, to which it is often owing, this self-described "tragicomedy" represents certain types of love while lovers wander in an enchanted wood at night. Daphnis has the naive innocence of his namesake but none of his passion. Cloe is a comically love-hungry shepherdess: "It is impossible to ravish me, I am so willing" (3.1). Yet if Fletcher had been reading Longus, it doesn't show except in the names.

Like Greene, Fletcher requires that in pastoral romance, rusticity serve mostly as a comic foil to courtly refinement. He burlesques Daphnis and Chloe by making them moral opposites; probably if he had read Longus, he found something absurd in their relationship. That his theme of chastity—anticipating that of Milton in *Comus*—is so exclusively female chastity, distances his play even further from the Greek romance. Fletcher's couple may scarcely resemble their namesakes, but Fletcher must have counted on his audience's knowing these names for his ironic effect. Already we see the consequences of making Longus a sophist.

The court play *The Faithful Shepherdess* has a long history of association with Shakespeare's romances of the same period, *Cymbeline*, *The Winter's Tale*, and *The Tempest*, in their pastoralism and tragicomedy and in those allegorical overtones that so many audiences detect. Carol Gesner has undertaken the most thorough exploration of Longus's presence in Shakespeare's romances, but the connection had already been observed by Villemain in an essay of 1828 in which he compared the charm of Longus's lovers with that of the Ferdinand-Miranda scenes in *The Tempest* (187). Evidence that Shakespeare knew Longus is admittedly shadowed with circumstance: parallel images that could originate elsewhere, though it would be hard to find them all in a single text other than Longus (see also Wolff).

The very idea of putting romance on stage challenged Shakespeare in ways he probably liked. Romance narratives notoriously violate classical decorum, with their leisurely structure and unlikely plots. How, for example, could a playwright handle a foundling story on the stage without falling into the faults of the old plays censured by Sidney in his *Apology for Poetry*? Sidney writes: "for ordinary it is that two young princes fall in love. After many traverses, she is got with child, delivered of a fair boy, he is lost, groweth a man, falls in love, and is ready to get another child, and all this in two hours' space" (76).

Shakespeare handles the accommodation differently each time, not because he was groping toward success, I think, but because he disliked doing the same thing twice. *The Winter's Tale* simply breaks the action in two, wittily smoothing over the "fault" of the long time-lapse by calling attention to it. In *Cymbeline* prolonged exposition accounts for the childhood of the lovers and princes (compare Aminta's recollection of his childhood in Tasso's play). The neat temporal economy of *The Tempest* masks rather lengthy exposition in scene 2 of act 1.

The Winter's Tale employs Longus's story, chiefly by way of *Pandosto*. As Wolff's and Gesner's source studies show, Longus, Greene, and Shakespeare all have children abandoned and, in a seeming divine retribution, the birth parents' other children die (Longus 4.24)—though only Longus presents two foundlings. A herdsman takes the infant home to his wife in Longus and Greene—to his son in Shakespeare—declaring that the find must remain a secret. The child grows old enough to tend the herd, which prospers; the child, being of aristocratic origin, is more beautiful and talented than other rustic offspring. Even Polixenes confesses that Perdita is "Too noble for this place" (4.4.159). When the foster father can at last tell the story and reveal the birth tokens, child and parent are reunited.

However, Shakespeare must have read Longus in addition to Greene. When Shakespeare's shepherd, about to find Perdita, complains about young hunters scattering his sheep down to the seaside, he echoes a passage found in Longus (2.13) but not in Greene. Rustic dances in act 4 evoke the nature-imitating dances in Longus (2.36–37). In particular the "dance of twelve Satyrs"—among them, "three neatherds" wearing animal skins (4.4.319–21)—calls to mind the neatherd Dorcon's disguise in wolf skin. Finally, the definite seasonal division in the play resembles the seasonal structure in Longus, which is not evident in Greene.

Shakespeare restores to the story Longus's twin themes of art and nature, downplaying Greene's of fortune and nature. Longus's ecphrasis echoes in the living statue, as if, in a play so apparently dominated by nature, art must have the last word. All three plays, in fact, feature prominently a variant of the speaking picture. The masque of *The Tempest* is a living tableau, while in *Cymbeline* the description of Imogen's bedroom wall-paintings allows Diana and Philomel to express the themes of wronged virtue and honor in the play; near the close of *Cymbeline* appears a masquelike vision of Jupiter. Static scenes occupy the climax of all three romances and therefore impress themselves on the spectator's memory; Longus's painting, unmentioned after the preface, is easily forgotten. In either case, though, the idyllic poet's balance of nature and art ("culture," as Schiller calls it) survives: is Hermione, after all, a being of art or nature?

It is easy to see why Villemain would think first of *The Tempest* as a Shakespearean echo of Longus. There are the similarity of lovers on an island and the parallel between Shakespeare's Ariel and Longus's Pan. There is even a verbal link when Ariel scolds the villains in the speech beginning, "You are three men of sin" (3.3.53). With a similar opening line Pan reproaches the Methymnian general Bryaxis and his men for their violations of nature: "O most unholy and most impious of all men" [ô pantôn anosiôtatoi kai asebestatoi] (2.27). Just after this speech, Pan uses his storm to imperil the boat full of wicked men, as Ariel does in *The Tempest*.

Shakespeare, however, extends the foundling motif in new directions: Miranda and Ferdinand are both "lost ones found," and the island brings to both a new identity through love. And ultimately in *The Tempest* the foundling comes to symbolize all the major characters' conditions, as Gonzalo says in his summing-up:

> In one voyage
> Did Claribel her husband find at Tunis,
> And Ferdinand her brother found a wife
> Where he himself was lost; . . .
> . . . and all of us ourselves
> When no man was his own.
> (5.1.208–13)

In *Cymbeline* Cymbeline's sons are male orphans, and in *The Winter's Tale* Perdita is a female, though again people are "found" in various senses at both of these plays' ends. Imogen's wish to be "a neatherd" (*Cym.* 1.1.148) reminds the audience of her type's pastoral associations without actually making her a cowgirl.

Among these three Shakespeare plays, the lapses of time between loss and return range from twelve years (*Tempest*) to sixteen (*Winter's Tale*) to twenty (*Cymbeline*). None of the foundlings know their origins before this time—even Miranda remains ignorant of Prospero's story until her moment of readiness. The song "Full fathom five," occurring when it does, expresses Ferdinand's loss of the old self, the father, in preparation for the new. Cymbeline's sons, perfect specimens of the Renaissance pastoral hero, find their identities not through love, despite their tender words about Imogen, but through their desire for honor and heroic action. Posthumus, too, is orphaned, meeting his family only in the vision of the play's last act.

Shakespeare's romances also feature the hallmark idyllic images of chthonic cave, paradisal garden, and demonic storm. The nymphs' cave in Longus and the enclosed gardens of Philetas and Dionysophanes find counterparts in *Cymbeline* with the princes' cave and Cymbeline's garden, where the play opens. All Britain acquires a garden symbolism, in contrast to Rome, the city world where Posthumus loses faith. Shakespeare resembles Longus in suggesting a feminine symbolism of the cave, since the feminine returns to the world of the princes when they receive Imogen into their cave. In *The Winter's Tale* the floral imagery of the sheep-shearing feast creates a garden to be "torn down" figuratively when Polixenes harshly interrupts the feast and Perdita's rule. The cave is the site of the oracle or, displaced, the chapel where Hermione returns to life—where the feminine returns to Leontes' sterile patriarchy. In *The Tempest* Prospero's island embodies the Renaissance garden symbolism of art balancing nature, wholly consistent with the garden's meaning in Longus.

Prospero's cell, often represented as a cave on stage, is the center of the creative energy on the island, as is the cave in Longus. At the cell also the young lovers declare their troth. Gesner proposes that the very idea for the title storm in *The Tempest* came from the turbulence Pan raises against the invaders, both events being followed by ethereal music symbolizing harmony.[15] In *The Winter's Tale* a storm takes the lives of the sailors who bring infant Perdita to Bohemia, the final divine retribution for Leontes' crimes against nature. Almost all these images serve the themes, crucial to idyllic romance, of the union of masculine and feminine in nature.

More than his other plays, Shakespeare's romances bring the feminine into the human struggle. Marilyn French finds the romances to be "experiments in achieving a vision in which 'feminine' values are triumphant within the world of earthly power" (286). Incorporating such qualities as "well-being, harmony, love, and elation," the feminine is "exiled in the romances, just as it is in the tragedies; but in these plays, it endures its exile, while the males suffer its absence" (289–90). To choose this approach is to see Miranda's exclamation "O brave new world" (5.1.183) as something more than ingenue enthusiasm; the world is as new to the Italian politicians as it is to her. Miranda's first speech—her compassionate plea for mercy and her declaration "I have suffered / With those that I saw suffer!" (1.2.5–6)— makes her the necessary complement of love to Prospero's justice and power.

In *The Winter's Tale* Leontes' jealousy, a vice "rooted in the need to control" (French 309), lays waste a family and a crown by driving out mother and daughter. As we might expect in the romance most dependent on *Daphnis and Chloe*, this play most obviously enacts the feminine healing of self-obsessed masculinity. In *Cymbeline* the crisis of mutuality turns on the inner, spiritual division of the two who were one, Imogen and Posthumus. Lamenting her father's cruelty, Imogen reminds us that sexual symmetry exists in the pastoral world, but not the court:

> Would I were
> A neatherd's daughter, and my Leonatus
> Our neighbor shepherd's son.
> (1.1.148–50)

Male-female discord soon deepens. The husband rails not just against his "unfaithful" wife in act 2, scene 5, but against all women. The wife similarly turns against men in act 3, scene 4, though she falls well short of Posthumus's neurotic, Hamlet-like posturing. Her disguise—"forget to be a woman" (3.4.155)—signals the loss of the feminine in the court world and the weakening of sexual unity owing to such masculine disorders as Cymbeline's uxoriousness and Iachimo's cynical misogyny. Events both public and private render sexual harmony impossible until the end of the play. The jailer's comment at the end of act 5, scene 4—"I would we were all of one mind, and one mind good"—refers to Romans and Britons but also to courtier and commoner, and beyond these levels to the elemental division between the male-female principles of creating nature, which some have seen as the mythic center of these romances (Garber 115).[16]

Yet male and female create through nature and nurture alike. Britain being the garden world, act 1 of *Cymbeline* reveals that as children, Imogen and Posthumus were—like Miranda and Perdita—nurtured in nature. The "nurture-nature" phrasing, so important to the idyllic motive, and so familiar in sociological parlance, is in fact specifically imported from Prospero's language in act 4 of *The Tempest* where Caliban is "one on whose nature / Nurture can never stick" (4.1.188–89). In 1874 the scientist Francis Galton, in his book *English Men of Science: Their Nature and Nurture*, said he was using Shakespeare's phrase as "a convenient jingle of words, for it separates under two distinct heads the innumerable elements of which personality is composed. Nature is all that a man brings with him into the world; nurture is every influence from without that affects him after birth" (quoted in Freeman 9–10). In the late 1800s the debate over priority—Galton was a "nature" man, while Franz Boas a bit later championed "nurture"—renewed a dispute that absorbs Perdita and Polixenes in *The Winter's Tale*. It lies at the heart of idyllic literature, which typically assumes that nothing can perfect humanity the way nature's nurturing can.

Already in *As You Like It*—a play with an anti-Lycaenion in Rosalind (she meets her lover in the woods but only to preach *against* the "wicked bastard of Venus" [4.1.195])—Shakespeare has one of his wisest characters proclaim of the life in nature, the shepherd's life, that "in respect of itself, it is a good life; but in respect that it is a shepherd's life, it is naught" (3.2.13–15). Cymbeline's son, having without his knowledge a royal nature that instinctively abhors mere nature, can say in response to Belarius's praise of the country life:

> Haply this life is best,
> If quiet life be best; sweeter to you
> That have a sharper known, . . .
> . . . but unto us it is
> A cell of ignorance.
> (*Cym.* 3.3.29–33)

Perdita, too, is a reluctant rustic, as her foster father observes when she shirks her duties as mistress of the feast:

> Fie, daughter! When my old wife lived, upon
> This day she was both pantler, butler, cook,
> Both dame and servant; welcomed all, serv'd all;
> . . . .
> . . . You are retired
> As if you were a feasted one and not
> The hostess of the meeting.
> (4.4.55–64)

This knowledge instinctive to nobility explains Perdita's confutation of artificial flowers in the dialogue on art and nature. Her own interests should favor grafting base to noble, but her royal wisdom makes her demand natural flowers in her garden. Polixenes uses art, or cunning, to draw out her true feelings about "nature's bastards," while Perdita speaks from her heart, or nature.

Shakespeare held the mirror up to nature, but he also imagined that in nature exist, as French says, "threats to human harmony and cultivation"— adding even that "emotionally he feared nature and those he associated with it to a degree that seems pathological to some of his twentieth-century critics" (340). Perhaps the same diagnosis applies to most Renaissance authors of idyllic romance: Day, Greene, and Spenser all look uneasily on nobility stranded in the country. Nature proved "servile" in cooperating with Lear's wicked daughters. While *Daphnis and Chloe* contains memorable episodes of sympathy between people and nature ("pathetic fallacy"), *The Tempest* is less about sympathy with nature than control of it. The period's instinctive need to substitute a pastourelle couple for a pair of rustic lovers testifies unequivocally to its uneasiness outside the town or castle walls. So much Renaissance romance sets characters apart from nature—melancholy lovers who cannot enjoy life, court exiles who return to court at first chance, travelers in search of instruction—that during this period romance itself seems defined by its characters' need to transcend the created world.

≼ ≼ ≼

Wit and Innocence

SOPHIST AND LIBERTINE

When *The Tempest* returned to the public stage after the Restoration, the play usually appeared in the revised version by William Davenant and John Dryden called *The Tempest, or the Enchanted Island* (first acted in 1667, first printed in 1670). The playwrights invent a second daughter and a second lost son, "a Man who had never seen a Woman," says Dryden in his preface, "that by this means those two Characters of Innocence and Love might the more illustrate and commend each other" (4). Caliban also acquires a sister, Sycorax, allowing male-female counter-images of these qualities. Prospero keeps the foundling prince, Hippolito, in a cave, away from his daughters, Miranda and Dorinda, warning both them and the prince against the monstrous opposite sex.

The cave becomes the trysting place for Dorinda and Hippolito, who bring to the play the amusing innocence of Longus's lovers as they try to understand their new feelings:

Dor. I've touched my Father's and my Sister's hands
And felt no pain; but now, alas! there's something,
When I touch yours, which makes me sigh: just so
I've seen two Turtles mourning when they met;
Yet mine's a pleasing grief; and so methought was theirs;
For still they mourn'd, and still they seem'd to murmur too,
And yet they often met.
Hip. Oh Heavens! I have the same sense too: your hand
Methinks goes through me; I feel at my heart,
And find it pleases, though it pains me.
(2.5.65–74)

The revision brings out the latent possibilities of the original *Tempest* as a comedy of wit regarding innocence—possibilities inherent in Longus. Shakespearean Miranda's innocence, like Perdita's, betokens her pristine and princely virtue; innocence in the Dryden version signifies ignorance.

The Renaissance and Restoration *Tempest*s differ most in Shakespeare's greater seriousness toward pastoral, which "carries us into a higher state of identity than the social and comic world does" (Frye 149). The comic, childish behavior of Dorinda and Hippolito contrasts with Shakespearean Miranda's unguarded love for Ferdinand. Dryden and Davenant, nevertheless, continued to shape productions of the play well into the eighteenth century. The French knew Shakespeare's play mainly in this guise. Harny de Guerville drew from it in his one-act play *Georget et Georgette* (1761) about two young people in a peasant village who have never had contact with the opposite sex. Seven years later came *Hilas et Silvie*, a "pastorale en un acte" by Rochon de Chabannes that is set on an island whose resident nymphs have never seen men (Monaco 46, 54). Amused at the expense of innocence, these playwrights have taken *The Tempest* far from the idealism of Renaissance romance.

To understand further the changed prospects for idyllic romance since the 1500s, we can turn to Andrew Marvell's "Daphnis and Chloe," printed about a century after Tasso's *Aminta* and Remy Belleau's *La Bergerie*. In contrast to the lovers in Shakespeare's romances, Marvell's couple retain little mutual feeling or Greek idyllic sweetness. As in Fletcher's comedy, the "Longus Sophista" persona created with Jungermann's edition colors the text. Marvell conveys the brittle ironies of passion, countering the coyness of women with the cynical practices of men. Love is unattainable, eros and friendship impossibly dissociated:

> *Daphnis* must from Chloe part:
> Now is come the dismal Hour
> That must all his Hopes devour,
> All his Labour, all his Art.
>
> Nature, her own Sexes foe,
> Long had taught her to be coy:
> But she neither knew t' enjoy,
> Nor yet let her Lover go.

> But, with this sad News surpriz'd,
> Soon she let that Niceness fall;
> And would gladly yield to all,
> So it had his stay compriz'd.
>
> (sts. 1–3)

Females learn from female Nature to be "coy," pointedly rhymed in antithesis with "enjoy." Yet in so teaching, Nature betrays her own womankind—presumably because if women never land their Daphnises, the shepherd race will cease to be. Chloe stands, then, as synecdoche for Nature herself in the poem, especially in Nature's timeless, easy-going cycles (recall the woman's slow "vegetable love" in "To His Coy Mistress"). Daphnis represents the "dismal Hour"; to him belongs the sense of time that later begets the image of the lover as under a death-sentence (again a reminder of "Coy Mistress").

Longus's characters inhabit a world not divided in this way; for long stretches they seem untouched by human artificial time. J. B. Leishman describes Marvell's "Daphnis and Chloe," somewhat reductively: "Daphnis . . . is simply performing a series of elaborate variations on the theme . . . that the moment of parting is not the right moment for consummation" (128). What this leaves out is the characteristic Marvellian presence of Nature personified as woman:

> Nature so herself does use
> To lay by her wonted State,
> Lest the World should separate;
> Sudden parting closer glews.
>
> (st. 4)

A typically simple yet maddeningly profound Marvell scrap: what kinds of "sudden partings" can keep the world from separating? And is the verb "separate" used in the intransitive sense of dissolving on its own, or does it mean separating the world from nature, as Daphnis is separating from Chloe? The lines seem to say that sometimes Nature quits playing coy and shows her true self, in order to keep things on course. Nature's "wonted State," her customary appearance, keeps us from truly seeing her.

Yet there are moments of spectacular beauty that the world experiences from time to time—flowering spring, autumn colors, thunderstorms—events that leave people closer to Nature than before. Such sudden partings with Nature's everyday appearance draw us closer to her, as Daphnis's sudden parting from Chloe (which causes her to "lay by" her coyness) draws them closer to each other. The trouble is that we, like Daphnis, are shallow, fickle, unreliable lovers. Daphnis's ensuing long speech leads up to the narrator's cynical surprise at the end:

> But hence Virgins all beware.
> Last night he with *Phlogis* slept;
> This night for *Dorinda* kept;
> And but rid to take the Air.
>
> Yet he does himself excuse,
> Nor indeed without a Cause.
> For, according to the Lawes,
> Why did Chloe once refuse?
> (sts. 26–27)

Critics—who rarely discuss this poem in relation to Longus—seem to agree that the last two lines refer to "laws" of the women's "court" of love, as burlesqued in comic literature. The stanzas seem to make Daphnis a sophist hypocrite, a man of the "World" (stanza 4) who abuses the natural woman Chloe. As in "The Nymph Complaining," a female-nature figure, playful but sincere, contrasts with ungentle, worldly maleness.

Has Longus's narrator become Marvell's Daphnis? Daphnis's long speech —for Leishman, a series of witticisms—is for Elizabeth Donno traceable to the "libertine" persona in Drayton's sonnets (43), and she might bolster her case with the resemblance between that poet's famous sonnet "Since There's No Help" and Marvell's Daphnis when he pretends to be near death:

> But he came so full possest
> With the Grief of Parting thence,
> That he had not so much Sence
> As to see he might be blest.
>
> Till Love in her Language breath'd
> Words she never spake before;

> But than Legacies no more
> To a dying Man bequeath'd.
>
> For, Alas, the time was spent,
> Now the latest minut's run
> When poor *Daphnis* is undone,
> Between Joy and Sorrow rent.
>
> (sts. 6–8)

In this last stanza, the adjective "poor" is either an ironic truth (Daphnis is turning his back on spectacular beauty) or an utter deception in view of what the end of the poem reveals. The Daphnis of the "Hour" is now of the "minut," a word repeated in stanza 13. But as with most busy people, his being pressed for time is mostly his own doing (he has a date back in town with Dorinda).

In this speech Daphnis unwittingly identifies Chloe with Nature in a familiar pun reinforcing the earlier identification: "Could departure not suffice, / But that you must then grow kind?" (st. 12). He pretends that "kind," or natural, Chloe is his enemy, when actually he is the one deceiving her—much as, in "The Mower against Gardens," artificial men cunningly paint tulips and enlarge carnations. Daphnis is too clever by half in pretending to be the "condemned Wight" (st. 14) going off to the "Heads-man" (st. 25), since as a fallen man he is indeed under a death sentence. Another inadvertent self-revelation by the libertine Daphnis is:

> Rather I away will pine
> In a manly stubborness
> Than be fatted up express
> For the *Canibal* to dine.
>
> (st. 18)

The situation of the cannibal's dinner, familiar from voyaging romances, strikes a chord of truth in that the cannibals embody a most revolting instance of fallen humanity's unnaturalness. Perhaps Marvell is thinking of Serena in Spenser's sixth book, where her voyeuristic cannibal captors stand for worldly males who feed on women's flesh and reputation.

One need hardly dwell on the next stanza, with its lurid suggestion (a witty *reductio* of the conceit Drayton used to end "Since There's No Help") of an even more unnatural sin, when Daphnis explains why he cannot yield and stay with Chloe:

Whilst this grief does thee disarm,
All th' Enjoyment of our Love
But the ravishment would prove
Of a Body dead while warm.
(st. 19)

In a passing glance at this poem, Pierre Legouis says it is "implicitly placed under the invocation of Saint Longus, the patron of libertine naïvety" (29). Longus's sophist narrator in *Daphnis and Chloe*, the libertine manipulator of innocence and our own experience, becomes the patently specious Daphnis in Marvell's poem, his victim being Chloe-Nature.

Contemporaneous with this poem, George Thornley's 1657 translation of *Daphnis and Chloe* reflects a wrier wit, beginning with the title-page description: "A Most Sweet and Pleasant Pastoral Romance for Young Ladies." Not all young ladies (or their parents) would have welcomed the book if they had known it contained all the naughty bits of the original—a liberty not even allowed to Paul Turner's Penguin translation on its first publication in 1956 (see Turner's preface to the 1968, uncensored edition). Although Thornley omits Longus's name on the title page, the preface invokes "Longus Sophista." His dedication "To Young Beauties" implies an element of sophistry even in the characters' innocence: "Chloe knew well enough (though the Author makes her simple) what and where her Fancie was; and Daphnis too, needed not Lycaenium's Lanthorn to a plakit, or to follow Will with the wispe" (9–10). In other words there is something sham about the young lovers' naivety. Jungermann's affixing of "sophist" to Longus's name in the edition from which Thornley translated has once again informed the reading of the romance.[1]

Thornley's raciness and frankness show the kind of reputation Longus's book had been acquiring for the past century. Amyot left his name off the 1559 translation, and in the first published Italian translation (1643) G. B. Manzini warns "that if by chance his pen has allowed (which he believes it has not) to let fall into this work some loose phrase or so, or one liable to evil interpretation, then it should be seen to be far from the true and usual nature of his heart" (quoted in Barber 26). The contemporary historian of romance Pierre Daniel Huet thought the story shameful (53). Thornley informs his "young beauties" that his book "is so like your owne either simplicitie, or Art, you cannot but approve it here. You do not know what we meane, when we speake as plain as day. And now you have an Author too (which you never had before) to prove you do not counterfeit; The sophist in his third book; a man of great Authoritie; a Magistrate among the maids" (10–11).

The illustration facing Thornley's title page also advertises a sensual story, picturing a couple copied from the title page of the 1626 Paris edition of the Pierre de Marcassus "translation"—which is actually Amyot's (Barber 21)—with Chloe wearing a provocative décolletage. In a prefatory poem to Thornley, one James Wright pretends to wish the Lycaenion episode had remained safely in Greek:

> Only I wish Lycaenium and her Goose
> Had still spoke Greek; and not her selfe prov'd loose,
> And publike too: For sure a dimme eye may
> See through her thick dark Grove too much of day;
> And I, who yet am young, thus censure can,
> The Book thee Scholar speaks, the Grove a man.

Actually, the most serious moral objection that Thornley raises (in his preface, "To the Criticall Reader") has to do with the abandoning of the children: "To imagine Children exposed, (the very basis of the book) is not at all for this Age, an Age far wiser then that. It may be so; for Aesculapius had always a great beard, though his Father Apollo never had any. Did you never leave any [children] your selfe to Saint Antholin's or Greggs? Then read the Stories of the East and South, and you shall find many Children, both exposed, and Fortunate" (15). Here speaks the physician Thornley, a member of a profession that must keep secrets and that handles such problems with equanimity. Perhaps experience with the fruits of his young beauties' amours disposed him toward the sophist's skepticism about innocence.

The physician also lists his text among the "Stories of the East," romances with sometimes exotic settings that were, in his century, becoming "novels." At the same time he places *Daphnis and Chloe* above "the other Romances . . . , those of the affected twirling tongue" (11), presumably French. He often fleshes out Longus's narrative by expanding descriptive phrases that heighten the sense of place or character. When Chloe accepts Daphnis's pledge of love, she does so not just as "a herding maid" but as "a poor and harmless maid, and one that was bred a Shepherdesse" (2.39, Thornley 106). Daphnis "still having a pastoral outlook" becomes "Daphnis, who still had a childish, Pastorall mind" (3.19, 130). Lampis "an unruly cowherd" becomes "an untoward, blustering, fierce Herdsman" (4.7, 162). Gnatho, hiding "fearful . . . as a suppliant" in the temple, is Gnatho "in a mighty feare, . . . a sneaking suppliant" (4.25, 184). The cumulative effect of many such minor amplifications moves the story toward the character-centered fiction of the later seventeenth century. As in the Dryden-Davenant *Tempest*, comedy prevails over pastoral—maybe for the first time since Longus's rediscovery. Thornley's diction, the most attractive feature of his style, helps more than anything to, as he puts it in translating Longus's prologue, "rouze him that is in the dumps" (*lupoumenon paramuthêsetai*; literally, "to encourage him who is grieved"). Distinct also to Thornley are undertones of ribaldry missing from Amyot or Day.

Writing on the eve of the Restoration, both Marvell and Thornley respond with amusement to pastoral innocence. Thornley, physician-realist in matters of the heart, moves the comedy closer to satire than romance. With Marvell we can just see over the next horizon the era of sentiment: the idylls of Salomon Gessner or Bernardin de Saint Pierre's *Paul et Virginie*. While Thornley seems to deny the couple's innocence outright, Marvell stands at the margin between irony and sentiment with the thought that, if the innocence of Daphnis was once possible, in this corrupt age it would have to be a sham.

MILTON'S COUNTER-IDYLL

On she came,
Led by her Heav'nly Maker, though unseen,
And guided by his voice, nor uninform'd
Of nuptial Sanctity and marriage Rites.

Paradise Lost 8.484–87

We usually think of the pastoral element in *Paradise Lost* in terms of the classical eclogue, without regard for the particular innovations that Longus brought to the Renaissance, when *Daphnis and Chloe* showed poets a way from the lyric form of Virgil to a narrative pastoral of heterosexual love. Unlike the classical idyll or eclogue, idyllic romance has to do with courtship and marriage, not to mention the state of innocence that so preoccupied Milton from *Comus* and *Areopagitica* to *Paradise Lost*. The translator Thornley—a contemporary of Milton's at Christ's College, Cambridge—reports Longus's romance enjoyed a quiet vogue among educated readers of his generation: "The Pastorals of Longus Sophista, to my knowledge have bin signed with the Youthful Emeralds of some of our own, most excellent, sparky, astral Wits. But Those have kept within their own Ingenious, quiet Cortina, and have not come abroad by their Pens" (13). Is Thornley thinking of Marvell, excellent enough wit to have become Milton's assistant in Cromwell's government the same year, 1657?

Milton never mentions Longus's romance, but traces of it crop up in his early poems. In *Lycidas*, a palimpsest of earlier pastoral literature, scholars credit the name Amaryllis (line 68) to Virgil, but the context ("sport with Amaryllis in the shade") rather more closely resembles the scene in Longus where Eros reminds old Philetas of his youthful love for Amaryllis—"you played your Pan-pipe underneath those oaks, when you were in love with Amaryllis" (2.5). Since Longus's many Theocritean motifs are shopworn by the time of *Lycidas*, no one source can be argued for such a passage as the reproach of the nymphs in Milton's poem (Daphnis blames them for allowing the Methymneans to kidnap Chloe).

In *Comus* a solider connection exists. The Lady sings the "Sweet Echo" song when she is about to meet the false shepherd Comus; only Longus in antiquity says it was Pan's shepherds who destroyed the nymph Echo, and Comus invokes the name of Pan just after this song. Comus and Pan both insist that virginity yield to nature's passions and appetites. In *Paradise Lost* an ironic hint of Longus occurs just before the Fall when Adam weaves a floral garland for Eve while awaiting her return (9.838); weaving such crowns [*stephanoi*] for each other is a favorite pastime of Longus's couple. Later, when Michael shows Adam the way cities make war on shepherds and plunder their flocks (11.638–59), Milton may be remembering the Methymneans' raid on Longus's shepherds (2.20), which results in Chloe's capture.

Writing *Paradise Lost* with a knowledge of Longus, Milton would have compared Daphnis and Chloe with his own innocent couple. A memorable feature of Greek lovers' innocence is their amusingly (or distressfully) prolonged attempts to find out how to make love. Longus probably aimed beyond mere arousal in these scenes; they fit with his recurring theme of human dependence on imitating nature for every kind of need. Milton, by contrast, thought that in the important matters, including love and lovemaking, humans possess innate knowledge. Thus Eve, going to Adam, is

Led by her Heav'nly Maker, . . .
. . . nor uninform'd
Of nuptial Sanctity and marriage Rites.
(8.485–87)

Milton insists that knowledge of sexual relations (also called "Rites" in *Paradise Lost* 4.742) comes with this knowledge ("inform'd" in the Platonic sense of form) that we bring to the world. Adam and Eve could not, then, behave like Daphnis and Chloe, worrying why they feel the way they do. Male-female love, all love, is instinctual.[2]

The first reader to compare Milton's couple with Daphnis and Chloe seems to have been Alexander Pope. About two weeks before the poet's death, his friend Spence brought to the sickbed a copy of Longus, containing the French regent Philip's suggestive illustrations. Pope remarked, "They are very innocent Loves; like those of Adam and Eve in Milton: I wonder how a man of so infected a mind as the Regent could have any taste for such a Book" (525). The similarities do not end with "innocent loves," however. Equally important is the filtering of innocence through sophisticated observers—Longus's narrator and Milton's Satan—though Satan's viewpoint is skewed by malice, not just by superior knowledge. Milton would not have shared Longus's uncritical naturalism and nostalgia, his fondness for mere innocence, humanity lacking experience and the test of will. To distance himself from the adolescent idyllic, Milton makes marriage not the end but the beginning of the story—a gesture in some respects novelistic.

This critical distancing conforms with Milton's characteristic valuing of the inner over the outer person. *Comus*, like all the Greek romances, accentuates the heroine's chastity throughout. Yet the Lady represents more than the virtue of sexual restraint: she speaks for the whole complex of inner moral propositions that "chastity" represents. As the rectifier and husbander of nature, she opposes Comus's profligate abundance. Adam and Eve perform this restraining influence in the overabundant garden—especially Eve, the woman, who esteems the simplicity and restraint that belong to the Lady's "chastity" in *Comus*. Yet the magical power of Greek-romance chastity makes way for the gorgeous language of sexual love in the bower scene of book 4 of *Paradise Lost*. The couple's moment of union occurs much too early for Greek romance: in effect, the reader has nothing left to desire. From the standpoint of love and self-knowledge, Milton's epic almost constitutes a romance in reverse. His couple begin where Daphnis and Chloe end, in an aura of innocent wedded love. From book 5 on, they become increasingly perplexed, requiring instruction from an angelic sage, their Philetas. Finally, they become like orphans in the world outside the enclave, cut off from their true parentage.

So the wedding does not, as in *Daphnis and Chloe*, end the story, but, in the complex temporal organization of *Paradise Lost*, it does not exactly begin it. Adam and Eve appear in such various stages of courtship and postmarital life that the poem offers a virtual repository of type-scenes, fitted more to Milton's tonal shifts than to chronology. In *Daphnis and Chloe* and *The Tempest*, where the marriage bond is never tested, mutual love exists potentially but not fully. Literally, Adam and Eve are "married" when God presents Eve (complete with innate knowledge of sex) to Adam. In book 4, however, they behave as if enjoying their first night in the bower. In book 9 the scene of lust plus "morning after" recrimination suggests a sexual relationship outside marriage, though earlier in that book the two argue about their plans like a longer-married couple. When, finally, they set out into the world hand in hand, they resemble a young couple launching into the future. Courtship, wedding night, married life, maturity—all the stages seem potentially at any moment present in the poem.

Milton echoes the Greek romance by presenting both lovers in nature, but he imparts a typical Renaissance twist when he injects into the rural scene a pastourelle roving gentleman, Satan:

> As one who long in populous City pent,
> Where Houses thick and Sewers annoy the Air,

> Forth issuing on a Summer's Morn to breathe
> Among the pleasant Villages and Farms
> Adjoin'd, from each thing met conceives delight,
> The smell of Grain, or tedded Grass, or Kine,
> Or Dairy, each rural sight, each rural sound;
> If chance with Nymphlike step fair Virgin pass,
> What pleasing seem'd, for her now pleases more,
> She most, and in her look sums all Delight.
>
> (9.445–54)

The knight of pastourelle has become the Restoration city-rake, a merely cosmetic difference. Satan's decadent sophistication recalls the poem's earlier condemnation of "Court Amours" and "Serenate, which the starv'd Lover sings / To his proud fair" (4.466–70). Such moments depreciate the legacy of the chivalric love story (still indigenous to Shakespeare's romances) as compared to the image of simple, natural lovers. Emilia Pardo Bazán would later complain, even while adapting Milton's Eden to her own Galician landscape, that Adam and Eve have lost all their "nobility." Exactly. As fallen, therefore sophisticated, observers, Milton's readers may not share Satan's malice, but they do reflect his detachment from the naive couple. In his classic essay "Adam Unparadised" Frank Kermode works from the premise that we cannot understand the joy of innocence except by being without it. The bower love scene in book 4 meets its reverse image in the couple's lust after the Fall in book 9. In his preface to Longus, Thornley casts doubt on the pastoral lovers' authenticity. Satan similarly contributes to our doubts on the strength of Adam and Eve's love.

Readers will also acknowledge the ambivalent feelings aroused by Adam and Eve's innocence as new man and wife: beautiful but certain not to last. For Schiller this dual perspective on innocence is identical with the "modern" response to nature, or the created world. Schiller's *On Naive and Sentimental Poetry* defines the problem of the modern writer as "how to overcome the separation of creative mind and external world brought about by man's self-consciousness" (Sharpe 170). Milton's double vision measures the distance not just between prelapsarian and postlapsarian but between something called paganism and a Christianity that, as Coleridge puts it, had created the "under consciousness of a sinful nature" (245), wholly foreign to authors like Longus. Milton thought of our losing oneness with nature as equivalent to the loss of innocence that comes with self-consciousness.

To recognize this dual vision is to see why *Paradise Lost* was Schiller's quintessential idyll: "A loftier satisfaction is aroused by Milton's superb representation of the first human couple and the state of innocence in paradise: the most beautiful idyll known to me of the sentimental type. Here nature is noble, spirited, at once full of range and depth, the highest meaning of humanity clothed in the most graceful form" (*Naive* 151–52). Schiller never wrote his projected separate treatise on the idyll, but one commentator has proposed that the perfect idyll for Schiller "would make real the serenity which in conventional idylls is only an escapist illusion" (Reed 75); it would unite the real with the ideal. In Milton's words, "If true, here only," (*PL* 4.251). Nature, innocence, love—the principal subjects of idyllic romance—all achieve a realization in Milton's poem that Schiller found unique among the seventeenth- or eighteenth-century texts he knew.

Since the 1960s Milton's readers have found in the Adam-Eve relationship a major interpretive crux, but none have improved upon Coleridge's description of the couple: "The love of Adam and Eve in Paradise is of the highest merit—not phantomatic, and yet removed from everything degrading. It is the sentiment of a rational being towards another made tender by a specific difference in that which is essentially the same in both; it is a union of opposites, a giving and receiving mutually of the permanent in either, a completion of each in the other" (245). A key word here is *mutually*, and the description fits rather closely with the "sexual symmetry" in the Greek romances (Konstan). James Turner, who calls *Paradise Lost* a "troubled idyll" (287), assembles much patristic and Reformation evidence to validate the couple's equality in marriage. The apparently demeaning term "help-meet" actually comes from a Hebrew word that is, Turner explains, "most frequently applied to God, as in Psalm 70: 'Thou art my help and my deliverer'" (16).[3] Opinion and, even more, practice surely varied, but it was possible to find seventeenth-century people who believed, with the followers of Jacob Boehme, that union in marriage commemorated the original union of humanity in the hermaphroditic Adam (Turner 143). Readers are returning, it seems, to Coleridge's understanding of Adam and Eve as joined at least in mutuality, if not equality. The desire of each, as Mary Nyquist shows, is lost in the other.

Awareness of the idyllic romance tradition enlarges appreciation of Milton's art. Coleridge and Schiller made much of the lovers' idyllic aspects, their apparent embodiment of the ideal in the real. What perhaps draws the most critical interest in the poem nowadays is the psychology of marriage, the after-the-wedding characterization of Adam and Eve—the way the real constantly reinterprets the ideal in, for example, the quarrel in the garden. Perhaps Arthur Miller may serve to typify modern rewriting of Genesis in *After the Fall* (1964), when his Adam figure longs, near the play's close, "To know, and even happily, that we meet unblessed; not in some garden of wax fruit and painted trees, that lie of Eden, but after, after the Fall, after many, many deaths." The melodramatic phrase "lie of Eden" and the repetition of "after," slip into the elegiac key. This is heard in Milton, too. But as Schiller recognized, *Paradise Lost* also rises to celebrate both the romance of Eden and the wisdom that can follow love—or the wisdom that love can follow.

A BOOK FOR CYNICS, A BOOK OF NATURE

Pope's observation about *Daphnis and Chloe* shows the paradoxes of wit and innocence that confront Longus's readers. The two lovers are like the sinless Adam and Eve; how can they attract a sinner like the prince regent? Reading innocence into the story, Pope parts company with those many who have found Longus immoral. Three years after *Paradise Lost* Huet published his *Traité de l'origine des romans*; one of the earliest attempts to chronicle the development of prose fiction, it was influential throughout the next century, if only because of its firm moral premises. "The chief purpose of romance," Huet proclaims, "or at least what it should be, and which its authors should set for themselves, is the education of readers, who must always see virtue triumphant and vice punished" (5).[4] While Huet condemns Longus's plot (simplistic because it begins with birth and ends with marriage) and his style, he seems disturbed chiefly by the book's immorality—"so obscene . . . that one would have to be a bit of a cynic to read it without blushing" (53).[5]

Huet wrote during (and may have contributed to) a temporary eclipse of Longus's vogue, in contrast to the enthusiasm of the Renaissance and the increased readership of the 1700s (see Barber 27–29). Even in the abundant romance vogue of seventeenth-century France, despite Amyot's prestige, Longus seems to have made little impact (Magendie 24). Huet acknowledges the Greek romancer's earlier celebrity: "for although most of the wiser sort in previous times have praised [*Daphnis and Chloe*] for its elegance and charm, fitted to the simplicity appropriate to the subject, nevertheless I find nothing in it but simplicity, which sometimes descends to puerility and silliness" (52).[6] The now-established notion of Longus as a "sophist" underlies Huet's attack on Longus's style—"un stile de Sophiste"— which is "full of metaphors, antitheses, and those glittering figures that surprise the simple, and that please the ear without replenishing the spirit" (54).[7] It was a lewd book, then—appreciated perhaps by the barbarians of the last century but not by enlightened taste, which will not so readily submit to playful punning, antithesis, and alliteration. As a kind of afterthought, Huet adds that he has translated the romance himself but that he did so "dans mon enfance," at the only age when it can be appreciated. (Recall the tirades against romance in *Don Quixote*, followed by the speaker's evidence of wide knowledge, even admission of authorship, in the accursed genre.) Almost certainly the "simple" people whom chaste, neoclassical Huet has in mind are women, since he later comments on their prevalence as romance readers.

Especially in France, the classical age favored the sprawling, Heliodorus-derived "heroic romance," which was peaking even as Huet wrote. Honoré d'Urfé's endless *L'Astrée* helped propel the vogue for vast episodic narratives based on pseudohistorical events. Partly inspired in France by Sir Philip Sidney, the fashion returned to England with compound interest. Katherine Phillips ("Orinda") conducted a salon whose members took fictional names from French romances. By 1700 the word *novel* had become a label to distinguish other fiction from these long narratives (McDermott 120, 126). The baron in Pope's *The Rape of the Lock* owns no fewer than "twelve vast French romances neatly gilt" (2.38).

It was not just length that distinguished Longus from D'Urfé, however. Chloe's naivety, the very source of her charm for many later readers, was an occasion for scoffing in Pierre Bayle's *Dictionary*: "she loves too hastily, and presents her kisses too soon" (an odd reading, Daphnis being her lifelong companion). Bayle judges the scene of Daphnis's bath as not just textually defective: "This poor girl, seeing him stark naked melts with desire: she saw nothing but what was amiable in him; she was so little startled at this object [presumably Daphnis], that she boldly approached it, and having kissed her shepherd, she helped him on with his cloaths. . . . These things would be monstrous in the romances of our time. People will not forgive the marquis d'Urfé the little favors he makes Celadon obtain. The pleasure he procures him of seeing Astrea naked is charged on him as an unpardonable crime" (866–67).

This judgment agrees, assuming it is not ironic, with Huet's: the reader "of our time" must learn that sexual gratification is dearly purchased, that Chloe's innocence in discovering sexual difference absurdly misrepresents human nature.

Other grounds than moral or aesthetic could explain Longus's partial eclipse between about 1660 and 1710, in particular the questioning of his pagan sense of nature. In England, this period straddles what Keith Thomas calls "the confident anthropomorphism" of the Tudor era and the eighteenth-century belief "that all parts of creation had a right to live; and that nature itself had an intrinsic spiritual value" (301). In France, D. G. Charlton has traced a shift in emphasis from the seventeenth-century mechanistic *order* of nature to a vitally active nature. By the preromantic later 1700s, when this vitalism was distributed through all levels of society, the natural imagery of Milton's epic and Thomson's *The Seasons* appealed to readers all across Europe (see Charlton 70–78). In the decades that launched the Royal Society, however, humanity is seen as existing on earth to control nature, not to admire and imitate her ways (Glacken 494).

The last European edition of Longus in the seventeenth century came in 1660, but the eighteenth century saw four times the number of all editions and translations previously published, with much of the impetus coming from popular illustrated editions (see Barber 23–24, 45). And no illustrations aroused more interest than those of the regent Philippe, Duke of Orleans, whose "infected mind" Pope thought so ill-matched with the book. In 1719, Pope's friend James Craggs brought out *Daphnis and Chloe* in an English version reprinted throughout the century—a project no doubt suggested by the first French edition of Amyot containing Philippe's illustrations, which had been published the previous year (Barber 36). Craggs was secretary of war in 1717 and secretary of state from 1718 until his untimely death from smallpox in 1721. He visited Paris not long before French edition appeared, writing a gossipy letter back home to Pope.

Craggs's translation lacks the idiomatic appeal of Amyot's or Thornley's, but it held an audience in its time. An edition of 1764, entitled *The Pastoral Amours of Daphnis and Chloe: A Novel*, reminds us of the flexibility of the term *novel* in that age. Like some other translators, Craggs plugged the lacuna of book 1 with a scene of his own invention. While Annibale Caro, two centuries earlier, imagined the couple playing hide-and-seek like children, Craggs dwells on the sight of their nakedness and its arousal of passion:

> Accordingly they went both together to the nymph's grotto, where they bathed themselves in the presence of the deities that dwelt therein. Daphnis washed first, whilst Chloe held his cloaths and scrip; and she in turn committed her robe to the custody of Daphnis. It was at this instant that they discovered in each other such piercing beauties, that Daphnis could not forbear kissing Chloe, much less could Chloe withhold herself from kissing Daphnis. What did not those young unexperienced lovers see! with what tender raptures did they not mutually glow! It was in that moment they began in earnest to feel a reciprocal passion for each other. The uneasy Daphnis never reflected on the wonders he had beheld, without sighing and languishing after he knew not what; whilst Chloe kept continually in her thoughts the charms she had discovered in Daphnis. (14–15)

The exclamations sound totally out of Longus's register. The insinuated "wonders" and "charms" of the lovers' bodies recall erotic epiphanies in other love stories of this century, but Craggs cannot deliver the payoff that usually follows such revealings: this is, remember, only book 1. All in all, the translation appears far more a text of wit than innocence.

A too-solid text of pastoral innocence, at the other extreme, is Allan Ramsay's *The Gentle Shepherd: A Pastoral Comedy*, which echoes Longus and the second half of *The Winter's Tale*. This play demonstrates the popular appeal and endless flexibility of the idyllic romance plot, with all its potential for sentiment. When John Dunlop reports that Ramsay heard about Longus at second hand (74), he may be trying to exonerate his fellow Scotsman from the charge of having read so "reprehensible" (72) a romance as *Daphnis and Chloe*. Printed in 1725, *The Gentle Shepherd* was staged as a ballad-opera four years later. Throughout the century this silly play stayed alive in print and in such stage adaptations, one at Drury Lane as late as 1781. The oxymoronic theme of shepherd-aristocrat appealed to later eighteenth-century devotees of a primitive Scottish nobility. Dreams of glory in poverty came easily to Scots during this period: Ramsay had been an active Jacobite in his younger days—one reason why he is still venerated in his homeland.

The patriarch of this comedy, Sir William Worthy, returns home after Charles II has restored to him the lands he had lost during the Civil War (Worthy thus resembles Virgil's lucky shepherd, Tityrus, in the first eclogue). An old tenant reports that the ruined manor house belonged

> To ane that lost it, lending generous aid,
> To bear the head up, when rebellious tail
> Against the laws of nature did prevail.
> (Ramsay 76)

Sir William, disguised as an Autolycus-like fortune-teller on the village green, learns that his long-lost son, Patie, the "gentle shepherd," has lived a virtuous, if humble, shepherd's life. As in *The Winter's Tale*, the audience eventually hears of but does not witness the reunion of father and child.

Also like both Longus and Shakespeare, Ramsay throws a momentary scare into his audience when Sir William refuses to let Patie marry his longtime love, Peggy, because she is beneath the family's station. The onstage recognition scene occurs when the now-revealed Sir William has to adjudicate a supposed case of witchcraft. The "witch" turns out to be the former nurse of Sir William's sister, who died, leaving the infant Peggy to a cruel stepmother. It is now thirteen years since the old nurse left Peggy at the door of a poor, honest farmer. Although Patie may believe that "poor and rich but differ in the name" (86), the happy ending can occur only with recovery of Peggy's aristocratic identity.

A recent scholar of Scottish culture sees Ramsay's characters as "transitional between upper-class Augustan portraits of 'the happy and the good' man or woman, and Burns's man of independent mind, who 'looks and laughs at a' that'" (Crawford 94). Yet the aristocratic, patriarchal world of this play fixes it in an earlier time, one untouched by those new ideas of nature and society that would reshape the body politic. Ramsay's play acquires its Arcadian aura by linking up with the time of Charles II, the golden age of the Stuart past that, like other golden ages, was largely a mental construction.

The scene of nakedness in the bath, occurring in Longus and reported in Ramsay, represents a freedom of the body that was out of vogue in the 1700s; even shepherds could not heed the sage's advice to lie naked and embrace. Among the idyllic narratives embedded in James Thomson's *The Seasons* (1730), the story of Damon and Musidora in "Summer" in the final (1746) version makes the scene of Musidora's bathing a test of Damon's fidelity and hence of his love. Damon happens to be sitting by a stream when his love Musidora appears, thinking she is alone:

> Ye prudes in virtue, say,
> Say, ye severest, what would you have done?
> Meantime, this fairer nymph than ever blest
> Arcadian stream, with timid eyes around
> The banks surveying, stripped her beauteous limbs
> To taste the lucid coolness of the flood.
> (1298–1303)

In Thomson's first, more sensual, version of the story (originally published in 1730) the scene ends as the naked Musidora, who is accompanied by two other women, is about to enter the water, with the unseen Damon still watching: "And Musidora fixing in his heart / Informed and humanized him into man" (cited in Thomson 102, editor's note on line 1333 of "Summer"). The lines needed revising for other reasons than propriety. Crouching and peeping, Damon is hardly in a posture of mutuality, of "esteem enlivened by desire" (to use the phrase of Thomson's that becomes Jean Hagstrum's title). The last line also absurdly implies that Damon becomes a "man" by seeing a naked woman. Altering and expanding, Thomson has Damon withdraw from the scene, "Checked . . . / By love's respectful modesty" (1334–35). The youth leaves a note, however, which earns Musidora's grateful answer: "the time may come you need not fly" (1370). In Longus's bathing scenes, it is Chloe who first sees her beloved's naked body—an image that plants the first stirrings of passion in her heart. But Thomson's readers would not have wanted female eroticism to equal that of the male.

Thomson's great poem of natural description appealed to many outside of Britain; it furthered in no small way the increasing appreciation of nature that scholars have noticed in mid-eighteenth-century France. The English poem gave rise to translations and imitations, such as Saint-Lambert's *Les Saisons*, which Voltaire praised in a letter of 1769 as superior to the original. Somewhat closer to plagiarism than imitation is Nicolas Léonard's "L'Amour discret" in *Idylles et poëmes champêtres* (1775): Damon sits thinking of Lucinde, when she unexpectedly appears and prepares to bathe; the gallant Damon, like his namesake in Thomson's revision, then departs, leaving a note. Léonard's volume also includes an imitation of Goldsmith, "Le village détruit." His poems "Syrinx et Pan" and "L'Hyver," in which Daphnis rejoices in the winter landscape and his beloved, owe their existence quite directly to Longus.

One of Thomson's Swiss admirers contributed enormously to the developing poetry of nature: the prose-poet Salomon Gessner, born the son of a prominent Zurich publisher. At the age of nineteen, Gessner traveled to Germany hoping to break into the ranks of poets, only to be told that he lacked talent for verse and should stick to prose (see Hibberd 4–28). An early result was Gessner's *Daphnis* (1754), a loosely structured narrative in three books, marked by pensive wandering and reflection on nature-philosophy. In one episode Daphnis pauses in his love complaints to hear an old exile, Aristus, praise rural simplicity over the hopelessness of life under tyranny. While this work's affiliations with Longus are slight, not so the *Idyllen* (1756), Gessner's collection of prose-poems that made his reputation and signal a turning away from the vogue of "wit" in European poetry.

Gessner declares that the idylls of Theocritus, his chief model, belong "far from the epigrammatic wit in which we are schooled," adding that Theocritus "has comprehended the difficult art of bringing a pleasant carelessness into his songs, which poetry must have had in its first childhood" (2:xii).[8] Sophist wit has no place in poetry that evokes the "childhood" of the race. Gessner's shepherds own the sincerity of unfallen humanity—whether in "Chloe," where the shepherdess prays that the nymphs of the cave will help draw Lycas to her; or in "Mirtil, Thirsis," which recounts another Chloe's near-despair at the thought that Daphnis may have drowned; or in "Menalcas und Alexis," where a grandfather instructs young Alexis on the beauty of virtuous behavior. The imagery of idyllic romance—caves, gardens, storms, flocks—abounds, even though narrative scarcely occurs.

One idyll, "Daphnis, Chloe," confirms Gessner's expressed admiration for

Milton (see letter of 8 January 1763 in Gessner 3:158), echoing the famous Eve-Narcissus scene in *Paradise Lost* (4.460–91). Milton's Eve discovers her beauty in a reflecting pool and then takes flight when she sees, for the first time, the less-beautiful Adam approaching her. Gessner's Chloe admires her own beauty and wishes it could attract Daphnis; love and narcissism can coexist in this golden age. Meanwhile, the shepherd lover has slipped behind her and breaks the reflection by casting rose petals on the water (2:50). The two fall into each other's arms and declare their love. Milton's complex myth of the feminine utterly dissolves (like virtually all difference) in Gessner's rose petals. The *Idyllen* exists to gratify every heart's desire in a naive utopian fashion. Still, Diderot, Rousseau, and other *philosophes* openly appreciated Gessner. He had circumvented Christianity in a classically grounded vision of uncorrupt humanity. Schiller praises Gessner for uniting the naive with the sentimental, but he cautions that because the Swiss poet "is neither wholly nature nor wholly ideal, he cannot for that reason be quite acceptable to a rigorous taste that cannot forgive half-measures in aesthetic matters" (*Naive* 151). In other words, Schiller finds Gessner all too typical of "the abstract reflection and self-sufficient feeling that the age and its poetry were addicted to" (Reed 78).

These brief lyric prose pieces had already established Gessner's remarkable reputation when he published his brief play, *Evander und Alcimna*. Grouped as it was, in its first publication, with the "poems" of Gessner in *Gedichte von S. Gessner* (1762), this pastoral comedy seems intended as a closet morality play or philosophical dialogue rather than a text to be enacted on the stage. In reading the work, it helps to remember that the publishing date lies midway between Rousseau's *Discourse on Inequality* and Diderot's *Supplement to Bougainville's Voyage*. A reader of both philosophers, Gessner nonetheless acknowledges that *Daphnis and Chloe*—along with Virgil and, chiefly, Theocritus—had formed the basis of all his pastorals.[9]

The play sweetens the foundling story: an oracle tells the couple's fathers, both princes, to leave their infants with shepherds. For eighteen years Lamon (a foster father's name retained from Longus) has cared for Evander (a name recalling Virgil's Arcadian "good man"), while Chloe has looked after Alcimna (a name that derives perhaps from *alkimê*, "she who is strong") for sixteen years. Both royal offspring are exceptionally beautiful, virtuous, and deeply in love. The play follows the last part of Longus's story, as the two fathers return to claim their children and to see them joined in marriage. After some brief misunderstandings (including the possibility that Evander cannot marry Alcimna because she is of low birth), the two leave in royal robes to celebrate a rustic wedding. The heart of this play is a series of dialogues between the two lovers and some character types from their fathers' civilized world. These figures embody the usual antipastoral vices: overindulgence, vanity, military ambition, servility. The nobleman who addresses Evander in act 2, boasting of his amorous escapades, may descend from Longus's Gnatho, but he and the other stereotypes undergo no change of heart, no comic reintegration into the society. These dialogues, so engaged with life according to a philosophy of nature, recall Sir Thomas More's *Utopia* more than *Daphnis and Chloe*, in keeping with the unstrenuously philosophical tenor of Gessner's other writing.

Such ideological content explains the limitations of Gessner's idyllicism as Schiller sees it when he says that "One of Gessner's shepherds . . . cannot delight us as nature by the fidelity of imitation, since for this he is too ideal a being; he can as little satisfy us as an ideal by infinitude of thought since for this he is much too inadequate a creature" (*Naive* 181). Ramsay's Scottish shepherds, with their folkish songs, superstitions, and dialect, are less ideal and superficially more natural—perhaps even, to use Johnson's famous word for pastoral, "vulgar." These Scottish characters, steeped in old ways, living on a ruined estate, committed to a lost political cause, readily adopt the elegiac tones of sentimental poetry. Gessner's idyllicism moves in the opposite direction, approaching satire: the praise of nature serves to expose the vices of civilization. Gessner may have gained favor with the *philosophes* because his characters raise the era's issues. Diderot helped introduce him to the reading public in France, and through French and English translators he became yet another idyllic "best seller," reaching across the seas to American writers such as Harriet Beecher Stowe.

John Hibberd neatly summarizes the forces at work behind the Gessner phenomenon, so difficult to understand today:

> To a Europe increasingly conscious of the evils of civilisation he became a symbol of natural virtue, reminding his readers that innocence might still exist in the countryside. Largely through his influence his

native Switzerland came to be seen as a haven of rural happiness and true morality.... Many of the thoughts and sentiments now associated with the name of Rousseau became familiar to the reading public of Europe through Gessner's works; they seemed all the more convincing and appealing because expressed by a man who was utterly genuine and untainted by civilisation and formal education. The simplicity of his writings appealed directly to the taste of the age; they were taken as proof that great poetry, rivalling that of the Ancients, could be written in modern Europe. (1–2)

NATURE WITHOUT WIT

Gessner's first French translation in 1760 rode a wave of fashionable upper-class pastoralism. Long before Marie Antoinette's "Hameau," the pretended farming community near Versailles, the court enjoyed rural themes in entertainments, as with the 1757 *fête champêtre* at Bagatelle honoring the Polish king and featuring a village fair and peasant musicians (Charlton 20). As printings of *Daphnis and Chloe* grew more frequent, the story underwent a musical adaptation performed at the opera in 1747. A witness reports that this "ballet" opened with an old gardener's recollection of early love, interrupted by a visit from Cupid. When Chloe was captured by pirates, Daphnis took a boat to rescue her. After Pan revealed everything to Chloe's true father, the couple's marriage was arranged. It seems that the weakness of the poetry, by an eighteen-year-old named Laujon, was exceeded only by the poverty of Joseph Boismortier's music (see Grimm 1:95–98). Whatever its defects, this composition begins a long line of works that exploit Longus's frequent incidents of music and dance, a tradition that continues with Christoph Gluck (who composed music for the Longus-based one-act "opéra comique" by Charles Favart, *Cythère assiégée*, printed in 1760), Rousseau, Offenbach, Tchaikowski, and, of course, Ravel.[10] As recently as 1996 a musical score for soprano and violin based on the romance was published by Dimitris Terzakis, a Greek composer living in Germany.

Taste and mentality have changed since the earlier 1700s, when the naivety of Gessner's pastorals and this opera would have been unendurable. In earlier dramatic uses of Longus, couples fall in love but, not knowing what love is, are comically beset with conflicts and anxieties (see Munro). Playwrights may wittily complicate Longus's situation by putting two couples into this state, as Dryden does in *The Tempest*. Jacques Autreau's *Les Amans ignorans* (1720) makes Arlequin and Nina objects of laughter when love takes them by surprise. Pierre de Marivaux's *La Double inconstance* (1723), a wonderfully crafted play about courtly and rustic visions of life and love, "poses the problem," as James Munro puts it, "of what happens to Daphnis and Chloe [called Arlequin and Sylvie] if they are brought into contact with the world outside their village, and concludes that this enlarging of their horizons would lead them to realize the inadequacy of their adolescent affection for each other" (133). The comic roots of *Daphnis and Chloe* thrive again in the theater. But by the century's end the fate of innocence under love's spell becomes matter for pathos, not wit.

Early in the Gessner vogue, Jean-François Marmontel wrote a story set in a contemporary but Arcadian Switzerland, "La Bergére des Alpes"—one of the "moral tales" that he began publishing in 1755 in the *Mercure de France*. In a sentimental mode, two young refugees from the world's cruelty become Swiss shepherds. The story took on a life apart from the 1761 collection of these stories, *Contes moraux*, and achieved a remarkable publishing history all its own.[11] But it is Marmontel's "Annette et Lubin" that most recalls Longus, a tale of two cousins raised together who, orphaned, fall in love and make love, being unaware of the possible consequences. Like Longus's couple, they are inseparable; they think alike; they live only for each other and their flocks. Annette is utterly without wiles, and Lubin weeps as readily as she does. When the village magistrate notices one day that Annette is pregnant, a condition of which she was ignorant, he is horrified to discover that the child was conceived in an incestuous relationship. At last the wise lord of the estate settles the problem by persuading the Vatican to allow the cousins to marry.

In isolation this *conte* would pose a complex problem of interpretation, but in the context of the other tales and the author's professed intentions, there is no argument for irony here. Marmontel inhabits a marginal zone between wit and sentiment. Although his world is in its way as utopian as that of Gessner's primitive Greeks, his rustics need the shaping influence of civilized institutions. A moralist first, Marmontel parrots Huet's opinions concerning *Daphnis and Chloe* in his own *Essai sur les romans*: "Nothing more vain, more frivolous, less intelligent; nothing, above all, less delicate in matters of decency. And yet this is the flower of ancient romance!" (10:294).[12]

Gessner's pseudo-Greek idylls profess a love of nature anchored in no actual space or time. As such, they retain the innocence of humanity without history. Gessner's young French admirer Jean-Pierre Florian introduces into this sensibility a deep attachment to actual places, to nature specified. "I will celebrate my country," he promises at the beginning of *Estelle* (1787). "I will paint those pretty lands where the green olive, the deep red mulberry, the golden clusters grow together beneath an eternally blue heaven" (287).[13] The author grounds his natural description in actual places of his homeland in the south of France. The Gardon River, the village of Massane, the ancient town of Sauve, the valley of Beau-Rivage—this is a real landscape traversed with a love of place that anticipates the rural settings of George Sand, R. D. Blackmore, Emilia Pardo Bazán, and Thomas Hardy. Although his narrator wears the mask of sentimental exile, Florian enjoyed the patronage of Voltaire and the royal family, who would soon see him enrolled in the French Academy. There, on 14 May 1788, he delivered a eulogy for the recently deceased Gessner, hailing him as the poet of "filial devotion, fatherly tenderness, discreet affection, pure and bashful love" (Grimm 15:265).

All these domestic qualities converge in the prose narrative of *Estelle*, a pastoral romance grafted to the adventure-romance style of Montemayor or Cervantes's *Galatea*, which Florian had recently translated. The story blends heroic with pastoral, folk ballads and lyrics with the prose. But whereas Renaissance romance shepherd-heroes and heroines are always disguised aristocrats, these are and remain common shepherds: Némorin, orphaned in childhood; Estelle, his love and companion since that time; her parents, Raimond and Marguerite. At the beginning the lovers must part because Raimond has promised Estelle to Méril, son of an old friend. The separation allows the usual sad songs, exiles, and reunions, interspersed with Raimond's capture by Catalan "pirates" and a war between France and Aragon, in which Némorin distinguishes himself under the heroic Gaston de Foix. When the lovers finally do marry, Estelle has endured war and the loss of her husband, Méril, while Némorin has rediscovered and lost his boyhood friend Isidore. Obviously the story has more in common with the Heliodorus tradition than with Longus's idyllic romance, but the elegiac tone, the pathos, the emphasis on the countryside and on the fidelity and sacrifice of its inhabitants anticipate Bernardin's *Paul et Virginie* more fully than anything in the previous canon of romance.

The "Essai sur la pastorale," published with *Estelle*, reveals how carefully Florian had thought out his relationship to the tradition. From his praise of Gessner, whose pastorals he says had first inspired him to translate *Galatea* (273), a reader might expect more lyric than narrative. Gessner, Florian continues, may not have Virgil's power to charm the ear, but "he speaks as well to the heart, and inspires in it the purest sentiments. We form our taste reading Virgil; we nourish our souls reading Gessner" (278).[14] The pastoral eclogue, Florian thinks, lacks something found only in the narrative. Because eclogues merely present two or three speakers discussing an idea, a collection of eclogues resembles a collection of opening scenes of plays. Guarini and Tasso recognized this defect when they wrote their pastoral dramas—a problematic form, observes Florian, since theater requires strong passions that are inconsistent with pastoral. *Daphnis and Chloe* is a case in point: "This inimitable model of grace, of naivety, has always pleased more than Theocritus and Guarini, and would do so even more, without certain excessively bold images that ought to be banished from every work of this genre. Shepherds' love should be as pure as the crystal of their fountains; and just as the chief attraction of the most beautiful shepherdesses consists in their modesty, so the principal charm of a pastoral should be to inspire virtue" (281).[15]

Huet had said much the same a century earlier, followed by Marmontel and Dunlop. Yet no one paid Longus the respect shown here by Florian, who seems to think that the modern (Christian) poet must strive for Longus's grace without his pagan iniquities. Sannazaro, the first modern to "put the eclogue into a romance" (281), started a tradition lasting through Sidney and D'Urfé—though the latter's work offends in its great length, "a terrible fault in almost any kind of literature and moreover one indefensible in pastoral" (281). Finally, Florian takes special exception to the multiplicity of episodes in the Renaissance romance tradition, since these distract readers from the main characters. He objects to the appearance of characters from distant lands, since everyone knows shepherds scarcely ever leave their villages and valleys. The genre, in other words, requires that sense of a particular region which permeates his own *Estelle*—and which would characterize Wordsworth's pastoral narratives such as "Michael" and "The Ruined Cottage." Pastoral romance should strive for the same unity of place that is required in drama, says Florian (282)—a comment that acknowledges the form's roots in the conventions governing new comedy. The readiness with which Sand could adapt her romans champêtres to the stage suggests again Florian's forward-looking sensibility.

The view of innocence will always vary with the observer, but it is possible to trace a development during the period covered in this chapter, from the mid–seventeenth to the later eighteenth century. For the most part, Longus belongs to France. However, in England, where the French *libertin* pose had its moment, three works—the Thornley translation of *Daphnis and Chloe*, the Dryden-Davenant revision of *The Tempest*, and the Craggs translation of Longus, *Pastoral Amours*—suggest the same tendency of wit at the expense of innocence that invests the French regent's illustrations and the comedies of Marivaux and his contemporaries. After the mid–1700s, coincident with the renewed enthusiasm for nature in much of Europe, nostalgia for an age of innocence increases, a softened sensibility that encourages the Gessner phenomenon. Gessner himself disparaged the taste for "epigrammatic wit" but failed in an excess of idealism—or a dearth of intellect. While a Gessner shepherd, as Schiller says, "is too ideal a being" (*Naive* 151), Marvell's "Daphnis and Chloe" contemplates a fallen world where only the feminine part of humanity belongs to nature. For this era, at any rate, like Schiller we are left with the example of Milton and his critical understanding of the state of innocence. Milton accepts innocence as an ideal in the divine mind but despises, again in Schiller's words, "the unworthy evasion of cheapening the meaning of the ideal in order to accommodate it to human inadequacy" (153). It remains to be seen whether there were other ways to bridge the gulf between the ideal and the humanly inadequate.

❧ ❧ ❧ ❧

Paul, Virginie, and George

FRENCH PROPERTY

The moralists never managed to remove the earliest idyllic romance from the shelves. A significant moment in Longus's reputation occurred ten years before Florian's *Estelle* with the publication of Jean Baptiste Villoison's masterful edition of *Daphnis and Chloe*. The lengthy "Prolegomena" defends the Greek author against Bayle and especially Huet, arguing first that Longus was no "Sophista" (ii–iii) and that his work resembles earlier more than later Greek literature. Longus's Greek "flows forth like a silvery stream shaded by green woodlands, and is so resplendent, so vivid, so polished that every grace of word and thought is woven into it" (xxxvi).[1] Villoison finds in Daphnis and Chloe an open sincerity and simplicity that must appeal to every class of reader. His textual notes and commentary run to over three hundred pages, the fruit of collating eight manuscripts, seven editions, and Amyot's translation. Villoison's important scholarly work, communicating a new awareness of Longus's significance, contributed to the surge of Longus in print during the 1780s and 1790s. In 1785 F.-V. Mullot obtained a new translation of *Daphnis et Chloe* (included with the Byzantine romance *Ismene and Ismenias*) for his series Bibliotheque universelle des dames. Amyot's language, says the translator in his anonymous preface, is becoming unintelligible, especially for women (168). For their sake the translator omits the "indelicate" parts, the Lycaenion episode being replaced with an invented chaste tale of Agnotis and Edonis (the names mean "Without-knowledge" and "leisure"). "Our aim," he writes, "is to produce for our readers an entertainment that amuses the spirit without corrupting the soul" (172).

By about 1800 most European readers who knew Longus were indebted to French publishers for that reading; even the newly available Annibale

Caro translation was also soon published in France. By the century's end an anonymous reviewer of the Angel Day translation could observe in the *Atheneum* of 16 August 1890: "while English readers neglect 'Daphnis and Chloe,' our lively French neighbours are constantly issuing new editions" (219). The lively French had in fact secured custody of Longus, first with Amyot himself and then with Paul-Louis Courier's discovery of the long-lost lacuna—the scene of Daphnis's bath—in a manuscript in Florence. The aged Goethe had been reading the Amyot-Courier *Daphnis and Chloe* when he commended the book to Johann Peter Eckermann in 1831. It is, Goethe said, a story

> so beautiful that, amid the bad circumstances in which we live, we cannot retain the impression we receive from it, but are astonished anew every time we read it. The clearest day prevails in it, and we think we are looking at nothing but Herculanean pictures; while these paintings react upon the book, and assist our fancy as we read. . . .
>
> The whole poem shows the highest art and cultivation. It has been so well considered that not a motive is wanting: all are of the best and most substantial kind; as, for instance, that of the treasure near the dolphin on the shore. Then there is a taste, and a perfection, and a delicacy of feeling, which cannot be excelled. . . .
>
> It would need a whole book to estimate properly all the great merits of this poem; and it would be well to read it every year, to be instructed by it again and again, and to receive anew the impression of its great beauty. (398–400)

Longus's "poem" appears to answer both the classic and romantic in Goethe's sensibility—it has form, organic wholeness, and a balance of feeling and imagery; it is "beautiful," but it also "instructs" in a morality both close to nature and superior to convention. Beauty is truth.

Later in the century the classical scholar Erwin Rohde, Goethe's countryman, sought an explanation for this praise of a work he himself despised: Goethe must have been applauding not Longus's poem but Amyot's translation, a masterpiece in itself (see Rohde 516–17 n.3). Rohde does not account for Goethe's imitation of Longus in act 2, scene 3, of his *Faust*—an Arcadian episode of caves and oak forests where the infant Euphorion is nursed on ewe's milk while Pan and the nymphs keep watch. The strong visual sense of this scene has been attributed to the influence of Nicolas Poussin, though he was only one in a line of French painters, beginning with Paris Bordone, who made *Daphnis and Chloe* a familiar subject of French art.

Bordone's rather generic painting of Daphnis and Chloe dates to his stay in the city of Paris at about the time of Amyot's first edition. Venetian pastoral landscape in the style of Giorgione had already begun to make its way from Venice into French painting with the work of Claude Lorraine (1600–82). Book illustrations exist as early as Crispyn de Passe's copper engravings for Marcassus's 1628 "translation," far surpassed by the regent Phillipe's designs, reprinted throughout the eighteenth century. The same period saw paintings by Etienne Jeaurat (or Joras), Charles-Joseph Natoire, and Jean-Jacques Lebarbier (six designs, 1798).[2] In the nineteenth century Jean-Georges Vibert's *Daphnis et Chloé*, a large (fifty-four by eighty-seven inches) canvas showing Daphnis teaching Chloe to play the syrinx, indicates the conventionality of the subject by this time (1866), the painter having made his Salon debut three years before. Jean-Léon Gérôme's 1898 painting of the couple leading their flocks signals an impatience with the traditional sensuousness and intimacy toward Longus's lovers. It has an oddly epic grandeur in its landscape, owing to the painter's imposing mountain looming over the plain.[3] The book illustrations of Aristide Maillol (fifty-three woodcuts executed in 1937) and Marc Chagall (paintings done in 1965) reveal in the modern era a tendency toward primitive simplicity and nature displacing sensuous, romantic passion. Chagall in particular recovers the pagan feeling of the text whereby, as noted earlier, the mythic, animal, and human—"above" and "below"—seem indistinguishable.

Passion colored the representations of Daphnis and Chloe in the art of Baron François Gérard, beginning with his six designs for engraving struck in 1800. The pictures are remote from Longus's world. *Mélancolie de Daphnis* shows the shepherd in the wintry landscape of book 3, though it is difficult to read "melancholy" in Longus's own scene, however much intervening centuries of European romance may require it. Similarly, when Gérard illustrates the scene of Daphnis's near-faint with joy when Chloe returns from captivity (2.30), the image puts Daphnis in a posture not of exuberance but of unrequited love (or desire) and Chloe in an attitude of Milton's "sweet reluctant amorous delay." Twenty-four years later, when Gérard returns to the subject in paintings, passion yields to sentiment

Daphnis and Chloe Embrace by Aristide Maillol. Wood engraving, printed in black, page: (irregular) 7⅞ x 5¼". Taken from Longus, *Daphnis and Chloe* (London: A. Zwemmer, 1937), title page. Courtesy of the Museum of Modern Art, New York, The Louis E. Stern Collection.

and Lying naked on the ground. It's cold indeed; but after Philetas we'l endure it. This, to them, was a kind of nocturnal play, and entertainment. When it was day, and their flocks were driven to the field, they ran to kisse, and embrace one another with a bold, impatient fury, which before they never did. Yet of that third remedy, which the old Philetas taught, they durst not

Daphnis and Chloe Sitting under an Oak Embracing by Aristide Maillol. Wood engraving, printed in black, page: (irregular) 7⅞ x 5¼". Taken from Longus, *Daphnis and Chloe* (London: A. Zwemmer, 1937), 72. Courtesy of the Museum of Modern Art, New York, The Louis E. Stern Collection.

(Moulin 108): Chloe sleeps, her hand resting on her lover's knee while he is about to crown her with a wreath—he above, she below, in submissive content. Both the lively innocence of Longus's original couple and, what is more important, their mutuality in love are very distant from these images of grand passion.

LONGUS BAPTIZED?

The idyllic tradition produced one great work of revitalization in France at the end of the eighteenth century; it is to literature almost what the contemporary revolution is to political life. This was *Paul et Virginie* (1788), written by a naturalist and former military engineer, Jacques-Henri Bernardin de Saint-Pierre. A text that was widely reprinted and almost immediately translated, it was also made into a successful drama that was still drawing audiences as Louis XVI faced the guillotine.[4] With its fusion of sentiment, exotic Arcadia, and Rousseauistic philosophy, it captured readers everywhere. Well received at once, it was long cherished in the European imagination. Within a year, five editions appeared, along with an anonymous English translation entitled *Paul and Mary*, probably by Daniel Malthus, Rousseau's English disciple and the father of Thomas (Toinet 63). Then in 1796 came a version by Helen Maria Williams, who undertook the work to keep her sanity, hiding in Paris during the Terror. Paul Toinet counts, in France alone, as of 1900, editions numbering in the hundreds; by then in England the romance had seen at least sixty printings. In the United States twenty-five editions of Bernardin appeared during the nineteenth century: the Houghton Mifflin 1885 edition of Jewett's *Marsh Island* includes a catalog listing the title in two different issues, one bound with Frédéric de La Motte Fouqué's *Undine* and *Sintram*.

Such company marks the text as romance, even though its author may not have aimed that way. Indeed, *Paul et Virginie*—which first saw print as an illustrative tale in the author's expanded *Etudes de la Nature* of 1788—aims to be many things. Its mixed genres were first recognized a century ago by one of Bernardin's chief scholars: "We do not hesitate to admit, then, that *Paul et Virginie* is one of the most mixed productions there has ever been in any literature: novel, if you will, since there is action that weaves and unweaves, but also a poetic handbook of the apprentice encyclopedist, for one finds there a political economy, a pedagogy, an aesthetic, a moral philosophy, and a theodicy all in one" (Maury 531).[5] He forgot to mention travel narrative—and, of course, idyllic romance.

Jean Fabre, in an indispensable essay, sees the combination of aims as more creative than mechanical. Bernardin's purpose was "that of joining to the vision of the shipwrecked maiden the theme of childhood lovers, traditionally cherished by the grand idyll and the delicate [mignarde] idyll of that century, along with the theme of the education of two 'children of nature,' tirelessly reworked by the philosophical literature of the time in the form of experiences more or less absurd" (232).[6] To Fabre the text is a new creature, utterly unlike the moralizings of Marmontel or the derivative pastoral of Florian.

As an appendage to a work of natural science, the novel (or novella—about one hundred pages of text in the Garnier edition) anticipates the nineteenth-century practice of intertwining fiction with nature writing, loving descriptions of actual rural scenes.[7] Familiarity with Bernardin's novel was so widespread that it became a byword throughout the nineteenth century for certain sentiments about nature, if not life. On the one hand François-René Chateaubriand, who had almost memorized the book, celebrated it as the consummate Christian idyll; on the other, its melancholy tone satisfied the tragic bent of some romantics—Schiller's elegiac voice again.

Realists did not treat it kindly. *Paul et Virginie* is the favorite novel of Flaubert's Emma Bovary. Thomas Hardy's schoolmaster Phillotson in *Jude the Obscure* associates Jude and Sue with Paul and Virginie (horribly wrongly, it turns out). And in 1878 William Mallock published a satirical *The New Paul and Virginia*, featuring a positivist Paul and an Anglican ritualist Virginia. By the end of the century, people had undoubtedly endured so many operatic, musical, dramatic, painterly, and other renderings of this story that it badly needed a rest—though it still had enough life for silent films made in the United States (1912) and on the island of Mauritius (1923–24).

Can we still share early readers' admiration for a story that extols a heroine who chooses to drown rather than swim for her life because she would have to remove her clothes? It helps to remember that the work first appeared virtually as an afterthought in a study of nature. The "new image of nature" that Charlton outlines fed people's interest in this Rousseauistic account of two young lovers, children of two abandoned women leading solitary lives on Mauritius, victims of "the cruel prejudices of Europe" (Bernardin 89). Virginie's mother, Madame de la Tour, marries a man of lower class, against her family's wishes, and goes with him to the colony to start a new life. The young husband dies in Madagascar on a slave-buying expedition. Paul's peasant mother, Marguerite, who has been seduced and abandoned by a nobleman in her native Brittany, comes to Mauritius to escape her shame, having borrowed just enough money to "acquire" an old Negro (82).

The cruel prejudices of Europe thus infect the characters despite their isolation. People cannot escape the class divisions of mistress and slave, aristocrat and peasant. Throughout the narrative, Paul's mother is only "Marguerite" (as common as the daisy whose name she bears); Virginie's mother, "Madame de la Tour" (whose name means "the lady of the tower"). Although these two mothers and their children are poor, the islanders praise them for their charity toward both whites and Africans. Marguerite, ever conscious of her low rank, bluntly reveals to the lovesick Paul, using a word he has never heard, that he is a bastard. He bears this stigma in his heart throughout Virginie's subsequent absence in France, imagining her in social circles he can never enter. Although Madame de la Tour seems to want the lovers to marry someday, her socially induced fears about their poverty lead her to postpone a wedding until they are better prepared. It is in the context of this social constructedness that most recent critics read Virginie's famous death, refusing to disrobe on the sinking boat and thereby displaying the "outstanding, climactic example of social conditioning" in a narrative about the impossibility of returning to nature (Cherpack 251).

European social codes, represented by the mothers' doubts and the island governor's promptings, conflict with what others know to be natural happiness. The result is an unusually writerly text, a forest of uncertainties. Did Bernardin himself know what he was doing? Cherpack questions why the children attend Sunday church services when so much is made of their living by a natural religion. Nature, the supposed root of happiness, turns out to be violent and destructive. A frame narrator hears the story from an old man of the island who befriended both families while the children were growing up. The old man is perplexing in his narrative, full of surprises. He finds only "un bonheur négatif" reading about others' unhappiness, yet he thinks being a man of letters is a noble calling (Cherpack 248). His "consolation" of Paul rests on the argument that the couple would have had a dreary, miserable life as farmers and would have died eventually anyway.

Hence the problem with readings since Chateaubriand's that declare this a Christian romance. If the narrator follows any philosophy, it belongs more with Epicurus than Christ. Straight from Lucretius, in fact, is the old man's self-description: "Like a man on a rock saved from shipwreck, I contemplate from my solitude the storms that rage in the rest of the world; my tranquillity is even redoubled by the distant sound of the tempest" (169).[8] He advocates as the best life one without the cares of family, limited to a few friends, books, a garden. He even gestures toward the Epicurean disbelief in a personal God when, after Virginie's death, he proclaims himself "doubting, after the sad end of such a virtuous girl, that any Providence exists; for there are evils so terrible and so little deserved that even the hope of the sage is shaken by them" (203–04).[9] Far from Christianizing the idyll, Bernardin leaves it unresolved.

Although Bernardin had made Rousseau's acquaintance long before 1788, and although his story supposedly preached Rousseau's ideas of life according to nature, even the vision of nature in *Paul et Virginie* is none too clear. Like many classical thinkers, Bernardin starts with nature as the principle of order in human experience. During her childhood Edenic state, Virginie appropriately expresses this principle in terms of obedience: "We should do nothing, not even good, without asking our parents" (103). After her death, in the dialogue with Paul, the old man declares nature's moral rule inevitable: "one excess always balances another" (185)—"misfortune in the midst of pleasures is for the rich a thorn in the flowers. For the poor, on the contrary, a pleasure amidst their misfortunes is a flower among thorns, and they taste its delight enthusiastically. . . . Nature has balanced all things" (188).[10] Leaving aside the Panglossian outlook on wealth and poverty here, nature's balance sheet is never squared for the lovers in the story. Their happiness ends the moment they discover who they are, the moment of the idyllic-romance "second birth": Virginie, a young aristocrat who must be socially indoctrinated; Paul, a "bastard" who should not aspire to Virginie or, finally, to anything except death. Philip Robinson argues for consistency in Bernardin's view of nature (43–59) but blames Paul's "weaker animal nature" for his "failure to show the courage of virtue in his reaction to the final catastrophe" (58). Where else is nature to be found if not in the animal?

The only way to save appearances here would be to make the narrator as misguided as Madame de la Tour, her aunt, the governor, and the smarmy priest. It doesn't occur to anyone that if the mothers could survive happily on the island with few means, Paul and Virginie could have gotten by at least as well. Narrator's consolation soon lapses into something very like *contemptus mundi*, which would not have pleased the late Jean-Jacques. Again, the problem may lie with Bernardin himself, for he sometimes forgets narrator entirely—as when reporting all Virginie's inmost thoughts while she is in her bath (Mylne 248). Author's and narrator's philosophies sometimes appear indistinguishable, particularly in preferring death to life in this world (Gooden 565). The author's very image of nature on the island is suspiciously Arcadian—for example, in the apparent lack of bothersome insects. Although the novel describes lush foliage shading the island, Bernardin's letters from Mauritius report scorching heat in a sometimes treeless landscape.[11] And even though they have supposedly attained paradise on earth, the two mothers and their slaves often express their homesickness on foreign soil.

So much about these island lovers resembles *Daphnis and Chloe* that it comes as a surprise to find that nowhere in his writings does Bernardin ever mention Longus. The Garnier editor of *Paul et Virginie*, Pierre Trahard, takes this silence as the determining evidence that "the chaste author" would not have read the romance, since he would have been offended by certain pagan scenes—"by the bold depiction of the bath in the grotto, by the pasture scene beneath the familiar oak, by the suggestive nudity, by the search for remedies to the burning call of the senses, by the fruitless attempts at physical love following the example of the animals, by the crudity of details, in short, by the atmosphere of sensuality that bathes Longus's so typically Greek, so frankly, so naturally pagan work" (iv-v).[12] If Bernardin had read Longus, Trahard continues, "any comparison with the Greek writer would have been painful to him" (vi).

This denial of Longus as source conflicts with opinions of Bernardin's early readers. Chateaubriand saw in Bernardin a Christian response to Longus, whom he thought "too free" to quote for a proper comparison in his *Génie du christianisme* (209). Villemain's "Essai sur les romans grecs" of 1828 digresses at length on the superiority of Bernardin to Longus, not only because of the children's chastity but also because of their exemplary charity: "How touching is Virginie when she goes to ask pardon from the barbarous master for the poor Negress!" (189). Sand and Sainte Beuve were perhaps most responsible for linking Bernardin and Longus, followed by Anatole France in a much-read preface to Longus and by Alexandre Dumas *fils* in his preface to Amyot's translation of Longus, attempted in the language of Amyot himself (Dumas excoriates Bernardin's God, who "barbarously would unite [the lovers] only in the grave"). Trahard grants the parallels between *Daphnis et Chloe* and *Paul et Virginie* that are identified by a modern Longus editor: similar plots, the same chaste lovers with their excessive ignorance, modesty, sensual dreaming, the same "secret concupiscence that distances us from true purity" (iv). But these he dismisses as coincidental.

Since this kind of story had existed for several centuries in the culture, for my purposes it makes little difference whether or not Bernardin consciously adapted Longus's romance. Like all such stories, this one ultimately echoes Longus. Yet Trahard overlooks many details that weaken his case, and he perhaps misconstrues Bernardin's moral sense. On balance, Bernardin apparently baptized the pagan story into his own idiosyncratic faith of Christianity, Epicureanism, and Rousseauism, substituting Providence for Pan and the nymphs and lapsing finally, without regard to his philosophical inconsistencies, into the fashionable melancholy and *Liebestod* of European romance.

Similarities exist, then, in the use of a frame to create narratorial distance, in the island setting, and in the break in the story between childhood and the time of courtship. Longus's opening ecphrasis has also been compared with Bernardin's opening, when the narrator interprets the scene (landscape, ruined cottages) for the young traveler (Cherpack 255). The couple bathe together only as little children, and it is during a solitary bath in their childhood washing place that Virginie feels the first strong pull of passion, the same undefined yearnings as Daphnis and Chloe. In recasting the original bathing scene, Bernardin perhaps aimed at imposing Christian modesty, but the passions that sweep over Virginie in the dark water create a sexually provocative episode.

Although tropical Mauritius lacks the seasonal changes of Lesbos, the rainy season punctuates the narrative in the same way that winter and harvest time do *Daphnis and Chloe*. After Virginie's bath a great storm destroys Paul's elegant little garden, recalling the destruction of Dionysophanes' garden. Paul's garden, explicitly called a work of art and nature, is described with the same care and detail as the gardens in Longus. The second storm, after the aunt has deliberately sent Virginie home during hurricane season, takes Virginie's life. In Longus the storm is providential; in Bernardin it is (as I understand providence) anything but.

A telling similarity, one that brings to mind Shakespeare's romances, is the value placed on the feminine in both works. Near the end of the "preambule" to the fancy 1806 edition, Bernardin writes a long panegyric to women. Women contribute more than philosophers to humanity; they are responsible for families and society; they restrain masculine ambition and have abolished bad schooling, slavery, torture, and other barbarism. The matriarchy in his novel serves the function of Longus's nymphs. Both authors share an understanding of the feminine as the beauty and harmony of the natural order, the love and tenderness of the supernatural. The runaway slave whom the children care for appears all the more pathetic in being a female victim of a male institution. Moreover, her intent to drown herself identifies her with Virginie, who will drown after a period of virtual enslavement in French aristocratic society. Probably this desire to establish a rudimentary utopian matriarchy (Bernardin had already started and left unfinished a Rousseauist utopia, *Arcadie*) explains why he did not make the two children foundlings, although they are as "lost" to European society as any orphans could be.[13]

A subtle displacement from Longus is Virginie's "captivity," echoing the kidnappings of both Daphnis and Chloe. Paul pines away in his beloved's absence, just as Daphnis does, and sounds the familiar elegiac apostrophe to nature—"Poor birds, no more will you go to meet your dear protector" (157). The lament resembles the moment when Chloe thinks Daphnis is leaving her and deserting his goats (4.27). These are stock scenes in modern as in ancient pastoral. But Paul shares another moment with Daphnis and Chloe when he thinks his beloved will marry someone of a higher class. Several other small but telling similarities also deserve mention. Daphnis's climb to the treetop to bring Chloe the last most beautiful apple (itself an echo of a poem by Sappho) suggests little Paul's habit of climbing to bring Virginie "some nice fruit or a bird's nest from the very top of a tree" (90). Both couples take roles in mimes for entertainment (2.37; 124–27), though Bernardin, consistent with his "baptism" of Longus, has the children enact biblical pastorals, not Pan and Syrinx. They dance the roles of Moses and Zipporah or Ruth and Boaz not to the panpipe but to Domingue's tom-tom.

Finally, while the prophetic dream is familiar in romance, the double dream is rarer: one occurs near the beginning of *Daphnis and Chloe* when both fathers dream that Love has blessed their new children. At the end of *Paul et Virginie*, Madame de la Tour and Marguerite both have the same dream of the dead Virginie clothed in white, standing in a paradisal garden. Harriet Beecher Stowe would use a similar double dream in the melancholy ending of her *Pearl*. The difference between ancient and modern in this detail bespeaks the difference between a romance of eros and one of thanatos, as befits the elegiac tendency of idyllic romances in the nineteenth century.

Love unites, death separates. Countering the drive toward unity in Longus, Bernardin represents a profoundly dissociated world (Billaut 80). Yet a romance of love in death leaves the feeling that the lovers would not have lived had they not loved. Of the many motives that might guide a story to this outcome, one must be the conviction that ideal love and mutual affection die quickly in a depraved civilization. Milton acknowledges this dark romance element after the Fall, when Eve pleads with Adam, "Let us seek Death, or he not found, supply / With our own hands his Office on ourselves" (*pl* 10.1001–04). Adam recognizes the noble self-sacrifice behind her offer—

Eve, thy contempt of life and pleasure seems
To argue something more sublime
And excellent.
(10.1013–15)

But more closely scrutinized, suicide

                                      implies,
Not thy contempt, but anguish and regret
For loss of life and pleasure overlov'd."
(10.1017–19)

Behind the death wish of certain romances, then, lies "pleasure overloved," a kind of hedonism that rebels against mortal limitations. The divine, the "correct" love story of Genesis insists, as *Daphnis and Chloe* does, that life goes on, even though Genesis is burdened with the kind of knowledge that never comes to the Greek lovers. Bernardin weeps on the shoreline of childhood innocence. Because his couple cannot have love's joys to perfection, they must taste none of them. They are martyrs to the curse of finitude. In William Henry Hudson's *Green Mansions* Abel merely takes this logic one step further when he rebels against God, vowing "to show my hatred by being like Him" (286) when he loses Rima.

Reading *Paul et Virginie* in the light of its chief source and genre archetype may eliminate or explain at least one or two uncertainties of interpretation, though the 1788 preface creates its own uncertainties about models by praising Virgil and Theocritus. Classical pastoral meant for the most part males living alone or in small groups, singing and having erotic crises. It seldom involved the presence of women, and while it was familiar with death, it never admitted dead women (Goodden 565). These pastorals of self and solitude do not sit well with idyllic romance, which aims at the union of lovers. In Bernardin's construction, Virgilian pastoral melancholy conflicts with the buoyant new-comic strain in Longus. The strangeness of the novel also owes something to its Renaissance antecedents, to Sannazaro's and Tasso's fusion of romance with pastoral solitude and melancholy. The result is women living without a community, solitary travelers, solitary old men, lonely Paul, lugubrious Paul, a dialogue between Youth and Age, Virginie as matter for panegyric. Incidents come and go languidly, almost inseparable from reflection, in contrast to the quickly unfolding episodes in Longus.

Comparison of Longus and Bernardin also shows thematic cruxes more sharply. Eros tends Philetas's garden; nature destroys Paul's. The difference between the two sages—Philetas with his discourse on love, the old man with his homily of duty—encapsulates the difference between the two works. The handling of the divinely aroused storm at sea is also revealing. In Longus, as in Shakespeare, the storm is spiritual retribution for unjust men, pure and simple. The problem is not simply that the pagan sensuality of Longus "allows him to have innocence and eroticism coexisting without the proscribed sensuality" (Racault 180) but that Longus is a more literate writer than Bernardin, whose couple begins in a pastoral world, but ends in one that is "indisputably of romance" (Racault 192).

The uncertainty of genre parallels that of ideology. Bernardin indicates the numinous origins of the fatal hurricane by having Virginie drown on Christmas Day. It is well known that his historical source-story—in which not a young maiden but the ship's captain refused to take off his clothing and consequently drowned—occurred in August 1768. Try as one might to make Bernardin a Christian Longus, the Christmas dating is a patently contrived irony like the storm itself, calling into question, as indeed the old narrator does, the works of Providence in a benighted world.

Bernardin's elegiac idyll set off its own echoes in the nineteenth century, beginning with Chateaubriand's melancholy romances of nature in New World settings, *René* and *Atala*. In *René* the restless hero flees to the banks of the Mississippi to avoid the temptations of sex with his sister-beloved, a relationship that amplifies an incest theme only faintly discernible in Bernardin. In both novellas an insightful priest provides the wisdom of Bernardin's old man. A sibling couple also appear in *Atala*, as do the trek through the forest, the heroine's angelic death, and the consolatory sermon (Logé 887). Chateaubriand later affirms in *Génie du christianisme* (1828) the value of Bernardin over Longus on the grounds of the French story's self-evident Christianity: the Christian author imitates biblical pastorals; he excels, too, in representing nature because Christianity banished the gods from the forest, leaving the wilderness in all its primitive mystery for human contemplation (209–11).

While Chateaubriand's American romances gained readers throughout the earlier 1800s, Bernardin's story, with its many haunting ambiguities, suggested to other writers far different possibilities. Like Chateaubriand, Alphonse de Lamartine knew *Paul et Virginie* by heart, creating in his *Graziella* a heroine who identifies deeply with Virginie (see Guyard). Together, Lamartine, Bernardin, and Chateaubriand all had a hand in Jorge Isaacs's brilliant Colombian romance, *María*. But an author with far more impact on the literature of her time, whose intimate knowledge of idyllic romance from Longus to Bernardin, led to her creating a new chapter in the tradition, is George Sand.

REVENONS À NOS MOUTONS

With all its vexing charm, Bernardin's story falls short of the sustained achievement in idyllic fiction by George Sand, a novelist who shows a fuller understanding than her predecessor of the genre's profound human implications. *Paul et Virginie* had already left its mark on Sand's first novel, *Indiana*, which ends in a setting evocative of Bernardin's. Future idyllic romance-writers would know her commitment to the ideal of nature mediated by the actual rural life of her own region: Eliot, Hardy, Pardo Bazán, Jewett, and Cather among them. In the United States, while Sand biographies continued to flow, her novels stayed out of print from the 1940s until the 1970s. Her increased availability today is one of the many achievements of feminist literary scholarship.

To commemorate the first anniversary of Sand's death at the age of seventy-one, Matthew Arnold paid tribute to the woman who many years earlier, at her country home, had entertained him as an obscure young traveler in France. Arnold wrote that Sand's ruling thought throughout her life was "the sentiment of the ideal life, which is none other than man's normal life as we shall some day know it" (240). Idealism is a much-discussed quality of Sand's fiction, evident in her prefaces to *La Mare au diable*, where she declares that "the dream of pastoral life has always been the ideal of cities and the courts of kings" (4) and that "Art is not a study of positive reality; it is a search for the ideal truth" (12).[14] The idealism of believing that the normal life will one day become the ideal life paradoxically aligns itself with a kind of realism. In Sand the result is a kind of fiction different from Bernardin's model yet one grounded, as his is, in the observation of nature. Sand spent most of her childhood and youth in the country, but she saw enough of Paris to appreciate country-city differences. Growing up in the country gave her an understanding of rural people and, most especially, of what chiefly escapes Bernardin, their communities. Her optimism, as it is shown in Arnold's description of the ideal—the "normal life as we shall some day know it"—also differs from Bernardin's bleak nostalgia for lost paradise. During the 1800s few idylls managed to liberate themselves from the elegiac strain of *Paul et Virginie* so completely as Sand's pastoral novels do.

Bernardin's example, however, weighed on the mind of the author in *Indiana* (1832), superficially a formula romance about a wealthy older industrialist's young, beautiful wife, who takes a libertine lover. What distinguishes the novel is the heroine's feeling for her native land, the island of Reunion (then Bourbon), located a hundred miles west of Mauritius. There, Indiana had enjoyed a tranquil childhood with an older cousin named Ralph, born to her mother's sister in the same valley where she was born. Having come to live with her after the marriage, Ralph is her constant companion, a brother-figure like Paul who happens to be an English aristocrat. Eventually, despondent and rejected by her faithless lover, she follows Ralph back to Reunion and talks him into a suicide pact. At the last moment, however, when Ralph confesses his love for her, they turn away from the abyss to find a cottage in their home valley. In this climactic chapter 30, they reflect on *Paul et Virginie*, the descriptions of the faithful dog, the songs of the "faithful Negro," the intimate conversations of the two young people.

Sand thus begins her career engaged with Bernardin's novel (Didier 217–19). Her couple, however, survive the battle with passion and civilization before returning to a happy-ever-after ending where they began. Fifteen years later, Sand's thought about nature was to progress beyond the early, rather simple derivations from Bernardin. *François le Champi* opens with a dialogue between the author and a friend on the difference between the "primitive" and the "artificial" life. The primitivist friend wishes "never to think of a painting when I look at the landscape, of music when I listen to the wind, of poetry when I admire and enjoy them together.... I would like to be a peasant; a peasant who does not know how to read, whom God has given good instincts, peaceful inclinations, and a well-formed conscience" (210).[15] Sand replies that the peasant is also an artist, with his own music and poetry, though his art may be inaccessible to the city dweller—unfortunately, for "From the shepherds of Longus to those of Trianon, pastoral life is a perfumed Eden where souls tormented and abandoned by the world's tumult have sought refuge" (212–13).[16] As the phrase "perfumed Eden" implies, Sand dislikes the citified art of ancient and Renaissance pastoral. Longus's sophist narrator may exemplify one way of conveying nature's ideal truth, but the consequent amused irony offers nothing to Sand or her reader. It grants too much to sophistication; it is classic, not romantic.

To allow for peasant art, Sand conceives of her rural fictions as "tales of a hemp dresser," imagining a narrator quite unlike Longus's, a rustic witness to events who mediates between city reader and country character, speaking in a modified dialect of Sand's region, understandable to both country and city audiences. The three chief tales—the romans champêtres—were written close together in time, and all first appeared in serialization: *La Mare au diable* (*The Devil's Pool*) in 1846; *François le Champi* (François the waif) in 1847–48; and *La Petite Fadette* (*Little Fadette*) in 1848. In sequence, they became longer and more novelistic in their social complexity. Yet all three share the diction of the peasant storyteller.

In *François* the author's friend recalls hearing a recent story from the hemp dresser. He encourages Sand to write it down, but in a language spoken "clearly for the Parisian, and simply for the peasant" (217), inasmuch as the local dialect of the province of Berry would elude the general reader. Sand sprinkles the narrative, accordingly, with words that are "not French," as her friend says, such as the title word *champi*—"Obsolete," admits Sand, "but Montaigne uses it, and I do not pretend to be more French than the great writers who have made the language" (219). What begins to sound like a Wordsworthian diction now sounds more like Spenser's search for a "pure well of English undefiled." Old words are "pure" words. A peasant's plow is not a *charrue* but an *areau* (*La Mare* 17), which is not only the regional dialect of Berry (the superficial "local color" explanation) but also carries the ancient authority of its Latin root *ara*. Knowing that diction was an issue in ancient pastoral literature, Sand thinks as carefully about the linguistic as about the social theory behind her novels.

The compact, single narrative line of *La Mare au diable* makes it more a long tale than a novel. Germain, a widower, sets out to find a new wife in a village several hours distant, where he will court Catherine, a widow reputed to have a good head for business. At the last minute he agrees to escort Marie, a poor woman's daughter taking a job as shepherdess on a farm near his destination. He also takes his mischievous little son, Petit-Pierre. Losing their way, the three spend a chilly night beside a pond locally called the Devil's Pool. Marie uses her shepherding skills to build a fire with wet wood; she shows care and affection for Petit-Pierre, and as the night passes, Germain falls in love with her. Because he is twenty-eight and she is sixteen, Marie cannot reciprocate when he makes known his love; to her he is more like an uncle or godfather. The next day, when he meets the widow, Germain finds her an unpleasant, self-centered woman with no lack of suitors. When Marie reports to the farm, her new employer tries to seduce her. She and Germain return home disappointed—not before Germain thrashes the seducer in a fight—but neither mentions the possibility of love. Germain's mother-in-law observes his lost appetite and learns of his love in a "youth and age" dialogue.

She and Marie's mother manage to bring the two together, the novel ending with several chapters on folk customs in the wedding.

If the opening ecphrasis of Holbein's plowman recalls the one in Longus's prologue, the last chapters of *La Mare au diable* echo the concluding folklore at Longus's lovers' wedding. Petit-Pierre also acts as a "winged boy" bringing the couple together. With its sinister reputation the "devil's" pool is Pan's sacred place, the natural-magical site of Germain's falling in love (Sand probably knew that early Christians had reconstructed Pan as the devil). But this is an idyll of second marriage. Germain's Daphnis period happened long ago, for "Married at twenty, he had loved but one woman in his life, and since being widowed, although he had had an impetuous and playful temperament, he never laughed and joked with another" (36).[17] For this reason, although he does benefit from Marie's reviving his "inner feminine," it seems wrong to cast Germain as "a study in male passivity" (Grant). Marie and the wise mother-in-law represent the female contribution to renewing the long-depressed Germain—to a victory of eros over thanatos.

At the end of *La Mare* Sand also balances the feminine sensibilities of Marie, her mother, and Germain's mother-in-law against the well-meaning but faintly stupid masculine discourse at the beginning. In chapters 3 and 4, Germain and his father-in-law plan his courtship of the vain widow. The father-in-law's two-page speech is not clumsy writing, I think, but exemplifies rough-hewn masculine thinking: you're not getting any younger; your children will need a parent if anything happens to you; a wife will take some worries from our shoulders. Find a solid, older woman, not someone young and pretty who will bring us grief; find one with a little money, too. In fact, I've already lined something up with a certain father. The reader discovers only at the end of chapter 4 that the agreeable Germain conceals his deep feelings for his dead wife, that not a day passes when he does not secretly weep for her. What father Maurice has planned for him is a "froid projet" (37), but being a simple person, he accepts it as his fate. The romance of the journey changes all that—romance supported by the eerie experience of being lost in the forest, even if only a small forest. When the story closes, it is April, and "Everything in nature was laughing and happy for him" (175).

Emotionally both Marie and Germain are lost children found through love—poverty separates the one from her community; death, the other. *François le Champi* is about a literal foundling adopted in infancy from an apparently dying mother. The child's coarse foster mother plans to make him tend her few sheep and then to hire him out as a servant for her own profit. The sympathetic image of childhood illustrates amply the difference between Sand's world and the rarefied atmosphere of Gessner or even Bernardin. Ill-treated but patient and sweet-tempered, François draws the attention of a miller's wife, Madeleine, who takes him in, educates him, and shows him human affection for the first time. When François grows to adolescence—chapter 6 includes the idyllic-romance lapse of years between childhood and second birth—he continues to embrace and kiss Madeleine as if still a child. "He was the most innocent boy on earth, and never suspected what boys his age learn so quickly in the country" (262), an innocence that leads some to think him simple-minded.

If the boy's innocence rings truer than does Daphnis and Chloe's, it may be because it belongs to his character. When the miller's mistress, a vain beauty named Sévère, cannot seduce François, she tells the miller he has tried to make love to her. Banished to another miller's employ, François receives unexpected money from his true mother, whose agent recognizes him from a strawberry birthmark. The money hints at an aristocratic lineage, as does François's having greater strength and courage than other boys. François returns to Madeleine as an adult friend, ultimately as lover and husband. The miller having died, Sévère has tied up his estate in litigation. François cleverly extricates Madeleine from her troubles, and when she recovers her health, he realizes that she is "as beautiful as Our Lady" (392). She accepts François's proposal beside the very fountain where he had first seen her in childhood and where they had parted when the miller sent him away. In this last scene, as in *La Mare* and *Fadette*, the would-be groom must wait for some time upon the woman's assent. Sand's sexual politics did not escape Matthew Arnold: although the (male) English reader would respect Sand's ideas on love in general, "when he finds that love implies, with her, social equality, he will begin to be staggered" (253).

Sand's philosophy of love crosses dangerous yet not unfamiliar ground in the idyllic romance. Along with her other two rustic novels, *François* explores the blurred margins between kinds of love. Madeleine awakens in François an understanding of love. She shares the stage with him, changing imperceptibly from a maternal to an erotic relationship with the boy—to the scandal of many readers.[18] The narrative is in fact almost too brief to make the transition convincing. Hints of incestuous love keep returning to these stories of love in nature. Paul and Virginie call each other brother and sister before they discover sexual desire. Chloe's parents behave toward Daphnis as if he were a brother, since it never occurs to them that he would become her husband or that he might take her virginity. Shakespeare hints at incestuous love in *Cymbeline* when the two princes unwittingly appear to be falling in love with their sister in the cave. The subject is most fully explored in Pardo Bazán's *La madre Naturaleza*. The reason for this recurrence may have to do with the idyllic romance's descent from stories of paradise, the place where innocence knows no limits, the scene of undifferentiated affection. There, in the state of absolute harmony among the natural, the human, and the divine, humans follow the ways of Mother Nature; incest, a moral concept, is a consequence of the Fall. Sand's approving tone may owe something to the narcissistic coloring of romanticism (see Thorslev), but it also derives from a liberal intellect, purposefully unhampered by convention in analyzing *l'amour champêtre*.

La Petite Fadette, the latest and longest of the three country novels, deepens and complicates Sand's reflections on love in nature by weaving the story of young love into that of a narcissistic, homoerotic love between twins. Sand published the novel in serial form at the end of 1848, hoping to dispel the evil humors of that revolutionary year: "an appeal to fermenting passions is not the way of salvation; better a sweet song, a sound of rustic pipe, a tale to put children to sleep without fear and suffering" (16).[19] Since there has been so much suffering, "revenons à nos moutons" [let us return to our sheep] (10). The publisher's advertisement declares the novel "a pure and fresh composition," a relief from "our sad realities," written in "the style of nature whose secret only genius knows" (vii).

The Barbeau twins, Sylvinet and Landry, grow into adolescence with contrasting temperaments: the former is dainty, high-strung, intensely jealous of his brother's affections; the latter, stronger and more rugged, good-natured and patient. Like other villagers, the boys regard little Fadette with a mixture of contempt and superstitious fear. A mischievous, solitary waif, she lives outside the village with her lame little brother and miserly grandmother. The plot breaks neatly into four ten-chapter parts.[20] The first part is focused on the twins' story, with Fadette appearing only toward the end when she helps Landry find the runaway Sylvinet. The second part traces the beginning of love between Fadette and Landry, from the dance at the St. Andoche feast, when Landry defends her against the taunts of other youths, to their first embrace in chapter 20. A crisis occurs in the couple's growing love, and in chapter 30 Fadette, having decided they should separate for a year, takes a domestic position elsewhere as Landry resigns himself to his parents' wishes. The last ten chapters resolve the crisis as father Barbeau discovers Fadette's true character and learns that her late grandmother has left her a hoard of money. Sylvinet's jealousy leads to a near-fatal illness, cured only by the returning Fadette's wise words and healing touch. The lovers make their wedding plans, and Sylvinet departs to begin a successful career in Napoleon's army.

Sylvinet plays a central role in the first and last of these four parts. Although the twins' father never shows favoritism as the boys are growing up, he knows that Sylvinet "has a girl's heart" (3.42). As the boy nurses his jealous, self-pitying narcissism (to love his twin is to love himself), he comes to represent a negative image of the love between Landry and Fadette. During his illness near the story's end, a wise woman comes to examine him and declares, "He has an overabundance of affection [amitié] in his heart, and, from always having felt it toward his twin, he has almost forgotten his sex, and in this has strayed from the law of the good Lord, who wants a man to cherish a wife more than father and mother, more than brother and sister" (31.223).[21] Although not quite the greedy Gnatho of *Daphnis and Chloe*, Sylvinet represents the selfish lover. Holding a lamb when Landry finds him in chapter 10, he also symbolizes an infantile innocence (he is "enfant de corps et d'esprit" [7.61]), a parody of the innocence that preoccupies Schiller's "sentimental" poet.

Sand may not always succeed in joining the real to the ideal, but she effectively transmits her feelings for nature and the heart through her characters. Fadette—whose grandmother is a folk-healer often consulted by villagers—has become a complete student of nature. She sets out to instruct Landry in the things of nature, thereby dispelling his superstitious belief in Satanism. In many ways she typifies the solitary soul in nature dear to romantic pastoralism: "Flowers, herbs, stones, insects, all the secrets of nature would have been enough to occupy me.... I could have been alone forever without being bored" (18.142).²² Love of nature has turned her against the antinatural behavior of other youths: "they say I love evil creatures and that I am a witch, because I don't like to make a frog suffer, to tear off a wasp's legs, and to nail a living bat to a tree. Poor creature, I say to it, if everything ugly must be killed, I'd have no more right to live than you" (18.144).²³ Natural sympathy, not natural knowledge, gives Fadette both her healing powers and her special attraction for Landry, whose virtue allows him to see further than her tattered clothes and homeliness.

George Sand, who was Amandine-Aurore-Lucile Dupin in her girlhood, grew up playing with peasant children, absorbing their dialect and folklore. Like Fadette, she was something of an outsider, unconventional and lonely, but a free spirit—at least until she entered a convent school at the age of thirteen. Fadette's mother abandoned her and her brother to become a camp follower; Aurore's mother led a respectable life in Paris, often away from her daughter but winning her sympathies in the battles with the grandmother—though after the old lady's death, the girl came to know more of her mother's bad temper. The romance orphan figure may not loom so large as in *François*, but it lends Fadette much of her charm as a character who must depend on her own resources to navigate the reefs of adolescence. It is exceptional to find this character in the female rather than the male role: in Longus, Florian, and Bernardin the males are poorer than their sweethearts.

In *Fadette* Sand again experiments with the ways that varieties of love impinge on one another, comparing outward, selfless love with selfish obsession. While Landry and Fadette find separation painful, it pleases Sylvinet that Landry will go to work in a distant place where he will know no one. *Daphnis and Chloe* achieves much of its delight because the lovers feel love but do not know what it is. Natural feeling precedes its verbalization. Landry ponders the unnamed sensation of human love just when he and Fadette say farewell as she leaves for her year-long absence:

> never in all my life have I felt for father, mother, sister, or brother—nor certainly for the beautiful Madelon, and not even for my dear twin Sylvinet—a burst of affection [amitié] like that which this little devil caused in me for two or three minutes. If my poor Sylvinet had been able to see what I have in my heart, he would certainly have been eaten

up with jealousy. For the relationship that I had with Madelon did no harm to my brother, whereas if I had to remain only one day distracted and inflamed as I was for a moment beside this Fadette, I would lose my senses, knowing no one in the world but her. (20.158)[24]

The comparison of loves here acquires force because Sand has established Landry and his family as full of love for each other. Especially in coming after the friendship for Sylvinet and the infatuation with the pretty Madelon, Landry's love of Fadette appears utterly different in kind.

For her part, Fadette loves him "comme une folle," but (as Sand seems to think is typically feminine) she conceals the strength of her passion. With "a tranquil air she spoke reason to him, she even pretended she had not yet known love's fire, and she did not allow him to clasp her hand above her cuff" (25.184). In the last quarter of the novel, Fadette takes on a surprising maturity redolent of the "maternal tenderness" some have seen in Sand's actual love affairs (Karénine 676). Love takes a surprising turn at the end when, after Fadette has cured him, Sylvinet makes her such a close friend that he never acts without consulting her. In a way, Fadette becomes his mother in lieu of the woman who had excessively mothered him. When he leaves for the army, that mother recalls the wise woman's prophecy that he would love but one woman and none afterward. Sand thus closes the circle among self-love; maternal, fraternal, and amicable love; and the grand love that seems—as glimpsed in *François*—to encompass while surpassing all the other kinds. It may be that in this novel "male and female sentimental education are separate but only unequal in that the men have much more work to do" (Dickenson 60). The infantile male does seem to need the feminine in order to achieve psychic integration. But the "work" Sylvinet needs to perform transcends gender: to conquer a narcissism that the novel itself calls feminine, "girl-like" (3.42), and maternally encouraged. Sand resists generalizing about men or women, who as members of creation are all unique. "God," she says of the twins, "who has made no two things absolutely alike in heaven and earth, desired them to have very different fates" (2.33).

An excessively author-centered approach to this novel can remove both lovers from the scene. Karénine seems to have been the first scholar to call *Fadette* a new *Taming of the Shrew* (676)—a viewpoint that survives in a recent biography of Sand that calls this novel a "juvenile version of *The Taming of the Shrew*" about "an ungovernable young hellcat who is transformed by the miraculous alchemy of love from a village brat into a sweet, loving, and hardworking young woman" (Cate 608). Such an account of character and plot falls short: what about Landry and Sylvinet? We shall see that their story has fascinated later readers like Bruce Chatwin. Using the pattern of idyllic romances, especially as set by Longus and Bernardin, Sand writes of love reciprocated, of the stages by which this alchemy sublimates two very different people into one. All three of the romans champêtres retain the fairy-tale feeling of Longus's world, with Pan and the nymphs replaced by suggestions of haunted pools, changelings, witches—all of which have natural explanations. This playfulness with mysterious but finally explainable events descends more from Longus than Bernardin. In earlier romances, through the agency of the supernatural, characters like Daphnis and Chloe are reborn but do not grow; in this age of the novel the interest in psychological coherence replaces the old parental discovery scene with inner transformations.

THE LATER 1800S

As the century progressed, French writers from Baudelaire and Lautréamont to Francis Jammes and André Breton turned to Bernardin variously as an object of satire or of mythologizing (see Steinmetz). In *La Joie de vivre* (1884) Zola offers some of both. The hapless Lazare bathes in the sea with his young cousin Pauline, orphaned in Paris and raised as a little sister. The second chapter conveys a strong idyllicism: Lazare composes a symphony on the Earthly Paradise and teaches Pauline the piano in a scene evocative of Daphnis teaching Chloe to play the syrinx (2.73–75). Pauline satisfies her desire to know about sex not by experience but by determined study of medical books (2.88). Yet the natural affection between Pauline and Lazare clashes with Lazare's romantic attraction to the more feminine Louise so that his inability to choose between friend-woman and romantic woman threatens to undermine the lives of all three. Lazare dreams of escape to a Pacific island, where he and Pauline will live in paradise, eating fruit and cultivating a garden (9.323). The absurd dream at once degenerates into a scene of sexual passion bordering on rape.

But Zola, with his suspicions of human natural motives, is already among the moderns. Two earlier and more purely idyllic romances in the decade after Sand's three require special mention: Gérard de Nerval's *Sylvie* (1853) and Frédéric Mistral's narrative poem *Mirèio* (1859), which was written in the Occitan, or Provençal, language of southeastern France. The latter poem in twelve cantos made its author famous, helping him to achieve the Nobel Prize for Literature in 1904. Like Florian and Sand, Mistral dedicated himself to the geography and history of his native region—as well as to its language, whose metrical subtleties he reportedly understood better than any other living poet.

In Mistral's poem the fifteen-year-old lovers are Mirèio, a farmer's daughter, and Vincén—a poor basket-maker's son who is anguished by Mirèio's father's plan for her to marry a wealthy man. The leading candidate for her hand, Ourrias, breeds bulls, like Longus's Dorcon, and ultimately Vincén must fight with him for his beloved. Vincén, nearly killed and then healed by a witch, urges his father to speak on his behalf to Mirèio's father, who opposes the match. Beginning in the fall, the story has moved through spring to midsummer night, and the harvest feast of St. John, at the end of canto 7. Hearing of her father's opposition, Mirèio sets out by night on a fatal pilgrimage across the Rhône to the Church of the Three Maries ("li Santo," the three patron saints of the region), intercessors who resemble Longus's three nymphs. Her departure, like Vincén's fight, marks her break with childhood, signaled in the inventory of childhood treasures from her wardrobe (4.117). Like Bernardin's Virginie, Mirèio dies at her destination, though in a visionary ecstasy as the three saints come to escort her into Paradise.

On publication of his poem, Mistral sent a copy to Sand, who replied in a brief note hailing him as "in my opinion one of the foremost poets of France" (*Correspondance* 15:348). Sand probably read the accompanying French prose translation, and she heaped superlatives on many young writers who sought her approval. Yet her praise was not insincere. A few days later she told her countryman Charles Poncy that although she disliked Mistral's "dialect" (15), which was not as pleasant as their own of Berry, the poem was "magnifique" (369). In translation, at least, she could have appreciated especially the authenticity of place, with the feeling for actual nature, that she sought in her novels.

A few years earlier (on 22 November 1853), in a different kind of letter,

Sand received from Gérard de Nerval (the pen name of Gérard Labrunie) a request that she assist in publishing an illustrated edition of his recent novella, *Sylvie*. The letter drifts into a somewhat bizarre discourse on numerology and mysticism in which Nerval claims, for example, that he and Sand are linked by the *Ge-* in their names. Sand's reply, if any, is unknown. Nerval's story was well worth an investment, however. A limpid, haunting recollection of a haunted narrator, *Sylvie* became so famous that in 1922 a "Fête de Sylvie" was held in the Valois region of the country to promote the tourist trade.[25] The Parisian narrator, as a child, frequently spends holidays with his uncle in the village of Ermenonville, the scene of Rousseau's last days and of Nerval's own childhood visits. As an adult the narrator longs to return to this rural world, particularly drawn by memories of the friend and first love of youth, Sylvie. This simple, beautiful girl with an "Athenian smile" (41) danced with him at the Festival of Archers, which children celebrated "without knowing then that we were merely repeating from age to age a Druid's feast that had survived kings and new religions" (14).

The golden age of the human race (Druidic or Athenian) maintains an affinity with individual childhood. The longing for innocence led Nerval's lifelong friend Théophile Gautier to compare *Sylvie* with both Longus's and Bernardin's romances.[26] The *Sehnsucht* of Bernardin and Florian returns to the form; the narrator becomes hopelessly divided between Sylvie (the true idyllic heroine) and ethereal, blonde Adrienne, whom he first hears singing at the festival (the unreachable heroine of chivalric romance). Mysterious Adrienne, destined for the convent, captures half his soul. She and Sylvie are "two halves of a single love. The one was the sublime ideal, the other, the sweet reality" (66–67). Vivacious Sylvie eventually marries the narrator's good-natured, simple-souled foster brother and has children; Adrienne dies alone, quite young, in her convent—an end the narrator reveals only on the last page of his account.

Some declare this self-division an effect of the author's supposed schizophrenia, but the century offers too many bifurcated loves and lovers (Zola's Lazare is another), torn between a simple love and a complex life. The narrator can never quite imagine happiness with Sylvie; his thoughts always turn toward Paris, his actress friend, and the whirl of nightlife. His predicament foreshadows those of Pardo Bazán's Gabriel and Hudson's Abel. After 1900 Cather plays on variants of this self-division. Her "Far Island" employs the pattern straightforwardly. In *O Pioneers!* Alexandra's simple integrity competes with Marie's erotic complexity. The scene at the end of *My Ántonia*, when Jim returns to see Ántonia and her family, corresponds in interesting ways with the end of *Sylvie*—both stories representing strong, generous, maternal women in nature, with a wistful former lover seemingly reconciled to a solitary existence in the city. In France this self-division persists in the awakening, as well shall see, of Philippe in Colette's *Le Blé en herbe*.

This widening of the gap in sensibility that concerned Schiller and other romantics, a fissure between the mind and nature, the external world, takes many forms in the literature and thought of the century. Consider the far-flung controversies between science and religion. In 1880 Zola proclaimed, "The metaphysical man is dead; our whole territory is transformed by the advent of physiological man."[27] Yet in 1875 it was more schizophrenia than transformation that Zola portrayed in his idyllic *La Faute de l'abbé Mouret*. A priest suffers a shattering breakdown, loses all memory, and enters into a sexual relationship with a young woman in a garden called Paradou.

The age's increasing sense of self-division may explain Nerval's own feelings of such a schism: "A terrible idea occurred to me: 'Man is double,' I told myself. 'I am a double man,' wrote one church father. . . . In every man, there is a spectator and an actor, the man who speaks and the man who answers'" (quoted in Todorov 116). The supernatural or fantastic atmosphere of *Sylvie* participates in the ghost-presence, the spectator-specter, throughout nineteenth-century literature.[28] The succeeding era would redefine this large-scale split personality as a consequence not of competing natural and civilized selves, but of self-awareness. "What makes mankind tragic," wrote Joseph Conrad in a letter of 31 January 1898, "is not that they are victims of nature, it is that they are conscious of it."[29]

※ ※ ※ ※ ※

Ladies of Maine

STOWE'S SHAKESPEAREAN ISLAND

In America the conventions of idyllic romance traveled through channels other than Longus, including the romances of Shakespeare, frequently on stage and always in print. *Paul et Virginie* enjoyed a large audience in earlier nineteenth-century America. By 1814, translations had appeared in Philadelphia, New York, and Baltimore; Boston and Providence followed in the next decade (see Toinet). A farce adaptation by the English playwright James Cobb attracted theater-goers throughout the earlier half of the century and beyond, while a more serious dramatic version, subtitled *The Runaway Slave* was published in Philadelphia in 1864. In *The History of the Adventures, Love and Constancy of Paul and Virginia* (Plymouth, 1824)—perhaps intended as a children's book—the anonymous translator has Virginia saved from death by a black slave, the son of a king, who is then freed; Paul and Virginia marry (Robinson, "Traduction" 851–52). George Sand also, despite her personal reputation, had an eager reading public in America: *Indiana*, *La Mare au diable*, and *La Petite Fadette* all saw editions in the 1840s and 1850s.

One neglected line of idyllic fiction extends from Shakespeare's *Tempest* and Sand to several American writers from the mid-1800s into the 1900s. All of these authors work consciously within a tradition, with coastal Maine as a favored setting—a landscape isolated from urban society but endowed with the supposed values of a durable people. All use idyllic themes to join their sense of region with a perception of wider human experience. Most write at a time when Maine could approximate the idyllic island of Longus or Shakespeare or Bernardin, being remote from the corrupt world (Boston, New York) yet still accessible and recognizable to the reader as a community.

The earliest of these Maine pastoralists, Harriet Beecher Stowe, sets her *The Pearl of Orr's Island* on an island she visited, below Bath in the south. The first seventeen chapters—telling of Mara and Moses's childhood and ending when the two are, respectively, seven and ten years old—comprise part 1 of the novel, which was printed in the *Independent* during the catastrophic month of April 1861. This part of the work actually saw copyright as the whole novel in Britain on 4 July 1861. The rest of the novel appeared in serialized form the following December and April. This hiatus has led to the view that *Pearl* is really two texts, a "local color tale" followed by a "sentimental Christian romance"—though the break between childhood and young adulthood occurs regularly in these romances.[1]

Unlike *Uncle Tom's Cabin*, Stowe's most famous novel, *Pearl* avoids violence and the sensational as if reacting to the American turmoil. Stowe knew the idylls of Gessner, and as I have earlier pointed out, she was even the first to use the word *idyllic* in English. Such evidence—along with her appropriation of Shakespeare, Bernardin, and in a general way Sand (whom she read copiously)—suggests that Stowe was sensitive to her literary tradition, that her yoking a story of childhood to one of youthful romance was quite deliberate.

Shakespeare provides the starting point of *Pearl*: during a storm a father and daughter witness a shipwreck offshore. Later the daughter's daughter, Mara, discovers a tattered copy of *The Tempest*, which she cherishes as a mirror of her own life and world. Mara's grandfather, a retired sea captain named Pennell, had left sailing to help raise her mother, Naomi—then only five years old—on a farm on the island. Naomi, now dying from the shock of seeing the shipwreck that took her husband's life, gives birth to Mara, the Miranda of this story. Mara—"Call her not Naomi," her mother intones. "Call her Mara, for the Almighty hath dealt very bitterly with me" (8).

Both as name and character, Mara ("bitter") lies hidden in Shakespeare's Miranda ("admired"). Another retired seaman, Captain Kittredge, who brings some rare joviality to the novel, admits to Mara that he once saw *The Tempest* at an English theater, making her promise not to tell his wife. Mara herself hides her copy of the play, torn long ago from a collected Shakespeare. She soon meets her Ferdinand—Moses, a little boy washed up on Orr's Island still clinging to the body of his drowned mother. As if wishing to remake Moses into Ferdinand, she shares her secret text with him. While the children grow up as brother and sister, the play retains its hold on Mara's sense of their identity. The girl sometimes imagines Ferdinand as "much like what Moses would be when he was grown up—and how glad she would be to pile up his wood for him, if any old enchanter should set him to work" (133–34). Ariel's song, "Full Fathom Five," makes her wonder "if Moses had a father, lying deep in the sea with the sea-nymphs ringing his bell" (172). Captain Kittredge tells Mara that once, near the Bermudas, he had heard mermaids holding a funeral for a drowned sailor, "and I heard a kind o' ding-dongin'" (139). She persuades Moses to name his toy boat after Ariel, foreshadowing a time years later when Moses gives this name to a real ship in which he sails to find his fortune.

Stowe's knowledge of Shakespeare's romances including *The Tempest*, a prominent source of *The Minister's Wooing* (see C. Wilson), may explain why she so faithfully reproduces the characters of *Daphnis and Chloe*, even though she may not have read Longus. Besides the lovers, there are sages—both male (the old sea captains) and female (Aunt Roxy, a herbalist and something of a seer)—and a rival lover from the city, Thomas Adams, a young Bostonian whom Mara meets while Moses is at sea.

The pirates, a gang of heavy drinkers who smuggle goods from Canada, lure Moses, now an adolescent, into their company. Mara, spying while their leader, Atkinson, tries to corrupt Moses, "would think only of a loathsome black snake that she had once seen" (201). A nocturnal meeting turns into a drinking bout, and even though Moses refrains from alcohol (then prohibited by the "Maine Laws"), the presence of liquor horrifies Mara as much as the bawdy talk. Stephano and Trinculo would not have amused an Orr's Island audience.

Although she never praised Sand openly, Stowe knew Sand's rustic romances. She did not try to meet Sand during her travels through France in the summer of 1853, even though the French author had praised *Uncle Tom's Cabin* in a notable review the previous December. Stowe did wonder why she had never encountered Sand at one of the many Paris salons she visited, only to be told by Madame Belloc that French ladies simply could not be seen with Madame Sand (F. Wilson 430). Stowe's brother Charles bought Sand's *Consuelo* (not a *roman champêtre*) and read it with his sister, having been assured that it was "the most unexceptionable of the works of Madame George Sand" (Beecher 192). A few weeks later, still working through the novel, "Hatty [Stowe] said it was amazing that so corrupt a woman could describe so beautiful a character" (216). Stowe later judged Sand "the animalism and atheism of this century impersonated," though by this time she had read all of the novelist's works (in French).

For her own part, Sand privately exclaimed that Stowe was "not a woman of spirit, but a saint" and that "she bores me and makes me weep at the same time, with her Bible, her Negroes, and her urchins" (*Correspondance* 11:496–97).[2] It is a testimony to both authors' critical sense that they each could admire the other's fiction despite their reservations about one another as persons. Like Sand in her rustic fiction around 1848, Stowe consciously writes against the tide of violence in her society. Reviewing *Uncle Tom*, Sand recognized that Stowe's theme was "essentially domestic and of the family" (quoted in Fields and Stowe 153), a welcome counterweight to the sensationalism of much popular fiction. Both women, then, after a period of engagement with social issues and during a time of violence, remove their fiction to the countryside.

Addressing readers in the serialized *Pearl*, Stowe sounds like Sand in proclaiming that "our characters have no strange and wonderful adventures of outward life, and the changes that occur to them and the history they make is that of the inner life, that 'cometh not with observation'" (quoted in Fields and Stowe 287). As so often in the idyllic romance, the country setting helps create prospects of this "inner life." In *Pearl* the one experience with life outside Orr's Island comes in the night-world flashback narrated by the island's minister. Rev. Theophilus Sewell (*see well*) ought to qualify as sage, being at once minister, physician, and lawyer for his flock. His character is one of the subtler touches of the novel, however, for Mr. Sewell's reputed wisdom needs to be weighed against his actions in the past.

Sewell visibly falters when, at the discovery of the child Moses, he recognizes the dead mother's bracelet of hair embroidered with seed pearls. Years later, Sewell reveals to Moses that he had known and loved the boy's dead mother, born Dolores Mendoza, when Sewell was serving as tutor to Moses's mother and her father's other children in Florida. Dolores's natural gifts had saved Moses's mother from the depravities of her siblings, probably because the other children were the offspring of an irresponsible second wife. Dolores's father, "sensual, tyrannical, passionate" (258) resembles the Cuban plantation owner he plans to have Dolores marry.

At first Sewell is Dolores's Prospero, teaching her and the younger children the way of mind over passion: "A power of control was with me as a natural gift; and then that command of temper which is the common attribute of well-trained persons in the Northern states, was something so singular in this family as to invest its possessor with a certain awe; and my calm, energetic voice, and determined manner, often acted as a charm on their stormy natures" (249). If Sewell appears self-satisfied, his author surely means him to. Sewell-Prospero does not save Dolores from her evil fate, even when she begs him to take her away, knowing his love for her. First he temporizes: she would never be happy as a poor man's wife. By the time she persuades him otherwise, it is too late. As he is coming to take her to his homeland, he receives her message warning that their plan is discovered, that her father will kill him if he returns. At once Sewell abandons his beloved.

Years later, after a slave insurrection in Cuba, Dolores and her husband go to Boston; sometime afterward they drown at sea off Orr's Island. Sewell tells Moses all this in a letter that ends, "In some respects I am a singular person in my habits, and having once written this, you will pardon me if I observe that it will never be agreeable to me to have the subject named between us" (264). A revealing sentence. It supports the chill and vanity surrounding Sewell, who had already thought of himself as "singular" in describing his tutorial influence on his pupils. Why introduce this cruel prohibition with the palaver about his "habits" and what is "agreeable to me" if the intent is not to suggest cold, self-centered, and above all, self-protective qualities, no matter his talent and education? The first-person pronoun looms large throughout Sewell's narrative.

Sewell's adventure, in its brevity (about twenty pages), represents a range of passion and violence foreign to the rest of the story. Here is the romance underworld descent into the realm of the other—of the hot-blooded superstitious Spanish, the "half-barbarized negroes" (248), and above all the American South. Like Louisiana in *Uncle Tom's Cabin*, Florida (ironically Stowe's home state in her last years) is a rich stew of southern depravities—a state quintessentially "South," its southern disorders magnified by its Spaniards and Catholicism. As Persephone of this underworld, Dolores is married off by her father as though she were "one of his slaves" (251). She bears the foundling's token, the hair bracelet of her dead mother, "the only one that ever loved me" (256). And like the tokens in other foundling tales, it is associated with death but also with self-knowledge, for it will give Moses an identity.

Sewell's failures and Mara's death at the novel's end reflect authorial misgivings about the happily-ever-after tendency of idyllic fiction, perhaps after the example of *Paul et Virginie*. In both novels the melancholy follows from similar moral premises about sexual love: namely, that social attitudes weigh so heavily against women as to make an equal marriage impossible. Sewell's Florida adventure shows the impotence of the conventionally respectable man grappling with a vicious patriarchalism. Moses, too, seems to suffer from a male failing, a prolonged boyhood, despite his nineteen years—a fact of his character that keeps the feel of a childhood idyll incongruously alive in the latter half of the novel.

The boy-man quality in Moses parallels the girl-woman in Mara. Stowe betrays her intentions on this point in her inconsistencies about her heroine's age. As chapter 18 (the start of second part) begins we hear that the girl has "grown to the maturity of eighteen summers" (180), but shortly afterward she is "in her seventeenth year" (186). As the love story gets underway, is Mara sixteen or eighteen? The mistake discloses a wish that she be young and innocent yet a mature and likely prospect for marriage. Mara is thus "beautiful and childlike," with "that delicate pink tinting one sees in healthy infants" (181). Her sexual psychology fluctuates throughout the latter half of the novel between that of the child and that of the adult, but she finally seems unable to make the upward move. Daphnis and Chloe, Ferdinand and Miranda, Landry and Fadette—most of the lovers in this tradition inhabit the margins of adulthood, sliding evasively between pristine innocence and mature understanding.

Stowe also lingers over the elusive categories of gender and of love that engage Sand and other predecessors. As Mara and Moses grow, the narrator drops hints about their developing gender roles. Mara becomes increasingly maternal. Moses likes the history of Roman war-making; during his occasional raids on eagles' nests he thinks of himself as a conqueror. "I shouldn't want to spoil cities!" says Mara of his pillage. Moses responds: "That's 'cause you are a girl,—I'm a man, and men always like war; I've taken one city this afternoon, and mean to take a great many more" (162). When the narrator says that people such as shy Mara and mischievous Moses always end up hurting each other (148), one wonders whether she is not really thinking of the male and female at large. "Man's utter ignorance of woman's nature," says the narrator, "is a cause of a great deal of unsuspected cruelty which he practices toward her" (216).

Love, too, eludes Mara's grasp. "Like most shy girls, Mara became more shy the more really she understood the nature of her own feelings" (303). It takes a night of girl-talk with her childhood friend Sally Kittredge to make Mara realize that Moses loves her, a discovery that seems to deepen her self-understanding. But Mara's affections have a long history that starts in their childhood brother-sister relationship. Even after their courtship is underway, Mara continues to think of Moses as "brother" (220). Complicating the nature of their love is an explicitly maternal feeling that Mara has for her brother even though she is younger. Spying on Moses in the scene with the Atkinson gang, "She repressed herself as the mother does who refrains from crying out when she sees her unconscious little one on the verge of a precipice" (205). Mara seems a study in the subtle variations of woman's love for man. Wife, sister, mother: where does one love end and the other begin? George Sand, too, had asked such questions in presenting, not without scandal, a François both mothered by and married to the same woman.

Female sexual energy in the novel belongs to Sally Kittredge, who grows up to possess the familiar qualities of Sir Walter Scott's dark heroine: "a face with a rich Spanish complexion, large black eyes, glowing cheeks, marked eyebrows, and lustrous black hair" (181)—in temperament a "born coquette" (222). The unexplained "Spanish" feature echoes the story of Dolores, extending a faint promise of Mediterranean eroticism.

Sally plays the role of a genteel Lycaenion in this love story—*praeceptor amoris* in a psychological rather than physical way. She tells Mara of Moses's true feelings and does the same for Moses when Mara at first rejects his offer of love (312). Sally's moment of instruction sets the stage for the couple's declaration of love, again in *Tempest* fashion:

> "You see, Mara, that it was intended that you should be my fate," he ended; "so the winds and waves took me up and carried me to the lonely island where the magic princess dwelt."
> "You are Prince Ferdinand," said Mara.
> "And you are Miranda," said he.

"Ah!" she said with fervor, "how plainly we can see that our heavenly Father has been guiding our way! How good He is,—and how we must try to live for Him,—both of us." (320)

The lovers' piety recalls many moments in *Paul et Virginie*. (A character named Virginie appears in Stowe's *The Minister's Wooing* [1859], a French aristocrat who calls New England an Arcadia.) Both Bernardin and Stowe introduce God the Father, just where Longus presents brings in Pan or Shakespeare introduces the goddesses of earth and heaven. A particular religious vision, or revision, drives *Pearl* toward an unhappy ending. Mara's suffering blocks any movement toward mutuality; if the pale heroine must waste away with consumption, sexual gratification is an unpleasant afterthought. Only after a suitable period of mourning (four years!) will the pent-up eroticism of the unspiritual male be satisfied with marriage to the desirable Sally. The novel foregrounds nature in its occasional seascapes, especially when the children are young. But the older Mara usually reads, sews, chats with family and friends, or worries about Moses. So it comes as a surprise to hear later that "Mara had been all her days a child of the woods; her delicate life had grown up in them like one of their own cool shaded flowers; and there was not a moss, not a fern, not an up-springing thing that waved a leaf or threw forth a flower-bell, that was not a well-known friend to her" (341). These words occur just after the betrothal scene and the invocation of God the Father, and just before Mara tells Aunt Roxy she hasn't been feeling well lately.

Stowe wants to revitalize the theme of nature and the presence of God as she moves her novel into its most elegiac stage—to return death to Arcadia. Roxy's little sister comes to Mara's mind, long dead, known to Mara only by a grave, "overgrown with blackberry vines" while "gray moss had grown into the crevices of the slab which had served for her tombstone" (346). Nature will lead the consumptive virgin to her Father by way of Death. To someone's protest that Mara has such beautiful color in her cheeks, Roxy answers, "so does a rock-maple get color in September and turn all scarlet, and what for? why, the frost has been at it, and its time is out" (347). Shortly before Mara's death that autumn, "the early frosts had changed the maples in the pine-woods to scarlet" (371). When Moses returns from the sea horrified to find her dying, Mara suggests that perhaps it is better that they did not marry: "If we lived together in the commonplace toils of life, you would see only a poor threadbare wife. I might have lost what little charm I ever had for you; but I feel that if I die, this will not be. There is something sacred and beautiful in death; and I may have more power over you, when I seem to be gone, than I shall have had in living" (391).

In *Paul et Virginie* the old man tries to console Paul with virtually the same thought—that life's toil would eventually have dissipated their young love. Of course the "commonplace toils of life" include the simple joys celebrated by Longus and Sand. "Bitter" to the end. Stowe flirted with the pastoral life in *Uncle Tom's Cabin* and *Dred* but subjected it to her larger social vision. In *The Pearl of Orr's Island*, beginning with an idyll of childhood, she grows uneasy with this life in nature. "Are we Christians or heathen?" asks narrator, anticipating our resistance to the heroine's death. "We ushered in this history to speak of a class of lives formed on the model of Christ, and like his, obscure and unpretending, like his, seeming to end in darkness and defeat, but which yet have this preciousness and value that the dear saints who live them came nearest in their mission to the mission of Jesus" (366). *Pearl*—ending as it does with Captain Pennell's dream of finding a lost "pearl of great price" on the beach—shows the vast distance between the cult of duty that belongs to stoic Christianity and the cult of nature underlying Longus.

Mara's last words to her lover speak of "power" over him in death. The novel wrestles conspicuously with the problems of gender and feminine power—a theme already noted in the account of the children's developing sexual identity. While still an adolescent, "Moses, like many others of his sex, boy or man, had quietly settled in his own mind that the whole love of Mara's heart was to be his, to have and to hold, to use and to draw on, as he liked" (213). This ironic echo of the marriage vow and the banking metaphor of "draw on" hint that one reason for the failure of idyllic love lies in the male drive toward possession of women as property or commodities. In a quarrel shortly before their betrothal, Mara tells Moses, "You men must have everything, . . . the pleasure of feeling that you are something, and can do something in the world; and besides all this, you want the satisfaction of knowing that we women are following in chains behind your triumphal car" (304–05).

"Following" is woman's characteristic gesture in the story. Mara follows

Moses in their childhood games, trails after him for Latin lessons from Mr. Sewell—indeed, at first she was simply to "go along" to Sewell's and not receive schooling at all, for Mr. Sewell did not think girls had the mental strength to decline and conjugate. She also secretly follows Moses down to the beach for his meeting with the Atkinson gang. Poor Dolores, however, could not follow Sewell to safety, being left to follow her father's brutal command to marry a man she abhorred. Even Sally is left to follow in Mara's footsteps to obtain at last the prize husband. Although Stowe herself seems to have enjoyed a marriage of equals, her heroine's identity rests more on a desire to control her lover than on the need to become one with him.

A perceptive reviewer of *Pearl* (who liked it much better than Stowe's companion volume that year, *Agnes of Sorrento*) found in it "little versatility in the delineation of character and not much skill in the management of the plot." The complaint, which appeared in the July 1862 *North American Review*, sounds like the generic objection to idyllic and other romance—a criticism that even Shakespeare's romances (especially *Cymbeline*) cannot always escape. The same reviewer goes on to call this "a story of singular pathos and beauty. No one can read it without acknowledging its power and feeling all his sympathies awakened as if by some actual occurrence within his own knowledge and under his own observation." This too might be said of some famous romances, Shakespeare's in particular. The likelihood is that Stowe understood the form both intuitively and from studying such examples as *The Tempest*.

JEWETT'S ISLANDS

In 1889, when Stowe was nearing eighty and no longer writing, Sarah Orne Jewett wrote to her friend Annie Fields:

> I have been reading the beginning of "The Pearl of Orr's Island" and find it just as clear and perfectly original and strong as it seemed to me in my thirteenth or fourteenth year, when I read it first. I shall never forget the exquisite flavor and reality of delight that it gave me. I do so long to read it with you. It is classical—historical—anything you like to say, if you can give it high praise enough. I have n't read it for ten years at least, but *there it is*! Alas, that she could n't finish it in the same noble key of sympathy and harmony; but a poor writer is at the mercy of much unconscious opposition. (*Letters*, ed. Fields 46–47)

If she read *Pearl* at thirteen, Jewett would have come upon the book when it was brand new, marking one of those singular coincidences in literary history when a stray spark lights a great fire. This was a seminal book for young Jewett. As *The Tempest* is a resonant presence in *Pearl*, so Jewett would undoubtedly agree with a recent critic that *Pearl*'s "themes and imagery recur throughout Jewett's career, up to her greatest work, *The Country of the Pointed Firs*" (Sherman 27).

Although the same critic does not mention Jewett's *A Marsh Island* in her book, that novel participates in the same idyllic tradition. Neglected in modern Jewett criticism, it appealed to contemporaries: Blanck records Houghton Mifflin's running four thousand copies in three printings from May to August 1885, more copies than any of Jewett's earlier books had seen in their first year. Of course, being an idyllic romance, it struck some contemporaries as a great bore. "The mise en scene is perfect," noted a reviewer in the *Critic* (8 August 1885), "but the people are dull." One expects "something more to happen . . . than the eating of apples or the making of a pie." Just as in Stowe's novel, what "happens" here goes on inside the characters. The reviewer for *Harper's* (August 1885) showed more understanding of this point, describing the book as "a delightful prose poem," combining "the art of the poet, the painter, and the story-teller."

Like *Pearl*, *A Marsh Island* is set in coastal Maine, though the "island" of the title is sometimes joined to the adjacent land when the tide goes out. The marsh island images the condition of the characters, who not unlike classical shepherds alternate between joining the community of the farm and isolating themselves in the hours of deliberation and anxiety that occupy many pages of the book. Theorists of the novel such as Percy Lubbock would have scorned the fluctuating point of view in Jewett's narrative, and that eccentricity may help explain its later neglect by some of the author's strongest supporters. *A Marsh Island* is a book of selves, all analyzing, even plotting over, the motives and ambiguous gestures of the others. A typical page is solid with text, long paragraphs of rumination without action or dialogue. Dick Dale, the well-off young painter who finds himself stranded on the island with a hurt leg, catches a wagon ride with Doris, daughter of the island's leading farmer, and awakens, he thinks, to love. Dan, Doris's rustic boyfriend, worries that Doris is showing off this new city fellow. Doris's mother worries about the outcome of the couple's infatuation, while

Doris wonders why Dan is so chilly toward her. Stowe, though similarly preoccupied with her couples' minds, takes them down more conventional pathways. Jewett's *Marsh Island* seems a more writerly text than Stowe's, leading into marshy regions, opening on unanticipated experiences.

Among the variety of characters represented, Dick Dale probably receives the most attention. Others usually focus their own thoughts on him as, by a subtle process, these new, natural surroundings start to absorb him. This process begins when people remark upon his striking resemblance to his host's son, killed in the Civil War. By chapter 17, when his aunt happens to stop at the Owen farm, "he looked not unlike a farmer, himself" (226). The genteel aunt, fearing that Dick is about to go native, urges him to come back to town. Jewett's insertion of the aunt here serves to measure the change Dick has undergone, immersed in nature and love—or thoughts of love. Attracted to the purity of the people and the setting—what Sand called their primitiveness—he brings his heart to bear on Doris alone. She embodies the virtues of her surroundings as fully as Spenser's Pastorella or Shakespeare's Perdita. By the novel's end, though, while the cold Maine autumn deepens and, coincidentally, just before Doris chooses Dan over Dick, Dick grapples with a sense of alienation: "but where was his place?" he asks himself. "What had been the use of him and what would be his fate?" He returns to town an unsettled man, one friend hailing him as another pastoral fugitive, "melancholy Jaques" (287). Quite possibly the experience has enriched his identity, his sense of himself as an artist. And if, in the closing chapter, his paintings have been selected for an exhibition in New York, it may be because during his sojourn, despite its emotional turmoil, "He had at least gained a new respect for his own life and its possible value" (290). What sustains uncertainty on such questions is Jewett's manner of fusing omniscient narration with reported interior monologue, decentering the focus, keeping the reader from settling on a single meaning of any character's experience.

Rustic rival Dan exemplifies the subtlety of Jewett's characterization. From one perspective, he seems the hick—Longus's thick-brained Dorcon or Lampis. But he turns out to be a sensitive, courageous man who risked his life trying to rescue Doris's brother on the battlefield. He takes Doris for granted, then quails at the thought of losing her. He seems capable of using violence to defend his choice of mate, yet he is ready to withdraw generously if Doris rejects him. In retrospect these seeming contradictions coalesce as features of an authentic person.

If Jewett described *Pearl* as "classical," the *Harper's* review helps explain how that might apply to her own pastoral practice in *Marsh Island*. The Owen home, says the reviewer, is "equally removed from fashion and from rudeness, dignified in its simple freedom, in the frank independence of its primitiveness." Jewett outdoes Stowe in communicating these values, perhaps because she has, in keeping with the interests of the late nineteenth century, a more carefully honed appreciation for the "folk." Like Hardy (about whom she says virtually nothing in her literary correspondence), Jewett is adept at using her rustics' point of view both for choric commentary and ironic distancing. After Dick has shared his first meal with Owen's hired hay-cutters, they wait till he leaves the table, when "it was necessary to have a consultation upon the appearance of the stranger, and to make ingenious guesses as to his past history" (35). Exhausting that subject, Jim Fales, a young hired man who acts throughout as a generic dimwit, reports news on Asa, a former hand who has gone west to live with relatives. Asa, all agree, may be exploited once his family finds out about his savings (he has never spent anything, so he must be "snug"). Of course, Asa can always return if he wants to. "Some folks can't spend, and more can't save" (37). The Owens live well, someone says, and Jim Fales's clothes have gotten tight since he came to the island.

These characters, like the lesser folk of Hardy and Sand, belong to the atmosphere; they even blend into the natural setting, in a quintessentially idyllic pattern, with roots in the ancient device of the pathetic fallacy (see Ziff 289).[3] As in *Daphnis and Chloe* the inanimate, the animal, and the human seem forever about to merge. Newly arrived at the farm, Dick sees in the orchard "a sturdiness and royalty about the stout-stemmed fruit trees" (65). Later, the mainland hills in the distance appear "like the telling of some sad news, in their harsh, insistent presence" (129). Doris in particular acquires naturalistic qualities: "beautiful to look at as a fawn and unconscious as a flower," thinks Dick on first seeing her (72). Her father, advising Dan, says that "women's a kind of game: you've got to hunt 'em on their own track" (92). Later, as Doris startles a fox on the frosty morning when she is hurrying to Dan, she seems to agree—"Doris felt as if she were a wild creature, too" (272). At some level, Jewett suggests, these animal identities exist, distressing as they may be (just before his remark, Dick thinks Doris "a soulless creature").

Other characters help convey this feeling of old-world pastoral. Sheep stray on the downs, while the farm, a "thrifty estate," is "more like an old-country habitation than many homes of this newer world" (106). Patriarch Farmer Owen, "with his flocks and herds and his love for his lands" (109), has the sage's "uncanny gift for understanding secrets that were not told him" (238). The pastoral theme of concealed aristocracy reappears in Doris, whose "ancestors had been of gentle blood and high consideration in the old days of the colonies" (112). Like other idyllic romances, the novel follows the seasons, from high summer when Dick goes on his painting excursion, till October when he leaves the Owen farm, ending with the marriage of Dan and Doris and the news of Dick's exhibition in winter. The autumn cold sets in just after a critical encounter between Dick and Doris in chapter 14; apple-picking starts in chapter 16 when erotic anxiety runs high.

Longus had used the scene of apple picking at the end of book 3 to suggest that the lovers are ripe for love's picking in the next book—a scene grounded in an image from Sappho. From the top of a tree, Daphnis picks a beautiful apple, perhaps, says the narrator, "being kept in reserve for some shepherd who was in love" (3.33). He gets a kiss from Chloe in return, "better than any apple." In Jewett's novel Jim Fales, gathering the fruit harvest, offers Dick an apple from the tree outside the high window from which Dick spies on Doris; Dick leaves the beautiful fruit on his window sill uneaten. "This harvesting hinted at the spoiling of his beloved surroundings" (203). Later, when Doris realizes she has probably committed a fatal error in her love life, she comes across old, worn-out apple trees looking "like the fig-tree that was cursed." As she stares pityingly at the sight, "a withered, pathetic mockery of fruit fell on the sand at her feet. It was like a conscious gift from these outlawed growths; it somehow gave her a bit of sympathy" (271–72). The latter scene prompts Doris to seize the day, but in conjunction with the earlier one it also suggests the likely consequences of a life with Dick, the man of artifice.

The main turning point in love's progress, ultimately for all three lovers, occurs earlier in chapter 14 when Doris, coming to a small nearby island, discovers Dick sleeping by her boat, which he had taken there earlier at high tide. Their conversation turns to the question of place, so crucial in Jewett's fiction: would Doris like to live "where there is more going on?" " 'No indeed,' answered Doris simply. 'I like home better every year.' " At this, however, she cannot look Dick in the face, and she "wondered how she might escape, not so much from him as from her appalling self" (182). Dick eventually replies, "I don't believe I could stand the long winter [on the marsh island]. Town is the place when the snow comes" (184). But even as he says this, he is preoccupied by their present circumstances, and "Dale's thoughts were attacking him like an angry and desperate mob" (185).

In this episode both lovers appear to choose while remaining inwardly diffident. It is soon afterward that Dick's aunt tracks him down, shocked to find him turning farmer and thus surrendering to Doris's place as well as her person. As for Doris, her love of place also translates into one of person. Delighted with Dick's urbanity, she remains emotionally committed to Dan's familiar rustic ways. She worries over Dan's coldness. Unable or unwilling to recognize it as jealousy, she thinks, "Why could not people be more generous to you when they loved you than when they were simply friends?" (174). Then, in an unconsciously ungenerous moment, she thinks, "Poor Dan! he was really just as kind at heart and full of pleasant thoughts; but he was a country fellow and lacked the ways of the world and the gift of ready speech" (177–78). Finally, on a visit to a coastal town with her father, Doris, gazing out at the sea, "felt as if she were on the verge of a greater sea, which might prove either wonderful happiness or bitter misery; and confused and dismayed by her loyalty to both her lovers, she hid her face in her hands" (246). What follows navigates skillfully between the superficially happy ending (Dan and Doris marry, Dick succeeds in the art world) and the psychologically more consistent stopping point where three people, having learned something about the inner life, settle for the fated choice.

Jewett's analysis of the heart depends on a more searching approach to human love than Stowe's in *Pearl*, where love seems frustrated by differences in gender. Jewett resembles Sand (whom she mentions as early as 1877 in *Deephaven*) in exposing the self-shattering ambiguities of affection in her characters. Does anyone really love anyone? "Love is forever a mystery," says the narrator: "it is rooted deep in still greater mysteries, and the attractions and repulsions even of friendship are as inflexible as law can make them. Love and death are unknowable this side of heaven, but mankind is ever busy watching the signs of both with curious, unsatisfied eyes,—these strange powers that take possession of us against our will, and make us strangers even to ourselves" (128). Jewett, praising Arnold's essay on Sand in a letter of 1888, vowed to study French all winter in order to read Sand in the original.[4] What Arnold said of Sand can also be said of Jewett, a writer who regards "nature and beauty . . . as a treasure of immense and hitherto unknown application, as a vast power of healing and delight for all, and for the peasant first and foremost" (248–49). Quite possibly the character of Dick Dale owes something to Arnold's lesser artist, who uses beauty and nature "with selfish and solitary joy . . . for his own purposes" (248).

Jewett's last and best book of Maine fiction, *The Country of the Pointed Firs*, has received most of the critical attention paid her since Willa Cather's famous 1925 edition. This work, especially in its more conservative edition by Mary Ellen Chase, uncovers an idyllic strain but distances the conventional lovers, avoiding the sentimentality found in romantic pastoral. Is it Jewett's private joke on Wordsworth that the natural man of the book is a rather simple old fellow named William? Joanna Todd, a long-dead hermitess, would have made a suitably melancholy subject for Wordsworth, but the sadness of Joanna's story is mingled, like so much else, with a subtle humor. Mrs. Todd, her cousin, reports that Joanna left society because she thought she had committed "the unpardonable sin" and had "no right to live with folks no more," adding: "Yes, she was one o' them poor things that talked about the great sin; we don't seem to hear nothing about the unpardonable sin now, but you may say 'twas not uncommon then" (76).

The premise of this book, an outsider arriving to sketch various rural scenes and characters, trades on a common device of nineteenth-century fiction dating back to Sand's *Promenades autour d'un village*, Eliot's *Scenes of Clerical Life*, or the *Sportsman's Sketches* of Turgenyev (yet another of Sand's friends and admirers). Ultimately the type originates in the "little sketches" of Theocritus, who may account for the feeling of classical timelessness felt in such moments as the Bowden family reunion. Like Theocritus, Jewett has no obvious social agenda; as discursive as her narrative is, it never really advocates or condemns a viewpoint. Things always speak for themselves, with the result that one is sometimes at a loss to know what to make of certain figures—say, Captain Littlepage.

Old people predominate at Dunnet Landing as in *The Pearl of Orr's Island*. Old sailors like Stowe's captains populate the place, of course: Captain

Littlepage, Elijah Tilley, and the four old fishermen. Stowe's Aunt Roxy, with her wisdom and her never-ending search for herbal remedies, could be the model for the central character, Mrs. Todd—a skilled herbalist, the narrator's friend and hostess. If her "peculiar wisdom" (92) about people and nature qualifies her for the role of sage, she is virtually the only character-type surviving from the traditional idyllic cast. A recollection told by Mrs. Todd also recalls *Pearl*. In Stowe's opening pages the ill-fated Naomi and her father, Captain Pennel, watch the sea from "a point of elevated land" as her husband's ship is foundering. Pennel involuntarily voices a warning to the ship's captain: "*Don't* take the narrow channel today!" (2–3). In *Country of the Pointed Firs* Mrs. Todd takes the narrator to the spot on the cliff overlooking the sea where she had stood helplessly watching as her husband met his death in a shipwreck: "'twas just off shore tryin' to get in by the short channel out there between Squaw Islands, right in sight o' this headland where we'd set an' made our plans all summer long" (49). It says everything about the difference between Stowe and Jewett, and between their literary generations, that the young Mrs. Todd did not die on the spot (much less give birth) but simply went on living, as Maine sea-widows always had.

In her letter to Fields expressing her admiration for *Pearl*, Jewett said she considered the first part, the idyll of childhood, the best of the novel. In *Country*, though, Jewett chooses to write an idyll of old age. She celebrates nature not as creating but as created, in stories of the sexually quiescent time of life. Nature is fixed in time, an object of reflection. The impulse to withdraw from the active and violent, glimpsed in Stowe's uneasiness about the passions of Sewell and Dolores, Moses and Mara, revives in this visit to a world where heroic action, tragic loss, and passionate delight all belong to the past. It thus makes sense to exclude the story of William and Esther's romance from *Country*, for in so gray an Arcadia, that story seems a bit absurdly to hanker after Eros. It makes Esther (who tends the classic, pastoral-labeled "silly sheep" [154]) and reclusive William a displaced Daphnis and Chloe. When, near the end of the book, the narrator hears Elijah Tilley recount the story of his long life, Esther acquires, as Marjorie Pryse asserts in her introduction to the novel, "a new sympathy for and understanding of the world of men" (xvii). If this is true, then the sexes come a lot closer to oneness in this strange narrative than in *Marsh Island*, where marriage is less a resolution than a submission to the way things are. Pryse shows how the reference to *The Tempest* in the name of the old lobster boat, the *Miranda*, helps establish the image of shipwreck on a fortunate isle (see xvii and xx n.15). And the echo in *Pearl* works similarly.

The narrator recalls earliest memories of Dunnet Landing, among them "a childish certainty of being at the centre of civilization" (2). Reductive, dismissive labels such as "local color" may prevent our appreciating this theme of home-as-center throughout the sketches. If not a paradise, Dunnet Landing surely represents what the center of civilization ought to be, culminating in the visit to the Bowden family reunion. Here is a mystical body not of Christ but of humanity, of men and women in nature:

> The plash of [sea] water could be heard faintly, yet still heard; we might have been a company of ancient Greeks going to celebrate a victory, or to worship the gods of harvests, in the grove above. It was strangely moving to see this and to make part of it. The sky, the sea, have watched poor humanity at its rites so long; we were no more a New England family celebrating its own existence and simple progress; we carried the tokens and inheritance of all such households from which this had descended, and were only the latest of our line. We possessed the instincts of a far, forgotten childhood; I found myself thinking that we ought to be carrying green branches and singing as we went. (100)

The imagery of harvest and grove, sea and sky, expresses openly the intimated classical pastoralism in *Marsh Island*. Old age and childhood merge in the idea of a "forgotten childhood"—humanity's childhood in an ancient green world. The reunion casts the narrator in the role of the idyllic foundling discovering her place and family. William is one of several characters with an enviable certainty of their place when he declares, concerning the rugged prospect of sky and sea, "There ain't no such view in the world, I expect" (45). The narrator follows Mrs. Todd to a field of "such pennyroyal as the world could not provide" (48). Visiting the gravesite of Joanna the hermitess, she compares her pilgrimage with "paths trodden to the shrines of solitude the world over" (81–82).

Such moments in the novel follow the idyllic method, dissolving and internalizing complex civilization's sense of space and time. References to classical antiquity such as that in the account of the Bowden reunion serve the same purpose. Mrs. Todd is particularly memorialized in this way. She is like "Antigone alone on the Theban plane" (49), a "large figure of Victory" (40); she is "grand and architectural like a *caryatide*" (30). Most significantly, "She might belong to any age, like an idyl of Theocritus" (59).

There is no evidence that Jewett read Longus, but her mention of Theocritus implies another route into the ancient sources of the idyllic. At her death Jewett left notes for a story called "A Modern Idyll," in which an old couple go back to the country for a brief stay, talk over their long married life, visit a friend, and return home. Jewett made a note to herself: "Do all this in the manner of Theocritus" (Sherman 91). George Sand had fostered the modern vogue for idyllicism, but the astute and scholarly Jewett certainly had made her own acquaintance with some of the sources that Sand had tapped.[5]

AFTER JEWETT

Willa Cather befriended Jewett not long before the older woman died, and although Cather's pitches her rural fiction in the georgic mode, she sometimes toys with the idyllic, usually to show disapproval of it. Cather also absorbed Jewett's way of looking at her native place and learned from her the solitary devotion required for the writer's life—hence the Nebraska author's dedication of her first important novel, *O Pioneers!* (1913), to Jewett's memory.

With a good classical education, Cather knew Virgil's and Theocritus's pastoral poems (see Thurin), though she associated life on the land not with ease but with work, performed in a spirit of love. An interest in the idyllic appears with Cather's early enthusiasm for Sand's pastoral novels, so carefully traced by Dorothy Zimmerman, culminating in the year of *O Pioneers!* when the young writer hung a portrait of Sand above the fireplace in her New York apartment (Zimmerman 30). Reading and life had introduced her to the idyllic as early as "The Treasure of Far Island" (1902). Here Douglass, a successful New York playwright, returns home to Nebraska and rediscovers his first love, Margie. Before Douglass left home to attend school, the couple and their friends had buried a collection of childhood treasures on the river island where they had once played pirate. An island Arcadia, it stands outside of ordinary time, separating young innocence from the reality of the hometown itself, where its hollowness is reflected in the people who now come to hear Douglass read from his plays—the local Women's Christian Temperance Union harridan, an old deacon who once set a dog on him, an alcoholic lawyer, a niggardly banker.

Landing their boat on the island, Douglass tells Margie, "Descend, O Miranda, upon your island" (278), and the place becomes their brave new world, the scene of their self-discovery: "they had become as the gods, who dwell in their golden houses" (282). This apotheosis, playful or serious, recurs many times in the idyllic romance and supports Frye's theory of pastoralism's effects: "the pastoral . . . seems to represent something that carries us into a higher state of identity than the social and comic world does. The closer romance comes to the world of original identity, the more clearly something of the symbolism of the garden of Eden reappears, with the social setting reduced to the love of individual men and women within an order of nature which has been reconciled to humanity" (149).

In "The Treasure of Far Island" as in *O Pioneers!* the couple's mutuality is assured by their distance from the erotic; theirs is a mature love and a "comradeship" (273), not a passion. If Jewett's *Country* acquires an idyllic innocence by simply removing sexual passion from its people's lives, Cather's novels of rural life tend, as Sharon O'Brien says, to bring out "the insufficiency, even the danger, of sexual passion and the opposing grandeur of passion deflected from the personal to the impersonal object," such as the land (158). O'Brien makes this observation in an essay that treats *O Pioneers!* as a study in contrasts between the restrained Diana-Alexandra and the passionate Venus-Marie. Alexandra's story of chaste love amounts to an idyllic romance.

Erik Thurin's chapter on the classical roots of this novel (174–87) links it with epic, pastoral, even tragedy, and Longus's tradition could be included as well. Consider the scheme of foregrounding the seasons at the beginning of each part: winter, June, winter, June, fall. As in Longus, the first part of the narrative leads into a time lapse, here sixteen years, in the lives of the couple. The motif of concealed aristocracy surfaces in the story of Alexandra's grandfather Bergson, a wealthy and influential shipbuilder in Sweden until he lost everything in a disastrous marriage—an event that led to his son's emigration. Finally, a wedding ends the story, though a wedding with a calculated irrelevance, as befits Cather's Hardy-like skepticism toward conventional romance *and* pastoral (see, on the latter, her poem "Arcadian Winter"). A romance writer would have taken Cather's opening scene—with Emil's kitten up the pole, the mean townspeople, the determined big sister, the apt young rescuer—straight into a courtship and marriage. But by this novel's end, Alexandra is tired out, Emil is not there to applaud the marriage, and Carl is no longer fit to climb lofty heights against the storms of life. Arguably, Alexandra's brothers are not entirely wrong to see Carl as a fortune hunter.

Cather plays her couple against the idyllic pattern with merciless irony. An illusory idyll survives in Carl's memory of themselves as children doing the milking together, Alexandra approaching with "a bright tin pail in either hand, and the milky light of the early morning all about her" (117). But Alexandra comes to be much more than a milkmaid, and later in the novel Carl becomes not only the Daphnis-like moneyless suitor but a sort of transient—a failure spiritually as well as materially. His sense of failure comes quickly in life. By the time he was fifteen, his "lips had already a little curl of bitterness and skepticism" (8). When he returns after his long absence, he compounds his failure as an artist by denying that he ever had the instinct:

> "Paint?" the young man frowned. "Oh! I'm not a painter, Alexandra. I'm an engraver. I have nothing to do with painting."
> "But on my parlor wall I have paintings—"
> He interrupted nervously. "Oh, water-color sketches—done for amusement." (101)

The lapse does not register with Alexandra perhaps because, even more than Jewett's Doris, she retains to a fault the ingenuousness of the idyllic heroine. "Her mind was a white book, with clear writing about weather and beasts and growing things. . . . She had never been in love, she had never indulged in sentimental reveries" (185). The inability to know love, so often a matter for wit in the eighteenth century, here lends Alexandra an aura of pathos with her milky morning light. The sort of country person who takes things as they appear, she never acknowledges the dark side of human nature. Even when her younger brother, having fallen into the affair with Marie, is troubled, "She felt no anxiety about Emil. She had always believed in him, as she had believed in the land" (213). At the end, after her encounter with darkness, Alexandra has acquired a "disgust of life" (264). A full recovery seems unlikely.

Yet even at the elegiac end of the story, Cather humanizes and celebrates the land: "Fortunate country, that is one day to receive hearts like Alexandra's into its bosom, to give them out again in the yellow wheat, in the rustling corn, in the shining eyes of youth!" The sentence epitomizes the one pastoral theme that continues unabated through the novel: the sympathy between nature and the human. Like Jewett's Maine, the land here has a human face. But unlike rocky Maine, this land seems to cooperate with humans, a promised land—"The grain is so heavy that it bends toward the blade and cuts like velvet" (74). The grapes of *Daphnis and Chloe* hang so close to the ground that an infant could reach out and take them. Such images as Carl's memory of Alexandra at milking recall Jewett's merging of human with natural, momentarily dislocating us from time and place—removing us from novel to romance. Cather had already used the technique in "The Treasure of Far Island," where Douglass first reencounters Margie as she stands all in white lighting a lamp, her hair "red as Etruscan gold" (270) and where Margie appears a figure of the eternal feminine, uniting images of Venus, Diana's nymphs, and Penelope.

The timeless vision of the milkmaid incorporates the residue of longing from idyllic-elegiac romance. Throughout Cather's fiction, there persists a desire for escape from dour Protestant culture to (in this novel) the carefree French or (in *Song of the Lark*) Mexicans—ethnic incarnations of the conventional simple shepherds, figures more of literature than life. Cather lacks Jewett's capacity for distance and restraint, the subtle humor that often animates Jewett's scenes or characters. Jewett would not write "and the spring would come again! Oh, it would come again!" (182). Cather cannot leave alone a grotesque such as Ivar, who makes hammocks of twine and hears voices on the pond. Having created this memorable figure, she has to threaten him with institutionalization at the hands of Alexandra's sordid brothers. It is as if, at the end of Jewett's "The Queen's Twin," Queen Victoria's devotee Mrs. Abby Martin were to be served notice of eviction from her solitary cabin.

Mary Ellen Chase, fourteen years Cather's junior, departs from Jewett in a different way, in her pessimism about the capacity of the best-willed people to find salvation in their natural setting. Yet an event in Chase's childhood insured a lifelong devotion to Jewett. In 1900, four years after *The Country of the Pointed Firs* first appeared, she and her father, Judge Edward Everett Chase, of Blue Hill, Maine, paid the celebrated author a visit. To Jewett's inquiry what the thirteen-year-old girl wanted to be when she grew up, Chase answered that she would write books. "I'm sure you will," Jewett answered, "and good books, too, all about Maine" (Jewett, ed. Chase xxv). When Chase did begin to write, Jewett remained her model. Alan Nevins's review of her *Mary Peters* (1934) elicited an amiable letter from her on his mentioning "qualities which remind the reader of Sarah Orne Jewett" (E. Chase 102). But Chase was mostly a teacher. She taught elementary school while still in her teens and then, after graduating from the University of Maine, served on the faculty at a girls' school in Wisconsin. Having completed a PhD at the University of Minnesota in her thirties, she spent the rest of her life on the faculty of Smith College in Northampton, Massachusetts. In her writing, whether in books or magazines, she sought a popular audience, writing "good books," if not great ones, about Maine (especially *Mary Peters, Silas Crockett, Windswept*) and not about Maine (especially *The Bible and the Common Reader* and her still-valued doctoral dissertation, *Thomas Hardy from Serial to Novel*). Counting children's books and edited collections, the number of her published works comes to thirty-nine (E. Chase 181).

A novel that gets lost in this big mixing bowl is her second, *Uplands* (1927), a story set in "North Dorset," Maine, that is deeply informed by the author's study of Hardy, who haunts her fiction almost as pervasively as Jewett. She must have thrilled to the brief but astute notice in the *Saturday Review*, saying of *Uplands* that "The incidents are as tragic as those of Thomas Hardy, with never a suspicion of inappropriate softness or sentimentality" (15 October 1927: 223). Predictably for a disciple of Hardy and Cather, Chase also maintains a critical distance from the pastoral dream of nature reconciled with humanity.

The lovers, Martha and Jarvis, have been neighbors for six years, ever since the orphaned girl came to live as a ward (in effect a servant) with a pious hypocrite, Miss Wickham. Love comes to the pair imperceptibly one spring. A "strangled boyhood" (27) on a small farm has made Jarvis, now twenty-one, uncommunicative and diffident, but recently he has acquired an eagerness to live that seems both the cause and the effect of his feelings for Martha. Colin Holliday, perhaps the most interesting character in the novel, a young prospect for the Catholic priesthood, rivals Jarvis for Martha's affections. A city dweller visiting his grandmother, he seems to offer Martha, with her one year of school at the "village academy," a larger world of books and culture. Colin's Spenserian name reminds us that in the 1920s, Spenser still seemed the poet of airy Elizabethan fancy, sublimely detached from real experience—as is Chase's Colin. Colin also shares qualities with Dick Dale in *A Marsh Island*. Like Dick, he is recovering from an injured leg at the opening of the story, when he sits on a hill (a typical Elizabethan pastoral posture) watching the tide move into the marshlands below. His budding career as a devotional poet, like Dick's as an artist, seems planted in shallow soil. Like Dick, too, but with a repugnant edge, he is a portrait of male self-satisfaction; his idealism, including his religion, serves to cloak his egocentricity. By summer Martha has not only lost interest in Colin but has grown so in love with Jarvis that she and he slip off to town and get married. A short while later, just before their planned announcement of marriage, Jarvis is killed in a farming accident. Book 2 of the novel resurrects Colin as a suitor (he is still enrolled as a Jesuit seminarian), but his attentions and poetry become increasingly irrelevant as Martha discovers she is carrying her and Jarvis's child. After a stay at a convent in town, she reveals everything to Jarvis's parents and they welcome her to their home. Even though Martha dies in giving birth, the older couple's lives are revived by the prospect of a grandson.

As in Hardy's *Under the Greenwood Tree* or Cather's *O Pioneers!*, or *Daphnis and Chloe*, which the learned Chase could have read in Greek or in the English of the Loeb Library edition of 1913, this plot follows the seasonal cycle—here, from spring to summer (Jarvis's death), to September (the stay in the convent), to March (the child's birth). At the end, it is late April, and Colin has returned to visit his grandmother during a brief recess. In a gesture toward the consolation of pastoral elegy, the young poet tosses a spray of wild pear flowers on a brook, observing the petals float downstream. "He watched them quite out of sight," the book concludes, "wondering, as he did so, why his imaginative mind had never thought before of doing such a simple thing."

Nature's simplicity evades Colin, a prisoner of his and (to a limited degree) his religion's fictions.⁶ When he leaves his poem for Martha in a hollow birch tree, Jarvis, watching him, feels jealousy, with a "loathing of his own life," but at the same time, "he knew, in spite of his anger and contempt, that he too would like to put a letter for someone in the hollow of a tree" (63). The difference between the two young men is defined by the distinction between the longed-for letter, a simple communication with "someone," and the poem—in this case "To a Dryad in a Pink Dress"—a derivative "literary" communication with no one. After Jarvis's death, there is another moment when poetry, with the mythic appearance of beauty, conflicts with real life, as Martha awaits the train that will take her from North Dorset: "One who had seen her there curled up beneath the apple tree, her cheek in the palm of her hand and upon her eyelids as many graces as ever moved the poet of *The Faerie Queene*, could not have seen in her the prey of accident and chance" (206). The allusion to Spenser-Colin's vision of the graces suggests an impatience with both Colins' idealizing of women: "Colin did not forget Martha Crosby, or rather, to be more accurate, that for which Martha had stood in his imagination.... She herself faded away in the pastoral and Arcadian simplicity of the setting and the experience." Here Colin stops to recall a poem by Horace he has translated:

You shun me, Chloe, wild and shy
As some stray fawn that seeks its mother
Through trackless woods.
(84)

Even though it isn't Longus's Chloe, the association, following the phrase "pastoral and Arcadian," seems inescapable.

Martha now attends school in nature. Early in the novel, to escape Miss Wickham's relentless preaching, she takes a walk, pausing beneath a hemlock tree to examine a rose-tinted, delicate mushroom: "She had heard from some forgotten source that such an exquisite thing sprang sometimes almost at once from the most unlikely of places. Scraping away the brown pine-needles, she saw the coarse black earth in which it grew and the tough, invading tree roots around it. And suddenly the analogy occurred to her that she in her pink dress was like the mushroom, that, like it, she had all at once sprung into a new and radiant life" (40).

At first reading, this is an image of outer and inner nature as old as poetry itself, but the passage goes beyond the pathos of unacknowledged beauty. The mushroom is the rare and secret self, but the hemlock indicates a poison in the environment; the brief life of the mushroom foreshadows the couple's untimely death.

At several points North Dorset appears harsh and soul-destroying, like the tree roots. Jarvis's mother worries that her son will waste away there. Later Martha, waiting for their child to be born, tells his mother that she and Jarvis "knew we'd beaten North Dorset. It—it did n't have a chance against—against our love" (279). The stammer betrays a lack of conviction. Despite life's continuity at the end of the novel, it remains unclear whether Martha and Jarvis have "beaten" the hard climate and culture of the region. Like so many American novels of rural life, *Uplands* can never fully accept the soft primitivism of idyllic romance, the mode of *otium* over *agon*.

In effect, Chase has written an idyllic love story in the first half of her book and a Hardy-like love tragedy in the second. At harvest time, just before Jarvis dies, the idyll achieves a momentary fulfillment, described in the lovers' "spacious sense of sufficiency which forbade their living beyond the present" (123). It would be hard to find a better description of the idyllic-romance sentiment. Yet, echoing the idyllic-elegiac tones in Stowe or Cather, these feelings of love and sufficiency combine with "the fear of days in dull, steady succession, of nights whose mysterious ecstasy should ebb like a tide that has no turning, of poverty, of restraint, of slow despair" (125). Bernardin's old man lectured Paul in the same desolate tones, and Stowe's Mara repeated the message at the end of *Pearl*. Certainly Chase learned none of this from the more sanguine Jewett. What she and Cather did find in Jewett was the feeling for place, the art of conveying what Cather later described to Chase as "that indefinable spiritual atmosphere which certain places possess for those who understand them."[7]

Late in life (in 1962), Chase paid tribute to Jewett once more as the guiding spirit of her own and others' Maine novels: "Even the best of us distantly follow in her footsteps, stumbling and fumbling among the words which she so perfectly set down on paper, among the people whom she so unerringly portrayed, among the marshes and islands, the caves, the hills, the villages which she saw with a vision denied to all other Maine authors" ("My Novels" 15). Chase's later Maine sagas reflect a sense of history transcending the narrow focus of idyllic romance; her and her sister-in-law's few comments about this early novel suggest that the author held it in low esteem, perhaps because it lacked the temporal scope and spaciousness of those later writings.

Maine, with its splendid vistas and glimpses of pastoral life at the very back door of New England, has continued to produce notable fiction on rural life, most recently in the well-received work of Carolyn Chute. Two popular writers continued the Jewett tradition in the intervening century. Gladys Hasty Carroll's *As the Earth Turns* (1933), set on a Maine farm, is more georgic than idyll, filled with the details of working on the land and in the kitchen. It has a symmetrical, seasonal structure, with a part named for each of the four seasons, but it is preoccupied with tasks: clearing winter roads, curing infant croup, starting cabbages indoors. Picturing a variety of characters' lives, it focuses on no one couple. The dialogue often anticipates the conventional chatter of television versions of farm families. It was the second most popular novel of its year and assured the author a long career as a fiction writer (Seaton).

An author with a similarly wide public, but more thoughtfully inclined to write about solitary lives, is Elisabeth Ogilvie (1917–   ), who in the 1940s began her novels about Maine fishermen living on and around a place called Bennett's Island. Her many stories of coastal Maine include *Waters on a Starry Night* (1968), a narrative redolent of the idyllic tradition. The couple, Thora and Lyle, having met and married at sixteen and seventeen, now have four daughters and can barely survive on Lyle's income as a lobster fisherman. The plot turns on two tempests. The couple shelter a wealthy man whose boat has gone down in a storm, and while visiting, he notices that the books willed to Lyle by his uncle-guardian are rare and valuable; selling these becomes the family's salvation. Thora is a sensitive soul, intelligent despite her lack of education. As a child she would hide in a little cave on the island, and when her current anxieties as wife and mother drive her back there, she thinks of the place as a second womb. Seeking temporary refuge, Thora recalls the couplet from Marvell's "The Garden": "Fair quiet, I have found thee here, / And innocence, thy sister dear" (180).

The novel is more her story than Lyle's, but his near-death in another storm at the end of the novel brings the couple back together. The Wordsworthian title and the passage from Marvell offer a resonance that elevates this story above the ordinary romance plot. Nature as well as a sense of the past helps to restore harmony—represented not only by the legacy of books but by Thora's sage grandfather, whom her daughters enjoy visiting in his hermitage. As a "popular" writer, Ogilvie sometimes allows her formulas too much authority, but she has kept alive Jewett's feeling for the shaping influence of the Maine countryside. She has her own legacy of books, both as heir and testator, and a major part of her estate is the attachment to the ancient, mythical "island," a spot on the earth with a life that is its own.

Spanish Idylls

JUAN VALERA'S TWO TRANSLATIONS

Two undeserving victims of the Anglo-American neglect of Spanish literature, Juan Valera (1824–1905) and Emilia Pardo Bazán (1851–1921), survive in Britain and the United States chiefly in university Spanish studies. It was not so a century ago, when bookstores often sold translations of both and when no less a critic than William Dean Howells put their work in the forefront of recent European fiction. Reviewing Valera's *Pepita Jiménez* alongside Hardy's *The Mayor of Casterbridge*, Howells found that in Hardy "the allegiance to the lessons of life is so deeply felt" but that evaluating Valera's novel required "more purely literary criterions" ("Hardy and Valera" 40). Its achievement, continued Howells, lay in "the delicate irony, the fine humor, the amusing and unfailing subtlety" (41) that distinguished it from Hardy's tragedy.

Howells and Valera had already formed an acquaintance when this review appeared. Their surviving correspondence, issuing from the Spaniard's two-year residence (1884–86) as ambassador to Washington, reveals their differences over Howells's moral criticism, his (puritanical, Valera might have said) belief that novels communicate "the lessons of life," his conviction that "the first effect of the 'beautiful' will be ethical, and not aesthetic, merely" (40). To this position Valera responded, "Neither have I wanted to say that I am teaching this or that. A partisan of *art for art's sake*, I have not tried to teach anything" (see Duchet 100). This difference over moral purpose touches on a crucial problem with idyllicism, though the moral argument came easily at a time when novelists felt a need to justify their art on the grounds that they were recording, if not teaching, society's morals.

With Emilia Pardo Bazán, Howells was more firmly convinced of superior accomplishment. A few years after the Valera correspondence, Howells singled out her fiction for comparison with the stories of Sarah Orne Jewett. Her criticism of modern fiction and French naturalism he found "robust and vigorous," especially incisive in its chapter on English fiction. By 1908, in the essay "Lyof Tolstoy," Howells felt secure in ranking Pardo Bazán among the foremost contemporary novelists. Although any one of these novelists "shrinks and dwindles beside [Tolstoy]; behind him, in the same perception, but not the full perception or the constant perception, come Maupassant and Zola and Flaubert, Galdós and Pardo-Bazán, Verga, Björnsen, and perhaps Hardy—yes, certainly, Hardy in 'Jude,'—with, of course, Hawthorne from a wholly different air" (128). Since the "perception" meant is moral, Howells seems to place Pardo Bazán in a different line from Valera, but one that both novelists would have probably accepted. Idyllicism attracted Valera—half aesthete, half man of the world—for the same reasons that Tolstoy might have found the form insipid or that Pardo Bazán, as in *La madre Naturaleza* (Mother Nature), judged it fatally vulnerable to moral scrutiny.

Valera's 1879 translation of *Daphnis and Chloe* culminated his longstanding affection for the Greek story, mentioned as early as 1860 in his preface to a collection of legends and folktales ("Florilego" 86). A widely read man—in classics mostly self-educated—Valera often lectured on literary subjects ranging from medieval romance to Plato's philosophy of love to an attack on the Zola school's "new art of writing novels." Valera knew not only the Greek novel but its progeny: in his lectures in 1877 he called *Paul et Virginie* a "marvelous idyll" that imitated Longus's "ingenuous and delicate pastorals" ("Literatura" 239). Valera seems to have written the translation in about two months. It may leave something to be desired (García Gual 263), since aside from occasionally neglecting the Greek, Valera knowingly makes Gnatho pursue Chloe rather than Daphnis. Yet it is love's labor. Perhaps like that other Lothario-statesman-translator of Longus, James Craggs, Valera found Longus's guileless island an escape from sordid affairs, both the erotic and the diplomatic kind.

A long introduction (*Dafnis y Cloe* 9–45) situates Valera's ideas about fiction in relation to the idyllic tradition: "*Daphnis and Chloe*, rather than a bucolic novel, can be termed a rustic novel [cf. roman champêtre], an idyllic novel, or idyll in prose; and in this sense, far from passing out of fashion, it sets the fashion and even serves as a model, *mutatis mutandis*, not only for *Paul et Virginie*, but for the very fine novels of George Sand, and even for one that a certain friend of mine composed in Spanish a few years ago, with the title *Pepita Jiménez*" (43).[1] By saying "bucolic novel," Valera has in mind, I think, the earlier stories about disguised rusticating aristocrats; in any case, he has a clear idea of the contemporaneity of his own "rustic novel" type. Its qualities, he says, are that it takes its subject from ordinary life, "painting rural, rustic, or village scenes" (recall that Theocritus's poems were described as "little picture"). Instead of singing about heroes as the epic poets did, says Valera "in these modern idylls the themes concern the lowly state of life" (43). Modern examples exist in poetry as well as prose: Goethe's *Hermann und Dorothea*, Longfellow's *Evangeline*. With "the lowly state" Valera brings class back into the tradition, an element absent in Gessner's Arcadias and irrelevant to Sand. The rustic novel is both novel *and* romance (16), the fashion for romances changing from age to age—luckily for the novelist, who otherwise could not compete with early romances such as *Celestina* or *Amadis* (19).

Like Huet and Florian, Valera feels obligated to compare the earliest romances with those of his time. The ancients may not have felt or understood nature as deeply as the moderns, but in *Daphnis and Chloe* nature is lively, and the brevity of descriptions insures that they will strike the imagination of all readers without wearying them (21–22). As for the love theme, although franker in its sensuality, *Daphnis and Chloe* presents a more honest, selfless love than do modern novels such as those of Flaubert (22–24). Admittedly, *Paul et Virginie* raises love to a more spiritual plane, but there lurks also, "in the midst of its simple and natural beauties, an excess of feeling and an unwholesome sensitivity, owing to Rousseau, Bernardin's teacher, and a theosophical appetite to find in nature a religious revelation, while in *Daphnis and Chloe* there is positive (albeit defective) religion, and everything is more honest and less refined" (25).[2] In *Pepita* these doubts about nature combine with those about certain practices in religion to create the comic irony that so delighted Howells.

While hardly a religious story, *Daphnis and Chloe* is about divine care (40) but at an elemental level:

Daphnis and Chloe, in a complete state of nature, although one elevated and idealized by favor of the gods—but of gods seldom severe—love each other before they know that they love, are beautiful and ignorant, contemplate and understand their beauty, and from this contemplation and admiration is born an affection sufficiently refined for two who live an almost primitive life: he without school or the study of ethics, and she, without a vigilant Christian mother, without an English governess to tell her what is *shocking*, without anything of that kind. If the author, given his subject matter, had put into the loves of his two characters something more subtle, ethereal, and spiritual, it would have been totally false, stupid, and unendurable. (41–42)[3]

The first part of this passage exactly fits the two lovers of *Pepita Jiménez*, who love before they know love. The remainder certainly fits Pepita, impoverished in childhood with a coarse and mercenary mother. Luis is the antithesis of Daphnis, for his plight is precisely that he has too much schooling, particularly in ethics. The asymmetry will require further examination.

In his novel, Valera displaces godly powers with those created by mental and emotional states. Luis, a seminarian, visits his long-unvisited home village before he is to be ordained. He falls in love with Pepita, a young widow being courted by his own father. Love makes the priggish youth into a man, as he learns something of riding, fencing, and shooting, even defending Pepita's honor in a duel. Luis's father, glad to have a son who will continue his line, happily steps aside, and the two young people marry. Local characters enlivening the story include the old vicar and Pepita's maid, Antoñona, who function as sages representing the complementary wisdoms of Christianity and nature. Quaint details add those touches of local color (*costumbrismo*) that long sustained *Pepita* in American classrooms.

Yet the book's delightfulness owes at least as much to the characterization of the principals and to the comic irony surrounding a naive couple's loving "before they know that they love." The intelligent but unlearned Pepita and the bookish but inexperienced Luis (a combination that will reappear more comically in Pérez de Ayala's male scholar and female peasant) derive their mutuality from the symmetry of their graces and defects. Outwardly the pastourelle tradition, so influential in Renaissance literature, seems to be shaping the narrative: a young aristocrat travels to the country, fights a duel, and wins a handsome country girl. Yet Valera enjoys the play of forms as much as any author with his wide literary knowledge. The pastourelle soon proves a trompe l'oeil: only superficially does the story subordinate female to male. The author himself declared Pepita to be in the line of *Daphnis and Chloe*, *Paul et Virginie*, and Sand's novels, all of which place the lovers in a balanced relationship.

Much of the hero's comic self-revelation occurs in the first half of the book, a series of letters addressed to his father-superior uncle, the "Dean of the Cathedral of ——," brother of Luis's father. These letters, polite versions of the love complaints uttered by Daphnis, draw their enjoyment from the reader's superior feeling of knowing what is really happening in the anguished but innocent heart. The letters further show Valera rescripting the "discovery of the parents" motif into an exchange of the spiritual father for the earthly one. A reviewer in the *Nation* (4 November 1886), not fond of Valera's other work, found himself won over by Luis's letters with their "profound but not cumbrous analysis of his own heart."

These letters provide a frame, the narrative distance that Bernardin and others sought to imitate from Longus. Such distance helps make more credible the simplicity of idyllic love. A signal moment in Luis's development comes during a day of riding—with Pepita, his father, and others astride horses and with Luis and the Vicar on mules. That night Luis asks his father to teach him to ride because "Pepita has urged [*excitado*, which can also mean "aroused"] me to it" (*Pepita* 224); he had been especially impressed that day by her image mounted and carrying a whip (218). Not long afterward, the fencing lessons begin, accompanied by paternal, indeed patriarchal, lectures on women.

Scholars have suggested a self-dialogue between Valera the idealist and the realist at such moments. Valera, who often called himself an idealist, was a life-long student of Platonism and the Spanish mystics: among his many writings is a little book called *La psicología de amor*, which draws heavily on these readings. Still, during his diplomatic career he carried on some notorious love affairs that culminated, when he was sixty-one, in an ill-fated romance in Washington with the daughter of Grover Cleveland's secretary of state (the twenty-eight-year-old Katherine Bayard committed suicide in the Spanish embassy).[4] Platonic and mystical philosophies of love needed to be realized in experience.

A residue of aristocratic pride exists in Luis from the start, especially "a certain pride of family" (161 and n.21). It is at best a borrowed luster, since Luis seems to have been illegitimate (165 and n.25), a status that ties him to the foundling Daphnis and Bernardin's Paul. Pepita's fatherless plight similarly aligns her with Chloe and Virginie. As the novel progresses, Luis's false pride, along with his resistance, is worn away. The crisis comes during the folk celebrations of the "noche de San Juan," a summer solstice feast with overtones of pagan fertility rites. Earlier that month in an unguarded moment Luis and Pepita finally kiss, and the event sends him running from her house, vowing never to return. Antoñona visits him, leveling charges of cowardice unless he will explain himself to her mistress. Luis returns to Pepita the night of the festival. His planned courageous farewell, his self-defense, his seminary logic and theology wither against Pepita's common sense and impassioned appeals. Yielding, says the narrator, he "penetrated" the shadowy room, following after her (345).

The sexual innuendoes of "penetrate" [penetrar] accord with a pattern of associations leading up to this moment, as the word is used in both a spiritual and sexual sense, entailing both the union of the lovers and the idea of fusion in those mystical and Platonic philosophies of love that Valera knew so well. The seven places that Luis enters, ending with Pepita's bedroom, seem to correspond with the seven *moradas*, stages of mystical progress in Saint Teresa's writings (see Lott 14–18). Earlier, in his first letter to his uncle, after telling Pepita's history, Luis asks, "How to penetrate into the depths of the heart" of this young woman (158). Associating her with the beauty of nature, Luis recalls moments of mystical joy on hearing a nightingale or "on penetrating a luxuriant grove" (182). Such beauty is the means by which "the soul can penetrate a felt depth, and read and discover the beauty of God" (183). Planning his farewell visit to Pepita, Luis thinks that "it would be the work of a second to penetrate the entryway" of her house (311), and on arriving "he penetrated the entryway" (323). After the critical penetration the narrator describes how "The perfume of the flowers and the moon's brilliance penetrated through the window" (345).

Pepita is necessarily an object in Luis's letters, but she becomes a feeling subject in the second part when, the letters having stopped, we begin reading an account seemingly by Luis's father (see Ruano de la Haza). Without parents, married at sixteen to an eighty-year-old uncle with property, four years later she finds herself a beautiful land-owning widow, the most desirable woman on the local marriage market. In Luis's view, her widowhood adds to her imperious distance as he rides the sterile mule, and she, whip in hand, sits astride the spirited horse. Bathing in the erotic desire of his father, she is a "most dangerous woman," he thinks (247). Yet after the letters, a major reversal occurs in the novel with the shattering of this femme-fatale image.

For one thing, in this second part the shepherdess proves as perplexed as the shepherd. After the kiss, Pepita at first reproaches herself to the vicar and then finds the self-respect to exclaim, "If Don Luis loved me, he would sacrifice for me all his plans, his vows, his fame, his aspirations" (289). In preparing for Luis's "last" visit, she behaves artfully despite her sincerity:

> She had washed her face in lukewarm water so that the marks made by the tears would disappear to the exact point of not making her look ugly, but so that some hint that she had been crying would remain; she arranged her hair in a way that did not indicate painstaking concern, but that showed a certain artistic and pleasant carelessness without tending toward disorder, which would scarcely have been decent; she polished her nails, and since it would not have been proper to receive Don Luis in a dressing gown, she put on a simple house dress. In sum, she instinctively saw to it that all the particulars of the dressing table would concur to make her appear prettier and more elegant without there being apparent the least indication of art, of work, of time spent on these niceties. (326)[5]

The key word is "instinctively" in the last sentence. In spite of herself, natural Eros leads her on, as he does so many other idyllic lovers. While Luis struggles to maintain the appearance of heroic sanctity rising above temptation, Pepita keeps up appearances as a spirited woman who can survive being jilted. All the while, Valera insinuates their mutual desire, first by matching them with the comical old sages of the village: Pepita's confession to the vicar at the beginning of part 2 leads to Antoñona's scolding and counseling of Luis a few pages later. Far from being sophisticated, Pepita, we now learn, "had little communication with people and did not know how to mince words" (330). Luis, too, cannot communicate his feelings, but for the opposite reasons. When he finally does become hers, Pepita reacts like the country girl she is: "A woman from the city . . . will find strange what I am about to say of Pepita, even censurable, but although elegant in herself, she was very much a creature of nature . . . ; [thus, on hearing Luis's promise] she skipped and laughed and gave other signs of joy that, notwithstanding everything, had much about it that was childlike and innocent" (349).[6]

Such joy results from the resonance between the human and natural orders in a life well lived. The explicit support of Pan and the nymphs lends divine approval to the life according to nature, and such a providence is not absent from *Pepita*, even though the action might seem counter-supernatural. Luis finds himself in a subtle but vast conspiracy of nature to wean him away from a false ascetic spirituality. Within days of arriving in the country, he forgets his customary meditations in experiencing the beauty of the night sky, the fields, and the warbling birds—"almost sinful distractions," he calls them, "an unpardonable forgetting of the eternal for the temporal" (180). He first finds himself alone with Pepita when they are briefly separated from their walking companions, in a magically overgrown and secluded grove—one of many moments when nature seems to be in league with Pepita to bring him to her. The frequent and sensitive observations on nature, if always brief like those Valera admired in Longus, go beyond mere descriptive apparatus for the novel.

As a character, Pepita draws more from the idyllic tradition than Luis. When in part 2 we finally hear her own words, unmediated by Luis's letters, "She did not speak as a lady of our salons might have, . . . but with the idyllic nakedness with which Chloe spoke to Daphnis, and with the humility and total self-abandonment with which Naomi's daughter-in-law offered herself to Boaz" (330).[7] Pepita comes from a life of abject poverty yet almost prelapsarian virtue—and here it is worth remembering the epigraph, and for a while the working title of the novel, "Nescit labi virtus" [virtue knows no fall]. Even her old uncle-husband is said to have lived "innocently, without malice" (155). She belongs to the idealized Edenic countryside (far different from the Andalusia that Valera actually knew) full of delightful gardens, crystal streams, a thousand kinds of flowers, crowds of singing birds (146–48), more Theocritean than Spanish (146 n.7). Pepita represents what Yeats calls "unity of being," rooted in her natural habitat among people of nature:

"the sweet and pure light of her glances, everything coheres into a fit rhythm, everything is united into a perfect harmony, where one cannot find a discordant note" (202).[8] As with so many women of the male-authored idylls, Pepita owns more of nature's gifts than her lover, so much an object of love that her creator has to struggle to give her the selfhood and subjectivity that allow her to share the stage with her young man.

The mingling of Christian and pagan in the Chloe-Ruth allusion (Valera, who read Florian, may be thinking of that poet's Virgilian-biblical poem on Ruth) permeates the novel, and raises the question whether this sense of all-powerful nature constitutes a challenge to Christianity. Harold Spender, reviewing Gosse's translation of *Pepita*, observed that "If nature conquers religion, it is only because religion, in defying nature, had ceased to be true to itself" (*Bookman* [London] February 1892). Pérez de Ayala's Cástulo will later lament that we can no longer speak naturally about natural things. Ideas and feelings of the *pagus*, the open countryside, lend themselves to "paganism" of precisely the kind found in Longus. Valera's narrator reports concerning the village celebrations on the fateful evening, "The eve and morning of St. John [23–24 June], although a Catholic feast, retain I know not what bad habits of ancient paganism and naturalism" (321). Pepita's prayers to "el niño Jesus" give way to "the other infant," Cupid (327). In the brief, closing, third part, the now-married couple have grown fond of setting up little shrines around their house. Pepita's house serves as a sacred center, a cave of the nymphs. "But I must confess," Luis's father reports, "that both [lovers] also have their touch of paganism, like rustic pastoral love poetry that has taken refuge out of doors" (392). Among the shrines is a statue of the Venus de Medici with an inscription from Lucretius's famous opening lines to the goddess of generation: "Nec sine te quidquam dias in luminis oras / Exoritur, neque fit laetum, neque amabile quidquam" [And without you nothing rises into the divine shores of light, nor is there anything of joy and love]. Though Valera resisted any suggestion that he was "teaching," this is assuredly his novel's final statement on asceticism's excesses.

A garden—such as that of Dionysophanes in *Daphnis and Chloe*, in which nature seems a work of art (4.2)—brings a sharp focus to the art-nature theme. Pepita's garden and home suggest a balance achieved between the two, between spontaneity and structure. Water irrigates the garden in a network of ditches, cascading into "a path that Nature herself has opened" (186). Valera builds his description of Pepita's surroundings in a hierarchy of human relevance, ascending from grass and flowers to fruit and nut trees to vegetables, culminating in the gardener's cottage and the spot where Pepita will serve lunch, she and her maids being "dressed in country attire yet with great beauty and elegance" (187). This balance between rusticity and elegance in dress extends into Pepita's bedroom furnishings. Plants, birds, and flowers complement objects of art. The religious prints on her walls reveal "good taste . . . almost unheard of for a place in Andalusia" (273–74). On the eve of the Feast of St. John, the setting of Pepita's study composes a variety of sense impressions from the union of art and nature (moonlight "competed with" lamp and candle; merriment from a nearby house "mingled with" the murmur of the fountain).

Earlier, Pepita embodies the nature side of the dialectic in the novel, while the letter-writing dean incorporates the "art," the learned asceticism to which she is unwittingly a foe. In his argument with Pepita on the fateful night, Luis takes the dean's side at first, while to Pepita belong the seductive powers of nature. The dialogue merits attention as continuing the classical debate of pastoral opposites, evocative of that between Perdita and Polixenes in *The Winter's Tale* (4.4). The wedding of the two lovers restores harmony between humanity and nature much as does the wedding at the end of *Daphnis and Chloe* when the city parents recognize their country-bred children. Capturing this harmony, Pepita's wedding brings back the golden age, dissolving social barriers, as "Servants and masters, gentlemen and workmen, wives, maidens, and serving-girls of the village attended and mingled there as in the imagined first age of the world which, I know not why, they call golden" (381).[9]

A good point from which to assess Longus's contribution to this novel is the picture of Daphnis and Chloe on the couple's wall complementing the one of Cupid and Psyche. Together these constitute a diptych. Psyche, as in Goya's memorable painting *Cupid and Psyche*, holds her lamp, discovering the sleeping god. This represents the dark mystery of human passion reflected in Luis's fear—authentic, however amusing—on the eve of St. John; here also the mysticism of love that preoccupies both Valera and his seminarian. Compare this with the companion painting that "represents Chloe when the fugitive cricket deposits itself in her breast where, thinking itself safe in so pleasant a shade, it starts to sing while Daphnis tries to remove it" (392).[10] As an ecphrasis, this embodies the innocence (despite the compromising position of Daphnis's hand) and natural simplicity and spontaneity (the cricket's song), not to mention the theme of providence in nature (in Longus the cricket has just escaped a hungry bird) that the Greek romance has transmitted to later ages. In a way the two paintings are like Schiller's sentimental poet in negotiating the light and dark registers of Valera's novel: innocent and passionate, idyllic and heroic, pagan and Christian-mystical.

It would be well to consider here Valera's transformation of a Greek "romance" to a modern "novel," a distinction he seems not to have taken seriously. For Frye, realism—and thus much of what we call the "novel"—is "essentially parody-romance" (39): *The Great Gatsby* "parodies the success story," for example, which is "the romantic convention contemporary with it" (161). Characteristically romance gives itself away in its moral polarities, abandoning the gray shades of everyday experience for a world where people are consistently virtuous or, at least until an often unforeseen conversion, wicked (50). An effect of this moral dualism is that romantic heroes and villains inhabit, respectively, a happy world above the muddle of everyday life and an exciting, dangerous, or "demonic night world" below it (53). Most romances move in their narrative development from the idyllic to the night world and then back (54).

The relevance of this pattern to *Pepita* scarcely needs elaboration. Parody lurks in the subversive amusement at Luis's anxieties; the resulting distance resembles that created by Longus's sophisticated narrator. Equally comic is the seminarian learning to ride and fence. The "dangerous Pepita" image also proves an exaggerated figment of Luis's naïveté. Once Luis has "penetrated" the "dark room" after Pepita, he has descended into the shades of passion and unreason, the arena of romantic *Liebestod* and of contention with the night forces. In the logic of romance, for Luis to love Pepita means to face death from the Count of Genezahar, who simultaneously exists as a villain and as another object of parody, a city-goer and frequenter of the local casino that stays open all night. What self-respecting man of the world would devote his nights to such a village casino? Yet as part of the romance, Luis's powerful sexual drives may be viewed as projected onto the count, a kind of Jungian shadow to Luis. The count embodies all the qualities that Luis has never known until now—in his arrogant, oppressive courting of Pepita and in his insatiable love of women, horses, gambling, and alcohol. (Luckily for Luis, he has never pursued swordsmanship with the same energy.) Luis's cousin Currito is the count's sidekick, a kind of adjunct adversary who had earlier taunted Luis as a "theologian." If the count is a consummate nemesis in the story's polarities, Pepita in several respects represents a via media along which she is guiding Luis: between eroticism and sterility, between decadent civilization (suggested in the count's rank) and unaccommodated nature, between extreme worldliness and obsessive spirituality.

From the night-world struggle emerges a new identity or a renewed self-knowledge. Frye says that the hero's return to the upper world accompanies "the growing of identity through the casting off of whatever conceals or frustrates it" (140). This in part describes the movement of classical romance toward the revelation that the hero or heroine comes from aristocratic rather than servile or rustic parents. Just as beauty and innate grace set Daphnis and Chloe off from their country peers, so Luis seems exceptionally handsome and inexplicably quick to learn fencing and horsemanship. Because romance heroes are favored by the gods when not cursed by them, Luis so "unrealistically" strikes it lucky at both cards and dueling in his nighttime adventure. Frye writes that during the romance combat, the essential thing is not so much terror as "some kind of ritual," and we may recall the theory that *Daphnis and Chloe* was created to evoke initiation into a cult of Eros or Dionysos. In *Pepita* the ritual of the duel satisfies this requirement, though like other romance motifs it is tempered by an underlying sense of the actual, since the seconds decide (humorously, I think Valera would say) "that once the two combatants had sabers in hand, they might do whatever God should bring to mind" (370).

In his introduction to *Dafnis y Cloe* Valera remarks that "the novel is as old as the world" (27). Fundamentally his novel is a romance in conception and execution, though he delights in parodying such conventions of popular love stories as the duel, the dangerous woman, the rival lover. Needless to say, he was not the only novelist of his time to play with the older elements of storytelling. Nor is it inconceivable that Valera wrote *Pepita* with this critical heresy, "novel equals romance," in mind, adjusting the ancient requisites of the mythic and marvelous in romance to the dispositions of his audience. Still, in this idyll of natural sympathy and fortunate love, a supernatural presence is never far away.

PARADISE LOST IN GALICIA

Coming a generation after Valera, Emilia Pardo Bazán belonged to an age of "realism" in fiction. In Spain that meant the novels of Benito Pérez Galdós, with whom she had a long love affair, and in Europe it meant reckoning with the naturalism of Emile Zola (to whom she devoted much of her critical examination of modern fiction, *La cuestión palpitante*). To read her *La madre Naturaleza* is to be immersed in the questions of Zola's fiction—the determinism of "nature," humanity's inability to rectify its social and animal circumstances, the conflict between scientific and religious views of nature, the application of natural selection to human society.

Pardo Bazán was in her mid-thirties when she came to know the aging Valera, remaining friendly with him even after he campaigned against admitting women to the Spanish Academy. She visited him often during his last years of illness and blindness. They must have had interesting conversations—he who had scolded her for Zolaism in *Apuntes sobre la nueva arte de escribir novelas*, she who had remarked in print that his characters all sounded like their author (DeCoster 101). Yet it was Valera's *Pepita*, along with the novels of Flaubert, that helped Pardo Bazán see the novel's serious potential (Clémessy 1:47 n.11). She also agreed with Valera on the plight of the modern Spanish woman, though for quite different reasons. Valera thought that the ladies of the salons and cities, unlike their village counterparts, had lost their femininity, while she held that modern society had permitted only women of the villages to retain their independence and integrity (Clémessy 2:572).

The manifold ironies in *La madre Naturaleza* begin with the title and extend to the idyllic plot and characters. The heroine, Manuela—a girl in her late teens of seemingly prelapsarian character—is victimized by four different sorts of masculine illusion. Her father, the aging, morally decadent Marquis of Ulloa (a title he cannot rightly claim), neglects her because she reminds him of her sanctimonious mother, whom he alternately abused and neglected until her death in Manuela's infancy. That story also occupies the novel that some consider Pardo Bazán's masterpiece, *Los pazos de Ulloa*, published the year before this sequel, in 1886.

Since Manuela's infancy, her protector and devotee has been her father's illegitimate son, Perucho, who becomes her lover without their knowing that they are half-siblings. A pious priest, Julián, now curate of Ulloa, has never helped Manuela even though he virtually idolized her mother when he served the marquis as chaplain. Most significantly, in his other-worldliness Julián has never revealed to Manuela and Perucho their blood relationship. The central character is Manuela's Uncle Gabriel, who arrives at the beginning of the story aiming to marry her, now that he has retired from the army (recall that Pepita was first married to her older uncle). Gabriel will, he thinks, remake Manuela into a cultivated lady. The novel pulsates with sexually driven unconscious motives, cross-purposes, and contradictions, often anticipating the Freud-induced fiction of the next century.

Along with several other texts under discussion, *La madre Naturaleza* develops as a pastourelle struggling against an idyllic romance. Like Daphnis and Chloe, Perucho and Manuela spend whole days on their own, unnoticed by adults, wandering through a sometimes Eden-like landscape. Gabriel is the pastourelle's itinerant knight, Perucho the pastoral's lovelorn swain. But the author builds both characters by undermining their stereotypes. The less complex of the two, Perucho, once a big-brotherly protector, has evolved into Manuela's passionate lover. As the novel begins, an unacknowledged transformation has come over their relations: she looks at him "as if she had never seen him," and "he also looked much more, but fixedly, openly, with ardent, searching eyes, seeking in response a similar glance" (1.396). Perucho has recently returned from school in Orense and will soon show what he has learned about sex from other schoolboys. From the start he seeks a chance to put his learning into practice—as when he lies atop Manuela, urging her to play "like when we were little." "You're suffocating me," she yells, and in the final analysis her words prove true (4.417). Perucho's jealous and possessive love will in the end drive her into a (supposed) dead-end convent life.

The climactic confrontation between Gabriel and Perucho (chapters 27 and 28) works brilliantly through dramatic ironies produced by the two men's limited understanding. Gabriel knows, but not Perucho, that Perucho is Manuela's half-brother; Perucho knows, but not Gabriel, that he and Manuela have consummated their private vows. Perucho plays the role of the typical humble shepherd-lover, denying any interest in Manuela's wealth: "studies bore me; I was born a peasant and I'll die a peasant, with dirt all over my hands. A cottage, a little land, and a yoke of oxen to work it with—we won't be so miserable that we won't have that; and knowing that, let the world laugh at me as I laugh at the world" (602).[11] A literary formula to be sure—but Perucho's simple honesty is belied by the cunning with which, that morning—motivated partly by love, partly by the fear that Gabriel will take her away—he led Manuela to a desolate part of the Castro Mountains and seduced her. Perucho's speech, however, prompts in Gabriel a change of heart—Gabriel's "noble features breathed harmony and kindness" (27.603)—probably because he thinks he sees a fellow idealist.

Gabriel's idealism exists in tension with the power of nature. Gabriel is the angel sent to the virgin from on high; his army service leads him to be called "the artilleryman," the idealist in combat who kills from long distance (not to mention that artillery seems to have been the aristocratic branch of the Spanish army [see 447 n.24]). In the novel he most often appears sitting, musing, or lying in bed—quite in contrast with the peripatetic lovers. Gabriel's story, coming to the reader in his moments of reflection, begins with his worship of Manuela's mother Nucha, lost in his childhood when the marquis took her away. After his officer training, he leads an unsettled life. He holds contempt for the ideas of revolutionary Spain in the 1860s, dreaming of "an epic and glorious Spain made up of great captains and unconquered monarchs" (8.448). Temporarily leaving the service, he rebels against his former self; he immerses himself in German philosophy; returning to the army, he abandons studies and has an affair with a brigadier's wife, who leaves him, sending him back to books. But this time his interest is science, especially as it regards explosives, "which our era refines and perfects at every turn as if the supreme object of such progress were a universal conflagration" (8.455).[12]

Here the novel opens out beyond the idyllic space. Pardo Bazán seems to associate Gabriel's malaise with that of his whole society: soporific, rooted in an irretrievable past, mired in ideas and ideals untested by experience or honest observation. Frustrated idealism entertains destructive fantasies. (If this sounds like a Russian novel of this era, it may be because the author had been poring over that country's fiction in 1885 and 1886, preparing to write her ill-received *La revolución y la novela en Rusia*.) A glimpse of the social context occurs early in the novel when Gabriel is on a coach headed for the village of Ulloa, accompanied by an obese archpriest and a small-time political hack. In the afternoon heat, while all on board the coach including the driver are asleep, the horses, maddened by heat and stinging flies, run out of control and cause a crash. Gabriel's arm is injured when the archpriest lands on top of him.

Coldly received at the manor house by the marquis, his former brother-in-law, Gabriel hears that Manuela is "the picture of her dead mother." "If she looks like Nucha," he responds, "as far as I'm concerned she's an angel" (9.466–67). Gabriel now entertains pastoral daydreams about her:

> Why did he take delight in imagining the sylvan innocence of his niece, her somewhat unsociable personality and the submissiveness and tenderness with which, after her initial aloofness, she would very softly fall upon his breast; and why did he see himself dispelling her ignorance little by little, educating her, forming her, initiating her into the joys and goods of civilization; at other times, the tables turned, why did he see himself become a villager, and Manolita with her sleeves rolled up like Catuxa [the doctor's wife], feeding the chickens or—heavenly vision, ineffable sight! holding close to her white round breast a little creature half rolled up, all bathed by the sun? (11.476)[13]

In a profession and a society dominated by men, Gabriel is starved for the feminine; in Jungian terms he might be seen as seeking personal integration, trying to discover his anima. Yet he remains a child in this regard. Nucha is the only "mamita" he has ever known, and Manuela, her double, now offers him a last chance to find the satisfaction that Nucha represented. In his daydream of the nurturing and nursing female, he himself is the "little creature" at the breast.[14]

The artilleryman has his illusions dimmed when he first meets Manuela and notices her abrupt manner—an "infallible symptom of detestable upbringing," he thinks (15.502), but on reflection he finds that her boorishness makes her more attractive. The thought of how much he has to teach her inspires him with enthusiasm. In other words, the naturalness of this girl who has been "left to herself ever since she was born" (15.503), the unreflecting simplicity that will seal her fate, makes her desirable. Like unhewn rock or timber, she can be formed. Pardo Bazán allows her knight to test his powers in a typically idyllic orchard scene. On their first walk Gabriel gestures toward plum trees heavy with fruit. "Get me some. Have pity on a poor courtier," he jokes. When she does so, Gabriel urges her to have one. "I don't feel like it," she says; "I've had enough plums." She has a duty to have one, he says: "The duty of young ladies to make themselves agreeable and nice to everyone, and especially to guests in their home, and even more especially if they are uncles come to see them" (15.505).[15] The encounter begins to sound like a scene between Don Quixote and one of his village princesses: Gabriel calls her an angel, but "Even if you were a devil I'd love you." Then, "Before I saw you I already liked you," at which Manuela weeps with laughter (16.506–07).

Edenic intimations in this scene accumulate when, coming out of the trees, the two see a fat snake and Gabriel feels "the chill that comes with the reptile's presence," though Manuela, unperturbed, picks up the snake's skin, apparently just left behind, to take to Perucho, saying, "If only I had a rock to squash its brains" (16.513). From one point of view Gabriel is the snake, the outsider who brings turmoil into the lives of the idyllic pair and whose rivalry tempts Perucho into the fatal step, for both, of carnal knowledge. In Catholic tradition, it is the Virgin Mary who crushes the serpent's head; in the novel's terms, Manuela will crush Gabriel by refusing him even though, after the incest is revealed, he is "more than ever" determined to marry Manuela (28.609). In rejecting him at this point, she keeps her integrity intact, which the author probably values more than her virginity. The dejected, rejected Gabriel's famous last line of the novel—"Nature, they call you mother. They ought to call you cruel stepmother"—is on one level a reminder that we are all foundlings uneasy with our appointed place. More narrowly, it is a cry of benighted anguish from a former innocent, an orphaned and now permanently exiled heart.

If there is no blaming Mother Nature, there is also no absolving her. The narrator says, in that final scene, that Gabriel is looking at "life, indifferent, rhythmic, serene life," a description that makes Gabriel's cry all the more irrational—first, because it is misdirected (the blame ought to fall on the community around the young couple including, to some degree, himself) and, second, because it suggests a determinism that the author herself had condemned during her critique of Zola's naturalism in *La cuestión palpitante*. The juxtaposition of Gabriel's cry with an "indifferent" nature certainly clears Pardo Bazán of inconsistency here, but elsewhere the narrator describes nature as the couple's "protector and accomplice" (1.396). Nature's "accomplice" role, dear to the naturalist, is perhaps too often felt in Pardo Bazán for her to be completely exonerated of Zolaism. Consider the lovers' ascent up the Castros or, much earlier, the scene of sheltering in a grotto during a rainstorm. There, in the dim light of an opening that lets in enough water and sunlight for a luxuriant mass of plant life, "It seemed that Nature revealed herself more powerful and lascivious than ever, showing off her genesis-powers with a free immodesty" (1.396). Manuela notices among the plants a "secret rite of organic life"—an insect "sacrifice" caught in a spider's web and a procession of ants with a dead body (1.397).

Although the novel does slip at times into this rhetoric of natural determinism, even in its misleading title, I think Pardo Bazán aimed quite elsewhere—at the human egotism (Gabriel's idealism, Father Julián's convenient otherworldliness) that imagines itself wholly undetermined. An old bonesetter, a folk-healer—the nearest thing to the idyllic sage in this novel—tells the couple what no idealist wants to hear, that humanity lives and dies undifferentiated from other beasts (3.409); even the man of science, Dr. Juncal, agrees that the titles of physician and veterinarian are artificial, created by human pride (7.439). In *Daphnis and Chloe* the natural divinities do act as protectors and accomplices. In *La madre Naturaleza*, by contrast, unthinking, careless, human folly *permits* nature—now defined as the absence of civilization—to "take its course."

Seeking Manuela and Perucho on the fateful day, Gabriel imagines nature scolding him:

> Fool, let a beautiful couple go around unaccompanied from the time of adolescence, without protection, without instruction, wandering freely like Adam and Eve in the days of paradise through the hollow of a most pleasant valley, in the passionate season of the year, among sweet-smelling flowers and carpets of soft grass capable of tempting a saint. What barrier, what fence will keep them apart? An entirely illusory,

ideal one; a fence that my laws, the only ones they are subject to, don't recognize, for I have never forbidden birds born in the same nest from nesting together the next spring. (25.584)[16]

On the novel's last page Gabriel calls himself what nature calls him here, a fool. For him to wish nature to be his mother, in the last sentence, suggests that he remains just that. From one standpoint Gabriel is like Schiller's elegiac poet, who "seeks nature, but as an idea and in a perfection in which she has never existed" (127). But in view of Gabriel's quixotic touches, it may be more accurate to say that if nature really were a woman and could talk, she would not be the first of her sex to say to men of Gabriel's type, "I'm not your mother."

That people can see nature as sinister seductress-accomplice and as merely the voice of common sense associates *La madre* with both its romance and novelistic precursors. The deluded priest in Zola's *La Faute de l'abbé Mouret*, having failed to listen to common-sense nature (his normal instincts including his sex drive), slips into romance madness in his paradise fantasy.[17] In *Pepita* Valera sustains the romance elements of the novel by filtering events first through the young seminarian's eyes. In *La madre* Pardo Bazán's narrator oscillates between hints of romance (the supernatural, the fantastic) and declarations that these are simply illusion. From romance she draws such characters as the eccentric bonesetter and "La Sabia," an old witchlike woman who subsists in a ramshackle house that guards the entrance to the lovers' paradise in the Castros. Initially Gabriel appears to be the stock romance hero, the comandante with a mysterious, exciting past, ready to take the nubile virgin away from sordid reality. Pardo Bazán often tempts the reader into romance situations, as in chapter 26 when (in a moment reminiscent of *Wuthering Heights*) Gabriel sees Julián emerging secretively at night from Nucha's mausoleum. At La Sabia's, in chapter 19, Manuela and Perucho steal some milk, whereupon Manuela thinks they are under the witch's curse (537). The milk seems to bring on a kind of intoxication in Manuela as they climb the mountain, as if she has taken some magic potion. Gabriel undergoes similar disorientation that same afternoon, searching for the pair during the hot siesta hour, distracted by "the whispering silence of the woods, the hoarse murmurs of the millstream, the fragrance of the chestnut blossoms" (25.581).

Texts contributing most to *La madre* are *Paul et Virginie*, explicitly mentioned, and the story of Eden. In the background lie *Paradise Lost*, hints of George Sand, and even *Daphnis and Chloe*. Idyllic signals audibly reverberate in the opening pages of Pardo Bazán's work. The lovers, not yet quite lovers, take refuge under a vast chestnut tree, a "patriarchal tree," suggesting that of the Genesis story. Its counterpart in the final love scene on the mountain is a grand oak tree, the oak being a favorite resting place of Daphnis and Chloe. It guards the entrance to a place where "no human foot, but Nature herself had opened paths similar to the winding alleys of an English garden" (19.539). The ambiguity of active-passive nature continues in this image of the deceptively natural yet artfully made English garden. Another idyllic echo appears in the early pages when the couple, running for shelter from the rain, cover both their heads with Manuela's long plaid skirt, "acting out the pleasant and tender portrait of Paul and Virginia, which seems an early, bold symbol of confidence in love" (1.394). In Bernardin's scene, of course, the couple are still small children; here Manuela's "boldness," really ingenuousness, in covering them both with her skirt anticipates their later union. They then discover better shelter in the "rude and shadowy grotto" (394) that recalls the cave of the nymphs in *Daphnis and Chloe*. In addition to marking the genre, all three images of refuge—tree, skirt, and grotto—possess a certain irony that foreshadows the novel's counter-idyllic outcome.

Paul et Virginie's presence in *La madre Naturaleza* has been recognized at least since Armand Singer, over fifty years ago, found many correspondences between the two works, mentioning also echoes of the Genesis story and Valera's translation of *Daphnis and Chloe*.[18] While Longus is probably the source for the couple's scene of passion, Singer says, their excursions at the beginning and end are based on Paul and Virginie's expedition to return the runaway slave to her master. Manuela resembles Virginie in her command of natural lore and her charity toward her poor neighbors. One might add that Pardo Bazán's expressed admiration for Bernardin's landscape descriptions (*La literatura francesa* 1:31) helps account for her long, symbolically suggestive passages of natural description in *La madre*, as contrasted with the briefer, largely functional ones in Valera's *Pepita*. But the discovery of parentage plays no part in the French novel: Pardo Bazán looks back to Longus for this ancient romance motif, providing it with an ironic, novelistic twist.

La madre exists so much in the consciousness of Gabriel that it is difficult to find the shared male-female perspective of Longus, Bernardin, or Sand. Manuela often appears filtered through the reports of others, even at the end, when she chooses her bleak future. Maryellen Bieder has suggested a kind of mutuality in that Gabriel's views are countered by a "female voice" in the narrative. In certain episodes, however, especially those with Perucho and Manuela in the countryside, the views of the lovers alternate. Bieder points to Manuela's lingering thoughts about the beauty of Perucho's curly hair and to Perucho's loving reflections about her feet (108–09). Although Perucho is the guiding will in the ascent of the Castros, both he and Manuela comment on the scene and converse during this part (chapters 19–21), which constitutes a little idyll in itself.

The novel also paints scenes of the community at work quite similar to those of Longus, such as the one of the harvesters whom Manuela and Gabriel see coming back from Father Julián's house:

> Drawing near the [marquis's] house they heard the happy shouts of the reapers, and Gabriel, catching sight of his brother-in-law supervising the work, went toward the place where they were harvesting. He saw the whiteness of shirts and dresses, the red sashes and blue scarves of the men and women in the field, shining against the dark background of the soil; near a hedge sat an earthenware jug, and the crew—chanting their inevitable "ay . . . le le!"—were quickly tying the bundles of sheaves, using their knees to press down the stalks. The intoxicating smell of cut sheaves perfumed the air, and the artilleryman felt a rush of joy as, enchanted, he contemplated the picture. (18.531)[19]

A similar "picture" later shows the threshing work as a scene "worthy of a colorist painter, a student of Nature faithful to reality, enemy to the effeminizations of drawing and false light seen through the studio curtains" (23.569–70).[20] The scene-painting takes us back to Sand's plowman at the beginning of *La Mare au diable*, a static "little picture" against which the drama of these two weeks, the time of ripeness (Longus's *opôra*) unfolds. Also Sand-like is the character of Manuela, who roams as freely as little Fadette. Manuela's uncomfortably frank, blunt manner resembles that of Fadette more than the genteel sweetness of Virginie.

A decade before this novel, Pardo Bazán had published an introductory study of Dante and Milton entitled *Los poetas épicos cristianos*, showing her knowledge of *Paradise Lost*. Her pages on Milton (247–330) are mostly standard information probably gathered at the Bibliothèque Nationale, where she often worked. Although she did not read Milton's poem carefully (she changes Raphael into Gabriel [327–28], a mistake with potential significance for her novel), and although her critical opinions are often derivative (especially of Hippolyte Taine), she has some heartfelt opinions of her own, especially on book 4 of *Paradise Lost*. Here, she claims, lie exposed both Milton's greatness and his shortcomings. This epic, she writes, "is full of the bourgeois and prosaic personality of Milton and, at intervals, of his most sensitive poetic inspiration. There is a sovereign mastery in the joyous description of Eden and in the beautiful nightfall that encloses the amorous rite of our first parents" (323).[21] She recalls visiting a fog-shrouded London and being surprised when the mists suddenly lifted to reveal St. Paul's. So with *Paradise Lost*: "Perhaps a gloomy mist exhales from Milton's poetry that prevents me from admiring it" (329). Book 4 ought to have been "the nuptial hymn of the human race," but alongside the Song of Songs, it is merely British fog (324). What most bothers her about the fourth book was Milton's treatment of prelapsarian sexuality:

> How opposed to our own is this conception of paradisal life! We have all dreamed of the first couple; we have seen them roaming and wandering arm in arm along the rosy paths beside lakes surrounded by a flowery shoreline perfumed with violets and irises; we have numbered their sighs and swoons, their raptures in the shade of the palm trees, their ecstasies in the grottoes and beneath the willows. . . . For us impurity and work follow the Fall; they don't precede it.
>
> How preferable I find the chimerical creation of Tasso, a tale of knight-errantry forged from real deeds, to the domestic realism of Milton. (326–27)[22]

Spoken like a countess. Seen in this light, the unknowing love of Perucho and Manuela is reduced to "impurity." The comment might best be read in the light of personal setbacks at this earlier time in the author's life.

In view of her explicit comparison of Manuela and Perucho to Adam and Eve, it would be unlikely that Pardo Bazán did not think of Milton's story of paradise when writing her novel. The episode of Gabriel's urging Manuela to pluck the fruit resembles, more closely than the serpent's temptation in Milton's ninth book, the dream of Eve in his fourth book, when the seeming angel takes Eve to the tree and urges her to pick the fruit. Seen in this context, Manuela's refusal makes her even more Edenic than Eve, since it is based on simple lack of hunger. Gabriel's flattery and cajolery recall Satan's in both of Milton's temptation scenes. Gabriel sees himself, of course, as an instructing angel, like Milton's Raphael—whom Pardo Bazán in her book misremembers as Gabriel. The war stories that Manuela wants to hear from him approximate Raphael's story of the war in heaven, which according to Milton marked the invention of artillery, Gabriel's profession. Like Milton's archangel Michael, Gabriel also instructs Perucho after the Fall concerning his future life and then, in effect, runs Perucho out of paradise. His advice on passion bears a general resemblance to the counsels of Raphael in the long seminar that is Milton's eighth book. Perucho seduces Manuela in an "immense amphitheater" (21.555), a locus amoenus at the top of the couple's climb, not unlike the "woody Theatre / Of stateliest view" (*PL* 4.141–42) at the top of the mountain where sits Milton's paradise. In *Paradise Lost* we enter Milton's Eden through Satan's eyes as he makes his way over the newly created earth. In *La madre* the counterpart is Perucho's guiding Manuela and the reader to the desolate place and choosing to follow "the fox's path" (21.554) to get there—the fox being, of course, an ancient symbol of Satan. Manuela's seeming intoxication after drinking milk at La Sabia's recalls Eve's drunken feeling after she eats the fruit in book 9. At the end of Milton's epic, Adam and Eve leave paradise in the evening, "hand in hand." Lingering in the village cemetery, Gabriel sees Perucho and Manuela returning arm in arm (21.591) from the mountain. Like Milton's couple, they have already had their "fall," but unlike them, they don't know it.

Because they did not know, as Gabriel observes (32.627), their incest was no sin; and even if they had known, they would have violated no laws of nature. Their "crime" is all the more tragic in that it precedes knowledge and mutual recognition. Important similarities also exist between Gabriel's counseling scene with Perucho that night and the advice the old narrator of *Paul et Virginie* offers Paul after Virginie's drowning (Singer 40–41). Yet in

Perucho's uncontrollable passion at this moment, and in Gabriel's befuddlement, lies a more authentic perception of human nature, or of the human sensibility, a century after Bernardin. Pardo Bazán, Zola, and other novelists of their generation share an awful discovery: modern industrial civilization has entrapped people in the powerful structures that their own intellects have created. It seems unfair that, when Gabriel reveals to Perucho that he is Manuela's half-brother, the youth exclaims, "You've come here brought by the devil to deceive me and to deceive everyone" (28.605). Yet, self-deceived by a lifetime of idealizing and rationalizing, Gabriel fits better than anyone else the role of serpent in this garden.

Pardo Bazán began her career as a novelist after discovering, from *Pepita Jiménez*, that the novel could provide a framework for the study of humanity (Pattison 32–33). In her two-volume *La literatura francesa moderna* (which begins with Bernardin and Rousseau), she proves a careful reader of George Sand, whose contribution to the novel she declares to be the completion of the individual in the *couple* (emphasis hers: "Jorge Sand completa el individuo representándolo por medio de la *pareja*, el hombre y la mujer" [1:248]). Like Valera, and Pérez de Ayala afterward, Pardo Bazán recognized the thematic possibilities of the idyllic romance, with its dual perspective on nature and civilization. Both she and Valera approach the romance elements in their fiction with intent to undermine, though Valera finds the lure of romance hard to resist once he's there. The young seminarian—his illusions disturbed, if not exactly shattered—exchanges one kind of retreat for another. Only Pepita's practical wisdom sees them both through. Pardo Bazán creates a heroine truer to life, who seems to lack this wisdom, whatever her botanical and zoological knowledge.

A revealing point of contact between these two novels is Fray Luis de Leon's commentary on the Song of Songs. The mystic has helped distort the vision of Valera's Luis, but he has also helped him to rise as a lover and (if somewhat comically) a hero. All true love participates in the mystical experience. Pardo Bazán's Gabriel, searching for a book to read so he can fall asleep on a warm night, discovers an old copy of Fray Luis that foments in him an idealist's dream. Manuela leads him through a paradisal field, saying tender things in a biblical style, while Father Julián looks on paternally, giving Gabriel cool water from an earthenware jug (22.566). Psychoanalysts may wish to turn the jug into a female breast, linking it with the earlier image of Manuela nursing an infant. However this may be, it is clear that in Gabriel's unconscious mind, Manuela has been cast in a role no woman should want.

Although the idea might well have come from Valera, Pardo Bazán claimed to dislike the sensational, romantic novels of George Sand in part because they appealed to this kind of fantasizing: "It will be objected that the love made divine by George Sand was a transcendental idealism, but we know well how, in the thread of these idealisms, are concealed strands of the effeminization and decadence of a literary epoch, and even of a society" (*La literatura francesa* 1:249).[23] The novelist's suspicions of idealism are most apparent in the effeminized priest, Julián. He bears more blame than Gabriel for the evil outcome, and he does his final bit of life wrecking at the end when, as Gabriel's emissary to the despondent Manuela, he misrepresents the offer of marriage as Gabriel's gesture of magnanimity in spite of all he should know (35.640). Who wouldn't prefer to enter a convent?

The Catholicism that both Valera's *Pepita Jiménez* and Pardo Bazán's *La madre Naturaleza* confront belongs to the era of the first Vatican Council—triumphalist, antimodern, laying stress on doctrine and the supernatural. This temper helps account for some of the two Spaniards' preoccupations and the contrasts between their novels and those of British and American authors. For Valera and Pardo Bazán the ancient idyllic form, grounded in nature, stands against supernaturalist dogmatism while rectifying the more corrosive elements of modern life, Wordsworth's "fretful stir / Unprofitable, and the fever of the world" ("Tintern Abbey" 52–53). Like British novelists from Eliot to Hardy, they arbitrate the great dialectics of their century—simplicity and progress, religion and science, self and society. Valera sets his novel in a somewhat earlier, apparently simpler, decade of that century, in a place where the practices of simple folk still flourish. A cosmopolitan, he authentically longs for a simpler life. Like the aristocratic Tolstoy, Pardo Bazán (the countess actually refused to use the title) dislikes much that is modern, especially the common man's passion for newspapers. Wordsworth again comes to mind, disparaging "the craving for extraordinary incident, which the rapid communication of intelligence hourly gratifies" (Preface to *Lyrical Ballads*). Pardo Bazán satirizes this craving in Perucho's stepfather's newspaper reading, punctuated as it is by outbursts about the heat wave in New York, the Irish Fenians, and the doings of King Ludwig in Bavaria. Perhaps her closeness to life in Galicia, which is for her what the region of Berry is for Sand, meant that she did not need to set her novel in an earlier age. The effect of Gabriel's contemporaneity and Manuela's timelessness is perhaps all the more striking on that account—and her idyllic novel all the more urgently a means of evoking simple verities that time and a deluded civilization, as instanced by Gabriel's own brand of naturalism, have labored to forget.

ぎ ぎ ぎ ぎ ぎ ぎ ぎ

British Naturists

THE TEXTURED EVOCATIONS OF *UNDER THE GREENWOOD TREE*

In British literature of nature, the nineteenth century begins with Wordsworth's monumental narrative poems and ends with the fiction of Hardy. As Wordsworthian romantic nature tradition continues on its own course, it sometimes merges with poetry of the folk—the writings of William Barnes or the Manx poet T. E. Brown, for example. Brown found a large audience (and in public readings held on his home island, he still does so today) for his dialect verse narratives such as *Betsy Lee* (1872), about two children, one orphaned in a storm, who grow up together in a fishing village but lose the chance for marriage and happiness to an envious lawyer's clerk. Vying with Hardy's influence in the regional novel throughout the later 1800s and early 1900s is the more benevolent vision of Richard Blackmore's *Lorna Doone* (1869), a novel itself perhaps shaped by *Daphnis and Chloe* (Sutton 38). Since the example of French realism (Edwards 148) or naturalism did not start a flood of English Zolas, it is worthwhile using John Alcorn's term "naturist" to describe the line of late Victorian and Edwardian novelists whose view of things will not quite handle the baggage of "naturalist." Two of the authors discussed in this chapter, Thomas Hardy and W. H. Hudson, appear in Alcorn's lineup, and the third, the once-popular Henry De Vere Stacpoole, belongs there. In Darwinian terms we might say that all three of these authors, with their beliefs in instinct and sexual liberty, their aversion to the abstractions of commerce and religion, labor to produce Alcorn's final exemplar, D. H. Lawrence. In Alcorn's words, the naturist is "post-Romantic in his attempt to obliterate the observing, thinking, feeling first-person, the Wordsworthian 'I'" (4). Naturists ponder their age's "renewed interest in animality" (9) in human life, and their characters are "part of the landscape"—the landscape itself being a "principal personage," not just a backdrop (7). Birkin, in Lawrence's *Women in Love*, expresses the naturist creed: "Whatever the mystery which has brought forth man and the universe, it is a non-human mystery, it has its own great ends, man is not the criterion" (Alcorn 110).

The naturist sensibility may tend toward either the elegiac or the idyllic, but only Hardy maintains the capacity for both, imbued with an artfully concealed wit. *Under the Greenwood Tree* stands almost alone in the author's work as a Sand-like idyll. Hudson's *Green Mansions* is an idyllic romance gone terribly wrong. Stacpoole's *The Blue Lagoon* and *The Garden of God* attempt, without these other two authors' animus toward religion, to discover unmediated experience with nature. Each author was, in his way, a scientific observer of nature—Hardy in the tradition of the Victorian serious amateur, Hudson as a self-trained and renowned ornithologist, Stacpoole as a physician and environmentalist.

Naturism is hardly unique to Britain. Pardo Bazán, Cather, and Jewett often present characters bound to a landscape that acquires its own personality as the fiction develops. What Cather said about plots Hardy also might have said; feelings and thoughts, images and characters, all bound up with nature, seem to come first with him. Cather puts faith in nature, but if Hardy shares any belief with Cather, it is that some unseen power—Fate or "the Immortals" (in Cather, nature or providence)—shapes individual lives. For Hardy this power almost always yokes romantic love with suffering and death; not so, or not so often, in Cather and Jewett. They did not marry; Hardy did—twice. In this sampling, at least, Nancy Chodorow's theory of gendered loving holds true: "men do not become as emotionally important to women as women do to men" (197–98). Cather, it often seems, would like to banish romantic love from all decent company. Hardy could not have written a novel like *Death Comes for the Archbishop*, where the only loves are of God and friend.

While *Under the Greenwood Tree* marks a beginning for Hardy, the opening of his imaginary "Wessex" countryside, it also carries on the family of rural fiction represented by George Eliot's *Adam Bede* and *The Mill on the Floss*, and even Emily Brontë's *Wuthering Heights* and the rural novels of George Sand. What Longus gave to earlier English novels in this line came through echoes in Shakespeare, Bernardin, and Sand, though the Greek author obtained a low place at the Victorian table through a clergyman's bowdlerizing. A school friend of Samuel Taylor Coleridge and Charles Lamb, Charles V. Le Grice writes the dedication to his 1803 Longus translation, *Daphnis and Chloe: A Pastoral Novel*, by voicing the claim that "The streams of Helicon, from which Longus drank, were troubled with the muddy waters of sensuality. I took no small pains in cleansing him from all impurity before I ventured to introduce him."

A few years later the scholarly lawyer John Dunlop, in *The History of Fiction*, similarly harks back to Pierre Daniel Huet with the remark that "there are particular passages so extremely reprehensible, that I know nothing like them in almost any work whatever" (72), a comment one would have thought certain to increase Longus's readership. Dunlop's praise of Longus's narrative style, however, anticipates the century's interest in balancing actual against idealized life in nature. Longus refrains, says Dunlop, from trying to depict a vague golden age (meaning, no doubt, as in Gessner), "but attempts to please by a genuine imitation of Nature, and by a description of the manners, the rustic occupations, or rural enjoyments, of the inhabitants of the country where the scene of the pastoral is laid" (69). The poet, Schiller had said, must not sacrifice the real for the ideal; Dunlop's insistence on the actual anticipates the emergence of local color, regionalism, *costumbrismo*, and realism in nineteenth-century rural fiction.

From 1855 on, English readers could obtain Longus fairly easily through the Bohn's Classical Library translation by the Rev. Rowland Smith—that is, the translation by Le Grice that was edited and augmented by Smith—in *The Greek Romances of Heliodorus, Longus, and Achilles Tatius*. Bohn's translations, famous for their tiny print and literalness, were nevertheless the Penguin Classics of their day, valued especially by those without the then-coveted training in Latin and Greek. Smith explicitly resisted bowdlerizing, quoting a recent translator of Catullus: historical fidelity requires that the manners of the ancients not be suppressed "through a fastidious regard to delicacy" (xviii). As a compromise, Smith puts censored passages into Latin at the foot of the pages where they occur—namely, the couple's discussion of animal intercourse, much of the Lycaenion scene, and Gnatho's attempt on Daphnis in book 4. Smith's introduction quotes Dunlop's praise of Longus and adds some of his own observations about Longus's influence on *Paul et Virginie*. Anticipating today's feminist interest in the Greek romances, Smith commends Longus and the other authors for "the more prominent manner in which they bring forward that sex, whose influence is so powerful upon society, but whose seclusion in those early times banished them from participation in the every day affairs of life" (xii).

English idyllic fiction during this period found its most notable expression in George Eliot, linked to the tradition of Longus, if at all, through George Sand. Already in a laudatory article in the June 1842 *Monthly Magazine* Eliot found Sand "not only the most remarkable woman—but the most remarkable writer of the present century" (579). Certainly the later novels *Adam Bede* and *The Mill on the Floss* possess a greater density and complexity than Sand's rustic novels, but the French author was a real presence in some of Eliot's best work (see Blount 93–110 and Thomson 152–84).

Closer to the pattern of idyllic romance among Victorian novels is the love story of the younger Cathy and Hareton in the second half of *Wuthering Heights*, which Robert Polhemus has ingeniously dubbed "an eroticized and unsentimental version of a Wordsworthian vision" (90). The second-half couple neatly substantiates this interpretation. Both are orphans, both thrown together in the rustic setting of Heathcliff's and Catherine's earlier, darker passion. Young Cathy enters the novel as a Miranda-like figure: she has lost her mother and has been raised by her father "into an apt scholar" (233), as we hear at the start of chapter 18, which passes over twelve years of her childhood. On the threshold of adolescence, at thirteen, she meets Hareton, then eighteen, with so different a childhood. Yet Hareton has the traits of concealed aristocracy visible the first time Nelly Dean sees him since his boyhood—"Good things lost amid a wilderness of weeds" (241). No Ferdinand here, Hareton more resembles the disinherited Orlando of *As You Like It*, though not even knowing what he should know. In succeeding years, Heathcliff's plot almost draws the fatherless Cathy down its rat hole, as she joins Hareton in virtual slavery.

Wuthering Heights searches more deeply than *The Tempest* into the nature-nurture question, with nearly every child-parent relation framing the issues in a new way. How can old Earnshaw have fathered so miserable a son as Hindley? Is Heathcliff a product of his parentage or his adoptive family? Why is his son so unlike him? Is young Cathy's transformation into the slattern whom Lockwood first sees the result of a too-secluded nurturing, of an unstable mother, an unwise father? Are the characters inextricable from the baneful toils of their natural surroundings—a land supremely fit, says Lockwood in the novel's first paragraph, for misanthropes? Whether they originate in Longus or Sand (see Thomson 80–89) or Shakespeare, idyllic romance themes arise only to fade under Brontë's tragic irony, at least until the marriage at the end of the story. Even then, when the couple manage to break through their mutual animosity, their love lacks mutuality. Hareton has begun to read, in the novel's last chapter, but Cathy's superior learning and upbringing foretell a marriage of unequals. We hear that "she beguiled Hareton . . . to dig and arrange her a little garden" (397), as if he needed manipulating; Hareton's reported mourning at the tyrant Heathcliff's grave betrays a pitiable innocence.

A similar ambivalence eats at the roots of Hardy's idyllic romance, *Under the Greenwood Tree*, destabilizing the balance between lovers. Fancy Day shares center stage with her slavish admirer Dick Dewy; for the novel's entire first half, and a good part of the second, however, she exists as an object, not a thinking and feeling subject. Her mystery, her seeming complexity, begins with her distant image in the window and ends in her keeping a secret, but like most of the character-traits in this novel, it resolves itself into a familiar type. "At the same time," says the intrusive narrator, "it may be observed that when a young woman returns a rude answer to a young man's civil remark her heart is in a state which argues rather hopefully for his case than otherwise" (146). When she says no, boys, she means yes. The riddle of Fancy, on one level, simply masks a male stereotype of fickle, flirtatious womanhood.

This novel abounds in type-characters, who with its type-scenes (caroling, courting, beekeeping) help make it Hardy's happiest novel—and, for some, his most favored, as David Wright asserts in his introduction to the Penguin edition: "To this day *Under the Greenwood Tree* has been the best-loved if not the most highly-regarded of Hardy's novels. Minor in scale, it has often been called 'a prose idyll.' One critic even described it, rather incongruously, as 'a modern and exquisite version of *Daphnis and Chloe*'" (18). Not everyone agrees, and those who come to the novel with a profound knowledge of the author often read it as deeply ironic, not idyllic at all. The unnamed critic who compares it with *Daphnis and Chloe* is Charles Whibley, a popularizer of the classics and a literary historian who links the two works in an essay on Hardy from the June 1913 issue of *Blackwood's Magazine* (Cox 418). If Whibley draws the comparison "incongruously," perhaps it is because the sex in Hardy is more muted than in Longus. Whibley's comment, however, deserves a second look.

In Hardy's crucial chapter "Honey-taking, and Afterwards" ("Autumn") a bee stings Fancy on the lip. Longus uses the same image in Daphnis's love-complaint: "her mouth is sweeter than honey, but her kiss hurts more than the sting of a bee" (1.18). The labial bee sting makes its way, as was noted earlier, into Tasso's *Aminta* but perhaps by way of another Greek romance, one included with Rowland Smith's Bohn's Classical Library edition. In Achilles Tatius's *Clitophon and Leucippe*, the young man Clitophon pretends to be stung on the lip so that Leucippe will say a charm and put her mouth close to his, allowing him to snatch his first kiss (2.7).

When Fancy is stung, Farmer Shiner—the countrified rival type who usually chases the heroine in idyllic romance—steps forward to examine her lip. But Fancy turns toward Dick, who disagrees when Shiner says, "It isn't swelling" (178)—and Shiner could be right: Fancy may be trying to lure Dick into a kiss. The hartshorn, the remedy, which the two suitors stumble over themselves to retrieve, sounds like Hardy's joking with the Elizabethan sense of "horn," the badge of jealous lovers. Dick then asks Geoffrey Day for his daughter's hand and is rejected on grounds of low breeding. In fact, both lovers' fathers have an exalted opinion of their children. "She's good enough," says Dick's father, "but I can't see what the nation a young feller like you—wi' a comfortable house and home, and father and mother to take care o' thee, and who sent 'ee to a school so good that 'twas hardly fair to the other children—should want to go hollering after a young woman for" (136).

The mention of Dick's and Fancy's exceptional schooling recalls that given Daphnis and Chloe (1.8). The two fathers' initial coldness toward the marriage, their sense of latent greatness in their favored children, also parallels the behavior of Longus's Dryas and Lamon.[1] As originally written, the novel looked even more like *Daphnis and Chloe*. For one thing Dick and Fancy at first stood as nearer equals in class. Hardy also at first conceived only one rival for Fancy's hand, Farmer Shiner, thus setting up the typical hero-heroine-boor love triangle of idyllic romance; Maybold's love interest came later (Millgate, *Novelist* 43, 53).

The subtitle *A Rural Painting of the Dutch School* implies the origin of the word *idyll* as a diminutive of the Greek *eidos*, meaning "figure" and, hence, "little picture." Many of the novel's chapters describe picturesque moments:

Christmas caroling, the dance at the tranter's, the wedding feast. Hardy begins an "Autumn" chapter so as to suggest that he consciously shaped the novel in this way: "The next scene is a tempestuous afternoon" (183). A related technique is the freezing of such moments as the first entrance of Fancy (62), or the dance at the tranter's "like a picture in a dream" (83). The seasonal structure of the novel (four parts, "Winter" to "Autumn," with the epilogue marriage scene) led Millgate to suspect an origin in "Elizabethan pastoral," or James Thomson or William Barnes. But Longus, too, has a four-part organization, ends with a rustic wedding, and similarly orchestrates the characters' moods with the seasons.

Echoes of Shakespeare's *As You Like It* exist in the title *Under the Greenwood Tree* and in the subtler details that are explored by Millgate (see *Novelist* 44–54). The memo of a reader for the potential publisher of Hardy's novel suggests an additional source in urging the author to follow the example of George Sand as an observer of rustic life—advice that Hardy followed (Millgate, *Biography* 138). Leslie Stephen, a few years later, also urged Hardy to read Sand, "whose country stories seem to me perfect & have a certain affinity to your's" (quoted in Millgate, *Biography* 180). That affinity is most evident in the two authors' regional settings—the Berry of Sand's novels and the Dorset of Hardy's.

Under the Greenwood Tree, like *Daphnis and Chloe*, ends with an account of wedding festivities, but so does Sand's *La Mare au diable*, with its prolonged discussion of nuptial ceremonies and folk customs. The rustic musicians of the Mellstock Quire recall the rural bagpipers who give the title to Sand's *Les Maîtres sonneurs* (P. Thomson 188). What Hardy has in greater abundance, though, is texture. Sand's rustic novels could find a quick way to the stage because the cast is limited and so much is carried through the dialogue. Henry James complained in reviewing *Far from the Madding Crowd* that dialogue in Hardy does nothing for his plots. And even a short Hardy novel like *Under the Greenwood Tree* displays a canvas crowded with people other than the principals: tremulous Thomas Leaf, obtuse Shiner, the domineering wives Day and Dewy, smug Parson Maybold, even passersby such as the trio in the spring-cart. Sand observes her region's dialect, details of topography and local customs, but in spite of *Promenades autour de mon village*, she never quite imagines a whole village. Points of comparison are the village dance at the Feast of St. Andoche in *La Petite Fadette* and Hardy's dance at the Tranter's. Sand focuses on Fadette's extravagant dancing and the reaction of a few youths, Landry especially, but the angle is too narrow by comparison to Hardy's picture of wheeling dancers, ladies' earrings turning somersaults, grandfathers in the chimney corner. Fadette and Landry dance, and one or the other always appears onstage; Fancy and Dick dance but sometimes drop out of sight, being members of the larger community gathered at the novel's end under the broad tree.

The narrator's distance and ironic comments convey something like Longus's wit, but Hardy has a mean streak. Dick "arrived opposite her door as his goddess emerged," displaying "an audacity unparalleled in the whole history of village schoolmistresses at this date—partly owing, no doubt, to papa's respectable accumulation of cash, which rendered her profession not altogether one of necessity—she had actually donned a hat with a feather" (193). When Irving Howe speaks of the "easy, fraternal irony" of this novel (46), he is certainly right about the "fraternal" part. The problem with such narratorial comment, what differentiates it from Longus's "sophist" irony, is the resentful edge. Here and in the great novels Hardy's irony is that of someone who wishes that the reason for the irony weren't there, whereas Longus accepts it as in the nature of things. Generally, Sand's passion for rural virtues seems to have rendered her incapable of irony on the subject. The combination of what Howe calls "a tentative or usable nostalgia" with "a complicating irony" (45) aptly describes the Wessex style. It is a kind of magic trick and reminds us how few authors of idyllic romance can hold the sentimental and the ironic in balance throughout a narrative.

George Eliot wrote of Sand, as no one could say of Hardy, "She is full of faith, of enthusiasm, of noble aspirations" (589); Sand's earnestness inclines her toward traditional storytelling ("tales of a hempdresser") and romance. Hardy has the novelist's inclination to probe the affirmations of romance—again Frye's novel-as-parody-romance. Andrew Lang said Hardy was more like Eliot than Sand in his rural fiction because he saw his shepherds "with the eyes of a philosopher" (quoted in Cox 36). This mediated, ruminated vision creates a cast of characters far more ambiguous than Sand's young lovers, who are fully known to each other (and the reader) at the story's end. Finishing *Under the Greenwood Tree*, the reader is left with Fancy Day's secret—and with no clear indication whether it should stay a secret.[2]

Like Sand and Longus, Hardy ends the story with a wedding, but he also manages to imply a future at this point. As the couple leave the party, Dick tells Fancy, with the insufferable self-confidence he shares with other males in the novel (Shiner, Maybold, the fathers):

> "why we are so happy is because there is such full confidence between us. Ever since that time you confessed to that little flirtation with Shiner by the river (which was really no flirtation at all), I have thought how artless and good you must be to tell me o' such a trifling thing, and to be so frightened about it as you were. It has won me to tell you my every deed and word since then. We'll have no secrets from each other, darling, will we ever?—no secret at all."
>
> "None from today," said Fancy. (225)

Dick resembles no idyllic hero so much as Milton's Adam, a self-important, slightly condescending alazon-type. Fancy seems to know better than Dick that the world is fallen, that some things are better left unspoken. As a couple they may never share the mutual confidence of Longus's pair, but there is at least a strong chance—again, not all Hardy's critics will agree—that Fancy's slight advantage in the wisdom acquired from experience (for example, the experience of having plighted her troth to two men at once) will see them through.

Although the laughter is often male in this novel, a notable countermasculine element is the all-male Mellstock Quire. In his preface Hardy defends such amateur musicians as "trying their best to make [the Sunday routine] an artistic outcome of the combined musical taste of the congregation" (33). But this particular quire, like other males in the novel, is proud and shall be made low. As Harold Toliver points out, the quire "may represent a disappearing idyllic order, but their clumsiness and crudity, as much as their opposition of new ideas, cause the disintegration of the old ways" ("The Dance" 63). In their lofty gallery, their cacophonous music has to contend for the first time with the "intrusive feminine voices" below, the girls of Fancy's school, who dare to sing in unison and drown out their efforts. "Brazen faced hussies," come the male replies; "Shall anything saucier be found than united 'ooman?" (72). Their resentment participates in a traditional rural misogyny, soon to receive a painful jolt when all those male instrumentalists must give way to a single young woman playing a harmonium. Fancy leads a counterattack on behalf of her sex. A year later, these male malcontents will dance at Fancy's wedding. Her victory over men, gained with a modest advantage of wit, will be total.

Parson Maybold, perhaps Fancy's one permanent victim, occupies the role not of the idyllic rival lover but of the itinerant outsider. As newly arrived vicar, he is not of the Mellstock community, yet the Church of England expects him to preside over Melstock's most sacred functions. His vicarage represents an authority without compassion, a familiar image of official religion in Hardy's writing. The scene where the quire receives its "death" sentence, as Reuben puts it (112), enacts a typically nasty bit of church politics. Maybold lays the blame on "one of the churchwardens," Shiner. But the parson's own importing of the organ into the parish shows that this was his intention all along. "I see right in you, and right in Shiner," Maybold glozes. "I see that violins are good, and that an organ is good" (114). He impresses Fancy as offering her a rung up the social ladder. "That's he coming!" she informs Dick, on seeing Maybold approach. "How I wish you were not here!" (133). Maybold's proposal of marriage ("Don't refuse.... It would be foolish of you—I mean cruel!" [199–200]) betrays an ego to match, at least, Fancy's. He wants to take her to the other end of England—a parish in Yorkshire—where they would no doubt inflict their self-centeredness on some other rustic community. Yet he, more than she, stands for community-destroying egotism in the novel. The rivalry between Maybold and Dick amounts to a conflict between the nation and the village, part of the losing battle of modern life, as Hardy sees it, even if Dick wins this round. Both in the love story and the quire story, Maybold represents faceless power beyond the community, his vicarage a comic romance underworld in this novel.

Seen quickly and from a distance, *Under the Greenwood Tree* may look like an idyllic romance, but read as such, it yields too many pitfalls, blind alleys, and dangerous leaps. Fancy Day ends with the greater share of understanding, maybe the only share; Dick ends with the greater love, or maybe infatuation. Yet unlike those of *Paul et Virginie* and most idyllic romances of the 1800s, Hardy's ending can arouse the idyllic feeling—what Maurice Blanchot calls "un véritable bonheur sans parole" [a real and wordless happiness].[3]

W. H. HUDSON'S PARADISE FOR TWO

Authors of idyllic fiction write about nature, but not since Bernardin de Saint-Pierre was any such author so professionally a naturalist as W. H.

Hudson. Between these two men are measured the immense changes in Western thought about nature since the Enlightenment. Bernardin, born in 1737, a technician of war with thoroughly European roots, discovered nature voyaging in the Indian Ocean. Hudson, born in 1841, grew up on the Argentine pampas, a self-taught student of nature who then came to Europe, where he became an irrepressible lover of the English countryside. Both naturalists received public acclaim, even financial rewards, for their scientific work, though Bernardin's Rousseauistic philosophy shaped his sense of nature, while Hudson, both admirer and critic of Darwin, became an advocate of species preservation, a harbinger of later twentieth-century ecological movements.

Both authors came to fiction late, and *Green Mansions* shares the intense moral and erotic feeling of *Paul et Virginie*. Yet Hudson's nervous protagonist and aura of fantasy distance his novel from the conventions of European pastoral fiction that Bernardin knew. Bridging their differences, however, are two points of kinship: both men were naturalists before becoming novelists, and both arrive at a deeply elegiac vision of the human condition in relation to nature. Hudson acquired this vision from indigenous experience and, in a later spell of melancholy, concluded that his life had ended when he left South America at age thirty-two (Tomalin 101). The remembered land of his youth, moreover, no longer existed; a favorite boyhood haunt, once "alive with herons and spoonbills, black-necked swans, glossy ibises in clouds, and great blue ibises with resounding voices, is now possessed by aliens, who destroy all wild bird-life and grow corn on the land for the markets of Europe" (*Far Away* 197).

Such sentiments belong more to the Wordsworthian than the naturist end of the nineteenth century, as does the peaceable nature in the reflective oral history called *A Shepherd's Life*. Published six years after *Green Mansions*, when the author was a year shy of seventy, this book springs from conversations with a Wiltshire shepherd, Caleb Bawcombe (in reality, one James Lowes), whose keen recollections of fifty years' shepherding go back to stories of people his father knew fifty years before that. Bawcombe leads Hudson to a woman who can remember days of rural unrest in 1830, when mobs broke up threshing machines. In her company we travel to a time before the fiction of Sand and Stowe; it seems hardly possible that as she tells her story, the Great War is only four years away. Nature's slowness and sameness on the downs form the base against which Hudson, like Sand or

Hardy, plays out the lives of his rural characters: "For the labourer on the land goes on from boyhood to the end of life in the same everlasting round, the changes from task to task, according to the seasons, being no greater than in the case of the animals that alter their actions and habits to suit the varying conditions of the year" (*Shepherd* 54).

A Shepherd's Life observes humanity following the cycles of nature. Like *Country of the Pointed Firs*, the book seems determined to avoid youth and passion. It lives in the country of the old, among the least nature-offending members of the human species. Yet seven years earlier, as he was completing *Green Mansions*, Hudson himself began an extended amorous relation with a younger writer, Linda Gardiner, a clerical secretary of the Royal Society for the Protection of Birds (Tomalin 190–91). If the restless, tragic passion of Hudson's most famous novel clashes with the quiet of *A Shepherd's Life*, it may be because Hudson's spiritual breadth eludes us after so many decades during which his popular novel has slipped off the horizon. It is just possible that, old as he was, Hudson felt the anguish of his young lovers as fully as he knew the tranquil rhythms that pertain to life in nature.

"I had a look at the first few chapters," Hudson wrote to his editor Garnett after mailing *Green Mansions* in December 1903, "and was again struck painfully by the cumbersomeness of the form . . . : the story doesn't move at all" (Garnett 58). Since Hudson usually destroyed his manuscripts once they were in type, it is impossible to say how Garnett may have revised this text, if at all. The leisurely reflections on trees, bell-birds, mounting storms, or the fabulous hata flower typify the unhurried, nature-imitating pace of the book. These details merge with the desperate passion of Abel and Rima, punctuated with some moments of humor (Rima's curses called down on the cowering Nuflo, Nuflo's Sancho Panza–like discourses on God and the human condition, Rima's eagerness to explore the whole world). Reader after reader has fallen in love with this book, as young Alfred Knopf did when he set out to make the romance a best seller.[4]

Knopf recounts the publishing history of *Green Mansions* in his foreword to John Payne's bibliography of Hudson. In its first edition in 1904, *Green Mansions* saw publication on both sides of the Atlantic, but except for a London "Reader's Library Edition" in 1910, it seems to have been destined for oblivion. Then Knopf, newly graduated from Columbia and visiting John Galsworthy in Devonshire, discovered Hudson's book. Knopf overcame Hudson's disinterest in an American reedition; Galsworthy wrote a preface, and in 1916 the book saw the first of twenty-two printings that were to follow in the next nine years. In California, Knopf remembers, one bookseller alone ordered a hundred copies. The edition not only gave Hudson fame in North America but launched Knopf's own firm on its illustrious history. For decades after 1916, dozens of editions in unknown numbers of printings came from other presses in England and the United States, several editions being illustrated (by, among others, Keith Henderson and Edward A. Wilson). During the 1920s it was translated into Czech, Dutch, Finnish, French, Russian, and Swedish; versions in Japanese, Serbian, Turkish, and other languages appeared in succeeding years. The post–1916 dates of those early translations indicate that it was Knopf who cultivated the book's immense readership.

The *Times* (London) reviewer of *Green Mansions* in its first edition seems to err twice in calling it an "idyll." First, the pessimism of this tale of lost paradise, the fates of the birdlike Rima and her lover Abel, suggest nothing of idyllic joy. Second, to impute almost any interest in literary convention conflicts with Hudson's frequent disclaimers that he was not a "literary man." David Miller quotes Hudson to his friend Ford Madox Ford: "I'm not one of your damned writers: I'm a naturalist from La Plata" (10; see also Garnett 177).

This mask of unsophistication vanishes with knowledge of the author. When *Green Mansions* was published, Hudson already belonged to a circle of literary friends that included George Gissing, Morley Roberts, R. B. Cunninghame Graham, and the leading editor and critic Edward Garnett. Thomas Hardy he admired and once, in 1903, almost visited; after walking up and down a while in front of the novelist's home, Hudson decided against introducing himself (Tomalin 186). Edward Thomas became, Hudson would say after the poet's death, the son he never had. John Galsworthy, Henry James, Ford Madox Ford, and Joseph Conrad came to know him, Conrad praising *Green Mansions* in a piece published in his *Last Essays*. As a naturalist in an age of science, Hudson may have sought to conceal any taint of literature in his reputation, but his letters to Garnett show him widely read in recent fiction, with a well-honed critical sense.

Hudson, who traveled in the Banda Oriental and Patagonia, never ventured into the distant jungles of Guyana (then called British Guiana) and

Venezuela—a fact lending strength to the notion that he created his romance, as any romancer does, less from experience than from other literature. Discussing this novel recently, a Panamanian student was amused by the image of Abel lying on the floor of a tropical forest to meditate: in no time, she said, he would have been covered with insects. For *Green Mansions* scholars have found literary predecessors in Lady Morgan, Arthur O'Shaughnessy, and other minor authors.[5] Although he had some knowledge of Theocritus and Virgil, Hudson shows none of Longus.

Between Hudson and the Greek writer, however, lay the accessible example of *The Tempest*, which no one seems to have mentioned as a likely source for *Green Mansions*. Both plots begin with a political upheaval, one in Milan, the other in Caracas. In both a young man, isolated in a wilderness far from home, discovers a mysterious, seemingly prelapsarian virgin living with a fatherly protector in apparently supernatural circumstances. When Abel first hears Rima's voice, there are several hints of Shakespeare's play, including a repetition of the title word: "I began to hear a confused noise as of a coming tempest of wind," and "After that tempest of motion and confused noise the silence of the forest seemed very profound" (2.38). Hearing a mysterious voice—one "purified and brightened to something almost angelic" (39)—Abel resembles Ferdinand listening to the invisible Ariel's song after the shipwreck. In effect Miranda and Ariel fuse in Rima: she has Ariel's birdlike qualities, his Pan-like power over nature; she also shares Miranda's innocence and beauty. In chapter 3 Abel encounters the dangerous Pan-Ariel side of Rima when he enters the enchanted place. "Imaginary terrors began to assail me," he recalls. "It was distressing to have such fancies in this wild, solitary spot—hateful to feel their power over me when I knew that they were nothing but fancies and creations of the savage mind" (3.50–51). Rima is at her most dangerous when the coral snake at her foot strikes Abel, sending him into panic like that of Ariel's victims in Prospero's storm. When Abel awakes under Nuflo's and Rima's roof, the tempest continues outside.

Vital similarities also exist between Caliban and the "Guyana savages," especially Kua-kó. In both the play and the novel, the wild men harbor a special hatred for the virgin beauty, desiring to rape or kill her; in both, they suffer for their attacks. When Abel regains consciousness, Nuflo asks why he is "residing with these children of the devil" (7.96); Caliban's parents are the witch Sycorax and perhaps a devil. Like pre-Rousseauist Europeans, Abel and Rima resemble Prospero and Miranda (and, for that matter, Shakespeare's countrymen who colonized Virginia) in their contempt and mistrust for "savage" men. Hudson's Indians have Caliban's superstition and ignorance, his peculiar blend of vengefulness with childlike naivety. The magic that Abel brings them—the silver tinderbox used for a bribe, the revolver that Kua-kó plots to steal—belongs to the realm of fire that will bring Rima's death. Their destruction of Rima and their own apocalypse realize Caliban's would-be revolt on a large scale.

Like Shakespeare, Hudson builds on the motifs of the lost one found and of two lovers' discovering themselves in nature. Although Ferdinand and Miranda are not exactly the central characters of their play, they, like Abel and Rima, share equal roles in the plot. Two sons have lost a father; two daughters a mother. In psychological terms both Abel and Ferdinand enter nature seeking the feminine part of themselves. In the new birth of adolescence, Rima and Miranda desire to know their origins. Miranda's exclamation over the "brave new world" approximates Rima's excited response to Abel's geography lesson when she learns that vast nations and oceans lie beyond her enclave: "Come, let us go together—we two and grandfather, and see all the world; all the mountains and forests, and know all the people" (11.155).

In both Shakespeare and Hudson, finally, the heroine's dead mother represents both a lost, prelapsarian life and a break in the cycle of life that only the daughter's entry into that cycle can repair. Hudson alludes to Shakespeare seldom, but chapter 5 of his *A Hind in Richmond Park* develops a knowing comparison between Shakespeare the self-concealing poet and Chaucer the self-revealing one. It is the kind of insight that only someone with an intelligent grasp of both poets could make, and it leaves little doubt that Hudson would have known a major play like *The Tempest*. One of the sources for Rima suggested as early as 1926 (by Henry Salt in the *Fortnightly Review*) is the heroine of the Canadian novel *The Heart of the Ancient Wood*, by the then-popular Charles G. D. Roberts—a girl named Miranda. Why Salt, or someone since, did not think of the more famous Miranda is anyone's guess. My own is that Hudson's pose as the unbookish man of nature, unlikely to engage in literary imitation, succeeded completely.

Other presences, especially North American, haunt *Green Mansions*, though not so fully as *The Tempest*. In *Idle Days* Hudson reveals that he has been reading a biography of Hawthorne, whose way of mingling reality and romance must have contributed to Hudson's narrative. In the same text he digresses at length on Melville's thoughts about whiteness in *Moby Dick*—this well before the 1920 "rediscovery." Abel's questing spirit carries a Melvillean quality; his primitivist romance and ambivalence about life among the indigenous people recall the sailor's story in *Typee*. On another front, the atmosphere of forest mystery often resembles brooding scenes from Hawthorne's fiction—"Young Goodman Brown" and "Roger Malvin's Burial" especially come to mind. Abel's role as the initiate into bitter experience of human nature follows an established Hawthorne scenario.

Green Mansions manifests the caution toward erotic passion shown in Shakespeare, Stowe, and Cather. Hudson stressed man's need to contain "sexual rage" in a letter on utopian novels (Garnett 174–75), and his hero's tainted desire for Rima recalls a similar passion in his earlier utopian romance, *A Crystal Age*. *The Tempest*, of course, also contains a theme of sexual restraint: Prospero enslaves Caliban because he tries to rape Miranda; he admonishes Ferdinand not to violate Miranda's virginity before their marriage. When Abel's words link Rima with the Edenic snake (he describes his "astonishment and admiration at the brilliant being as she advanced with swift, easy, undulating motion towards me" [6.79]), the innocent girl reminds us of Rappacini's daughter. Both young women release a moral poison. And in Abel this poison continues to work after the snake's venom has faded. At one point, searching for Rima, Abel finds himself engulfed in a storm, symbolizing the desire that drives him: "Groping blindly along I became entangled in a dense undergrowth, and after struggling and stumbling along for some distance in vain endeavours to get through it, I came to a stand at last in sheer despair. All sense of direction was now lost: I was entombed in thick blackness—blackness of night and cloud and rain and of dripping foliage and network of branches bound with bushropes and creepers in a wild tangle" (10.146–47). Blindness, confusion, entanglement suggest the trope of the heart's forest, traceable back through Hawthorne to Spenser and medieval romance. The storm recalls Virginie's episode of passion while bathing as the hurricane mounts. In the darkness Rima finds him, but slips away when he tries to embrace her. Here and elsewhere in the novel, Rima perceives something unclean in Abel's love, despite her attraction to him. Only later, when she undergoes a transformation in the cave at Riolama, does she seem to reciprocate his passion.

The cave, the womb from which Rima is reborn, shares female symbolism with Longus's cave of the nymphs. In the same place where Nuflo tended her mother, Rima lies in a deathlike trance after hearing for the first time her mother's story. Her trance seems to follow a literary convention that Hudson elsewhere deplores as "The fashion set by Fouqué, . . . the childish 'Now-I-have-got-a-soul' transformation scene."[6] Fouqué's *Undine* ends with the sea nymph's becoming human; Rima in the cave, recognizing love, begins to respond through a dim recollection of her mother's own reported sorrow on losing her beloved. The new knowledge, enlivened with the memory of her mother's story—"she and another were like one, always, apart from the others"—enables her to see herself and Abel as lovers in the world: "But we are everywhere alone together, apart—we two" (17.248). The paradoxical language—"everywhere alone together, apart" acknowledges the Genesis mystery of "one flesh." The phrasing perplexes in linking "together" with "apart": like man and woman in Genesis, they will go apart from parents and cling together as one. Yet they learn the meaning of "together" only to feel the total force of "apart." While Daphnis and Chloe enjoy several moments of love and reunion in their sacred cave, these lovers experience only one.

A new Rima issues from the cave to prepare for marriage. Why she returns alone and ahead of the men has always puzzled readers, but it seems that Abel must repeat his first search for Rima in order to find her not as a forest sprite but as a woman. When you arrive, she tells Abel, "you shall find me, but not at once." She will be all in white, like her mother, saying, "Am I different—not like Rima?" (17.251). This image of Rima in white meets its counter-image when Abel finds the "finest white ashes" and kisses "each white fragment" in her funeral pyre (21.302–03).

As Rima's story, the novel breaks evenly into phases of stasis, when Rima is object, and of movement, when Rima is subject, undergoing her education, acquiring an identity. In the process she moves between bipolar images of woman. A paradise-woman, her mother, entered Nuflo's life as a sainted being; the old man remembers his first sight of her with an "aureole" around her head (15.213). Nuflo's story also associates Rima's mother with the apocalyptic Virgin, the woman in the wilderness about to give birth, and perhaps the virginal Astraea, the last inhabitant of the golden age, too good for a fallen world. With her unhuman, birdlike language, she cannot long endure life in the village where she goes to rear her child. The contrary female image, the crone, is the all-too-mortal Cla-cla, the chief's mother, ancient but constantly busy, putting everyone to sleep each night with her interminable stories. With all her limitations she is the one person in the community for whom Abel feels affection. His discovery of her bloody corpse, after his revenge violence, brings home the full horror of his crime, tilting him toward his prolonged insanity. Like the old people of *A Shepherd's Life*, Cla-cla represents humanity smiling through old age and suffering in ways that proud Abel could not understand, at least not until his final purgation.

Abel's discovery of Rima is also Rima's discovery, for new knowledge enters her paradise—knowledge of the outside and inside. Their encounter marks Rima's second birth, the time in other idyllic romances when the character leaves childhood and innocence behind. Hudson felt keenly this departure from childhood in his own life, an experience that he describes in his autobiography. After a long, serious illness from which he was just recovering at the time of his birthday, he had a kind of epiphany. "Fifteen years old!" he writes:

> This was indeed the most memorable day of my life, for on that evening I began to think about myself, and my thoughts were strange and unhappy thoughts to me—what I was, what I was in the world for, what I wanted, what destiny was going to make of me! Or was it for me to do just what I wished, to shape my own destiny, as my elder brothers had done? It was as though I had only just become conscious; I doubt that I had ever been fully conscious before. I had lived till now in a paradise of vivid sense impressions in which all thoughts came to me saturated with emotion, and in that mental state reflection is well-nigh impossible. (*Far Away* 305–06)

In the geography lesson Rima, too, wants to know her place in the world. Her complete innocence reflects the purity of Eden, and her mental state resembles that childhood condition Hudson describes—a period of utter spontaneity, of Wordsworth's "glad animal movements," but heightened by her uncanny knowledge of nature's (the birds') language. Her passing out in the cave may be a recollection of Hudson's own childhood illness, and she awakes, as he did, from being near death to achieving a sense of her own self.

Abel, by contrast, seems a case of failed Wordsworthian development. His pride and his tainted passion for Rima provide a key to his character and to the novel as a whole. Escaping from the city, he seeks a conventional heroic destiny. He will earn fame as an explorer or observer of Indian life—but his manuscript gets soaked with rain. Abandoning that ambition, yet with no sense of the incongruity of his next choice, he decides he will make his name by discovering the fabled lost gold that the Spanish sought. In another inadvertently revealing moment, he impresses the tribal chief, Runi, by shooting his pistol in the general direction of the village of Runi's enemy. Here Abel is like the gang of Englishmen from *The Purple Land*, who boast of bringing civilization to the country while they enjoy shooting off their revolvers to intimidate villagers during their weekly trips to buy liquor. Abel treats his Calibans with all the imperiousness that Prospero, or for that matter Stephano, bestows on Shakespeare's moon-calf.

Because Runi and his tribe show all the defects of "lower man" in popular anthropology circa 1900—ignorance and superstition, dishonesty, cruelty in seeking revenge—some see Hudson as engaged in racist caricature (D. Miller 157). Yet the text surely encourages reading Abel's version of things as counter to Hudson's. A proud man falls when he undertakes a crueler-than-"savage" revenge. In the months that follow his annihilation of Runi's village, who is more superstitious than Abel, with his crazed (Pan-induced?) fantasies after Rima's death? At the beginning he marks the Indians' "cunning or low kind of intelligence" (1.18). At the end he prides himself on his own "cunning" (18.262), exulting in their mistaken belief "that I was incapable of the cunning and duplicity they practiced." Abel unwittingly admits to his own "savagery" in the scene when he kills Kua-kó: "Could any white man," he imagines his enemy boasting, "meet the resolute savage, face to face and foot to foot, and equal him with the old primitive weapons?" Abel does "equal" the savage—in ways he does not yet recognize: "Quickly stooping, I once more drove my weapon to the hilt in his prostrate form, and . . . I experienced a feeling of savage joy" (19.279–80). Abel is now undifferentiated from his enemy: two become one in hate, not love.

David Miller has said of the last part of the novel, "Abel's anguished soul is caught up in a web of haunted and despairing ideas centring on the question of identity—the theme that was so crucial in his relationship to Rima" (160–61). Does Abel find or lose himself? The white ashes are what remains spiritually after Rima's death, the bloody revenge, and the betrayal of Runi's village. In a nightmare reprise subtly played out during the novel's last three chapters, Abel slips into a demonic reverse-quest, almost in symmetry with his earlier entry into paradise. Taking on the deviousness and cunning he earlier ascribes to the Indians, Abel becomes Cain, the killer of Kua-kó. Self-condemnation descends on him most forcefully when he sees the slaughtered body of grandmotherly Cla-cla. Earlier he ridicules Nuflo's secret feasts of animal flesh; now he is reduced to eating loathsome grubs. If previously he has scorned Nuflo's shack, he now makes for himself a still smaller enclosure that he shares with spiders and beetles. Having scoffed at Nuflo's superstitions, he now fears the ghosts of Nuflo, Rima, and the chimerical giant snake, an imagined magnification of the serpent that brought him to Rima.

The reflecting pool where Rima saw her beauty becomes the mirror where Abel finally beholds the wreckage of his face. Rima, the "Rima of the mind," whispers speech that recalls Hudson's New England forefathers, with their old Anglo-American Puritan sense of human isolation: "Austerities? Good works? Prayers? They are not seen; they are not heard, they are less than nothing, and there is no intercession. . . . Your life was your own; you are not saved nor judged; acquit yourself—undo that which you have done, which Heaven cannot undo—and Heaven will say no word nor will I" (21.309–10). This anticipates, if it does not fully explain, Hudson's turn toward theodicy at the end, when Abel proclaims that "outside of the soul there is no forgiveness in heaven or earth for sin" (22.323).

In the novel this theme makes sense if Abel is "a new Ahasuerus," or a reformed Cain seeking forgiveness for murder. Rima—at first unfallen nature, then prospective soul mate—now becomes Abel's mediator or intercessor. Abel has earlier scoffed at Nuflo for harboring similar superstitions about Rima; now Abel wants her death to expiate or ennoble his own brutality, thereby evading responsibility for his crimes. Rima's answer—*Abel's* answer—leaves him in Pascalian silence and solitude. Just as Hudson himself, by his own confession, never found love in his marriage (Tomalin 115–16), and just as he was known to friends as a solitary, even secretive person, so Abel emerges as a man with neither love nor country, with no attachments, approximating what a future generation will call the existential hero.

Because the soul is so sealed off from God or spirits beyond itself, the mysterious urn in the prologue may be interpreted as the soul's image. The prologue's brief ecphrasis of the urn on its ebony stand, in Abel's secret room, surely calls attention to itself. On its face the urn bears in epitome the story of *Green Mansions*, just as the picture in *Daphnis and Chloe* embodies that story: "a cinerary urn, its surface ornamented with flower and leaf and thorn, and winding through it all the figure of a serpent; an inscription, too, of seven short words which no one could understand or rightly interpret." Longus's narrator can find an interpreter for the painting, while no one in Georgetown, where Abel has died, can explain this design and motto. The words, as later revealed, are "Sin vos y sin dios, y mi" [Without you and without God, and me]. The motto means, Abel says, "I, no longer I, in a universe where *she* was not, and God was not" (21.304). The prominence of the word *without* links this gnomic line with the theme of apartness in the novel. Let flower, leaf, and thorn stand for the ideal, indeterminate, and demonic zones of nature imagery. They are the range of "good and evil" in Abel's experience of nature, both coming from God. Like the figures on the urn, these wind through the narrative without resolution, enclosing the mere ashes of Rima, the dead, voiceless past buried in Abel's memory.

The serpent—symbol of death and wisdom, healing and renewal—begins and ends Abel's sojourn in Rima's forest. Abel makes a comb of thorns to bring civility to his wild visage: renewal comes out of pain. But the thorn is also the serpent's tooth, the Indian's poison dart. Are "you" and "me" in the motto lover and beloved or viewer and serpent? Abel says on the book's last page that "outside of the soul there is no forgiveness in heaven or earth for sin." Perhaps the motto asks to be read in this context—that the soul must forgive itself unaided by God, the serpent, or the other (friend, beloved). This Hawthorne-like sentiment accords with the elegiac strain so often heard when Hudson laments civilization's abuse of nature.

STACPOOLE'S ISLAND COUPLES

Henry De Vere Stacpoole (1863–1951) met with success as a popular novelist when he discovered the idyllic romance, or to be faithful to his account of things, when the idea came to him: "Early in 1907, lying awake and pondering, not for the first time in my life, on the extraordinary world we live in, the idea came to me of what it must have been like to the cavemen who had no language and for whom a sunset had no name tacked on to it, a storm no name, Life no name, death no name and birth no name, and the idea came to me of two children, knowing nothing about any of these things, finding themselves alone on a desert island facing these nameless wonders" (*Men and Mice* 93).⁷ The thought is epidemic in the fascination of the early 1900s with the state of nature—whether imagined by the recent evolutionary biology and anthropology or by popular fiction like Jack London's *Before Adam* (1906). (London's novel was set in the Pleistocene era and influenced by another caveman romance, Stanley Waterloo's *The Story of Ab* [1897]). Yet Stacpoole thinks beyond the limits of popular Darwinism. We now live in an "extraordinary" world, demarcated by the "names," the language that has evolved; perhaps ours is a better world, but what was it like to experience nature, to live consciously without the mediation of language? Stacpoole's capitalizing the word "Life" restates the question: what would it be like to live Life itself?

Answering such a question in fiction requires moving away from the distractions of the mortal struggle with the jungle or an ice age. It invites an idyllic form, a tranquil setting such as the Pacific islands Stacpoole had seen while traveling as a ship's doctor just out of medical school. His night thoughts led to his enormously popular *The Blue Lagoon* (1908), which went through twenty-four printings in thirteen years, held the stage of the Prince of Wales Theatre for nine months in 1920 and became a silent film in 1923, hailed by *Variety* as "one of the best pictures ever made by a British company." Imitations were many, as Stacpoole observed in 1922: "The old *Blue Lagoon* has produced more bastards than any book I know of." He suspected a Transatlantic Films production, *Mother Instinct* (1916), of infringing on his copyright, while Alfred Gordon Bennett's *The Valley of Paradise* (1922) barely escaped a lawsuit. Stacpoole himself wrote several sequels, ultimately included with their prototype in *The Blue Lagoon Omnibus*, whereupon there were plans for another film in 1938 starring Margaret Lockwood and Michael Redgrave, which was perhaps scratched because of the war. In 1949 Jean Simmons and Donald Houston, more fully clad than Brooke Shields and Christopher Atkins in the 1980 film, acted in a Technicolor version.⁸

Throughout his life Stacpoole wrote more than fifty books, including poetry, comedy, mystery, and adventure, but none of his books received the acclaim of this Pacific romance. The 1980 movie of *The Blue Lagoon* makes a good starting point for discussing the book, if only because it is a late 1900s reading of an earlier 1900s idyllicism, accommodating an Edwardian romance to a postsexual-revolution audience. In most details the film follows the novel. Two children, cousins, Richard Lestrange and Em (not Dick and Em, as in the book; it's Michael and Em in the 1949 film—we Richards notice these things) are en route to San Francisco when a fire breaks out aboard ship. Separated from the elder Lestrange (Emmeline's parents are dead), the children and a sailor named Paddy Button—played by Leo McKern—drift in a lifeboat until they reach an uninhabited island that is flourishing with marine life, vegetation, fresh water, and a derelict cask of rum. In the movie's first half hour the foundlings enjoy life under the foster parent's easy sway until Paddy one day swims off with his rum and dies. When the children turn over his body, a small crab crawls from his mouth—an image Stacpoole found powerful but inexplicable (*Mice and Men* 93). The crab returns in Em's nightmares as part of the theme of death in nature that the film, unlike the book, never lets us forget. We are menaced with occasional interspersed shots of a spider, a skull, an octopus feeding, a centipede—all mingled with some spectacular photography of lagoon life.

Whether on page or screen, the story does not quite fit with Stacpoole's night thoughts of 1907. These children come to the island civilized; they have and use language. Only later, with the "second birth" of adolescence, do they begin to forget words, to go long periods without speaking. The film's facile naturalism does originate with the author: a physician and an admirer of Zola, in 1908 Stacpoole could hardly have handled the presentation of nature in any other way. Befitting the anthropology of the day, the children discover on the other side of their island a terrible artifact of "natural man," a crude idol encrusted with old blood. What Hollywood adds in 1980 is Freud: the idol is darkly phallic; Em's nightmares are interwoven with the observed onset of her menses on the screen; while still on the ship the children are caught looking at Paddy's photos of nude women. Paddy later scolds the innocents for "runnin' 'round naked all the time." Together, these details work against idyllic romance fulfillment.

Some years pass after the sailor's death, and with Shields and Atkins assuming the roles, children's play becomes sexually meaningful. Both the novel and, less subtly, the movie fulfill the potential for voyeurism latent in the tradition of *Daphnis and Chloe*. Shields and Atkins swim naked, eat significant fruit, then fall to kissing and intercourse while the camera intersperses shots of flora and fauna. Someone tells me that this movie is sometimes cited as a model of bad filmmaking. California sexology and naturalism don't help, but there are some small strengths: McKern's acting, the cinematography of nature, and sometimes even Shields, who oscillates convincingly between the attitudes of childhood and maturity.

The depiction of nature's menace on film requires an approach that is different from what is necessary for the printed page. And, except for a certain tendentiousness, the screen version of *The Blue Lagoon* is better than the book on this score. Stacpoole *talks* about nature, and he trots out several overworked motifs of its dark side. Em contemplates nature's beauty in the lagoon a moment before Dick is nearly killed by a giant octopus, for example. Fights with mollusks had been popular at least since one of Stacpoole's favorite authors, Victor Hugo, published *Toilers of the Sea*, not to mention Jules Verne's sensational episode in *Twenty Thousand Leagues under the Sea*. Stacpoole would himself keep the tentacles flying in *The Garden of God*. (The 1923 *Blue Lagoon* film seems to have done the octopus fight spectacularly.) Again, near the end of the novel, as the couple are leaving the lagoon, Dick barely survives battle with a giant ray. To suggest nature's demonic side, the 1980 movie provides subtly menacing images rather than unlikely monsters. And in view of Stacpoole's medical knowledge, his account of Em's giving birth in her sleep is one of the weak moments in the book. One wonders about the audience response in the Macowan-Mann play when Em enters holding her baby, saying, "I felt so bad. Then I went off to sit in the woods. And I remember nothing more. And when I woke up . . . it was there!" (118; compare the novel at 246). In the 1980 film, however, childbirth is an opportunity for excitement. Richard returns to their shack one day, horrified to find Em in the agonies of labor; the camera draws back for a distant shot accented by a scream.

Stacpoole lets nurturing nature transcend the nightmare nature of the marine monsters. After years of longing for rescue, the couple one day have the chance to attract a ship's notice, and spontaneously they decide not to. It is the moment of self-discovery for the foundlings, in a process begun with the child's birth. With the baby, nature "put everything to rights in her own time and way" (246). Not even the seasonal cycle of *Daphnis and Chloe* is in evidence in this Pacific Lesbos: so delicately are the seasons attenuated, so repetitious the pattern of life in the lagoon, that time vanishes through indefinition. The sheer bulk of natural description in the novel pushes aside the narrative, further undercutting the reader's sense of time. Conventions of romance such as the mysterious idol and the threat of the savages (complete with drums and secretly observed human sacrifice) lend a necessary minimum of fear and excitement to the story, but even less than in Longus. Instead, the story fixes attention on the growth of a couple, not of two individuals, to maturity. Read as an idyllic romance, *The Blue Lagoon* almost has to end at this point. If marriage, as in Longus, is unavailable as a conclusion, then death—though an ambiguous and almost imperceptible death—will have to do. Admittedly the 1920 playwrights chose to have the elder Lestrange find the couple alive and happy at the end, but they had also conventionalized the hero by having Dick rescue Em from rape by a castaway they invent named Guy Neborg.

Stacpoole's sequel, *The Garden of God*, well received in 1923, holds up better than its predecessor, I think. (Vulgarized, it too appeared on the screen following the 1980 film as *Return to the Blue Lagoon*.) The intellectual texture of this book may indicate that the established author had a freedom in 1923 that his publisher would not give him in 1908. *The Garden* has far more to say about natural life without language than *The Blue Lagoon*, faltering only at the end when the narrative slips into a tiresome formula.

The story picks up where *The Blue Lagoon* ends. For years Dick's father, Lestrange, has been hiring ships to comb the region in search of the children, whom he at last finds dead in their small boat, suicides by poisoned berries eaten in despair. Their child survives, however, and Lestrange persuades the captain of his ship, the *Rarotonga*, to leave him, the three-year-old boy, and the boatswain's mate, Jim Kearney, behind in hopes that Dick and Em will somehow return to life with them. The captain decides to leave Lestrange to work out his madness in the competent Kearney's charge, planning to return in a year. A few days later, however, unknown to the two men, his ship goes down in a storm. Kearney first broaches the subject of language, saying of the little boy, "He's the silentest kid I've ever struck—and I'm thinking those that brought him up mustn't have had much use for their tongues" (60). Yet a little later he is surprised to see Dick, as the men name him, carefully put a newly caught fish in the shade of the boat's thwart to keep the sun from spoiling it: "It was like a flash of light revealing the child's upbringing and the fact that the people of the wild begin their education in the school of necessity, which is not a school of languages" (72). So Dick is nearer the caveman's wordlessness than his parents ever were.

Even less languaged is Katafa, a young woman who has reemerged after a ten-year absence. A Spanish ship captain's daughter, she was an infant when her father and crew were killed in an affray with islanders on Karolin, some miles beyond sight of the lagoon. Her life was spared on the condition, imposed by a tribal medicine woman, that she be marked with the taboo of "Taminan": she cannot ever touch another person or be touched. Katafa ("the frigate bird") grows to adolescence cooperating unconsciously with the taboo, avoiding all contact—"a ghost in everything but speech" (109). The lapse of ten years calls to mind similar intervals (in Longus, Bernardin, Sand, Stowe) that allow the second birth of adolescence and identity to occur.

On the one hand, then, a solitary boy has almost lost interest in using language; on the other, a girl must live in an alien community experiencing human life virtually through language alone. By the time the two meet, Lestrange is long dead, and Kearney, uneasy about the female intruder, forms an irrational hatred for her. When Dick, still without romantic interest, gradually abandons his language for hers, the old man broods, "She's turning him into a —— kanaka" (145). Plotting against these two males, Katafa one night lights a signal fire on the reef beyond the lagoon. Kearney follows her with murderous intent, only to be killed by a monstrous "decapod" (a giant squid) aroused by her fire's light, "the most terrible of all seathings . . . barrel shaped, great as an oak tree, with two beaks, a tongue armed with teeth, eyes a foot broad and ten tenacles [sic], two of thirty or forty feet in length" (157–58). The toothed tongue and the dark sea-thing roused by a female power convey a Freudian symbolism absent from *The Blue Lagoon*.

The aggressive egotism of Katafa—she is almost a case study in her psychosis—contrasts with the tranquillity that Dick inherits from the lovers in *The Blue Lagoon*. Without Kearney, Dick slips further into the snare that the girl is only half-consciously weaving. The "labour of talking" becomes an impossible burden. He "could think up things from the past easily enough if they were recent, but to arrange them in the order of thought, dressed and connected by words, was becoming a hateful labour" (177–78). Yet when Kearney is out of the way, Dick manages to weaken Katafa's hate with an act of language rising from his unconscious. One night, just as she is about to set fire to Dick's hut, she hears him, in his sleep, cry out for help: "She could not understand in the least why she had held her hand, or why the appeal for help had so shattered her purpose" (181).

She continues to loathe Dick, the impulse to kill him coming "at times in great waves up from the darkest recesses of her mind, like the rollers from the storm that had destroyed the *Rarotonga*" (182). In the familiar pastoral trope, inner joins to outer nature. Katafa with her Taminan, "a creature beyond human sympathy," resembles the decapod, "in the sea, watchful, ever waiting to strike, ever fearful of being itself destroyed" (178). Physically, Dick seems to grow toward an unfallen state as he loses his words or exchanges his thin European vocabulary for a purely functional, emotively simple language of the present moment. The "namelessness" Stacpoole set out to describe in *The Blue Lagoon* is far more purposefully realized in this later novel about a couple who, having both lost their names, acquire an identity independent of any human name-givers.

This process also joins more convincingly with a story of love, both the parental love of the grieving father Lestrange and the erotic love of the young couple. In the novel as a whole, love between parent and child gradually yields to male-female love. Lestrange the stranger, the foreigner, enters this Eden driven by a quest for his lost children even though he has seen their lifeless bodies with his own eyes. The obsession with their return from death estranges him from his little grandson so that the buoyantly practical Kearney "takes Dick away" from him, just as Katafa will later take Dick away from Kearney.

Katafa's love, begun in hatred, emerges in an unforeseen moment when a bird, "stirred, maybe, by some old memory" of the birds that used to come to Emmeline, lights on Katafa's thumb and she strokes it: "It was the first warm-blooded living thing that . . . had come to waken the warmth of humanity in her heart" (184). Still, the girl cannot break through the Taminan: "The very intensity of her longing and her passion cast her more completely into the grasp of the subconscious power that had her in its charge" (197). A physician's and a traveler's experience (as well as that as a justice of the peace for Essex) allows Stacpoole some insight into the seemingly magical "power" that older people can have on young minds: "In the old romances we read of women spell-bound by witches and black magic. Le Juan [the Karolin medicine woman] had used no black magic. Working with no material but Katafa's self, she had moulded into it a law that had become part of self" (199).

In an earlier scene Dick grapples with and kills a Karolin hunter who has ventured onto the island. Now a war party, the entire fighting-age male population of Karolin, has beached its long boats seeking revenge. Katafa and Dick find their moment of attraction just as these men invade the island. In an unfortunate lapse into trite naturalism—part of the general falling-off of the last part of the novel—death hunt and love hunt take place simultaneously, for the attack comes just when Dick is first seized by desire for Katafa, who saves him from one of the spearmen and escapes with him to a hiding place. What happens next recalls nothing so much as the havoc raised by Pan in *Daphnis and Chloe* against the invading army from Methymna. A storm suddenly hits the island, the Haya è Matadi, "the great wind without rain that once in a decade swept Karolin and the sea for a hundred miles beyond, coming only at night, lasting only an hour, and more dreaded than a hurricane because more mysterious" (219–20). In the dark, wild confusion most of the warriors, who have divided in two groups, attack and kill each other, while others flee in Pan-like panic to be destroyed by the storm in their canoes or to be eaten by the sharks that the high winds have driven into the lagoon.

In the morning, when Katafa awakens in their hiding place, "her arms clasped themselves round the reality" (227)—whereupon the reader is confronted by a white space and a line of dots across the page. As in *The Blue Lagoon*, the couple need no instruction. A suggested equation of woman and nature, somewhat surprising in view of the more balanced portrayal of the couple in *Blue Lagoon*, intensifies when Katafa's love for Dick is called "a sexless love that is akin to mother-love—the one thing deathless if there is no death" (258). George Sand, too, explored the continuities between maternal and erotic love. Unfortunately, just when these themes might start to unfold, the author disengages, steering us toward an Edgar Rice Burroughs ending, as the loving white European couple, driven from their island by a shipload of mutinous New Hebrideans (potential Calibans) flee to Karolin so that Dick, slayer of the island's menfolk, can become the new king. On the last page, "the great knowledge came to him, as it came to the earliest men who fronted the wolf, that strength is possession and that without possession love is a mockery" (288). H. G. Wells had once urged Stacpoole to "think *harder*" (*Men and Mice* 106), and it is hard to think what that last bit of capitalist social Darwinism has to do with the rest of the book.

When Stacpoole's publisher T. F. Unwin received the manuscript of *The Blue Lagoon*, Unwin huffed that he'd rather have a book about London. Stacpoole remarks, "well, it was about London, in a way" (*Men and Mice* 94). The comment suggests that behind the novel lie motives akin to those of ancient pastoralists in distancing themselves from the city's complexities. *Daphnis and Chloe* probably left an impression on these books. Evidence of its imitation in *The Blue Lagoon* includes the dual foundlings, the time lapse, and the panic of the storms. At Malvern School in Worcester, Stacpoole learned some Greek.[9] After the war, while living in the Swiss Cottage district of London, he had as a neighbor Dr. Arthur S. Way, retired schoolmaster, translator general (Euripides, Theocritus, Virgil, and others) who, Stacpoole says, "infected me with the desire to translate Sappho" (*Men and Mice* 104). Stacpoole adds: "if you want to translate or render Sappho you have only twelve hundred Greek words to tackle and you may do a decent job of it if you have time and patience and a Greek lexicon and an old Dr. Way behind you—and the inspiration got from love of the subject and want of admiration for the way the subject has been translated by others, also a modesty that prevents you from dress improving" (105).

A comment Stacpoole makes in the second edition of his *Sappho: A New Rendering* (published in 1920, the year that Arthur Way published his own Sappho translation), puts him on a path that probably intersected with Longus.[10] Stacpoole hails the poet as "the voice of a world that has been, of a freshness and beauty that will never be again" (7). Further, having visited Greece, Stacpoole sets one of his novels, *The Street of the Flute Player* (1912), in ancient Athens. His poems, too, often reflect sentimental classicizing in the manner of Oscar Wilde, George Moore, or Algernon Swinburne. Stacpoole's poem "The Nightingale (in the Woods of Sicily)" ends by invoking Theocritus and Amaryllis. "The Pipes of Pan" joins the Victorian chorus on the death of Pan that dates back to Elizabeth Barrett Browning. Stacpoole again invokes Sappho and Theocritus in "The Almond Tree," and a reviewer of his *Poems and Ballads* singled out in the *Athenaeum* (22 October 1910) the Theocritean "Sea Pastoral" for special praise.

Stacpoole's love of nature originated as early as his mother's experiences growing up in the Canadian woods (*Men and Mice* 15), but it is tempered by a naturalist's understanding. The *Times Literary Supplement* reviewer of Stacpoole's *The Pools of Silence* (17 June 1909) applauded the novelist's jungle setting (based in part on his travels in Africa): "The scenery of the Congo is wonderfully drawn; we would especially mention a description of rainstorms seen against the primeval forest. The wild life of the forest, too, is portrayed vividly and with evident knowledge." While other popular romance-writers of the early 1900s indulge in scientific impossibilities, Stacpoole tries to bolster everything in his romance with a natural explanation —except for Em's giving birth, perhaps forced on him by a squeamish publisher. The lucky windstorm is a natural phenomenon. The bird that comes to Katafa is "maybe" prompted by an atavistic memory. The Karolin medicine woman who performs "witchcraft" on Katafa is using the actual resources of human psychology. Stacpoole lived at a time when nature itself still contained mysteries beyond anything in romance: "Under the sea surface lies a world ruled by laws of which we know little or nothing" (*Garden* 167), he could say then—as we no longer can.

In 1922 he went to live, write, and garden on the Isle of Wight, later founding an environmental society called the Penguin Club "to campaign against the oil menace" threatening marine birds (*Men and Mice* 122); the cause enlisted notable personages from his generation. Although Stacpoole's *Times* (London) obituary (13 April 1951) does not mention the Penguin Club, its existence, however tentative, attests to his active interest in nature conservancy. In 1934 he dedicated a pond at his home—Bonchurch in Ventnor on Wight—as a bird sanctuary. Speaking for an optimistic generation, this author of *The New Optimism* (1914, alas) never doubted that humanity could itself not only thrive but carry the other species safely through the ecological storm.

Alcorn proposes that "Of all the naturist writers, Hardy, Hudson, and Lawrence are closest to the spirit of primitivism; and Hudson is the immediate source, along with Hardy, of Lawrence's primitivism" (70). In some ways,

Lawrence belongs to his present, while Hudson owns the longer view—backward and forward: youthful reading of Gilbert White's *The Natural History and Antiquities of Selborne* (1789) helped make him as devoted an environmentalist as any today. Comparison of *Green Mansions* with most of D. H. Lawrence's fiction apparently supports Alcorn on the shared primitivism of the two. Yet Hudson knows nature in the lost Argentina of his childhood, and he infuses the landscape with a remembered vitality. Lawrence searches for untamed places sustained by Hardy's English mythology of people and the land. This land-people nexus dissolves on contact not with knowledge, the inherent sophistication of the civilized world, but with a combination of elements to be called not "civilization" but modern life. Of course, neither Hudson nor Hardy can approximate the buoyancy with which Stacpoole transcends the war (scarcely a subject in his many novels after 1918) and its aftermath. But then, modern life in general scarcely makes itself felt on his pacific islands.

Innocence and Radical Innocence

COWBOYS AND SHEPHERDS

By the earlier 1900s the American popular novel of backwoods life was already well established in books like Edward Eggleston's *The Hoosier Schoolmaster* (1871), the love story of a country schoolteacher and a hired girl. Owen Wister's *The Virginian* (1902)—in which an admiring narrator from the East observes, among other things, a romance between a cowboy and a schoolmarm—seems to merge images of pastoral romance with backwoods and "Wild West" novels in ways that will prevail on the screen for generations. Wister's cowboy has the classical shepherd's independence, humility, and unassuming plainness; he does not sing, though the era of singing cowboys is not far in the future. Unlike the ancient shepherd, he is capable of violence in defense of the right, and he wins his love with courage and straightforwardness. Like shepherd knights in Renaissance romances, he represents a wedding of opposites, the pastoral and the heroic. The lore of the West is that of the open range; since sheep destroy the grassland, the shepherd gets no welcome in the wide-open spaces.

A most memorable union of the shepherd with the cowboy is Lynn Riggs's well-received play *Green Grow the Lilacs*, first staged in New York by the Theatre Guild in 1931, then converted twelve years later into the musical *Oklahoma!*. Riggs, a scholarly graduate of the University of Oklahoma, all but acknowledges the classical roots of his play in calling it a "simple tale, which might have been the substance of an ancient song" (*Green Grow* viii); by the end of the first scene the familiar terrain of Greek and Shakespearean pastoral unfolds. The cowpuncher Curly McClain (first acted by Franchot Tone) is the shepherd-singer-lover with a repertoire of traditional songs such as "Get along Little Dogies"—to be displaced later, of course, by the great music and words of Rodgers and Hammerstein. Curly's sweetheart,

Laurey (he first saw her as a little girl with berry juice on her mouth), orphaned in childhood, lives with sage Aunt Ellen, a font of practical wisdom. Her boorish suitor is the brooding hired hand, Jeeter, and the couple's shivaree on their wedding night recalls the country customs of the marriage night described by Longus and Sand.

So-called Indian territory—*Green Grow the Lilacs* is set before Oklahoma statehood, in 1900—provides more than a folksy backdrop for the action. It is a last innocent frontier, in the last year of the old century, in an America not quite come of age. Its inhabitants like to think of the United States as a wholly other place. Aunt Ellen shames the U.S. marshal's posse hunting for innocent Curly by reminding them, "we're territory folks—we art to hang together. I don't mean *hang*—I mean *stick*. Whut's the United States? It's jist a furrin country to me. And *you* supportin' it! Jist dirty ole furriners, ever last one of you!" (161).

Oklahoma was also Riggs's place of the heart, to which he often returned for his dramatic settings, even though he left the state for good after college. In Arcadian obliviousness the settlers can both boast of their native Indian blood (161) and thrill to old man Peck's ballad of "Custer's Last Charge" (97). Unlike so many end-of-the-frontier stories in America, there is not a trace of melancholy in Riggs's play. Hints of change—the coming of barbed wire and the plow and of a civilized legal system—cannot dampen the spirits of newly married Curly: "Country a-changin', got to change with it!" (157). Especially when read from the other side of *Oklahoma!*, the play tells a story that scarcely needs beg a foremost place in the nation's social mythology. And a song line such as "All the sounds of the earth are like music" redoubles the spirit of Pan in the musical version.

As others have noted, even while Riggs's play was drawing its first audiences, events in Oklahoma and elsewhere were furnishing the material for John Steinbeck's *The Grapes of Wrath*. The imagined North Carolina of Riggs's friend Paul Green abounds in similar good country people with bad luck. The short story "The Humble Ones" (from Green's *Salvation on a String and Other Tales of the South*) begins idyllically with a couple marrying in their teens and starting a family in a three-room house they build far from the highway. In twenty-six pages, there follows a married life of death, depression, and disease. Idyllic romance must have offended writers like Green, who knew the misery of impoverished farmers. Robinson Jeffers, who probably shared Green's outlook, disliked pastoral. In his poem "Self-Criticism in February" Jeffers tells himself, "It is certain you have loved the beauty of the storm disproportionately," only to respond:

> But the present time is not pastoral, but founded
> On violence, pointed for more massive violence: perhaps it is not
> Perversity but need that perceives the storm-beauty.

The lines refer to the world of the 1930s, but they help explain the many hard-primitivist ironies of Jeffers's most pastoral poem, *The Loving Shepherdess*, which was written in 1929. Clare Walker, having lost father, lover, and home, wanders with her diminishing herd of sheep over the California Big Sur and Carmel country. A doctor has told her that if she carries her child to term in April, she will die. Her story follows the seasons from early autumn to her death, alone and in the pangs of labor, calling for her now-vanished flock. Outwardly Clare and her sheep appear as timeless figures in a landscape, "a pleasant picture, the girl and her friends, in the green shade / Shafted with golden light falling through the alder branches" (pt. 2). Clare lives in a green shade, but without a green thought. In an age "founded on violence," the picture belies the story of this woman whose lover murdered her father, then abandoned her to a predatory world. The themes of nature, love, and innocence collapse in a grim narrative of human cruelty, lust, and victimization.

The twelve parts of the poem, recalling the temporal organization of such traditional pastorals as Spenser's *The Shepheardes Calender*, begin by juxtaposing Clare's innocence with the taunts and mockery of supposedly innocent schoolchildren. Emerging from their one-room schoolhouse as Clare and her sheep pass, they have learned civilization's varied meannesses. The only child who will help her, a Spanish-Indian boy, foreshadows the coming of her only guide and protector, Onorio Vasquez, in part 4, a seer whose visions contain a wisdom that offsets Clare's increasingly sheeplike innocent ignorance.

Although Jeffers said he drew the story of the wandering shepherdess from a character in Scott's *Heart of Midlothian*, this devotee of Greek literature has created a parallel with *Daphnis and Chloe* in the episode (pt. 3) of Clare and the young cowboy Will Brighton. In an abandoned house the cowboy has his "will" with Clare at her own urging ("I want to leave glad memories"). Her openness, utterly without coyness, matches her with Chloe almost to the point of parody, and it would be comic, were the outcomes not so tragic. While she is with the cowboy her sheep wander off and fall into an unused well. Like cowherd Dorcon in Longus's wolf-pit episode (1.12), Will climbs down the pit to find that one sheep has been killed breaking the others' fall, then raises the animals to the surface.

The poem several times mentions the opposing interests of cowherds and the sheepherders: Will and Dorcon are of course both cowherds with dishonorable designs on the heroine. Clare met her would-be Daphnis, however, in an Arcadian past before she knew betrayal and violence. That love story, as Clare tells it, ends part 8:

> He lived on the next hill, two miles across a deep valley,
>   and then it was five to the next neighbor. . . .
>   We used
>   to meet near a madrone-tree, Charlie would kiss me
> And put his hands on my breasts under my clothes. It was
>   quite long before we learned the sweet way
> That brings such joy to most living creatures, but brought
>   us misery at last.

This narrative fugue lends but a glimmer of light to one of the darkest episodes of the poem, recalling the antipastoral heath scenes of *King Lear*. Onorio and Clare, seeking shelter under a little bridge on a winter night, have been joined by an old man who has lived thirty years with two hate-filled women. The old man wishes all humans would die young before they know unhappiness. He would burn all the houses, forcing people to take to the roads, "All young, all gay, all moving, free larks and foolery / By gipsy fires." Like Gessner's prehistoric Arcadians, Clare often seems a preconscious being devoid of mind. The narrator reports that "she was always either joyful or weeping," like a caricature of heroines in popular rural fiction. An impotent innocence thwarts her pastoral care. Clare responds to others "either not knowing or not thinking" (pt. 4); "Her pity poisoned her strength" (pt. 7).

Those who know Jeffers best have found in this poem evidence of the author's Hardy-like quarrel with the Almighty, in particular his skepticism of the "savior complex" as embodied in Jesus. The Good Shepherd's language sometimes interweaves with Clare's ("the birds have perches but we have no place" [pt. 7]; "Why have you forsaken me, father?" [pt. 9]). Yet, consistent with her absolute valorizing of innocence, Clare locates "The golden country that our souls came from" not in the Father's heaven but in the "all-enfolding love" of the mother's womb:

When I was in my worst trouble
I knew that the child was feeling peace and happiness.
I had happiness here in my body.
(pt. 10)

This land outside history—history being the province of the mad visionary Onorio—constitutes the most fragile of human fictions, a country of lotus eaters, where waking is dying: Clare's flock meets its first disaster while she is making love; two of her last sheep are killed and clawed by a mountain lion while she sleeps. *The Loving Shepherdess* poses a Nietzschean response to static, idyllic, isolated, innocent love; Clare's predictable sappiness, however, allows the author's skepticism to overpower the poem, weakening the very premise that Clare is supposed to confirm. Jeffers writes at a time when the myth of American innocence competes with one of power. (In "The Broken Balance" he writes, "life is not always good, but power's good.") Innocently complying with her first lover, the shepherdess participates in the ultimate crime against a patriarchalism that often hovers over Jeffers's work (*Tamar, Medea*). In a pseudomatriarchal counterfantasy of womb-life, she and her child die. Like so many other American writers, Jeffers found as much "broken balance" in relations between the sexes as in those between fast-fading nature and encroaching civilization.

In its anti-idyllicism, Jeffers's *The Loving Shepherdess* questions the "radical innocence" that Ihab Hassan found so essentially American. Because "all innocence amounts to a denial of death," argues Hassan, the theme of innocence is "a radical plea for the Self" (325). Stephen Spender has even concluded that for the American writer "his innocence [is] what he feels to be his real self" (22–23), an insight rich in implications for my subject. In Clare Walker, Jeffers satirizes this innocence with a character so conspicuously innocent that she has no self, or more accurately, she empties herself into the innocence of her flock and unborn child. *The Loving Shepherdess* recalls the failed-love romances of Stowe and Cather by virtue of its strong preoccupation with the self grappling against the odious, intrusive collective will. Like most ironists, Jeffers leaves his readers no place to stand.

A shipwrecked mob, seemingly the wreck of modern society, drives Clare out of her home and into her green world of death. By contrast, Mary Austin's more conventional heroine Jacinta in *Isidro* (1905) leaves the green shade of her guardian's wilderness home to recover the superior class origins that will protect her from society. Austin lived in Jeffers's Carmel country a generation before the poet and in later years cautioned him about the excessive sex in his poetry. Carmel is mostly the setting for *Isidro*, a novel that takes place in the last years of Spanish colonial rule in California. The title character, a young candidate for the priesthood, discovers a flock of sheep and their murdered owner while on his way to study with the friars. He also encounters a rough country boy, El Zarzo (whose name means "the briar"), who turns out to be the foundling girl Jacinta.

As historical fiction *Isidro* owes much to Scott, but the portrayal of the courageous yet naive seminarian-turned-lover recalls Luis in Valera's *Pepita*, which Austin could have read in English after 1891. The strong sense of the experienced landscape around Carmel helps make this first novel probably her best.[1] Jacinta's transvestism has a long history in romance, but Austin uses the motif to achieve a mutuality in the couple unlikely to have existed in Spanish colonial life around 1830 even to this limited degree. After their adventures and marriage, says the narrator, Isidro's "word of supreme endearment" for Jacinta is "lad," as if her authentic self remains her presexual boyhood. Jacinta's shedding her boy's clothes marks but one of the many passages and emergences in the novel. A similar watershed in sexual self-knowledge comes when Isidro renounces the celibate life. Yet identity is social as well as sexual. Like so many other hidden aristocrats (Chloe, Perdita, Pastorella), El Zarzo is attracted to Isidro by "a desire to mix with his own kind" (170). Her guardian, Lebecque—a trapper who lives with her in his "lair" inside a green thicket—represents the end of the primal land where even the Indians have evaporated into the mission settlements. (Lebecque dies fighting a bear.) The final dissolution of the missions, attended by violence and insurrection, represents a transition from security to a dangerous freedom not unlike that which the novel's couple undergo.

It is difficult to ignore the Anglo-Protestant strenuousness, with its antipastoral implications, coloring Austin's version of the Catholic colony. When Jacinta first observes the Indians' life in the mission, she is appalled by the locks and whipping post, yet she notes that here "if a man works not he is flogged; but in the forest if a man works not he goes empty, and that is the greater pain" (122). The libertarian Jeffers would also have chosen freedom over the cloistered virtues of mission existence. California is still "a lotus eating land" (326) when the troubles begin. Once the Spanish throne and church have departed, the land and lovers alike must come to their senses. The one false note in the novel sounds at the end, when the married couple, rather than remain in the dangerous new country, take ship for Mexico, where Jacinta will claim her vast inheritance.

At about the same time, *The Shepherd of the Hills* (1907)—a softer if more melancholy pastoral romance by a soon-to-be Californian, Harold Bell Wright—drew an enormous readership and movie audience from an increasingly urban America. On the screen in its third film version, *Shepherd of the Hills* became one of John Wayne's early successes. Wright has provided a living for many in the area of Branson, Missouri, where there is a religious monumental statue called *The Shepherd of the Hills* and where tourists annually watch a folklike play based on the novel. The book propelled Wright into public notice, and during the next forty years, his novels would sell over ten million copies.[2] In the town where I live, a used book store devotes a special section to Harold Bell Wright books. Even in Britain, cheap editions of *Shepherd* remained in print steadily from 1909 until the 1940s. Certainly for American popular audiences of the earlier twentieth century, idyllic romance held strong appeal.

With little formal education, Wright somehow acquired a sixth sense about literary structures, especially the forms of romance. Leaving home as a boy because of an alcoholic father, he received a brief remedial education at Hiram College in Ohio and then went west to become a minister in southeast Kansas and the Missouri Ozarks. Throughout his youth, he says in his autobiography, he loved reading "everything, from Nick Carter [a popular detective character] and the *Police Gazette* to Shakespeare" (*To My Sons* 94). Seeing Goethe's *Faust* profoundly affected the future minister, especially the character of Mephistopheles (114). Wright must have learned from fiction of the late 1800s the appeal of such formulas as golden-age nostalgia, country-versus-city living, or the orphaned hero. (In his *The*

Winning of Barbara Worth the heroine at age four becomes lost in a sandstorm but eventually marries into a wealthy Eastern family and is found to be of blue-blood parentage.) Popularity led directly to Hollywood, where Wright, having earlier abandoned his ministry, worked as a screenwriter, mostly of Westerns.

Convention's subterranean channels have left many traces of European pastoralism in *The Shepherd of the Hills*. The melancholy shepherd is Howitt, a mysterious white-haired exile from the city who offers to work for a local farmer. Is it a hard job? "Difficult, no," says farmer Matthews, "there ain't nothing to do but tendin' to the sheep" (21). If wolves still threaten sheep this late in the history of Ozark settlement, surely they are the wolves of literary pastoralism. An *Et in Arcadia ego* theme develops when Howitt, surrounded by sheep, discovers a small cemetery containing, he later learns, the grave of the Matthews daughter. "Moss had gathered on the headstones, and the wind, in the dark branches above, moaned ceaselessly" (30). The lovers are Matthews's son, Matt, and a "deep bosomed," "splendidly developed" (77) young woman, Sammy Lane. Howitt, educating the couple, becomes their sage Philetas. People describe them as extraordinarily beautiful, like Adam and Eve before the fall (17, 252, 292). Sammy has aristocratic blood (63, 94, 107)—southern aristocracy, that is, from a family ruined by the Civil War. Probably Sammy echoes Miranda in *The Tempest* when she talks with her father about her origins: "Tell me more. . . . Seems like I remember bein' in a big wagon, and there was a woman too; was she my mother?" (64). The "pirates" of this romance follow the outlaw Wash Gibbs, who has a sinister hold on Sammy's father and eventually kills him. Near the end is a Theocritean or Virgilian dialogue between youth and age when Howitt encounters a young painter from Chicago—"Very soon old age will rob you of your freedom, and force you to think, whether you will or no" (296). On the whole, one of the strongest points of resemblance between this romance and *Daphnis and Chloe* is the (at times gratuitous) recurrence of so many conventional scenes, characters, and images that belong to pastoral literature.

Howitt, later revealed as "one of the biggest D. D.'s [Doctors of Divinity] in the United States" (248), has deserted his wealthy city church, searching for true religion and for his lost son, Howard, who some years earlier disappeared while traveling and painting in the Ozarks. Howitt witnesses

Sammy and Matt's efforts to discover their love while young Ollie Stewart tempts Sammy to come live in the city. She is about to yield to Ollie (like Spenser's Pastorella and Austin's Jacinta, she has an aspiring mind) when truth intervenes. In a violent fight between these two giants, Matt bests Wash Gibbs, and after Sammy watches the spectacle ("her lips parted, her face flushed with excitement" [194]), she learns Matt had recently saved Ollie from a mountain lion. The populist author sees to it that she opts for the country. Comparing Matt in his ragged country clothes with Ollie, Sammy thinks, "the men who would work for Ollie in the shops would look like this. It was the same old advantage; the advantage that the captain has over the private; the advantage of rank, regardless of worth" (185). A pastourelle subplot develops in the pastoral setting when Howitt learns that his son, Howard, seduced and abandoned Matthews's daughter, who died soon after. Howard has lived secretly, a penitent in a nearby cave (sooner or later, there would have to be a cave), with a portrait of the girl he had, too late, come back to marry.

Longus spins the words of his story from a picture; likewise the portrait of Wright's dead beauty, ruined innocence as an icon of the spirit of the place, embodies his story. Comparison of the two paintings reveals fundamental differences between the two authors' worlds. Longus's painter envisions the whole pastoral cycle in the passage of time: babies born and exposed, pirate raids, youths in courtship and in love. Wright's painter leaves behind just the haunting individual portrait, as if everything beautiful in this world dissolves in a single death—again the melancholy romance tones of Bernardin, Chateaubriand, Nerval, Stowe, and Hudson. The elegiac theme rises to a climax when, at the end, "men were tearing up the mountain to make way for the railroad" (298). *The Shepherd of the Hills* begins as a wide canvas of life, with authentic glimpses of Ozark folk ways and landscapes. It finally surrenders (as *The Pearl of Orr's Island* does) to moroseness, oddly oblivious to the happiness of the newly married principal lovers.

The "night world" union between Howard and his now-dead beloved has resulted in the birth of a child named Pete. An innocent because of his mental handicap, Pete is the one person who befriends and secretly visits Howard in his cave. Pete's silence, his occasional mysterious allusions to undisclosed persons and events, give him a kind of omniscience, like one of

Wordsworth's simple seers. Silence and inaction again belong to the idyllic. Frye mentions the romance use of mute or inarticulate characters to express "the falling silent of the world in its paradisal or humanly intelligible phase" (115). Wright once more struck upon the right literary image. Compare the inarticulate Leaf in *Under the Greenwood Tree*, Hudson's silent Rima, the slipping away of language in Stacpoole's *Blue Lagoon* novels. Wright's unfortunate Pete follows his father in death so that life may go forward, but the residue of that death and other disturbing developments at the end leave less room for optimism than Wright's public, and even Wright himself, seem to think.

The nightmare side of mute paradisal innocence is disabling paralysis, the inability to control outcomes that belongs with the determinism of much naturalistic fiction in Wright's time. Such feelings hardly fit with the rugged, prelapsarian, deep-bosomed qualities of Wright's Edenic lovers. In his autobiography Wright says that he became a writer because he was a solitary escapist reader in his youth. He speaks of himself as if a character in a novel by Dreiser or Zola: "I was forced into authorship by life, by a combination of circumstances over which I had no control" (97). Wright himself had enough control to leave church life for the film studios, but his characters act less freely. Sammy's father cannot escape his outlaw past; no one can resist the coming of the railroad (a familiar symbol in American naturalism). Yet the doctor of divinity can move freely among his big-city church members, his rural pupils, and his sheep.

Wright the omnivorous reader ingested indiscriminately the nineteenth-century strands of the idyllic and elegiac, along with similarly inconsistent blends of American utopianism and nostalgia, Emersonian self-reliance, and Dreiserian helplessness against "circumstances." Unwittingly he allows these contradictions free play in an ending that tries to resolve itself in several directions at once: youth cut off in its prime versus youth happy ever after, Christianity versus natural religion, destruction of Arcadia versus rural virtues preserved. "Primitivism," says Hassan—and the term as he uses it applies perfectly to *Shepherd of the Hills*—"recognizes the validity of human instincts and seeks to defend their integrity against the encroachments of an order ruled by abstract social goals. But Primitivism seldom has the means of mediating successfully between the needs of the self and the demands of civilization" (51).

So it stands with the John Wayne film of *Shepherd*. It projects a Western hero (even the vistas look more like the West than the Ozarks) in a stereotypical situation that loses Wright's story but gains in consistency and flatness. Matt, Sammy's father, and others are wholly occupied with making moonshine and eluding revenuers. Hero and heroine have little use for each other at first. She gets his attention by slapping his face, and soon he is saying such things as "A blue-eyed filly is the most worrisome kind." Howitt comes to buy land, not to herd sheep, though flocks of sheep show up inexplicably; the locals call him a shepherd because he can heal the sick just like "the Good Shepherd," as Marjorie Main says at one point. Howitt, father of Matt (who has been raised by a cruel stepmother), has just finished a long prison term for killing a man; Matt, not knowing this, hates his father for abandoning his mother and causing her early death. The climax of the film is a shoot-out between father and son. Gunplay finally settles Hassan's "demands of civilization."

Wright's romance followed *Isidro* by just two years, but the books are a world apart. The huddling Ozarks are a hideaway land, an enclave apart from the America of railroads and cities. Austin's open canyons, arroyos, and forested mountains belong to her wider historical view. Wright's conventional pastoral setting is a place of refuge; Austin's landscape, a scene of destiny where the couple leave sheep country for heroic climes. Austin, too, understands sexual identity in ways that Wright's world, freighted with social mythology, does not allow. Wright's pastor-turned-shepherd abandons his church and never looks back, exchanging his theology for a sort of elemental American pantheistic unitarianism. Austin grants her characters freedom from their sage, Padre Vicente, who quixotically dreams of keeping Junipero Serra's missions alive. The author of a memorable book on sheep and herding, *The Flock*, Austin knew too much about real pastoral to write mere pastoral romance and too much about the native Americans of the Southwest to oversimplify them as romance primitives. She called herself a "naturist," meaning something like the term as I applied it to the British idyllic romancers—a role involving the spiritual as well as the scientific. Austin excoriated southern California for selling out to merchants and developers, while Wright would make his living from the movie industry there. Reading Austin's autobiography, *Earth Horizons*, one feels that if the railroad had been threatening her Arcadia, she would have known what to do about it. That the American public would prefer Wright was a foregone conclusion.

SHEEP WITHOUT COWBOYS

A signal episode in the history of *Daphnis and Chloe*'s reception in Britain during this period is the Irish poet and novelist George Moore's translation, planned as early as 1918. The date recalls other recourses to idyllicism in time of war (Sand, Stowe). Moore's fondness for things Hellenic extends from *Pagan Poems* (1881) to *Aphrodite in Aulis* (1930), written in his eighties. Moore thought Longus's romance "the beautifullest story in the world" (quoted in Hone 391). Looking back over his long and varied life in letters near its end, he said nothing had pleased him so much as his translation of *Daphnis and Chloe* (Hone 483).

Like Goethe and like Day, Longus's first English translator, Moore knew only Amyot's French version of *Daphnis and Chloe*, though he did confer with several Greek scholars. To one of these, Mary Somerville, he revealed an odd notion that his translation restored the beauty of a "story" held captive by bad writers: "I have redeemed the loveliest of stories from bad greek and bad english" (quoted in Hone 395). He knew of one imitation of Longus, Mistral's *Mirèio*, but in a letter to A. J. A. Symons, Moore dismissed it as an "oily" poem—"I am full of contempt for the critics who compare it with *Daphnis and Chloe*" (Hone 395). Probably he resented the Provençal epic's patriotism, a form of the moralizing that he held the bane of literature. When a lawyer acquaintance in Ireland objected that *Daphnis and Chloe* was an immoral book, Moore fulminated, "for seventeen hundred years the greatest minds in all countries have looked upon this tale as one of the most beautiful ever written. . . . I would remind you that Humanity has continued to go its way through the ages always the same, never better, never worse, taking to its bosom the writer who writes about Humanity for Humanity without troubling to point out which is the right road and which is the wrong and casting out the preacher as a bore and a humbug" (Hone 397–98). This response, as yet impossible when Huet first raised the moral objection in the seventeenth century, bespeaks a new readiness in Britain to receive Longus in the years after the Great War.[3]

Until Turner's Penguin translation, Moore's remained the principal twentieth-century English version of *Daphnis and Chloe* (though Thornley, being out of copyright, was more in use). After the first editions in Britain and the United States in 1924, there were British editions in 1927, 1933, 1937, and 1954; an American "Limited Editions Club" printing of 1934 remained in use till the 1970s. Early reviewers (one, for example, in the *Daily Telegraph [London]* of 2 January 1925) hailed Moore, with his paganophile credentials, as Longus's kindred spirit, eminently qualified for the task. In the *Guardian* (14 January 1925) Hugh l'Anson Fausset also took inaccurate pot shots at Thornley—"bald and uninspired" by comparison. A more discerning evaluation by Rachel Annand Taylor in the *Spectator* (31 December 1927) rightly objected to Moore's reliance on homespun words like "beastie" and "lassie": "The story after all has remoteness as an element in its beauty." But Moore's name, together with illustrations by various artists, carried the translation into the 1970s, when it was used with the beautiful Braziller Chagall edition. Moore's insistence that he was recovering "the story" despite the author may explain why Longus's name does not appear on early title pages.[4]

A sense of the beautiful drew Moore to the story without any of the feeling of lost innocence characteristic of American writers during this period. Nor did Moore's aestheticism incline him much toward reflections on nature. It was in more conventional fiction and poetry that Wordsworthian "nature" as a literary theme had persisted in the later 1800s. Nature, "the idea of 'the land,' the earth as tilled and cultivated by man, was a predominant symbol of harmony" (Cavaliero 3). In 1909 English readers were buying novels that appealed to lovers of such a countryside: S. R. Crockett's *Rose of the Wilderness*; Rosamond Napier's *The Heart of a Gypsy: A Romantic Tale of Exmoor*; R. Murray Gilchrist's Peak District romance, *The Two Goodwins*; J. E. Patterson's Suffolk coast novel, *Watchers by the Shore*; and Emma Brooke's *The Story of Hawksgarth Farm*.

True, major novelists of rural life increasingly emphasized the individual's survival "by a vital struggle with his environment" (Cavaliero 204). The comfortable old countryside was dissolving to reveal nature's real face in floods, drought, rage, and the like—though, of course, such conditions have no special priority as "nature" (see Meeker 26–35 and Lackner). Roger Ebbatson has said that D. H. Lawrence's fiction, with that of many others after 1900, "centres upon the clash between the rationalist-materialist reading of the Universe expounded by Darwinism and the transcendentalist-vitalist reading of the Romantic-Nature tradition" (258). One of Lawrence's most ironic Edenic stories, "England, My England," exemplifies this continuing of Hardy's critique of idyllicism, as do novels by two "heiresses" of Hardy, Mary Webb and Victoria Sackville-West.

The Shropshire novels of Mary Webb (1881–1927) follow Hardy in creating a comprehensive sense of place where tragic lovers struggle with nature and fate. Take the sentence beginning, "If the vast, vague Someone who created Robert and Gillian and Rwth has anything in Itself ironical." That clause, at once registering itself in Hardy's bleak school of theology, appears in Webb's counter-idyllic *Seven for a Secret* (269), a book published in 1922 and dedicated to Hardy with his permission. A hired man and shepherd-poet, Robert Rideout, and his employer's daughter, Gillian Lovekin, were playmates as children, but as Robert's affection has matured into love, Gillian's has diminished. In quite differing ways the two young adults retain a trace of childhood innocence. Robert is "as simple, as unselfconscious as a child, without a child's egotism" (31), while the self-centered Gillian has a "helpless, childish soul" (83). Like several of Hardy's heroines, she is a catastrophe waiting to happen.

The couple resemble Daphnis and Chloe in that Gillian's father does not think of Robert as a spousal candidate because of his poverty. They differ in that Gillian scarcely notices Robert's companionship except as a sounding-board for her own feelings. Robert lacks both future and tychê. Gillian lacks the capacity for love, and Ralph Elmer, who buys the nearby inn, quickly catches her eye. Elmer has a housekeeper, Rwth, apparently unable to speak, and a sinister hired man, Fringal. Time reveals that the supposed foundling Rwth is a gypsy princess whom Fringal stole at birth. By the time of this revelation, Ralph has seduced Gillian, whose father forces him to marry her. Ralph murders Rwth, then vanishes, leaving the way open for Gillian, now apparently wiser, to marry Robert. Hardy's Bathsheba and Gabriel linger at the edges of this novel, never so much as in this final stage of soldiering on despite the fall.

Mary Webb's eros is not Longus's winged boy but the cruel Venus of European romance. As Ralph is about to seduce Gillian, the narrator declares that the two "were bound for sacrifice on an altar older than mythology: the altar of one who reigns in fold and field, in town and village, in the castle and the hut, who is merciless and arrogant, . . . who hates virginity; who will be worshipped as long as there remain in the world maids and men; but whose worship is as mysterious as the forest, and whose name is unclaimed of any worshipper—for her name is unknown" (230). Nature and humanity conspire to keep this monstrous divinity supplied with victims. Robert represents the safe love of Eden, childlike in his lack of ego: "He saw the landscape, not Robert Rideout in the landscape" (31–32). It may be that in her novels Webb "is closer to Lawrence than to Hardy, for, like Lawrence, she saw in sexual wholeness the proof of a man's capacity to live and to experience" (Cavaliero 137). No "man" (or woman) displays this capacity in this novel—least of all the pastoral Robert, with his tedious poems and laconic manner. As in *Under the Greenwood Tree*, the wedding that ends the story leaves the reader uncertain of the couple's future. Gillian is a fallen Eve, Robert an unfallen Adam yet difficult to imagine as a man, except in performing indispensable farm work. Stella Gibbons's *Cold Comfort Farm* lies just over the hill.

Also like Hardy's novel and other idyllic romances, *Seven for a Secret* follows the changing seasons: it begins in early spring; Ralph plots his seduction for May Day; and the novel ends with the coming of winter as snow covers Rwth's body. Some splendid natural description helps authenticate the declared sympathy between nature and the human order (see, for example, the coming of spring, 55–56). Writing near the end of an era rich in rural fiction (and ripe for Gibbons's satire), Webb often shows pastoral sentiment just beneath the thin layer of tragedy. More than Hardy, she longs for the idyllic—or she does not manage to conceal her hankerings as well as he. The difficult task of idyllic fiction, however, remains unaccomplished in Webb: to instill nature's simplicity and freshness in the characters without depriving them of humanity.

Other idyllic motifs, the foundling and concealed aristocracy, find expression in the silent gypsy princess Rwth. During the early 1900s, besides their romance potential, literary gypsies retained their roles as figures of natural humanity, with antecedents in Emily Brontë, George Eliot, and Matthew Arnold. In *A Shepherd's Life* Hudson reflects on gypsies' "love of wildness and of eating wild flesh" (246). The gypsy lover and the woman of higher class meet in Victoria Sackville-West's *Grey Wethers: A Romantic Novel* (1923), a tragic idyll indebted to *Wuthering Heights* as much as to Hardy. For reasons of status, genteel Clare marries an effete husband even though her real affections go to Lovel, a gypsy man of all trades whom she has known since childhood. By the end of the novel the couple have eloped, to disappear forever. The setting in the Wiltshire Downs recalls Hardy's Wessex, a landscape strewn with earthworks and other memories of pagan England.

The novel's curious title, *Grey Wethers*, alludes to an anomalous cluster of gray stones that from a distance resemble a group of sheep and that provide the setting for the couple's meetings on the Downs. Because Clare and Lovel come together only in nature, "their friendship was like something pure, impatient; a very core of unity, all shows burned away." In their silence and spontaneity, these moments create an order of natural life that borders on the primitive, with Lovel as the shepherd-guide: "For hours together they might be silent; at times their talk was purely practical, when he would show her how to cast a fly, or how to throw a sheep for shearing, or how to twist a rough basket out of osiers. Quite abruptly, sometimes, he would break off and leave her. She never thought of asking him, next time, why he had done so, any more than she would have thought of asking the breeze why it had dropped" (51). Reviewers thought the novel "sound and penetrating," praising the author's descriptive power and sense of place (see Stevens 90). These latter virtues recur three years later much amplified in Sackville-West's book-length poem *The Land*, an account of the four seasons that imitates Virgil and James Thomson. But in her formidable years Sackville-West would disown *Grey Wethers* and her other romances, perhaps because they conflicted with her strenuous later vision.

Among Lawrence's stories and novels that have been approached as, at least in some respects, pastoral, one story most succinctly encapsulates the themes of idyllic romance: "England, My England," first published in 1915 and then in 1921 in the collection bearing that title. Lawrence wrote the story, which is partly based on people whom he knew, as a fable about the Great War and its causes in the soul of European civilization.[5] Like the novels by Sand and Stowe, Lawrence's story is yet another work whose author uses a pastoral situation to react against war. Egbert, mooching off his father-in-law, has to a fault the classical shepherd's humble vision: "It was not that he was idle," says the narrator. "It was that he stood for nothing" (16). The family lives in one of the "snake-infested places" where "the savage England lingers" (7)—the land also celebrated in the openings of *The White Peacock* and *The Rainbow*. Early in the marriage the wife,

Winifred, begins turning to her father for the "male strength" that Lawrence's women seem to need. Her dependence increases when their daughter is crippled after falling on a sickle that careless Egbert has left in the grass. The snake in this Eden is not the sickle but the enervating generosity of Winifred's father, coupled with Egbert's passive acceptance of things.

Lawrence portrays the malaise of Egbert (and, to his mind, of many other contemporary men) through the irony of Egbert's features—which with his Viking blue eyes and the "slightly arched nose of an old country family" (8) imply an English independence now buried under industrial slag and commercial waste. The daughter's crippling turns Winifred from Eve into the "Mater Dolorata" (28). Egbert begins to live apart as a wanderer "like Ishmael" (31) until the war breaks out. After he drifts into the army, "An ugly look came on to his face, of a man who has accepted his own degradation" (35). Rootless, he longs for the savage old spirit of the place: "the desire for old gods, old, lost passions, the passions of the cold-blooded, darting snakes that hissed and shot away from him, the mystery of blood-sacrifice, all the lost, intense sensations of the primeval people of the place, whose passions seethed in the air still, from those long days before the Romans came" (29–30).

Beneath this mythic language—with some of the same phrases Lawrence uses to describe the primal earth of Hardy's landscape in *Return of the Native*—lies an insight into the way social and economic forces in industrial civilization have helped depersonalize and unsex human lives. More than the other English naturists, Lawrence understands that once human and animal are indistinguishable, so are the natural and artificial orders, and the environment ceases to have definition, ceases to exist. An effective symbol of this transition is the "heap of earth" (40) near the dead Egbert's face after he is blown apart, comparable with the garden earth Egbert works at the story's outset.

Lawrence's fiction may serve as a proving ground for the difference between American and British fiction of the earlier 1900s as it handles the subjects of love, nature, and innocence. The optimistic Lynn Riggs finds all three compatible, while the ironic Jeffers renders them mutually defeating. Hassan believes that "What continues to distinguish the American from the European novel is its critical awareness of *loss*, its ironic cultivation of human *vulnerability*, its bitter generosity toward all things *quixotic* and infrangible" (60). This can mean that benevolent nature keeps its hold on the American imagination after it has lost out in Britain under the acid rain of war, freewheeling capitalism, and a population explosion that has lately culminated in the disappearance of pork butchers and poky shops. The chief "loss" in America, that of the frontier, finds a British parallel in the disappearance of the old Britain, in particular that of the country house and the empire. A difference that many can agree upon—between the perspectives of the historical, time-centered Europe and those of the geographical, atemporal America (Spender 15)—may explain why Europeans seem so much more capable than Americans of viewing the state of innocence with amused irony: they live constantly reminded of time's difference. But of loss and vulnerability in every land of the twentieth century, there is plenty to go around.

Novelists such as Webb and Lawrence, with their longing for natural reintegration of the self, afford one kind of check on the supposed American difference. But still another perspective on the state of innocence emerges from the French Canadian experience of love in nature as recorded in Louis Hémon's *Maria Chapdelaine*, written sometime before the author's death in 1913. Here one proves oneself with a kind of stoic Jansenism by following nature in a spirit of duty. If *The Shepherd of the Hills* ends with the foretelling of inexorable change as machinery breaks into the garden, Louis Hémon (who became an actual fatality of progress when a train struck him in rural Ontario) closes his *Maria Chapdelaine* with a declaration of permanence: "in the country of Quebec nothing has changed. Nothing shall change, for we bear witness to this" (15.187). In a land of snowy fields and endless forests, perseverance requires more heroic dimensions than do the milder climes of Wiltshire and the Ozarks. But Persephone, not paradise, inhabits the core of this novel. Maria's mother eventually dies in the winter, and Maria realizes she will someday follow her, despite the annual return of life in the spring: "To live that way in this country, as her mother had lived, and then to die and leave behind her a saddened husband and the memory of her race's essential virtues—she felt she would be capable of that" (181).[6]

The restless son of an illustrious father, Hémon lived for a while in England, where, after publishing a novel, he suffered the death of his wife. He sent their small daughter back to France, then traveled and worked as a farmhand in Canada for two years before his death. With an education and a literary family, Hémon is more likely than Wright to have had contact with the major texts of idyllic romance. A knowledge of Sand's rural fiction is suggested in the simple narrative style with the protagonist always in the foreground, as characters hear and deliver speeches on a set theme. The theme of change is enunciated in Maria's speech to herself in chapter 15, her urban lover's speech in chapter 12, and her country lover's speech in the next chapter. Maria herself resembles simple, good-hearted characters like Sand's François and Germain; she also displays the inarticulateness of souls close to nature: "Girls from town had found her simple-minded; but she was merely sincere and honest, close to nature, who knows nothing of words" (13.145). The idea recalls Stacpoole's insight into the conservatism with language in the state of nature: Hémon says that country people avoid "grands mots pathétiques"—instead of using a lofty word such as "loving," they would say "liking" (11.119).

In place of easygoing champêtre cheerfulness, however, Hémon conveys something more like Cather's earnest dedication to the people of a land unspoiled by passion and desire. Yet unlike Cather's Alexandra, Maria never matures as a woman. When a Quebec land-settlement venture in 1927 used as its poster girl Maria Chapdelaine "wife and mother" (see Deschamps 19–37), it was adding quite a lot to a novel whose heroine merely contemplates marriage at the end. Although Cather would have applauded Maria's choice to stay with the hard country life rather than live in the city, Cather also recognizes the impossibility of the kind of permanence that Maria (though perhaps not Hémon) anticipates in her final monologue and that Maria's French Canadian myth-makers emphasized in their propaganda. It is ironic that the land-settlement pamphlet pictured Maria as Demeter, in view of her Persephone thoughts in chapter 15 of the novel.

Hémon follows the practice of idyllic romance in organizing *Maria Chapdelaine* after the year cycle, with close attention to the seasonal changes. Ten of the sixteen chapters begin with reference to the time of year, making a virtual *calendrier des bergers*. Set in a land where the differences between summer and winter mean so much, Hémon's novel is able to articulate the sympathy between the human and the natural with greater persuasive force than perhaps any earlier idyllic romance. At the beginning Maria sees the trapper François Paradis for the first time since her childhood, seven years earlier. During the first three chapters, while the ice is breaking up outside, their love takes hold. François proposes to Maria while they are seated, as Longus's lovers often are, on a tree trunk, where Maria imagines they will sit again in the coming spring. Reminiscent of the harvest scenes in *Daphnis and Chloe* are the descriptions of clearing land, picking blueberries, and gathering hay (chapters 4 to 6). In the summer François comes to see Maria's family, sleeping with her brothers, as Daphnis does with Chloe's father in his winter visit. Autumn is "melancholy, charged with regret for what has slipped away and for the threat of what will come; but under the Canadian sun it is more melancholy and more unsettling than elsewhere, and is like the death of someone whom the gods have called too soon without giving him his due portion of life" (86).[7] This passage—coming in chapter 7, near the end of the conventionally idyllic half of the novel—foretells the death of François that winter, lost in the terrible cold, and of Maria's mother. The penultimate chapter announces the coming of spring "like a beautiful maiden delivered from a wicked enchanter by the wave of a magic wand" (15.173).

The name François Paradis creates tensions that inhibit our reading this novel as mere celebration of the motherland.[8] François represents the paradise that Maria might have found, the triumph of erotic love so often frustrated in medieval and early modern romances. But is it a lesser or greater paradise than Duty will bestow? Orphaned in childhood (an echo of Sand's *François le Champi*?), François is, for the climate, a perfect adaptation of Daphnis—a resourceful "survivor" Nicole Deschamps calls him, a *coureur de bois*, a fur trader, a guide, an interpreter, an amiable free spirit (58). The local sage, the parish priest, cautions Maria that with her lover's death she must forget the past, take care of her parents, marry, and raise a family.

Marry whom? Maria's choice is easy as long as it lies among the conservative Eutrope, Lorenzo (who would take her to a big city in the United States), and François. After François's death, though, it is as if Fancy Day were left to choose between Farmer Shiner and Parson Maybold. Lorenzo's diatribe against farm life sounds immensely convincing, perhaps reflecting the author's own feelings after his months as a farm laborer in Peribonka. Yet when Maria rejects the city because it is "an easy life almost without labor, filled with little pleasures" (15.184), she seems zombified by loss, dreariness, and suffering. Her settling on dull, hard-working Eutrope empties the novel of any residual romantic love. At least Wright's couple have an established friendship and an affection whetted by tattered Matt's longtime desire to wed Sammy—a desire that is eventually fulfilled.

The Canadian idyll collapses (or ascends) into georgic at the end, when Maria's father tells her for the first time the story of her mother's and his early life together, a story of heartbreaking struggle, including her mother's terrifying battle to keep hungry bears from killing their sheep. The great question of why someone would live this kind of life goes unanswered, except to the degree that the answer is self-evident in living the life. Hémon himself seems respectful but less persuaded than the land developers of 1927 who appropriated Maria's story (see Deschamps).[9]

Although both *Shepherd of the Hills* and *Maria Chapdelaine* could lend themselves readily to political agenda in their respective cultures, nature asserts itself far more in the Canadian romance than in Wright's story, where it is little more than a convenient setting for a tale of supposed folk.[10] Hémon's characters are understood almost solely with reference to the forests and farms and winters of the land. Passion merely obfuscates living. More convincingly than in most naturalistic fiction of the time, nature tyrannizes over human society. Deschamps's insight that realism and symbolism constantly work on each other in this novel (51), that action is always a pretext for rumination (56), holds true largely because of nature's overwhelming presence. This reflective content, not new to idyllic romance (for example, Bernardin and Hudson), takes us back to the allegorical overtones that some detect in *Daphnis and Chloe*. The vague but powerful ideologies controlling both Wright's and Hémon's romances, however, with their mythic open-endedness, their unrealized conflicts between helplessness and freedom, death and life, dissolve authentic allegory before it can form.

Hémon's world differs from Wright's, too, in the controlling presence of the French fathers, both familial and priestly. Through them the voice of Duty speaks. The American literature surveyed in this chapter differs in the noticeable absence of the powerful father from *The Virginian*, *Isidro*, *The Loving Shepherdess* (where he is murdered), *Green Grow the Lilacs*, and even from *Shepherd of the Hills* (where Matthews senior and Jim Lane are benignly oblivious to their children's marriage interests). To live without a father is to live without the restraints of origin, a well-known American dream.

Or rather a United States dream. Fatherhood stands quite otherwise in the Colombian Jorge Isaacs's *María*, the Latin American novel that most resembles, in idyllicism and immense popularity, the books by Wright and Hémon. In the first century after its publication in 1867, *María* was perhaps the most read novel in Latin America, seeing print in some one hundred and fifty editions and being used as the basis of films made in Mexico and Colombia. With critical praise from the likes of Rubén Darío and Miguel de Unamuno, it deserves to be taken more seriously as an artistic achievement than Wright's or Hémon's novels. (There is only one English translation of *María*; published in 1890, it is an inadequate work, omitting whole chapters.) Isaacs, son of a Jewish immigrant father, wrote under the spell of *Paul et Virginie* and its offspring—Chateaubriand's *Atala* and Lamartine's *Graziella* and *Rafael*.[11]

A novel of the region, of *costumbrismo*, *María* invites reading alongside the novels of Stowe, Hémon, Wright, and Valera. But it shares with Valera the strong father-figure that is lacking in its North American counterparts. Dedicated to "the brothers of Efraín" (its hero), the book announces its audience as masculine. María, an orphaned second cousin, comes to live with Efraín when he is seven and she is six. Although he comes to think of her as a sister, when he returns home from his distant school at sixteen, he realizes his love for her. Efraín's lyric reflections on the countryside merge with his thoughts of María: "Those lonely places with their quiet woodlands, their flowers, birds, and streams—why were they speaking to me of María? What of María was there in the damp shade, in the breeze stirring the leaves, in the sound of the river? It was as if I were seeing Eden but she was missing" (10.72).[12] Making María one with his landscape, the narrator in effect sexualizes his beloved Cauca Valley (see Cymerman)—one reason why the novel still retains such a strong hold on Isaacs's homeland.

Efraín's loving father readily approves of the couple's marriage plans, but their union is deferred by a series of narrative byways, some pastoral (such as the shepherd Tiburcio's love problems in chapter 49) and some heroic. In fact it is Efraín's manly achievements—encouraged by his wealthy, powerful father—that draw this novel away from the idyllic orbit. Efraín and María never achieve sexual symmetry—perhaps could not have done so in their culture. María arrives as a poor relative. While Stowe's Mara earns the right to be treated as an equal in Sewell's classroom, María with her "sisters" must sit at Efraín's feet as his pupil when he returns from school. (Efraín has them read Chateaubriand's *Génie du christianisme* (*Genius of Christianity*) but specifically warns María away from *Atala* [34.181]). She at least holds a right of refusal: Efraín worries at length that she might not return his love.

Finally, while the social rank of the couple in *María* is the reverse of that in *Paul et Virginie*, the outcome is the same. The love story ends not in marriage but death as María suffers a lingering illness that draws Efraín back from London in time for her final moments. Love finds perfection not in fusion but in loss. So compelling a death scene left Isaacs's more credulous countrymen with such a strong conviction that María must have been a real person that they have erected a monument to her in the cemetery where she is supposed to have been buried (321 n.). One recalls the afterlife of Paul and Virginie, Maria Chapdelaine, Nerval's Sylvie, and the Shepherd of the Hills. Yet the strong paternal presence in *María* sets the novel quite apart from these and especially from the other idyllic romances of the United States.

In the final analysis, *María* behaves more like a European novel in this regard. Consider the British texts, where the fathers all seem powerful: *Under the Greenwood Tree, Seven for a Secret* (Gillian's father forces Ralph to marry her), *Grey Wethers* (Clare must choose a husband under the stifling influence of her priest-father), and "England, My England" (where paternal wealth and "male strength" drive the weak Egbert to his death in a war begun by mad European patriarchs). Among many other things, the father—even a gentle, solicitous father such as the one in *María*—stands for structure and limits in the European romances. He embodies the all-pervading influence of class and history that Americans like to think they have eluded. Riggs's Oklahoma as a territory lies outside government, "duty free," by comparison with the duty-bound, class-bound lives of couples in the European fictions. Unfathered pastoral couples such as Curly and Laurey, Jacinta and Isidro, or Matt and tall, deep-bosomed Sammy have a larger-than-life quality as a result of living, like the gods, in a primeval world "innocent" of the crimes that Robinson Jeffers perceives from his end of the western shore.

Points of Departure

DAPHNIS AND CHLOE "REDIVIVOS"

While the twentieth century continues idyllic romance on page, stage, and screen, *Daphnis and Chloe* becomes an object of direct imitation in significant fiction for the first time since Bernardin. Almost simultaneously, and quite independently, both a French and a Spanish novelist began writing novels based on Longus. The celebrated Colette's adaptation, which followed that of the young Ramón Pérez de Ayala by a year, takes us into the kindred and increasingly prolific family circle of the Summer Sexual Awakening (visually explored in the film version directed by Claude Autant-Lara in 1954).

Le Blé en herbe (1923)—the title means "the unripe wheat"—reenacts elements of the Greek romance at a vacation site on the Breton coast. Philippe and Vinca (initials recalling Paul and Virginie), aged sixteen and fifteen, have since infancy lived together in nature, though only during their families' long summer vacations. This year, as summer ends, the two have begun to see themselves as lovers. Although they think they know what love is, they fare in their presumptuousness somewhat worse than Longus's openly clueless rustics. So when it is said in the fifth chapter (at one time entitled "Daphnis") that Philippe is less ignorant than Daphnis, we are not to infer that he is any wiser. Superficially his residual ignorance vanishes with his innocence, after his seduction by Madame Dalleray, an older woman vacationing nearby. Yet a crucial lesson remains until the novel's end, when still-virginal Vinca proves Madame Dalleray's equal by luring Phil into the hay. This climactic irony, from a detached narrator who enjoys the ironies of innocence, suggests that Colette is using Longus's technique along with his story.

Jean Duffy attributes Colette's narrative technique—whereby "the childish or adolescent reaction is qualified by a narratorial rider" (44)—to her age at the time she wrote *Le Blé en herbe* (in her late forties), in contrast to her couple's youth. But Colette often speaks in the tones of the ancient sophist-narrator. Madame Dalleray, more developed and sympathetic than Lycaenion, shares in the narrator's knowledge as rough-and-ready Lycaenion does not. She also plays the role of the fatal woman of medieval romance, seeming to cast a spell over Philippe. After his initiation, the detailed account of Philippe's psychic change (chapter 11) differs markedly from Daphnis's naive delight at the corresponding moment, but the novel uses mutual erotic desire, strong enough to overwhelm perceived infidelities, to draw the lovers into a closer relationship, ultimately one of equals. Innocence once again proves a mask, as it so often did back among the wits of the 1700s. Ultimately, whether we take as true Philippe's declaration, at the start of the long chapter 16, that he and Vinca have become one, or two as one, depends on our endowing Vinca with a measure of spirituality that Colette neglected to give her.

The casual allusion to Daphnis shows that Colette could count on many of her French readers to recognize the interplay between her novel and the Greek romance. In Britain, Spain, and the United States, however, Longus's reputation for prurience kept him off the horizon—at least until the late nineteenth century, when *Daphnis and Chloe* becomes noticeably more available. Hence two Longus-inspired novels that are *not* French, appearing thirty years and a world apart: Ramón Pérez de Ayala's *Luna de miel, luna de hiel*, published in pre–Civil War Spain, and Yukio Mishima's postwar Japanese novel, *The Sound of Waves*. At either end of an unloving and antinatural time, the two books reimagine, along diverging paths, the themes of innocence and love in nature. In so doing, they also shed the elegiac burden so prevalent in the literature of nature, even in popular fiction, of the preceding era.

Luna de miel, luna de hiel (1923) belongs in part to Pérez de Ayala's campaign against the instituted ethical rigors of his society.[1] The young writer had already incurred displeasure with a satire on Jesuit education entitled *A.M.D.G.*, banned in Spain throughout the Franco period and even omitted from his *Obras completas* in the 1960s. (The title is the abbreviation of the Jesuit Latin motto meaning "For the Greater Glory of God.") An admirer of Valera, Pérez de Ayala knew Valera's Longus: what better way to ridicule the ethic of denial than to bring Longus's couple into a modern setting, where their ignorance of sex would concur with official doctrine? Yet the resulting novel, *Luna de miel, luna de hiel,* transcends its satirical motives, drawing sympathy toward both the lovers and their domineering, repressive matriarch. It recapitulates, and manages wondrously to hold together, both the witty and the sentimental readings of Longus inherited from earlier centuries. Pérez de Ayala, like Valera and Pardo Bazán, writes of young people in search of identity at its most elemental.²

The novel's matriarch-idealist, doña Micaela, determines early that her son, Urbano, will be raised absolutely as an innocent—that is, as sexually uninformed. He will be "a perfect man" (40), coming to marriage in utter virginity. Hungering for aristocracy as well as innocence, Micaela arranges the boy's marriage with Simona, daughter of a profligate, near-bankrupt widow. As a respectable girl, Simona will necessarily be ignorant of sex too. The children grow up as each other's sole playmates, Urbano being tutored by Micaela's trusted old friend don Cástulo ("chaste little fellow"). When they marry as planned, Urbano has an anxiety attack. Their wedding night is comically uneventful; they separate and return to their homes, but they soon reunite at the country house of Simona's grandmother for a few Edenic days. Then creditors abruptly claim the grandmother's estate. Urbano's father, don Leoncio, has lent so much money to Simona's mother that he, too, loses everything. An angry Micaela removes her son, hoping to annul the marriage. Meanwhile, Cástulo marries one of the grandmother's corpulent servants, Conchona, and undertakes to start a school. He and Urbano conspire to steal Simona from the custody of seven old aunts, who have secretly placed her in a home for wayward girls. This latter half of the novel mostly exists in the romance underworld, with Simona imprisoned and Urbano meeting her by night. Following her rescue from the convent, exactly a year after the wedding, the couple enjoy a real honeymoon.

The classically educated Cástulo, who points out the links between the young couple and Daphnis and Chloe, best expresses the satirical point of the novel: "What is absurd is that we cannot speak naturally about these natural things" (126). The "ethical madness" of Micaela's scheme (Amorós 327) grotesquely exaggerates the idealism found in Valera's seminarian or in Pardo Bazán's melancholy Gabriel (with whom Micaela shares the archangelic source of her name). Along with these two novels, *Luna de miel* displays the characteristic double vision of idyllic romance: detached sophistication and natural innocence. But the novelistic tendency to parody romance magnifies the difference. Micaela's idealism-madness brings her to an impasse that she herself acknowledges on hearing of Cástulo's marriage, just before going magnificently insane: "'Either my mind is starting to wander or the world has gone crazy and the natural laws no longer apply,' said doña Micaela. In other days her eyes were imperious and hostile toward external reality. Recently they had altered to an expression of fear joined with an emotion of melancholy anxiety. 'The world is falling apart. Everything is going backward'" (241).[3] Appeal to the "natural laws" intensifies the irony; to go "backward" from these giddy heights is the only progress possible.

For the moment, however, Micaela speaks as a somewhat satiric figure, a caricature. Pérez de Ayala transforms Micaela into his "fullest study of woman to date" (Agustín 248), however, in the process of expanding *Luna de miel* from the short novel that was published in 1921 into the final version of 1922. Giving her a much fuller history (see Amorós 340), he creates a character that inspires a greater sympathy in the reader. Being raised by a single mother, the child Micaela is horrified to discover the fact of her illegitimacy. Then, as she is entering puberty, a gypsy woman tells her that one day a man will deflower her and she will scream like a rabbit (202). Her obsessions become the understandable response of a sensitive soul to a coarse, even bestial, sexual ethic of the sort described in Pardo Bazán's Ulloa novels or, for that matter, represented in Longus's wolfish Lycaenion. The irony of her situation—like, say, that of Bernardin's Virginie—extends to the irreconcilables of the larger society (even civilization) where antihuman behavior coexists with superhuman ideals.

The other characters help define the fallout from this idealism as a sort of schizophrenia. Cástulo, the wispy scholar, and Conchona, the huge peasant, visually typify divided life in the novel. Conchona herself is variously a goddess—Pomona (85) and Athena (270)—or an animal (a "bestia" [84, 241]). She puts life and spirit into Cástulo's plans for an academy, then gives birth to a baby mistaken for a pig. Of Leoncio's two loves, Micaela comes to represent refinement and companionship, while his vulgar mistress, María Egipciaca, is physical pleasure. "Why can't María Egipciaca and Micaela be merged into a single woman; the soul of one and the exterior of the other?"

he complains (260). Even Urbano comes to think of himself as a body, Simona as his soul (124). This disembodiment of the feminine recalls the way in which Valera's Luís and Pardo Bazán's Gabriel idealize Pepita and Manuela, thinking them incapable of passion.

Innocence remains intact, for Urbano and Simona are not Pardo Bazán's rustic unfortunates. During the second, most idyllic quarter of the novel ("cuarto cresciente"), Cástulo enunciates a central theme in remarking that "The man who does not have a child's soul [alma niña] is a soulless person" (127). The child-soul is more specifically the little-girl soul, not unlike Simona, the princess in the tower (77), awaiting union with physical life. The innocence of the *niña* constitutes a pattern in the novel, a symbol corresponding generally to that of the nymphs in Longus. Besides the soul mate Simona, we glimpse another young girl, Micaela, learning about her origins or about sex from the gypsy. In her madness, Micaela plans to give birth to a niña, a wonder child, who will be called Angeles. By this time, having thrown off her rigid masculine-power mask, she seeks a return to innocence. As for Simona and Urbano, they manage the juggling act of keeping the *alma niña* alive while exchanging the dependency of childhood for the liberty of a mature couple.

As a text of idyllic fiction, *Luna de miel* justifiably invokes Milton during this most Edenic of the four "cuartos." Simona's grandmother, nearing death, acts as sage for the still unenlightened couple: "Look at the garden, the park. Would you say this is Paradise lost? No, only limbo. And if it has been Paradise for you, which indeed it has, that is owing to your desire for happiness, which you have not achieved. But paradise is outside, further beyond these walls, in life's struggles" (160).[4] The Miltonic allusion recalls Micaela's amusing but significant error early in the novel when she compares Urbano and Simona to Adam and Eve. In reply Cástulo likens them to Daphnis and Chloe, the "amantes helénicos" [Greek lovers], which Micaela hears as "amantes edénicos" [Edenic lovers](24). The (con)fusion could apply to many other idyllic romance couples. Ideally viewed, two lovers like Urbano and Simona may appear Edenic in their happiness; comically viewed as a "Hellenic" pair, they are naïfs trying to make sense of what is unknown to them but known to readers like don Cástulo.

The tension of these two viewpoints creates much of the story's delight. Longus supplemented by Genesis opens avenues of play rather than melancholy in the novel. On the matter of sex education, Cástulo echoes Longus: "although Nature, no further away than the herds they [Daphnis and Chloe] grazed, offered them instruction and example, their innocence and ignorance of the activities of love were such that they could not figure out how to satisfy their desire" (24).[5] Micaela, with her Dantesque profile, takes a more orthodox view of such things: "We are dealing with a Christian marriage, between two innocent creatures, as God commands. And their Guardian Angel will inspire them in what to do" (25). Pérez de Ayala sees the world more as Longus than Micaela does. Yet traces of sympathy linger for Micaela, if only in that her iron high-mindedness has a source in her unpleasant childhood. Moreover, by increasing their *trabajos*, she enables Urbano and Simona to transcend the level of ordinary lovers. Micaela makes the novel work by sustaining the contrary currents of both sentiment and satire.

Besides the couple's sexual ignorance, the most notable feature imitated from *Daphnis and Chloe* is the four-part structure, suggesting the year cycle, with each part named for a phase of the moon. The novel begins in June, a month before the wedding, and ends just a year after that day. Urbano and Simona's troubles grow with the waning of the year; their marriage is at last consummated in early spring, and they win liberty in the new summer. Part 1 ends with Cástulo's mumbling, "Daphnis and Chloe reborn. There's nothing new under the sun" (71). Cástulo repeats the allusion a few pages later, then quotes (without acknowledgment) the end of Longus's preface: "But as for me, I hope the gods will allow me to manage other people's experiences while keeping my own sanity" (87).[6] In effect, Cástulo stands in for Longus's urbane narrator in the country, "hunting" for and soon finding erotic fulfillment. In part 2, Cástulo's young charges enjoy their paradise, Urbano supposing at first that they will walk forever in the garden and hunt butterflies. Like other idyllic couples, they frequently behave as brother and sister (see, for example, 96–97). At the same time, Cástulo and grandmother Rosita debate the implications of the idyllic predicament. The tutor maintains that the couple should follow the example of nature; Rosita, that nature must be fought, not imitated (81). Yet she is the sage who will guide the pair while Cástulo pants after Conchona (who, despite her massiveness, soon becomes "Conchita").

In the midst of this pastoral retirement occurs a memento mori somewhat like the scene of Dorcon's death in Longus. One Sunday the lovers visit a nearby fishing village where a courtship ritual is in progress. The mystifying behavior of the village folk reminds Urbano how little he knows of ordinary people's lives. All at once, a body washes ashore; a sailor identifies it as that of a suicide (106). The shock of seeing a corpse in the midst of celebration completes Urbano's lesson in the impossibility of timeless gardens. The young man returns and, to the puzzled amusement of the *peones*, embraces Adam's curse, assisting in the hard work of the land. He begins to understand himself. "I am making myself a man. Simona is making me a man. . . . My mother didn't want me to make myself a man" (109). He wonders about a baffling remark by the foreman that he should be looking after Simona these nights (108, 113). The couple's nightly, night-long visits on a balcony become more amorous; one night, for no reason that they can understand, they find each other almost naked. But just at the point where nature might have shown them the way, the grandmother's death propels the couple into their "trabajos," their ordeal.

Developing a theodicy of Eros, Pérez de Ayala first demolishes the obstacles to natural love: the chastity fixation, class differences, patriarchy—all the narrative impediments that the poets of chivalric romance had so carefully refined and cultivated centuries earlier, including the myriad ways of prolonging a story, of holding both the lovers and the reader in thrall. Yet he writes of love in nature while eluding the trap of the naturalist's "scientific" disdain for inner nature. "With you," wrote his friend Antonio Machado, "the novel of imagination is reborn and we forget the realistic novel of cold observation and prolonged detailing of what is external and anecdotal" (quoted in Amorós 346). A convincing account of the *inner* processes justifies the ways of Eros to man—processes that lead to fulfillment and transformation. At the end, as in every idyllic romance, the lovers find their identities—though not in any lost parents. When Urbano foils the coach robbery, he gives his grateful fellow passengers a false name because, he later tells Simona, "we have begun a new life. I am not the Urbano of before, nor are you that Simona. We have to find new names" (339). Francisco Agustín speaks for many readers who have found the first half—the "Dafnis y Cloe" part—of *Luna de miel* the most tender and sincere of all the author's fiction (246; see also Amorós 260). The classic pattern of idyllic romance, played out with ingenuity and sympathy in the first half of the novel, would seem to have fit perfectly Pérez de Ayala's continuing interest in the "intimate correspondence between Nature and the permanent or essential in man" (Amorós 327). Within a few years Pérez de Ayala's political fortunes would rise as his fellow Republicans came to power in Spain, sending him to Britain as ambassador. He was still in this post when the stirrings began that would lead to civil war and his own exile from Spain for the next two decades.

At this same time, on the other side of the world, Yukio Mishima (the pseudonym of Hiraoka Kimitake) was coming of age in a country torn by a different kind of political violence. Published less than a decade after Hiroshima, this young writer's *The Sound of Waves* (*Shiosai*, 1954) reminds us that the idyllic stories of Sand and Stowe were written to counter war's effects upon their societies. We earlier saw that Remy Belleau found uses for *Daphnis and Chloe* during the sixteenth-century French religious wars and that, simultaneously with the Reign of Terror, Parisians flocked to a dramatized *Paul et Virginie*. The modern publishing history of *Daphnis and Chloe* suggests a similar pattern, with editions appearing in Weimar in 1917 and 1918; in Hoogstraten, the Netherlands, in 1943; and in Berlin and Heidelberg in 1945, followed soon by editions in Hamburg and Munich. Readers in postwar Japan were also discovering *Daphnis and Chloe*: Ferrini lists translations in 1947, 1948, 1949 (two), 1951, and later. This vogue may have encouraged Mishima, not yet thirty, in his attempt to recreate Longus's Greek island in his own country.

Mishima wrote *The Sound of Waves* in an access of Hellenism, following a savored visit to Greece during the spring of 1952—he later dismissed the novel, however, as "a joke on the public" (Nathan 115). Because it does indeed conflict with both his homoeroticism and the crafted pessimism of his later fiction, the best guess is that his renunciation of the novel was an attempt to distance himself from this early stage of his life and art.[7] Nevertheless, as a "translation," *The Sound of Waves* outpaced its Greek source in Japanese bookstores. It set a postwar record for hardback sales, and well into the 1970s it continued to sell a hundred thousand paperback copies a year (Nathan 120–21).

Even more remarkable, it appeared at a time in world history when Longus's romance would seem to have run its course or to be capable of furnishing material only for sentimentalism or satire. Mishima's book stands among a small body of post–1945 literature (very small, as far as I can determine) that offers an affecting and human story reviving the possibility of an authentic idyllicism or joyous unity in love and nature. Now and then, one can glimpse the author's later fascination with cruelty, as in the description of Shinji's father's death in an air attack on his fishing boat (5.36), or the anecdote of the girl who loved her seducer for his sadism (8.80)—hints detectable only in retrospect.

Mishima refashions Longus's romance as deliberately as does Pérez de Ayala, but the results suggest different aims. Longus's narrator, with his sophist wit, makes way for an affirming but unsentimental voice. Mishima finds a way to put novelistic realism in the service of Greek romance material: scrupulous description and character psychology coexist with sympathizing nature, a tutelary shrine, even prophetic double dreams (12.122). In a gesture as old as Sannazaro's sixteenth-century "piscatory" eclogues, Mishima removes the setting from the world of shepherds to that of rural types more familiar to his readers, fishermen. The sleight of hand performed in the achievement is impressive in view of the many subtle details carried over from *Daphnis and Chloe*. Marguerite Yourcenar praises the Japanese novel as "infinitely purer" than the Greek romance: "above all, nothing in Mishima's novel betrays any wish to titillate the reader with the artificially prolonged sexual games of two children experimenting with love without discovering orgasm" (40). Pierre Huet's moralism and Samuel Johnson's antipastoralism aside, if Mishima's book is "typical of those happy books a writer often writes only once in his life" (Yourcenar 38), Longus did at least provide the novelist with a formal starting point.

Like Daphnis and Chloe, both of Mishima's lovers have lost parents. Hatsue, put up for adoption because her father wanted no more daughters, has returned to live with her father now that her mother and only brother have died (similar deaths appear in Longus 4.35). Her father, like Chloe's, owns ships and has become wealthy. She continues her "piscatory" work, however, as a diver with the island's other women. Shinji works on a fishing boat to supplement his widowed mother's small income from diving. (Mishima transposes the Greek novel's childhood phase to Shinji's little brother, Hiroshi, whose school excursion to the city allows the usual country-city contrast.) Like Daphnis and Chloe, the couple quickly fall in love; the rival—an ambitious, better-connected boy named Yasuo—never really has a chance, as far as Hatsue is concerned. Mishima converts the episode of Dorcon in the wolf skin to have Yasuo lie in wait at night to catch Hatsue drawing water; she is rescued when an angry hornet, not a pack of dogs (9.89–93), attacks Yasuo. From the start Shinji displays ignorance if not of sex then of courtship (5.34). Like the Greek couple, Shinji and Hatsue discover a new erotic desire on seeing each other naked, while retaining a Greek openness in their attitude toward their bodies. Instead of Pan, it is "perhaps" the sea god assisting the lovers (3.25, 6.44) when they come together in a lucky storm complete with "sounds like human shrieks and shrilling fifes" (8.64). A second storm (chapter 14) allows Shinji, as a cadet sailor, to prove himself by saving his future father-in-law's ship. The forbidding senex, Hatsue's father, eventually lets Shinji's courage compensate for his poverty, but before his heroic deed, Shinji's seeming ineligibility for Hatsue's hand nearly brings tears to his eyes. In managing "to avoid the double shame of having others see him cry," Shinji behaves more stoically than the openly emotional Daphnis.

The novel also follows the seasons, from love's beginning in the early spring to the couple's engagement in late August. Dominated by the shrine and the lighthouse, the island retains the Arcadian qualities of Lesbos. Shinji proclaims a naive belief in the island as enclave of perfection: "very bad things . . . will all always disappear before they get to our island"; "there's not a thief on the whole island—nothing but brave, manly people" (6.53). At the end, after his heroism, Shinji has acquired a more mature sense of his place in the order of things: in some way the island and the gods had protected him and Hatsue, but "it had been his own strength that had tided him through that perilous night" (16.183). No such revelation comes to Daphnis, whose salvation is from without. It may even be that this "assertion of male supremacy" breaks "the mood of wholeness and joy" in the book (Wolfe 103), but I think this overreads a single sentence. The conclusion's flaw, if it has one, lies not in the self-discovery but in the narrator's momentary forgetting of Hatsue.

The cooperation between inner and outer nature frequently speaks in Mishima's images of the sea. Shinji hears "the sound of waves" as "the surging of his young blood was keeping time with the movement of the sea's great tides" (6.45). When he and Hatsue stand naked before each other, "it seemed as though this unceasing feeling of intoxication, and the confused booming of the sea outside, and the noise of the storm among the treetops were all beating with nature's violent rhythm" (8.77). This episode in particular indicates the almost mystical "consummate accord" (44) between self and nature in the narrative, a feeling of oneness sustained in Mishima's remarkable meditation on weightlifting, *Sun and Steel*.

One reason that Mishima can rewrite the ancient Greek romance so convincingly must be that he retains the lively pantheism of Longus, while not relinquishing a modern sense of the inner life. For Shinji as for Longus's couple the gods exist, they answer prayers. A cave where his little brother and some playmates go—"one of the most mysterious spots" on the island—contains "a Sanskrit inscription some unknown hand had carved long ago on one of the moss-covered walls" (10.97–98). The unrevealed meaning of these ancient words matters less than their presence as a slender thread of Indic civilization linking Greece (Lesbos) with this little Japanese island.

The theme of inner accord with nature, so difficult to express after the discordant fictions of literary naturalism, coexists with a passion for the material surfaces of life that transforms moments of *The Sound of Waves* into imagist poems. There is the description of the catch on the fishing boat: "The black, wet bodies of the soles, their little eyes sunk deep in folds of wrinkles, reflected the blue of the sky" (2.17). As Hatsue talks with the other diving women, "A piece of green, transparent seaweed fell from her hair to the dazzling sand" (13.140). Visiting Greece, Mishima found that "The Greeks believed in the exterior and that was a noble philosophy" (Nathan 115). In the island of this novel, value exists on the surface, not in the depths visited by the divers or the lofty pinnacle of the lighthouse. A diving woman had recently perished, some said because she had seen below the waves what humans are not meant to see (8.68). These depths, which belong to the feminine, represent the islanders' most primitive fears in nature's least-known regions.

In the lighthouse, all is neat and bright, as befits the only place with electric lights after the village generator went out (1.9). But the lighthouse represents the modern excess of intellect. The keeper's wife, a former teacher, parrots miscellaneous information—the doings of film stars, the location of famous opera houses. Chiyoko, the keeper's daughter, attends the university in the city, where she has come to know about love in movies and novels (7.59) and where she has learned to absorb information, such as a list of Victorian women poets, none of whom she has read. Moving from lighthouse to lighthouse, the family has no home. Chiyoko displays the rootless modern's lofty arrogance toward people dependent on nature. Shinji, however, she loves in secret.

Such characters add actuality to the novel's romance structures; they amplify the sense of a living society, of young people as belonging to families and peer groups. Fidelity to social details in Japan means adjusting Longus's male-female mutuality to account for the realities of a largely patriarchal village. Mishima develops the feminine in several ways. Shinji and Hiroshi have only a mother to head their family. A self-appointed committee of village women, headed by the lighthouse keeper's wife, sways Hatsue's father to allow the couple's marriage. While they confer with the formidable shipowner his hands are "toying with a fan showing a picture of a beautiful woman advertising a drugstore" (15.173)—an image of the masculine fantasy's submissive woman comically at odds with the immediate pressure of the collective feminine will.

An episode that goes far to compensate for stretches of isolated masculinity (Shinji on the merchant ship, Hiroshi with his playmates) occurs in chapter 13, which is exclusively centered in the diving women at their tasks. Hatsue has already undergone a rite of passage in courage, since all young girls in this trade have to overcome their fear of the depths—"the strangling feeling of running out of breath, the inexpressible agony when water forced its way under the water-goggles" (135). The older divers—"those who had husbands"—pursue their trade, by contrast, in a spirit of play, with a light-heartedness that the younger ones envy. Into the midst of these women, cheerfully comparing their naked breasts as they dry themselves at a beach fire, walks an old peddler (a former grade-school principal fired for sexual misconduct), who acts as judge in a spontaneous abalone-gathering contest. As a prize he offers one of his "stylish" plastic purses—an object that recalls the many humble prizes in contests of pastoral literature.[8] Winning the contest, Hatsue hands the purse over to Shinji's mother, who finishes second. Her generosity overcomes the friction existing between her lover's mother and her own father. In this way, concludes the narrator, the "politics of the island" were always managed. If Mishima departs from Longus's romance in advertising the hero's courage, he takes pains to give the heroine a strong measure of virtue as well.

A MILDEWED STORY

The Homeric scholar Cedric H. Whitman provides an epigraph on the matter of recycled stories: "There is, in one sense, no such thing as a good story; there are only serviceable stories from which meaning can be built" (15). Does the core narrative of idyllic romance contain something of value in essential humanity? Or, if the "essential" is disallowed, does it perform cultural work in the way a "serviceable" story should? Is the idyllic plot a recurring infantile dream of escaping from history, from suffering, necessity, duty? The scorner of idylls (including some who have written them, like Mishima) may find them escapist, may see their eroticism as self-indulgent or narcissistic (as is at least arguable in the 1980s *Blue Lagoon* movies or in Pierre Louÿs's Hellenic sex fantasies, *Chansons de Bilitis*).

The charge of counterrealism or antinaturalism, though, does not account for the important role of natural contingency in the plots, however unnatural the paradises might be. Longus excels among Greek romancers in organizing his stories around nature rather than chance. All the Greek romances except *Daphnis and Chloe* exist in what M. M. Bakhtin calls "adventuristic time" (95), lacking in "any natural, everyday cyclicity" (91).[9] Foregrounding the cycle of nature, Longus avoids the regimen of tychê found in the other Greek plots. Some things do happen by chance (the intrusion of Lycaenion, for instance), but most events respond to nature. "Natural cyclicity" determines the winter visit, harvest time, even the war (resulting from a chain of events that begins with a hungry goat). Whether or not his setting really represents Lesbos, Longus communicates, to the Renaissance and beyond, a sense of life in nature that is rare in other ancient romances. He helps reshape the conventions of romance from its medieval contours to introduce an unaccustomed sympathy between the human and the natural.

The story of a couple's self-discovery through love in nature seems less common now than it was a century ago. Recently the meaning of nature has entwined itself with the political and biological consequences of civilized exploitation. In two 1980s novels set on Mauritius that are echoes of *Paul et Virginie*—J.-M. G. Le Clézio's *Le Chercheur d'or* (published in English translation as *The Prospector*) and Geneviève Dormann's *Le Bal du dodo*—Europe has uprooted Eden. Le Clézio's couple grows up on the island near a great tree that they call "the tree of good and evil" (140). A hurricane sweeps away their home, ending the childhood idyll as the narrator is drawn into an aimless life that includes the horrors of the Great War, while his sister, several times associated with Virginie, devotes herself to social work. The wanderer, "le chercheur," attempts a primitive life with an island woman who, like Hudson's Rima, mysteriously appears and vanishes, ridiculing his quest for gold. He can never settle, nor can his sister leave her island.

Dormann's *Le Bal du dodo*, winner of the French Academy's Grand Prix du Roman in 1989—while more exacting in its analysis of postcolonial society and while transcending the nostalgia of Le Clézio's novel—still leaves us with divided lovers and divided souls. "The Dodo's Ball" is the New Year's Eve gala for a Franco-Mauritian society, whose members are as flightless and stupid as their patron bird. Much of the novel surveys the island's past, which the heroine, Bénie, pieces together from old newspapers, letters, and diaries. Her "Paul" is her near-twin cousin, Vivian, her inseparable companion in childhood and her lover in adolescence. During a storm they take shelter in an abandoned lodge. Bénie remembers that Vivian's mother, catching them in a passionate embrace, sundered them with a broom in much the same way that the angel drove Adam and Eve from Eden with a flaming brand. After "the abomination" (105) the family ships Bénie and Vivian off to schools on different continents. In Africa, Vivian discovers his homosexuality, while Bénie, studying in France, eventually marries a respectable Frenchman, having refashioned herself into "a simple, plain woman, without a history" (196)—in other words, an idyllic woman, another Virginie.

In Bénie's absence from the island, her love for it grows more acute. When her grandmother dies and leaves Bénie her home, Bénie returns to the island—here the novel opens, the plane becoming a satirical ship of state with Bénie speaking up for the rights of the nonwhites aboard. Soon she undertakes research on her family history, beginning with an ancestor who arrived on Mauritius in 1768—the same year as Bernardin. There, he found a place "cruelly different from the Eldorado that the young man was expecting" (267). The critical moment of Mauritian history comes with the inhabitants' surrender to the one-crop agricultural economy of sugar, a commodity produced since 1830 by Bénie's male ancestors. Modern Mauritius, having lost most of its agriculture, now depends heavily on the tourist trade, on "dish towels imprinted with Paul and Virginie" (314). Economic history is thus interwoven with an account of the family patriarchate, who must take much of the blame for the island's setbacks.

While the men in Bénie's family have a history of succumbing to the lure of powerful women, the women in this family live at their best without men. These women, like those in *Paul et Virginie*, find private ways to circumvent masculine dominance in public affairs. Bénie's father married an English baronet's daughter, Maureen Oakwood, who bathes naked in the lagoon at night and otherwise scandalizes the French. Although a disastrous mother, Maureen retains a hold on her daughter's mind with her eccentric independence. Bénie's grandmother, having shaped her in her childhood, draws her back to the island with the legacy of her house. The nurse, Laurencia, is a sage of folk magic and plants. Bénie's great grandmother never read anything except *Paul et Virginie*, even though her lover (named Paul) called it "a miserable trifle, an inanity" (289). Male-female conflict runs deep in this family's history.

Dormann retains features of traditional pastoral, while at the same time questioning its premises. Hints of Edenic nature appear when Vivian's lover, Stéphan, befriends a tiger shark that enters the lagoon to be fed by hand. Does this mean that homoeroticism brings harmony to a world torn by male-female passion, or is it an obviously tall tale that betrays its unlikeliness merely in the telling? *Le Bal du dodo* begins as a pastoral text in the way of Milton's *Lycidas*, "Yet once more" [Une fois de plus]; it ends with the two cousins reunited, Vivian declaring that "they will never separate you and me." If their relationship can survive Vivian's capriciousness (does he find in her merely a source of material support?), they may indeed be together always, but if this is the case, theirs will be a friendship without passion. In a way, Bernardin's matriarchy furnishes the germ for this novel of pastoral skepticism, but the work is nourished by the feminist and postcolonial critique of culture ongoing at least since 1960, the date of Dormann's first novel, *La Fanfaronne*, a love story partly set in Algeria during the war. Published in English translation as *The Seasons of Love*, the work was well received in the United States, the author being compared favorably with Françoise Sagan.

These echoes of Bernardin follow other postwar literature in representing humanity as alienated from peaceable nature. Thus an authentic naturelover like the Canadian Fred Bodsworth in *The Sparrow's Fall* (1967) writes a survival story of a couple whose conversion to Christianity has driven them to the no-man's land between tribe and white society. The novel regards theism and naturalism, which are more or less synonymous in Lesbos or in Hémon's Canada, as irreconcilable opposites. Solitary labor to survive in the wilderness is, of course, a well-worked theme in literature since 1945, but Bodsworth takes up the rarer situation of two lovers isolated from the close ties of a traditional society. While the story of the male survivor-in-nature continues to have its appeal (as evidenced by James Dickey's *Deliverance*, for example), more recent American fiction has seen the development of the "female pastoral," featuring solitary women, or a community of women, struggling with nature in various novels that "share a vision of rural female autonomy" (Harrison 12).

The initiation story of the lone female or male responds to a range of desires (to prove oneself, say, or to take one's place in the community) quite unlike that of the couple searching for identity in one another. And in the twentieth century the couple need not be sexual opposites. Andre Gide's novella *La Symphonie pastorale* (1919) presents a love triangle among a blind girl, a Swiss pastor who rescues her from neglect as an orphan, and the pastor's son. The male-female love story here partly disguises Gide's own love affair with Marc Allégret, the son of an actual pastor. Truman Capote takes another path around sexual difference in his semiautobiographical novel *The Grass Harp* (1951), which in 1952 enjoyed a brief run as a play in New York and in 1996 became a movie. In Capote's work, the couple is an adolescent boy and a postmenopausal woman (a character whom Capote based on his spinster cousin). Bearing the venerable pastoral name Collin, the boy is being cared for by his two aunts—the slightly scatterbrained Aunt Dolly, whom he loves, and the rigid, business-like Aunt Verena. One summer Collin and Dolly escape for a sojourn in the tree house that serves as their island. Though their story is not centered in romantic love, the deep affection of this innocently naive pair, combined with their episodes of self-discovery, still locates Capote's work within the idyllic romance tradition. Dolly's inseparable friend Catherine—an outspoken woman of African and American Indian origin who has a penchant for secret natural remedies—provides the primitive spirit in this southern pastoral world. The novel expresses the commitment to the private life characteristic of pastoral: "No matter what passions compose them, all private worlds are good, they are never vulgar places" (4.51). The grass harp—the wind rushing through the tall Indian grass below the local cemetery—provides the natural music for the boy and older woman's private world. The grass "knows the stories of all the people on the hill" (1.9), and the act of narration merges the boy-woman couple into this knowledge. What Yourcenar said of *The Sound of Waves* also applies to *The Grass Harp*: it is the author's once-in-a-lifetime happy novel.

Like the narrator in Longus or in Theocritus, the narrator Collin now belongs to the city, though he can recall warm rural experiences, the "famous landscapes of youth and woodland water," that he now sees only "trailing through the cold rooms of museums" (5.72). The retrospective view can understandably lead one to read *The Grass Harp* as "a pastoral elegy to irrevocable innocence" (Hassan 250), but this is to overlook the joy of the novel. A more solid point of contact with ancient pastoral in this novel is Judge Cool, who reads Greek every morning before breakfast and woos Aunt Dolly as "a spirit, a pagan" (3.49). Both the Judge and Collin-narrator are preoccupied with the uncalculating, loving, female pastoral figure Dolly. She displays innocent openness in all matters, though in "all natural things Dolly was sophisticated" (1.14). At the novel's end, after Dolly's funeral, when older and younger man briefly reunite, Dolly becomes a nymphlike spirit moving across the Indian grass.

A more fully human character than Dolly, Judge Cool has searched for love and innocence ever since his wife died, early in their marriage. He speaks of having "surrendered myself to strangers—men who disappeared down the gangplank, got off at the next station" (3.41). A few years earlier his quest has led to a strange episode when, happening upon a children's magazine, he began a pen-pal correspondence with a young girl in Alaska, pretending to be a boy her age. The counterfeit letters, like the one-night stands, partake of the search for a soul mate, "a person to whom everything can be said," and the wish to stop "hiding"—"afraid as we are of being identified" (3.41). Here Capote introduces his own plight as a gay man in a homophobic society, suggesting that the special American fixation on innocence—which existed at least until the past few decades—may reveal itself most deeply in stories of this kind. On reflection, the love story of the boy and older woman masks the admiration, sympathy, and love that Collin holds for the more believable character in the story, the older man.

A particular tree marks the lovers' meeting place in many idyllic romances (such as those by Hémon, Chase, Hardy). In *The Grass Harp* it is the broad "china tree," or chinaberry, with its old tree-house platform where Collin, Dolly, the Judge, and others gather for a few days and nights. Calling this a "raft in the tree" brings to mind Huck and Jim's fugitive vessel; it is a place where Collin could "sail along the cloudy coastline of every dream" (1.16–17). In contrast, a half-sunken houseboat sits in a nearby river, once belonging to an old white man who wanted to marry a young black woman and spend his days fishing—the townspeople would not hear of it. The juxtaposed tree house and boat represent voyages of innocence and love taken in imagination, where "all private worlds are good." When the sheriff, set on by Verena, tries to dislodge the dreamers from their tree house, Dolly asks in her usual tone of prelapsarian dismay, "is it that after all the world is a bad place?" (4.50). The Judge will later answer affirmatively, looking "at once his age, autumnal, bare" (4.56). Critics who have faulted Capote for taking refuge in dreams and fantasy simply ignore his assumptions about the need at some point to create private worlds against "the world."[10] This is surely in line with Stowe's "history of the inner life," a life offered without irony, in risky earnestness.

Capote sets before us a small southern town where people's grotesqueness results from their inability to reconcile their sordid lives with their longing for innocence. An apt symbol is a huge deputy with a babyish voice, his throat once torn by a mad dog. A relevant incident is the story of Collin's friend Riley, who as a boy of ten saved his little sisters from their insane mother's attempt, one Christmas morning, to drown them in the bathtub. The gold fraternity ring that Catherine found cleaning a hog's intestine may be merely a whimsy, but it may also signify the ironic implications, at many levels, of "fraternity." Innocence and the grotesque meet in Little Homer Honey, a child evangelist who does rope tricks. He and his fourteen siblings, all from different fathers, travel with their mother, Sister Ida, in her lifelong quest for love, which is sparked by her passion for her sister's husband—one man has the same freckles, another the same eyes. Yet Ida is also a natural life-force. "I can't get on," she confesses, "without another life kicking under my heart" (5.76). Her family's shows, combining God with carnival, stand in opposition to the mean, conventional religiosity of Mr. and Mrs. Buster, the preacher and his wife, who urge the attack on the tree house.

In recent literary history the innocence envisioned in Capote's world seems to have become a scarce condition. Fiction since 1945 tends to exchange "the problem of evil" for "the problem of innocence," as if the world's enormities call into question the possibility of a guiltless life, even among children. Recall the "abomination," as Vivian's mother refers to it, between Dormann's kindred pair. Three examples may illustrate the range of modern aversion to idyllic innocence, ranging from bitter to mildly comic irony.

Jeux interdits (*Forbidden Games*), the French film of 1951, is a nightmare reprise of the childhood idyll that replaces Dionysos with Death as the presiding deity. The foundling Paulette, her parents killed in a Nazi strafing, seduces Michel, the son of her new peasant family, into a cult not of nature but of the funereal. René Clément, adapting the story by François Boyer, foregrounds the Christian cross as principal icon of the death culture. The secret animal cemetery at the mill parodies the cave of the nymphs as meeting place; the children's solitary rambles in the countryside are filmed as classic idyllic gestures. The requisite erotic scenes occur also at the mill, between Michel's older sister and her boyfriend. This adolescent couple's quarrelsome senex-fathers inflict far more family misery than Chloe's father, however. Little Paulette, raised in ignorance of religion by Parisian parents, delights in the rituals of death, while Michel, his family's religious expert because he can recite all the prayers, enjoys having a convert. (By presenting Rousseauistic, insightful children in a world of stupid adults, the film's anthropology paradoxically supports religious orthodoxy.) The film's deepest ironies originate not so much in death-affirming as life-denying qualities, detailed in a country setting worthy of George Sand. When a member of Michel's family slowly dies from a farming accident, the children's quiet, eager curiosity about death matters less, in moral consequence, than the skinflint patriarch's refusal to pay money for a doctor. Predictably, the film ends not in self-discovery but in disunion and alienation.

For its ironies, *Forbidden Games* depends on popular notions about pastoral life that conflict with its realist premises. In the United States, confidence in nature's nurturing must compete with a similar realism in the pioneer memories of nature's mindless discipline. American georgic pours acid on anything savoring of Arcadianism. Examples occur in such serious regional fiction as the novels of the North Carolina writer John Ehle. *The*

Land Breakers (1964) covers the lives of a few frontier settlers from 1779 to 1784 in the register of classic georgic realism. When his first wife dies, Mooney Wright considers marrying the ready-witted but immature Pastorella of the neighborhood. Instead, however, he chooses Lorry, "a pretty woman, and quick to work" (86). Work Lorry does, in the absorbing accounts of the sheer labor of daily life then, such as the ordeal of wool preparation (107)—it's a book that makes you want to go out and cut the grass. Into the settlement come Paul and Nancy Larkins, lighthearted newlyweds who will soon taste the fruits of their carefree outlook on the wilderness. They unknowingly build their cabin with the hearth beside a snake hole, and once they are snug in bed the fire's heat draws a roomful of venomous reptiles. Idyllic love vanishes when Paul dies from their bites and Nancy goes insane. Yet men and women alike live in such hard circumstances in this world that georgic seems about as unprofitable as pastoral. At the end, when Mooney and his boys begin another spring planting, it's hard to know whether to hope or to cry.

The Land Breakers begins a historical series by Ehle centering on the Wright family. In a later installment, *Winter People* (1982), a newly bereft father seeking work in the Depression courts a young back-country woman, a Mooney Wright descendant. An ambassador of the machine age, he builds the town a church clock, bringing social renewal and clock-minding to a desolate spot. Ehle's fiction sustains a strong sense of place, and as in many American novels of this kind, the work of progress must not yield to such idyllic, time-insensitive values as leisure, sufficiency, or nostalgia.

Yet a third response to idyllic innocence in modern, especially European, fiction subjects it to comic, even absurdist treatment. The stereotyped young lovers Chloe and Colin in Boris Vian's *L'Ecume des jours* gaily inhabit an artificial world without a sheep in sight. Nature, the lily growing in Chloe's chest, destroys; nurture comes only through artifice—it takes human body warmth to make the gun barrels grow out of the ground. Measuring the comic difference between past innocence and present, Friedrich Dürrenmatt makes his mismatched couple of *Grieche sucht Griechin* (published in English as *Once a Greek . . .*) plan a honeymoon to Greece while sitting before a mildewed statue of Daphnis and Chloe. Arnolph Archilochos is a bookkeeper of Greek origin, even though his last real Greek ancestor fought beside Charles the Bold at the battle of Nancy. Chloé Sa-

Ioniki, his beloved, once a child-refugee from Greece, answers Arnolph's newspaper ad for a wife. Unknown to Arnolph, the beautiful Chloé is an expensive whore whose marriage is being sponsored by several leading-citizen clients, including the president. The fairy tale shatters when Arnolph discovers the truth and nearly becomes a presidential assassin. He finally decides to take the good luck of having found a reformed woman prepared (apparently) to be a good wife. Whether as fable or novel, the story's hints at idyllic romance constitute a more cheerful version of the irony in *Forbidden Games*. If the world ever had the requisite innocence for Arcadia, that time is long past—hence, perhaps, the naive Arnolph's association with a medieval ancestor.

The interplay of wit and innocence in *Once a Greek . . .* takes us back to the age of Marvell and Marivaux. Dürrenmatt writes of innocence in a world that trades on beauty and ideals as commodities. Yet fools and whores still dream of the pristine world faintly visible in mildewed statues. Recognizing the nature of things does bring the couple both a foreseeably happy marriage and a measure of self-knowledge, but the story's very improbability seems to indicate that Cold War Europe looked coolly upon idyllic endings.

Faced with the need to draw conclusions from the large range of material covered in this book, I am consoled by Edmund Burke's maxim that a clear idea is a little idea. In coping with the imponderables of love, nature, and innocence, we could add that a clear idea is also a forced idea. A historical summary is more appealing. If George Sand had written her projected study of the "uninterrupted series of pastorals" in the history of art, she would have lingered for some time in the Renaissance. Alongside the renewal of the pastoral eclogue, the romance of lovers in nature accelerates when the West discovers *Daphnis and Chloe*.

Idyllic romance enters literary history first as a valued complement to the already thriving Virgilian pastoral tradition: it extends the range of pastoral from lyric to narrative and drama; it provides a narrative centered, unlike the eclogues of Virgil, on the experience of courtship and wedded love. Yet Renaissance adapters seem unable to translate the two lovers as authentic rural youths, both male and female on an equal footing. As a result, Longus's excessively rustic lovers get mixed up with the more familiar errant aristocrat and country girl (or boy) of the pastourelle tradition. The comic spirit of Longus's romance also cannot quite survive after contact with established European romance, characteristically inhabited by destroyer-heroes, cruel love, Eros and Thanatos. Poets contemplate nature in a spirit either of melancholy (because nature is lost in the Fall or in social upheaval), or of skepticism (as in seventeenth-century witty excursions into pastoral), or of idealism (most famously in *Paradise Lost*).

In the later eighteenth century, consistent with Samuel Johnson's dictum that romance should strive to "increase prudence without impairing virtue" (*Rambler* no. 4), idealistic love stories in nature vie with witty or parodistic stories of rural fools and disguised aristocrats. With Gessner, Florian, and Bernardin, a cultivated, naive idyllicism opens a vein of elegiac reflection in sympathy with the Rousseauistic search for nature. During this period of idealism, echoing through Sand and Valera, lovers return to a relationship of mutuality rarely seen in the Renaissance: actual landscapes replace generalized settings—real places dear to the author and conveyed as such in the narrative. After Darwin, in the mid–nineteenth century, natural determinism restores the Pan-ic threat of an overpowering nature that either can destroy love and personal identity or can direct readers in sympathy with nature toward a recovered wise innocence—if, that is, any way into nature exists, a doubt that haunts some of the most recent examples of the tradition.

Endless literary forms, themes, and motifs have woven their way through the novel over time, independent of such extraliterary influences as theories of biological determinism. By the end of the twentieth century the fiction of love in nature can take the form of survival narrative, nature utopia, return to paradise, family saga, georgic, anthropological romance-of-the-other, adolescent comedy, naturalistic tragedy, pastoral satire, pastoral of the self, summer excursion, autumnal elegy. Familiar qualities of idyllic romance may surface, recede, and reemerge for a page or several chapters at a time. The relative scarcity of pure idyllic romance nowadays perhaps means nothing, since the universal fiction factory is constantly and unpredictably fusing and separating parts and retooling itself. What remains is the theme, the "desire for union or merger, both physical and emotional" without which romantic love cannot exist (Harris 102), grounded in a world undistracted by civilization.

A novel that most wittily recombines and recreates the traditional idyllic elements is Bruce Chatwin's *On the Black Hill* (1982), about twin boys who grow to old age as shepherds in the Radnorshire borderlands in Wales. From one perspective, their home remains unspotted by the outside world. On the day Hitler's war ends, the local front-page headline reads: "51½ lb. Salmon Grassed at Coleman's Pool: Brigadier Tells of 3-Hour Struggle with Titanic Fish." Britain still has her demiparadises, even in 1945. Yet one theme of this novel by a great travel writer must be that private enclaves never escape the outsider's touch. Benjamin and Lewis Jones's mother was raised in India, and despite her long life in Radnorshire, that experience subtly shapes her and her family. World War I draws one of the twins into uniform and misery as an object of cruelty and abuse. In World War II, the night of the Coventry raid, Benjamin, seeing a red glow in the sky, exclaims, "And a good job 'tisn't we!" (183), then returns to bed. This scene typifies the many moments when the author's wit is imposed on a character's innocence. The absurdity speaks for itself, however endearing. "We" soon includes a German prisoner forced to work on the twins' farm, dubbed "The Vision," but quickly accepted as a friend and advisor, visiting the Joneses after the war. Even the Beat Generation comes to the farm when Theo, an Afrikaner immigrant turned Buddhist, lives there in a tent and enjoys quoting *As You Like It*: "Who doth ambition shun, / And loves to live i'the sun."[11]

Shakespearean pastoral and the Bible belong in a region suffused with sheep. Turn-of-the-century Radnorshire farmers prefer the Old Testament over the New Testament because in the former, "there were many more stories about sheep-farming" (33). Benjamin and Lewis "always recognized their affinity with twin lambs" (45). Their neighbor Jim comes to love his sheep so much that he cannot send them to market. Like Jeffers's shepherdess, he treats them as friends; the flock grows decrepit; the farmyard fills up with sheep graves. An artist, Nigel, wants to sketch the brothers at work for a series of etchings he will call "The Sheep Farmer's Year," to be graced with a sonnet for each month. The twins' mother's favorite author is Thomas Hardy (she especially loves his *Woodlanders*), whose shepherds' lives cause her to identify Wessex with her own Radnor Hills.

The presence of Hardy, the Bible, and Shakespeare needs no argument, but the claims of idyllic romance also surface in the resemblance between this story of identical twins and Sand's *La Petite Fadette*, especially regarding the brothers' sexual inclinations. Lewis, like Landry, is the conventional pastoral lover. From the age of ten he hankers after Rosie, but later, in her teens, she enters service as a chambermaid to the wealthy Bickertons, whose son eventually leaves her pregnant and alone. End of idyll, end of pastourelle. After other loves, but never a wife, Lewis comes to suspect his mother and brother of conspiring to keep him a bachelor. Like Sand's Sylvinet, Benjamin acquires feminine traits in boyhood. He secretly tries on his mother's clothes and perfume; he enjoys mothering Lewis; he wants to live with Lewis always, "to eat the same food, wear the same clothes, share a bed" (88). Like Sylvinet, Benjamin is raised protected by his mother in privileged idleness while Lewis works hard. Young Lewis must leave home, as Landry did, to work on a nearby farm, helping to support his family. Benjamin nearly faints on hearing they will be separated, recalling Sylvinet's fits of illness whenever it looks as if he will have to live apart from his brother.

One more bit of evidence exists that Chatwin had been reading *Fadette*. He studied case histories of identical twins in one of the standard works on the subject by René Zazzo, *Les Jumeaux, le couple, et la personne*, and he even conferred with Zazzo while writing the novel. He would not have overlooked the French scholar's citing *Fadette* as one of the most noteworthy novels about twins and love (see Zazzo 485).[12] Although the absence of a Fadette or Chloe distances this novel from the idyllic romance tradition, the twins' biological status creates a "two as one" relationship that engages the conventional themes of identity and quest for completion in the other (Zazzo's title translates as "twins, the couple, and the person"). A salient image of Chatwin's novel is the imprint of bodies in the old men's beds, side by side, the very beds where their parents had slept.

This deeper meditation on identity frames and sets off what John Updike, in his *New Yorker* review, calls the "mosaic" of *On the Black Hill*. Since the novel might also be seen as a cleverly assembled series of snapshots, he might also have called it an idyll, in the "little picture" sense. Each life in the brothers' lives has its own story: an irascible father, a lonely and odd old woman, a venal lawyer, a legacy-hunting nephew—a community of people being born, growing old, living idiosyncratic lives but without tragedy, suicide, high romance, or the other stuff of traditional British rural fiction. Rosie, the childhood sweetheart, is finally just an event in Lewis's life and in the twins' community, where she lives on with her illegitimate son. No wedding ends the story, as it does in Sand's *Fadette*, because the story does not end: even when one ancient twin dies in a mishap, the other lives on. Change comes, but imperceptibly or in short bursts, with a death or an unexpected visitor; even the permanence of nature—the land, the flocks, the hills—is partly illusion. Still, this realistic story had the power in the 1980s to fix and celebrate a place as fully realized as Sand's Berry, Hardy's Wessex, Cather's prairie, or Hémon's Quebec. *On the Black Hill* continued to find acclaim as a play (1986) and a film (1987).

Jo-Ann Mapson's suggestively titled *Hank and Chloe* (1993), with a stronger claim to idyllic romancehood, resembles *On the Black Hill* in its cast of idiosyncratic characters and its authentic sense of place, here the American desert Southwest. No mosaic, this represents the lives of two people during the several months that they travel on their way to loving union: Hank, a junior-college mythology and folklore teacher, and Chloe, a breaker of horses. Much prevents this first novel from sinking into formula romance: Mapson's playfulness with Longus's story; the comic juxtaposition of a tough, life-battered Western woman with an aimless young academic; the author's characteristically American insistence on the retrieval of identity in a rebirth of innocence. In Chatwin's fictive world, innocence merely defines a faintly amusing stage of life: when Lewis admits, in his seventies, to a boyhood dream of marrying Nancy Bickerton, Nancy laughs, "He has grown up. What are we waiting for?" (218). Perhaps for this reason, Mapson's world, compared with Chatwin's, seems oblivious to history, tightly focused on the couple. The heroine is orphaned in early childhood; the hero is cut off from his spiritual parent—his dead grandmother, on whose Arizona ranch he experienced during his boyhood summers the only happiness of his life.

While wearing her learning almost not at all, Mapson updates several episodes of *Daphnis and Chloe*, in addition to employing the motifs of the foundling and the recovery of origins. Hughville, Chloe's community, hardly more than a collection of shacks and mobile homes in the boondocks, contains a miscellaneous citizenry including illegal immigrants, presided over by a pleasantly dissolute rancher. The "war" that sends them all into captivity (in the local jail) or exile (for the illegals) is a drug bust concocted by a sheriff in league with a corporation seeking the land for development. As Chloe watches Daphnis bathing after they have rescued and revived an errant goat, Chloe and Hank shower together after finding and doctoring Chloe's battered lost dog—though this Chloe does more than admire the male body. Hank shares not only Daphnis's readiness to cry in a crisis but also his resourcefulness in winning Chloe back when she is lost to him. Chloe's birth token, a symbol of both identity and innocence, pops up at various points: a photograph of herself at age two on a toy horse. Although she never finds her mother, she takes her place by the end of the story, first by mothering Kit, her boss's daughter, from childhood into adolescence and then by following her mother's example and choosing to have the baby by Hank that she is now carrying. With her faithful dog (identified as a "shepherd"), Chloe leaps into her pickup and tracks down Hank, who has left his stuffy parents and the college to restore his grandmother's Arizona ranch.

Read in the context of some works discussed earlier—*O Pioneers!*, *Shepherd of the Hills*, *The Loving Shepherdess*—Hank and Chloe fits into an American pattern, with its absent fathers, its lighting-out-for-the-territories, and its turning away from the destroyer, civilization. Despite Chloe's apparent toughness (and a resilience that may strain credibility), the heroine sustains the narrative's attachment to nature—to horses and dogs, in particular—resisting the cruelty of men with a force of sentiment absent from the cool, detached voice of Chatwin's narrator. Mapson uses some of the deeper mythic resonance of the name Chloe to support this feeling, as Hank early links the name with "one of the personas of Demeter—wasn't she the 'green' one, the caretaker of young crops?" (49). Demeter and Persephone exert as much influence over this novel as Daphnis and Chloe. Mapson's Chloe is a Persephone, relegated to an underworld of loss, waste, sterility. The novel begins with the loss of a mare that has just foaled. Chloe's own health is so marginal that she usually misses her period. "Developers" in this underworld destroy; homelessness and disrupted families are the rule. The reform-school boys whom Chloe teaches to ride in the country represent a truly lost generation's last chance at entering nature. When these jaded boys find spontaneous delight during their hours outdoors, Mapson reminds her readers of the wisdom of nature's recovered innocence.

Such wisdom is earned by the couple in Ursula Le Guin's fantasy novel with a drably realistic frame, *The Beginning Place* (1980). Le Guin suggests a possible future of idyllic romance in which a renewed male-female complementarity helps to renew nature itself. In a society cluttered with cars, all-night supermarkets, TV ethics, and TV dinners, two young people have separately discovered a parallel world resembling the traditional societies of European folk and fairy tales. Irene first discovers the secret "beginning place" as a girl in a dysfunctional family; Hugh comes along later in a momentary escape from his bullying, divorced mother and his dead-end job. The "beginning place" translates as "genesis" and recalls the imagined enclaves in so many stories of this kind, places where time seems magically changed: Hudson's forest, Nerval's Druid-haunted landscape, Prospero's island. The fact of Irene's prior discovery (at thirteen she began performing fire worship and "the endless dance") seems to link her, like Mapson's Chloe, with the ecofeminist premise that "from a historical perspective, woman has been associated with nature"—an association that "has led to the domination and exploitation of woman and nature as resources in patriarchal society" (Devine 29). Yet the monster that terrorizes Mountain Town, threatening to destroy this natural society, is also female (a giantess bearing some resemblance to Hugh's nagging mother).[13] Oneness with nature belongs to the male experience, too. After Irene tries to banish him from her secret place, Hugh washes his face in the clear creek water. "'This is my home,' he said to the earth and rocks and trees, and with his lips almost on the water, whispered, 'I am you. I am you'" (55).

In Mountain Town, people have such jobs as shepherding or stonecutting; in real life Hugh works as a supermarket checker, his mother as a loan company clerk, Irene as an "errandperson" for Mott and Zerming—"You never really *do* anything. Go and go and get nowhere" (167). Hugh's father abandoned him and his mother (for Canada) years earlier. Hugh recalls that they have moved thirteen times in the past seven years: "and the oftener she moves, he thought, the more she doesn't get anywhere" (59). More than anything else, stillness and silence define the natural life as distinct from a world of confused noise and aimless motion. In *The Beginning Place* time literally stops, just as human time does (according to Shakespeare's Touchstone), in the forest. The lovers are not only half-orphans but foundlings in being without a guide, virtually lost souls in the lonely crowd. Hugh discovers himself in the way of heroes in Spenser or medieval chivalric romance, battling with the dragon—he is even called "Saint George" at one point (134). The episode also brings Irene her new identity: "I have passed the place of the dragon and I can't go back. . . . I was the daughter, but it's gone. Now I'm only the dragon's daughter and the king's child, the one that has to go alone, go on, because there is no home behind me" (160). Le Guin joins the medieval quest theme and the pastoral "beginning place," with its lovers' shared self-discovery. Ancient pastoral's ludic inquiry into the priorities of art and nature becomes a serious meditation on human survival, which will probably be a concern of any idyllicism for years to come, though Le Guin admirably circumvents the easy resolution of melancholy withdrawal.

A final point can be made about the service performed at a fundamental level in this story pattern, which combines uniquely the experiences of nature, childhood, and love. When Irene calls herself the dragon's daughter, she remembers her initial hostility toward Hugh when he first intruded into her space. Then, she was the solitary, outraged Amazon. Love, coming not at first sight but somehow bound up with Hugh's significant act, changed her. "With love," says Kenelm Burridge, "the assertion to autonomy is invited to realize itself through others" (35). The experiences of adolescence and puberty "reflect physical birth as moral rebirth" so that this stage becomes the type of many possible rebirths (34). Le Guin's social concerns —about family, environment, the plight of youth—may sound very contemporary, but her theme continues an old American quest to redeem and reconcile the values of love and innocence with the experience of nature. As long as beginning places exist, beginnings are possible.

NOTES

1. IDYLLIC ROMANCE

1. Dans les temps où le mal vient de ce que les hommes se méconnaissent et se détestent, la mission de l'artiste est de célébrer la douceur, la confiance, l'amitié, et de rappeler ainsi aux hommes endurcis ou découragés, que les moeurs pures, les sentiments tendres et l'équité primitive, sont ou peuvent être encore de ce monde. . . . [M]ieux vaut . . . un conte pour endormir les petits enfants sans frayeur et sans souffrance, que le spectacle des maux réels renforcés et rembrunis encore par les couleurs de la fiction.

2. Schiller himself writes: "The poets are everywhere, as their very name suggests, the *guardians* of nature. Where they can no longer quite be so and have already felt within themselves the destructive influence of arbitrary and artificial forms [such as cities] or have had to struggle with them, then they will appear as the *witnesses* and *avengers* of nature. They will either *be* nature, or they will *seek* lost nature" (*Naive* 106). Juliet Sychrava has argued persuasively in *Schiller to Derrida: Idealism in Aesthetics* (Cambridge: Cambridge UP, 1989) that "naive" and "sentimental" are historically determined categories rather than transcendental ones—a position that does not exclude, I think, my own use of Schiller, which at any rate has to do with a type of the "sentimental."

3. In addition to Hagstrum's *Esteem*, which is an encyclopedic survey of couples showing continuing ideals of love from the Greeks to Shakespeare, a relevant work is Allan Bloom's *Love and Friendship* (New York: Simon, 1993), which perhaps distinguishes too sharply between its title concepts. On the supposed end of the novel of love, see Gornick.

4. Convincing evidence for the influence of "Orphic-Dionysiac" theology in Longus is marshaled in H. H. O. Chalk, "Eros and the Lesbian Pastorals of Longos," *Journal of Hellenic Studies* 80 (1960): 32–51. A full commentary from this perspective is Reinhold Merkelbach, *Die Hirten des Dionysos: Die Dionysos-Mysterium der römischen Kaiserzeit und der bukolische Roman des Longus* (Stuttgart: Teubner, 1988).

5. Colin Still's *Shakespeare's Mystery Play: A Study of "The Tempest"* (London: Palmer, 1921) was celebrated by G. Wilson Knight in his 1931 essay "Mystic Symbolism" (see Knight, *Shakespeare and Religion: Essays of Forty Years* [New York: Simon and Schuster, 1968] 65–68).

6. The patterning sometimes seems excessive—for example, in the *kai* and *kata-* ("down") repetitions in the funeral rites of Dorcon: "they also [kai] poured [katespeisan] milk as a libation, and [kai] pressed [katethlipsan] grapes, and [kai] broke [kateklasan] many pan-pipes" (*Daphnis and Chloe* 1.31).

7. On affinities between this romance and new comedy, see Erwin Rohde 504–05 and Hunter 67–71. The most obvious are recognition scenes and stock characters such as the prostitute and the parasite. Rohde believes (and he is echoed in most later Longus criticism) that after the breakdown of the polis in Greek civilization, attention was given more to private and personal affairs than to public life—a fact manifested in the rise of new comedy and romance. In *The Nature of Narrative* (New York: Oxford, 1966) Robert Scholes and Robert Kellogg say that Longus anticipates Henry Fielding in his desire to "bring romance back to the comic earth from which it originally sprang" (226).

8. In his chapter in *Constraints* titled "The Education of Chloe: Hidden Injuries of Sex" (101–26), Winkler says that the pain of sex, foretold by Lycaenion, shows that the charm of the relationship is deceptive (121) in "a sexual order that inexorably translates females into victims" (104). In "Junk Bonds and Corporate Raiders" (*Arion* 3rd ser. 1.2 [1991]: 139–212) Camille Paglia points to Winkler's neglect of "the brutal biological absolutism of sexual anatomy and sexual intercourse" as represented by the violent breaking of the soil in the ritual of the couple's wedding night (168–69). Winkler's Longus seems to think it a shame that men and women cannot be sexual equals; Paglia's Longus, at ease with sex, is unperturbed by woman's suffering.

9. Hagstrum provides ancient testimony supporting this view in his notes, 433–38.

10. In "A Typology of Ecphrases" (*Classical and Modern Languages* 13 [1993]: 103–16), Rodney Stenning Edgecombe notes the value of ecphrasis as a key to the author's sensibility. In Longus's prologue, one might point to the undifferentiated suffering and joy of the painting as a clue to the author's "pagan" naturalism. Taking a gendered approach in *Museum of Words: The Poetics of Ekphrasis from Homer to Ashbery* (Chicago: U of Chicago P, 1993) James A. W. Heffernan sees in it evidence of Longus's masculinity (55–57).

2. RENAISSANCE REDISCOVERIES

1. On the pastourelle and its origins, see Alfred Jeanroy, *Les Origines de la poésie lyrique en France au Moyen Age*, 4th ed. (Paris: Champion, 1965), 1–44, 515–17.

Jeanroy concludes that pastourelle, like pastoral wherever it occurs, is "l'amusement d'une societé élégante, qui se repose d'elle-même en sa travestissant sous un amiable costume" (38)—the elegant society in this case being that of Provençal aristocrats in the earlier twelfth century. Jeanroy emphasizes as the lyric heart of the pastourelle the debate between the knight and the maiden, so I take some liberty with the label in applying it just to the narrative situation.

2. Accepi nuper ex Bibliotheca ornatissimi viri Graecarumque literatum peritissimi, Aloisii Alamannii, inspicienda Longi Poemenica. Quae cum diligenter legissem, & cum doctis sane viris lectionem illam communicassem, ita nobis arridere coepit hic Auctor, tum ob sermonis puritatem atque elegantiam, tum ob materiae festivitatem, ut prope facinus nos admissuros fuisse duxerimus, si (quantum in nobis esset) huiusmodi opus diutius in tenebris delitesceret: praesertim cum scirem illud a studiosis vehementer desiderari.

The same delight was voiced by Heinsius, as quoted in Jungermann's Longus: there was "nothing simpler, nothing more charming" than *Daphnis and Chloe* (prelim. fol. 5).

3.
Daphnis ho pais ekeinos alla kai Chloê
triseutuchôs sunêpsan autous eis gamon.
Daphnis ekeinos ho glukus, poimên monon,
ou tôn erôtos adaês toxeumatôn,
philoumenos men, antiphilôn de pleon,
kai mêden eidôs tôn erôtôn ti pleon.
têi parthenôi Chloêi gar ek tôn spargamôn
erôtikon sunêpto sumpoimên brephos.
Tautês erôn ên tês aplastou parthenou,
hês pur men ên to blemma tôi neaniai,
logoi de toxa, kai periplokai belê.
Chrusoun genos pros philtron ên to prophthasan.
ho gar philêtheis antephilei meizonôs.
ouch hoion esti touto chalkeion genos.
philoumenon gar antiphilein ou thelei.
tis logos, ti pragma kai tis hê phusis,
hêmas turannein tas erôsas parthenous
blêtheisas anterôti daknokardiôi?
gar pros hêmôn ouk erôsi parthenoi?
Erôsi, plên gemousi tôn akkismatôn.
philousi, plên truchousi tous philoumenous,
poiousin autois ekkremê tên kardian.

4. Of special interest to textual scholars is the fact that these poems allude to incidents in the lacuna of book 1, indicating that Estienne had read the missing passage long before it was discovered in the early 1800s. See Alice Hulubei, "Henri Estienne et le roman de Longus," *Revue du seizième siècle* 18 (1931): 324–40; and Georges Dalmeyda, "Henri Estienne et Longus," *Revue de Philologie* 3rd ser. 8 (1934): 169–81.

5. No one seems to have noticed that the Caro translation had been published already—as *Gli amori innocenti di Dafni, e della Cloe* (Bologna, 1643), which was supposedly translated by G. B. Manzini. Actually Manzini merely rephrased Caro's version and claimed it as his own. The fact that the work is Caro's is clearly evidenced, for example, in the following quotation from Manzini, describing Daphnis's beauty: "Ciascuna parte per se stessa bellissima, e tutte insieme piene di leggiadra, formavano una persona, che come di nobile tenea del delicato, e come di Pastore, havea del robusto" (19). The passage is exactly the same in Caro (311) except for "avea" instead of "havea." This sentence comes from Caro's invented episode inserted at the point of the great lacuna in book 1, which Manzini simply lifts.

6. The publisher August Renouard notes that this edition is an inexpensive printing of the Bodoni text (Parma, 1786). The introduction by Francesco Daniele of Naples, dated 1786, gives the year 1538 in a letter from Caro to Benedetto Varchi. According to Daniele, Caro's enemy Castelvetro said the translator knew no Greek (6, 9–10).

7. Lebègue also mentions these parallels: the destruction of the garden by a jealous swain, the Pan myths, the goats dancing to the flute, and the winter scene on the farm.

8.
>
> tu cognois bien son pere,
> Ianot ce bon fleuteur, & Ianotte sa mere:
> Ie l'ay fait amoureux de Catin son souci,
> Et la gente Catin de lui esprise aussi.
> Va le dire à son pere, à fin qu'il les assemble,
> Et d'un estroit lien ces deux coeurs ioigne ensemble.

9. Ainsi ie passé ce beau iour, & ceste douce nuict. Ie vous prie, si toute nostre vie estoit dispensee en ceste facon, mesnageant les iours & les heures en tels plaisirs, sans offense, sans malheur, sans apprehension fascheuse, sans alteration de nostre naturel, francs & libres d'avarice, d'envie, & d'ambition, aurions-nous regret en mourant d'avoir vescu si doucement en ce monde?

10. Day fait subir à ces paroles une transposition subtile, de façon à en éliminer

l'esprit de sensualité païenne qui les inspire et à les réconcilier avec les exigences de la morale chrétienne.

11. On the inherent ambivalence in pastoral, see Richard Cody, *The Landscape of the Mind: Pastoralism and Platonic Theory in Tasso's Aminta and Shakespeare's Early Comedies* (Oxford: Clarendon, 1969); and Peter Lindenbaum, *Changing Landscapes: Anti-Pastoral Sentiments in the English Renaissance* (Athens: U of Georgia P, 1986).

12. For earlier discussions of Spenser and Longus, see the various sources (Upton, Greenlaw, Hughes) cited by Doyle, who argues that in *FQ* 7, Faunus's voyeurism and wolf skin are based on Longus's Dorcon episode.

13. Although another hand may have made some of these markings, Robert Evans's case for Jonson's ownership of the British Library copy of Longus (call number C.79.a) is virtually conclusive. Pen and pencil marks and signs are consistent with those in other books known to have belonged to the poet. I wish to acknowledge Professor Evans's helpful discussion and correspondence on this subject, in addition to his article.

14. Jonson, in whose British Library copy of Longus the Echo story is underlined (119–20), may be thinking of Longus in his allusions to Echo in *Pan's Anniversary* (for example, hymn 3: "Echo the truest oracle on ground, / Though nothing but a sound, . . . / Beloved of Pan the valleys queen"). On Jonson and the Echo myth see Loewenstein, who also finds Longus contributing to a "complex of issues" in *Cynthia's Revels* (90).

15. Gesner's long chapter on *The Tempest* enumerates many more parallels: island setting, theme of nature, supernatural guidance of lovers, structural tightness, Prospero as Philetas, Caliban as Dorcon in his wolf skin, the nymphs and reapers of the masque (see 125–39). To these might be added the scene, at the end of act 4, in which Prospero sets his hounds on Caliban and the fools as, in book 1, Daphnis's dogs attack Dorcon in the wolf skin.

16. The question of Shakespeare's patriarchalism has preoccupied many scholars, and I don't think anyone can untangle that knot to everyone's satisfaction. In *Patriarchal Structures in Shakespeare's Drama* (Berkeley: U of California P, 1985) Peter Erickson can even say that the statue scene in *The Winter's Tale* leads only to "patriarchal closure" as "Leontes returns to the role of dispenser of bounty" (164).

3. WIT AND INNOCENCE

1. I discuss Thornley at greater length in "A Romance for Young Ladies: George Thornley's Translation of *Daphnis and Chloe*," *Classical and Modern Languages* 15 (1994): 45–56, showing that the translator is working from Greek as well as from Jungermann's Latin. The excellence of Thornley's translation is attested by its fre-

quent reprinting, including its adoption (with augmentations) in the Loeb Library edition of J. M. Edmonds (1916).

2. Science has not determined whether Milton or Longus is right, but some rhesus monkeys, it seems, reared in all-male surroundings, cannot figure out the sex act on their own when they are presented with their first opportunity. In "The Effects of Isosexual Rearing on Adult Sexual Behavior in Captive Male Rhesus Macaques," *Archives of Sexual Behavior* 17 (Oct. 1988): 381–88, Fred B. Bercovitch et al. reported that among male monkeys raised apart from females "43% did not mount with intromission(s), but only 7% of heterosexually reared males failed to achieve an intromission" (385–86).

3. The Hebrew word is *'ezer*. James Turner's learned and persuasive book could pay greater heed to the extensive ancient belief outside the Jewish tradition that marriage was a sacred union.

4. La fin principale des Romans, ou du moins celle qui le doit estre, & que se devoient proposer ceux qui le composent, est l'instruction des Lecteurs, a qui il faut toûjours faite voir la vertu couronnée; & le vice chastié.

5. [S]i obscene . . . qu'il faut estre un peu cynique pour le lire sans rougir.

6. [C]ar encore que la pluspart des Savans des derniers siècles les ayent loüez pour leur elegance, & leur agrément, joint à la simplicité convenable au sujet; neantmoins je n'y trouve rien de tout cela que la simplicité, qui va quelquefois jusqu'à la puerilité, & à la niaiserie.

7. [P]lein de metaphores, d'antitheses, & de ces figures brillantes qui surprennent les simples, & qui flattent l'oreille sans remplir l'esprit.

8. Sie sind weit von der Epigrammatischen Wiz entfernt, und von der Schulgerechten Ordnung. Er hat die schwere Kunst gewusst, die angenehme Nachlaessigkeit in ihre Gesaenge zu bringen, welche die Poesie in ihrer ersten Kindheit muss gehabt haben.

9. "I sought my rules only in Theocritus and Virgil, and read Longus" [Ich suchte meine Regeln allein in Theokrit und Virgil, und las den Longus] (see letter of 29 November 1754 in Gessner 3:143).

10. Schönberger (47) lists sixteen compositions, the ballet music of Frederick Ashton (1951) and Leo Spies (1958) being the most recent. Barber recounts Oscar Wilde's plan to write a libretto for the composer Dalhousie Young (71). I have not discovered whether Longus gave Gus Kahn the idea for his popular 1927 song "Chloe" (later revived by Spike Jones).

11. For the European theatrical career of "La Bergére des Alpes," see L. M. Price, *The Vogue of Marmontel on the German Stage* (Berkeley: U of California P, 1944); and Michael Cardy, *The Literary Doctrines of Jean-François Marmontel* (Oxford: Voltaire Foundation at the Taylor Institution, 1982). In America separate transla-

tions of "La Bergére des Alpes" were published at Wilmington in 1794 and Baltimore in 1797. One translation of it by "an officer of the army who fought under Gen Wolfe" is included in a selection of Marmontel (New York, 1801) and is entitled "Adelaide, or The Shepherdess of the Alps." In Britain, Charles Dibdin made the story into "a comic opera in three acts" for the Theatre Royal in Covent Garden (1780). It was also picked up by the *Weekly Amusement* of London in 1763, and separate printings in the later eighteenth and early nineteenth centuries survive from York, London, Manchester, Newcastle, and Durham.

12. Rien de plus vain, de plus frivole, de moins ingénieux; rien sur-tout de moins délicat sur l'article des bienséances. Voilà pourtant la fleur des romans de l'antiquité.

13. [J]e veux celébrer ma patrie; je veux peindre ces beaux climats où la verte olive, la mûre vermeille, la grappe dorée, croissent ensemble sous un ciel toujours d'azur.

14. [I]l parle aussi bien au coeur, et lui inspire des sentiments plus purs. On forme son goût en lisant Virgile; on nourrit son âme en lisant Gessner.

15. Ce modèle inimitable de grâce, de naiveté, a toujours fait plus de plaisir que Théocrite et Guarini. Il en ferait encore davantage, sans quelques images trop libres qui doivent être bannies de tout ouvrage de ce genre. Il faut que l'amour des pasteurs soit aussi pur que le cristal de leurs fountaines; et comme le premier attrait de la plus belle des bergères consiste dans sa pudeur, de même le principal charme d'une pastorale doit être d'inspirer la vertu.

4. PAUL, VIRGINIE, AND GEORGE

1. [P]rofluit, tanquam amnis argenteus virentibus utrinque sylvis inumbratus, & ita florens, ita picta, ita expolita est, ut in ea verborum omnes, omnes sententiarum illigentur lepores.

2. On pastoral landscape painting, see Cafritz et al., though these historians utterly neglect Longus in discussing the various literary-based pictorial themes, such as teaching the flute. A reason for this neglect may be that the history of Longus in art has yet to be written. A list of (mostly nineteenth-century) works—including sculpture, lithography, photography, porcelain, and book illustration—is appended to the edition of *Daphnis and Chloe* (Paris: Quantin, 1878) in the Petits romans antiques series. See also Schönberger's edition of Longus. My daughter Jennifer Hardin, who is an art historian, finds a medal sculpted by J. E. Roiné pictured in the May 1907 issue of *Putnam's Monthly* and accounts of paintings by P. A. Cot, Elizabeth Gardner (an American in the Paris Salon), and Raphael Collin in the *Art Amateur* for November 1879, September 1882, and June 1889 respectively.

3. On Vibert and Gérôme see Gerald M. Ackerman's introductory essay in Eric Zafran, *French Salon Paintings from Southern Collections* (Atlanta: High Museum, 1982), 164–65; and Gerald M. Ackerman's commentary (96) in *Jean-Léon Gérôme*

(1824–1904) (Dayton, Ohio: Dayton Art Institute, 1972), the catalog of a Gérôme exhibition held in 1972–73.

4. From 1791 to 1793, seventy-eight thousand tickets were sold for sixty-eight performances of Edmond G. F. Favierès's dramatic *Paul et Virginie*. See Emmet Kennedy et al., eds., *Theatre, Opera, and Audiences in Revolutionary Paris: Analysis and Repertory*, Contributions in Drama and Theatre Studies 62 (Westport, Conn.: Greenwood, 1996), 6.

5. Ne craignons donc pas de confesser que *Paul et Virginie* est une des productions les plus mêlées qu'il y ait dans aucune littérature: roman, si vous voulez, puisqu'il y a une action qui se noue et se dénoue, mais aussi manuel poétique de l'apprenti encyclopédiste, car on y trouve tout ensemble une économie politique, une pédagogie, une esthétique, une morale et une theodicée.

6. [C]elle de lier à la vision de la vierge naufragée le thème des amours enfantines, traditionellement cher à la grande idylle, et plus encore à l'idylle mignarde du siècle, et celui de l'éducation de deux "enfants de la nature," inlassablement repris, sous forme d'expériences plus ou moins saugrenues, par la littérature philosophique du temps.

7. Mauzi along with Donovan provides most of the facts in this paragraph.

8. Comme un homme sauvé du naufrage sur un rôcher, je contemple de ma solitude les orages qui fremissent dans le reste du monde; mon repos même redouble par le bruit lointain de la tempête.

Compare the famous opening of the second book of Lucretius's *De rerum natura*, in which, from a safe haven on shore, the poet takes joy in watching others struggle.

9. [D]outant, d'après un fin aussi funeste d'une fille si vertueuse, qu'il existât une Providence; car il y a des maux si terrible et si peu mérités, que l'espérance même du sage en est ébranlée.

On the dispersion of Epicureanism in Europe from the Renaissance on, see Howard Jones, *The Epicurean Tradition* (New York: Routledge, 1989). Classical Epicureans thought that children and spouses brought only grief, either because they became unpleasant to live with or because, if they were loving people, they would die.

10. Un excès y balance toujours un autre excès.... Un mal au milieu des plaisirs est pour les riches une épine au milieu des fleurs. Pour les pauvres, au contraire, un plaisir au milieu des maux est une fleur au milieu des épines; ils en goûtent vivement la jouissance.... La nature a tout balancé.

11. Mauzi quotes from one letter, "Ici le paysage est sans verdure, les promenades sans arbres" (15).

12. [P]ar l'audacieuse peinture du bain dans le grotte, par la scêne de pâturage

sous le chêne familier, par les nudités provocantes, par la recherche des remèdes au brûlant appel des sens, par les essais infructueux d'amour physique où les bêtes donnent l'exemple, par la crudité des détails, bref par l'atmosphère de sensualité qui baigne l'oeuvre si typiquement grecque, si franchement, si naturellement païenne de Longus.

13. Jordanova, however, sees in Bernardin a flawed feminist at best. For him, she says, "Women as *sexual beings* carry danger; it is really only as *mothers* that they are safe" (59, n.7)—a position that needs mitigation, I think.

14. In this second sentence, Sand goes on to call *The Vicar of Wakefield* "a book more useful and healthy" [sain à l'âme] than *Les Liaisons dangereuses*. On Sand's idealism see Schor.

15. [N]e jamais penser à la peinture quand je regarde le paysage, à la musique quand j'ècoute le vent, à la poésie quand j'admire et goûte l'ensemble. . . . [J]e voudrais être paysan; le paysan qui ne sait pas lire, celui à qui Dieu a donné de bons instincts, une organisation paisible, une conscience droite.

16. Depuis les bergers de Longus jusqu'à ceux de Trianon, la vie pastorale est un Eden parfumé où les âmes tourmentées et lassées du tumulte du monde ont essayé de se réfugier.

17. Marié à vingt ans, il n'avait aimé qu'une femme dans sa vie, et, depuis son veuvage, quoiqu'il fût d'un caractère impétueux et enjoué, il n'avait ri et folâtré avec aucune autre.

18. Karénine recalls that a friend's young daughter was horrified on reading *François le Champi*, her first Sand novel (673). Biographical critics see Sand's own wish-fulfillment in Madeleine's mother-to-wife transition: Sand supposedly took a young friend of her son's as both son and lover (see Salomon's introduction to *François le Champi* [184–85], which also scoffs at Sand's predilection for the "facile pathos" of romance motifs such as foundling stories [183]).

19. [L]'appel aux passions qui fermentent, c'est ne point là le chemin du salut: mieux vaut une douce chanson, un son de pipeau rustique, un conte pour endormir les petits enfants sans frayeur et sans souffrance.

20. Chapter divisions of the manuscript and serialized versions differ from those in the 1858 base text used by Salomon and Mallion in their one-volume edition (see variants, 274–314), in which Sand was free from arrangements dictated by periodical publication.

21. Il a une surabondance d'amitié dans le coeur, et, pour l'avoir toujours portée sur son besson, il a oublié quasiment son sexe, et, en cela, il a manqué à la loi du bon Dieu, qui veut que l'homme chérisse une femme plus que père et mère, plus que frères et soeurs.

22. Les fleurs, les herbes, les pierres, les mouches, tous les secrets de nature, il y en aurait eu bien assez pour m'occuper.... J'aurais toujours été seule, sans connaître l'ennui.

23. [O]n dit que j'aime les mauvaises bêtes et que je suis sorcière, parce que je n'aime pas à faire souffrir une grenouille, à arracher les pattes à une guê et à clouer une chauve-souris vivante contre un arbre. Pauvre bête, que je lui dis, si on doit tuer tout ce qui est vilain, je n'aurais pas plus que toi le droit de vivre.

24. [J]amais dans toute ma vie je n'ai senti pour père, mère, soeur ou frère, non pas, certes, pour la belle Madelon, et non pas même pour mon cher besson Sylvinet, un élan d'amitié pareil à celui que, pendant deux ou trois minutes, cette diablesse m'a causé. S'il avait pu voir ce que j'avais dans le coeur, mon pauvre Sylvinet, c'est du coup qu'il aurait été mangé par la jalousie. Car l'attache que j'avais pour Madelon ne faisait point de tort à mon frère, au lieu que si je devais rester seulement tout un jour affolé et enflambé comme je l'ai été pour un moment à côté de cette Fadette, j'en deviendrais insensé et je ne connaîtrais plus qu'elle dans le monde.

25. See Raymond Jean's introduction to his edition of *Sylvie*, xxv–xxvi.

26. See Jean's introduction to *Sylvie*, xx and xxiii. Jean also mentions that Anatole France observed resemblances between *Paul et Virginie* and *Sylvie*. Béatrice Didier writes that *Paul et Virginie* combines the myths of the primitive and of the island, a place where "a primitive purity, a simplicity in human relations has been able to be miraculously preserved" [une pureté primitive une simplicité dans les rapports humains ont pu être miraculeusement préservées] (902).

27. Zola, "The Experimental Novel" (quoted in Alcorn 27).

28. On the ghost story and self-division in the nineteenth century, see Harold Fisch, *A Remembered Future: A Study in Literary Mythology* (Bloomington: Indiana UP, 1984), 50–60.

29. Conrad's statement is quoted by Maurice Hemingway in "Naturalism and Decadence," 46 n.1. Hemingway persuasively links this theme in Hardy's *Tess*, Zola's *Abbé Mouret*, and Pardo Bazán's *La madre Naturaleza*.

5. LADIES OF MAINE

1. On the composition of *Pearl* see Kirkham. Gessner, Bernardin, and Sand apparently wanted to retain Longus's values of love and nature while modernizing his morals, "Christianity" quite aside.

2. Il me semble que je serais compétente pour parler de cette brave femme qui m'ennuie et qui me fait pleurer en même temps, avec sa Bible, ses nègres, et ses moutards.

Fields and Stowe quote Sand's laudatory review in translation (see 151–57), noting a resemblance of "character" between the three "women of genius" of their age—Sand, Eliot, and Stowe.

3. Cary mentions the haymakers on the marsh island as showing Jewett's technique of blending human figures into the landscape (430).

4. On her long interest in Sand see Jewett, *Letters*, ed. Cary 22 n.6. Jewett mentions Arnold and Sand in *Letters*, ed. Fields 38.

5. Magowan reports James Russell Lowell's comparing Jewett's *Tales of New England* with the idylls of Theocritus (72–73).

6. Chase retained throughout her life a lively interest in Catholicism, maintaining long friendships with several nuns. She must have been disturbed by the groundless attack on her novel as anti-Catholic in the *Boston Transcript* of 20 August 1927.

7. Cather, quoted in Mary Ellen Chase, "Portraits" 513. A copy of *Uplands* in the Smith College Archives is inscribed "To Margaret whose book this is," with the date 8 August 1927. This must refer to Margaret Macgregor, whom Chase helped to get a position at Smith and with whom she collaborated on an English textbook soon afterward. A few years later, Chase and others edited Macgregor's University of London dissertation, mentioning in the preface her sudden death. Chase had apparently taken back the inscribed copy after Macgregor's death.

6. SPANISH IDYLLS

1. *Dafnis y Cloe*, más bien que de novela bucólica, puede calificarse de novela campesina, de novela idílica o de idilio en prosa; y en este sentido, lejos de pasar de moda, de la moda y sirve de modelo aún, *mutatis mutandis*, no sólo a *Pablo y Virginia*, sino a muchas preciosas novelas de Jorge Sand, y hasta a una que compuso en español, pocos años ha, cierto amigo mío, con el título de *Pepita Jiménez*.

2. [E]n medio de sus sencillas y naturales bellezas, sobrada afectación y *sensiblería* malsana, propias de Rousseau, maestro de Saint-Pierre, y teosófico prurito de buscar en la Naturaleza una revelación religiosa, mientras que en *Dafnis y Cloe* hay religión positiva, aunque sea mala, y todo es más candoroso y menos alambicado.

3. Dafnis y Cloe, en completo estado de naturaleza, aunque sublimado e idealizado por el favor divino, pero por el favor divino de dioses poco severos, se aman antes de saber que se aman, son bellos e ignorantes, contemplan y comprenden su hermosura, y de esta contemplación y admiración nace un afecto bastante delicado para dos que viven casi vida selvática: él sin colegio ne estudio de moral, y ella, sin madre vigilante y cristiana, sin aya inglesa que la advierta lo que es *shocking*, y sin nada por el estilo. Si el autor, dado ya el asunto, hubiera puesto en los amores de sus dos personajes algo de más sutil, etéreo y espiritual, hubiera sido completamente falso, tonto e insufrible.

4. See DeCoster 26. The event was hushed up at the time (see *New York Times* 17 Jan. 1886: 1) and has never been fully explored—going unmentioned, for example, in modern biographies of Bayard's father. An edition of the young woman's love letters by Sáenz de Tejada—described over twenty years ago on the jacket of Valera's *Cartas Intimas* as being underway—has never materialized.

5. Se lavó la cara con agua tibia para que el estrago del llanto desapareciese hasta el punto preciso de no afear, mas no para que no quedasen huellas de que había llorado; se compuso el pelo de suerte que no denunciaba estudio cuidadoso, sino que mostraba cierto artístico y gentil descuido, sin rayar el desorden, lo cual hubiera sido poco decoroso; se pulió las uñas, y como no era propio recibir de bata don Luis, se vistió un traje sencillo de casa. En suma, miró instintivamente a que todos los pormenores de tocador concurriesen a hacerla parecer más bonita y aseada, sin que se trasluciera el menor indicio del arte, del trabajo y del tiempo gastados en aquellos perfiles.

6. Una señora de ciudad . . . hallará extraño y hasta censurable lo que voy a decir de Pepita; pero Pepita, aunque elegante de suyo, era una criatura muy a lo natural . . . ; brincaba y reía y daba otras muestras de júbilo, que, in medio de todo, tenían mucho de infantil y de inocente.

7. No habló como hubiera hablado una dama de nuestros salones, con ciertas pleguerías y atenuaciónes en la expresión, sino con la desnudez idílica con que Cloe hablaba a Dafnis, y con la humildad y el abandono completo con que se ofreció a Booz la nuera de Noemi.

8. [L]a suave y pura luz de sus miradas, a todo se concierta en un ritmo adecuado, todo se une en perfecta armonía , donde no se descubre nota que disuene.

9. Criados y señores, hidalgos y jornaleros, las señoras y señoritas y las mozas del lugar asistieron y se mezclaron en él como en la soñada primera edad del mundo, que no sé porqué llaman de oro.

10. [R]epresenta a Cloe cuando la cigarra fugitiva se le mete en el pecho, donde, creyéndose segura, y a tan grata sombra, se pone a cantar, mientras que Dafnis procura sacarla de allí.

11. [L]os estudios me revientan; paisano nací y paisano he de morir, con la tierra pegada a los manos. . . . Una casita, una heredad y una pareja de bueyes con que labrarla, no hemos de ser tan infelices que eso nos falte; y entiendo eso, que se ría el mundo de mí que yo me reiré del mundo.

12. [Q]ue nuestro siglo refina y concreta a cada paso, lo mismo que si el objeto supremo de tanto adelanto, de tanto progreso, fuese una conflagración universal.

13. Por qué se deleitaba en imaginar la inocencia selvática de su sobrina, su carácter algo arisco y el rendimiento y ternura con que, después de las primeras esquiveces, le caería sobre el corazón más blanda que una breva, y por qué se veía

disipando poco a poco su ignorancia, educándola, formándola, iniciándola en los goces y bienes de la civilización, y otras veces volvía la torta, y se veía a sí propio hecho un aldeano, y a Manolita con los brazos arremangados como Catuxa, dando de comer a las gallinas o . . . , ¡celeste visión, espectáculo inefable!, arrimando al blanco y redondo pecho una criaturita medio en pelota, toda bañada de sol?

14. See the thoughtful feminist reading of this novel by Ruth El Saffar, who finds in Gabriel a questing everyman and argues that after he loses Nucha, "Gabriel's subsequent life story is that of every novelistic hero: it is the story of deep desire for the sister/mother/spouse repressed, transformed into a grab bag of intellectual confusion, fantasy, military activity, solitude, and derailed erotic ambitions" (96). This seems to me an overdetermined reading of "every" novel, but Gabriel is perhaps more deliberately designed to seek the feminine than are most heroes. El Saffar's study appears in the same issue of *Anales Galdosianos* with the equally relevant articles—also of a feminist perspective—by Bieder and Diane Urey.

15. El deber de las señoritas, que es hacerse agradables y simpáticas a todo el mundo, y con mayor razón a los huéspedes que tienen en casa, y todavía más si son sus tíos y vienen a verlas.

16. Necio, pon a una pareja linda, salida apenas de adolescencia, sola, sin protección, sin enseñanza, vagando libremente como Adán y Eva en los días paradisíacos, por el seno de un valle amenísimo, en la estación apasionada del año, entre flores que huelen bien y alfombras de mullida hierba capaces de tentar un santo. ¿Qué barrera, qué valla los divide? Una enteramente ilusoria, ideal; valla que mis leyes, únicas a que ellos se sujetan, no reconocen, pues yo no jamás he vedado a los pájaros nacidos en el mismo nido que aniden juntos a su vez en la primavera próxima.

17. For a suggestive comparison with Zola's novel, see Hemingway, who cites several earlier discussions of *La Faute de l'abbé Mouret* as the "major source" of *La madre Naturaleza* (31). I am interested less in the longstanding discussion whether Pardo Bazán is a naturalist than in the kinds of concerns central to Hemingway's reading: Gabriel as disillusioned fin-de-siècle man and Pardo Bazán as distinguished by her irony and her detachment from her characters' viewpoints.

18. Besides Singer see Baquero Goyanes (73–79), who uses Longus and Bernardin to show that Pardo Bazán's novel is not really naturalistic but a highly artificial text. To Baquero Goyanes's evidence of the anomalous insertion of a Bernardin-like tropical element in the Galician landscape, one might add Manuela's hatred and fear of wolves (*La madre* 512). The rarity of wolves in the region at this time invites the question whether her phobia derives more from literary shepherdesses than the naturalist's "faithful observation of nature."

19. Al acercarse a los pazos oyeron el alegre vocerío de segadores y segadoras, y Gabriel, divisando a su cuñado, que presidía la faena, tomó hacia el camino donde

segaban. Sobre el fondo oscuro de la tierra vio blanquear las camisas y sayas, las fajas rojas y los pañuelos azules de labriegos y labriegas; contra un matorral descansaba un jarro de barro, y la cuadrilla, entonando su inevitable "¡ay... le le!" se daba prisa a atar los haces, sirviéndose de las rodillas para apretar la mies. El olor embriagador de los tallos cortados embalsamaba el aire, y el artillero sintió una ráfaga de alegría, y contempló embelesado el cuadro.

20. [D]igno de un pintor colorista, alumno de la Naturaleza y fiel a la realidad, enemigo de afeminaciones de dibujo y falsas luces cernidas por cortinas de taller.

21. {E}stá lleno de la personalidad burguesa y prosaica de Milton, y a trechos de sus más delicada inspiración de poeta. Hay una maestria soberana en la riente descripción del Edén y en la hermosa caída de la noche que envuelve el rito amoroso de nuestros primos padres.

22. ¡Cómo pugna esta concepción de la vida paradisíaca con la nuestra propria! Hemos soñado todos a la primer pareja; la hemos visto discurrir y vagar enlazada por entre sendas de rosas, a la orilla de lagos que circunda una margen florida y embalsamada por violetas y lirios; hemos contado sus suspiros y sus arrobos, sus deliquios a la sombra de las palmeras, sus éxtasis en las grutas y al pie de los suaces.... Para nosotros, la impureza y el trabajo siguen a la caída; no la preceden.

¡Cuan preferible encuentro la quimérica creación de Tasso, novela andantesca forjada sobre hechos reales, al realismo casero de Milton!

23. Se objectará que el amor divinizado por Jorge Sand fué un idealismo trans-cendental; pero bien sabemos cómo por el hilo de esos idealismos se saca el ovillo de la afeminación y la decadencia de una época literaria y hasta de una sociedad.

7. BRITISH NATURISTS

1. Hardy also plays with the rustic illusion of concealed aristocracy in *Under the Greenwood Tree*. Fancy's father, not without a lofty image of himself as the Earl of Wessex's gamekeeper, thinks he married up, to "a teacher in a landed family's nursery" (181). Mrs. Dewy thinks herself "a person of decent taste" who can barely keep her husband "respectable" (87). Mrs. Day resents having to show her fine silverware to common visitors (128). In *Tess of the D'Urbervilles* concealed aristocracy has more tragic consequences.

2. Comparisons of Hardy with Sand are now rare in Hardy criticism, but they were not so during his lifetime. Hardy's friend Horace Moule, reviewing *Desperate Remedies*, found a resemblance (see Gittings 154–55), as did Havelock Ellis in an article in *Westminster Review* (April 1883) that links *Under the Greenwood Tree* to *La Mare au diable* (see Cox 109).

3. Blanchot, *Après coup*, quoted in Bonnet (6), who adds, "un véritable malheur

aussi" [a real unhappiness too], though I would say that our expectations on this score are too colored by the elegiac tendency of nineteenth-century idyllicism.

4. Knopf tells the story of his youthful enthusiasm for Hudson in the foreword to Payne's bibliography (see xiii–xv).

5. Haymaker 331 mentions some of these studies while making the important point that Rima owes her existence equally to the general figure of the romantic nature-child from Wordsworth on.

6. Hudson, "The Serpent in Literature," in *The Book of a Naturalist* 164. This essay by Hudson again demonstrates the breadth of his reading in fiction, especially romance. On serpents, also see David Miller 139–44.

7. For biographical information on Stacpoole, see the article in *The Dictionary of National Biography 1951–60*, ed. E. T. Williams and Helen M. Palmer (Oxford: Oxford UP, 1971); and more generally, my "The Man Who Wrote *The Blue Lagoon*," *English Literature in Transition* 39 (1996): 205–20.

8. Stacpoole's comments and information on the supposed imitations are in "Correspondence" 121–22 and 189–221. On the films, see the entry for 26 April 1923 in vol. 2 (1921–25) of *Variety's Film Reviews* (New York: Garland, 1983); the entry for 5 June 1938A in vol. 3 (1937–40) of *The New York Times Encyclopedia of Film* (New York: Times Books, 1984); Jay Nash and Stanley Ross, *The Motion Picture Guide* (Chicago: Cinebooks, 1985), 1:249. The play, written by Norman Macowan and Charlton Mann, was produced by Basil Dean, with Edward Rigby as Paddy, Faith Celli and Harold French as the couple, and Hesketh Pearson as Lestrange.

9. In a 1921 interview, Stacpoole claimed that he got a "very considerable amount of classical learning" at Malvern College (quoted in McQuilland 126), but he later wrote that Malvern had emphasized modern rather than classical learning (*Men and Mice* 30–31).

10. This is apparently the second edition. It has no date on the title page, unlike the first, which is dated 1920. Stacpoole mentions a second edition in his list of books prefatory to *Of Men and Mice*.

8. INNOCENCE AND RADICAL INNOCENCE

1. Lawrence Clark Powell takes this view, saying *Isidro* "is compact, lyrical, and faithful to landscapes and seasons of a country she knew and loved." See Powell, "The Land of Little Rain: Mary Austin," in *California Classics: The Creative Literature of the Golden State* (Los Angeles: Ward Ritchie, 1971), 48–49. The novel has drawn almost no critical attention.

2. For a brief discussion of the Wright phenomenon, see James David Hart, *The*

Popular Book: A History of America's Literary Taste (New York: Oxford UP, 1950), 218. The subject is treated at length in Ferré.

3. Moore worried about his translation's fate in the United States, where he hoped, if the courts adhered to their practice of not interdicting classical literature, to sell a hundred thousand copies (Gerber 626).

4. Edwin Gilcher chronicles in *A Bibliography of George Moore* (DeKalb: Northern Illinois UP, 1970) the fortunes of this translation, which Moore sometimes published with his *Peronnik the Fool*, a version of the Parsifal story. In *My Life with Dreiser* (Cleveland, Ohio: World, 1951) Helen Dreiser reports that Moore bestowed a copy on her husband, Theodore, when the couple visited him late in his life (183).

5. The characters in "England, My England" are modeled on the Meynell family, whose hospitality Lawrence enjoyed for some months. Wilfrid and Alice Meynell housed their daughters and sons-in-law on their property, supporting them as Winifred's parents do in the story. One of the husbands was killed in the war, though in circumstances quite different from Egbert's.

6. Vivre ainsi, dans ce pays, comme sa mère avait vécu, et puis mourir et laisser derrière soi un homme chagriné et le souvenir des vertus essentielles de sa race, elle sentait qu'elle serait capable de cela.

7. [M]élancolique, chargé du regret de ce qui s'en va et de la menace de ce qui s'en vient; mais sous le sol canadien, il est plus mélancolique et plus émouvant qu'ailleurs, et pareil à la mort d'un être humain que les dieux rappellent trop tôt, sans lui donner sa just part de vie.

8. As Héroux notes, the tone of *Maria Chapdelaine* is anything but optimistic, and the early reviewers who hailed it as such (helping to propel the "myth" of Maria Chapdelaine herself) had not read the novel carefully or at all (for examples, see Deschamps 96). Deschamps explains: "Hémon describes his characters as social entities scarcely individualized and summoned daily to efface themselves before the values of a coercive and rigid society that reduces them to submission and impotence" [Hémon décrit ses personnages commes des entités sociales à peine individualisées et apelées quotidiennement à s'effacer devant les valeurs d'une societé contraignante et rigide qui les réduit à la soumission at àl'impuissance] (95). Héroux goes on to describe the (misread) novel's consequent appeal to the protofascist Action Française.

9. In *Reflections on the Canadian Literary Imagination* (Rome: Bulzoni, 1991) Northrop Frye lists *Maria Chapdelaine* among several texts demonstrating the idyllic tendencies of Canadian literature as a whole. Although "a pastoral myth" lies at the heart of every social mythology, he writes, the "nostalgia for a world of peace and protection, with a spontaneous response to the nature around it, with a leisure and composure not to be found today, is particularly strong in Canada" (87). The

strength of the "Canadian" over the author's European outlook, after so little time in Canada, bears witness to the power of nature to override cultural heritage in creating social mythology.

10. Wright's providential, idealized nature too often collides with naturalistic nature: for example, as Howitt teaches Sammy, "there was opened before them the great book wherein God has written, in the language of mountain, and tree, and sky, and flower, and brook, the things that make truly wise those who pause to read" (136). Yet a moment later the region is laid low in a prolonged drought (see 139–42).

11. For the publishing history and sources of *María*, see McGrady's introduction to the novel (Isaacs 13 and 15–21).

12. Aquellas soledades, sus bosques silenciosos, sus flores, sus aves y sus aguas, ¿por qué me hablaban de ella? ¿Qué había allí de María? en las sombras húmedas, en la brisa que movía los follajes, en el rumor del río. Era que veía el Edén, pero faltaba ella.

9. POINTS OF DEPARTURE

1. I use the title *Luna de miel, luna de hiel*, which means "honeymoon, moon of gall," for the whole work that is sometimes called *Las novelas de Urbano y Simona*. The whole was split in two at the publisher's insistence, the second half being titled *Los trabajos de Urbano y Simona*. Most agree that the two books constitute one novel. See Barry Eisenberg's translation of the whole, *Honeymoon, Bittermoon* (Berkeley: U of California P, 1972).

2. Pérez de Ayala claims, in one of several essays on Valera in his *Divagaciones literarias*, that the older novelist took to heart the aim stated at the end of Longus's preface: "May the gods allow me to handle the emotions of my characters without becoming myself over-emotional or carried away!" [Ojalá que los dioses me permitan manipular las emociones de mis personajes sin yo mismo emocionarme ni entusiasmarme!] (864). The translation seems to be his own; it is not from Valera's version. Pérez de Ayala's point in this essay is that Valera could convey great emotion while retaining the stability of reason.

3. O mi razón comienza a extraviarse o es que el mundo se ha vuelto loco y las leyes naturales no rigen ya—comentó doña Micaela. En otro tiempo sus ojos eran imperativos y hostiles hacia la realidad externa. Recientemente habían cambiado en una expresión de susto, junto con una movilidad de ansia melancólica—El mundo se desquicia. Todo anda al revés.

4. Mirad el jardín, el parque. ¿Diráis que es el Paraíso perdido? No, sino el limbo. Y si para vosotros fue Paraíso, que sí lo fue, débese a vuestros congojas y anhelo de dicha, que no habéis logrado. El paraíso está fuera, más allá de esos muros, en las luchas de la vida.

5. [A]unque Natura, no más allá de los rebaños que ellos mismos apacentaban,

les ofrecía doctrina y ejemplo, su inocencia e ignorancia de las prácticas amorosas eran tales que no acertaban a satisfacer el deseo.

6. Ayala's translation from Longus's preface is that quoted in note 2, above, though in the novel Ayala substitutes "manejar" for "manipular." Ayala's idiomatic tone in the sentence contrasts with Valera's cooler classicism: "Concédanos el Numen que nosotros mismos atinemos a contar, sanos y salvos, los amores de otros" (48).

7. When Mishima returned from his trip to Greece, he immediately enrolled in a university course in classical Greek and also began a two-year, probably platonic, romance with a young female student (Nathan 115). Nathan proposes that Mishima wrote *The Sound of Waves* to escape from himself and his world, then later pretended it was a "joke" (121), implying that Mishima's increasingly sadomasochistic tendencies led him to distance himself from his early work.

8. The peddler seems in part modeled on Autolycus in *The Winter's Tale*. Seedy and dishonest, he has fallen from better days and now sells ribbons and other trinkets, yet he holds the "guileless" (143) rustics enthralled. Both characters also help reconcile a lover's parent to a future spouse.

9. Although Bakhtin discusses *Daphnis and Chloe* in his study of Greek romance (86–110), he describes a formal pattern that is irrelevant to Longus: Daphnis and Chloe do not meet unexpectedly, they never flee, and there is no "varied geographical background" (88).

10. For the classic critique along these lines, see Cynthia Ozick, *Art and Ardor: Essays* (New York: Knopf, 1983), 80–90, though she does not mention *The Grass Harp*. A decade later Capote would provide plenty of the "world" in *In Cold Blood*.

11. Murray shows that Theo is an ironic self-portrait of the author, who based his feelings for Wales chiefly on holiday visits (80–81).

12. On Zazzo and Chatwin, see Murray 65.

13. Ursula Le Guin comments in the essay titled "Woman/Wilderness" in her *Dancing at the Edge of the World* (New York: Harper, 1990): "Where I live as woman is to men a wilderness. But to me it is home" (162). The claims of ecofeminism, a theme of recent interest that would seem to bear significantly on my subject, are in my opinion troubled by such theorists as Jordanova and the various other authors of the essays in MacCormack and Strathern's *Nature, Culture and Gender*, who question the woman-nature equation from several perspectives.

WORKS CITED

Agustín, Francisco. *Ramón Pérez de Ayala: Su vida y obras*. Madrid: Hernández y Sáez, 1927.
Alcorn, John. *The Nature Novel from Hardy to Lawrence*. New York: Columbia UP, 1977.
Alpers, Paul. *What Is Pastoral?*. Chicago: U of Chicago P, 1996.
Amorós, Andrés. *La novela intelectual de Ramón Pérez de Ayala*. Biblioteca Románica Hispánica 2; Estudios y ensayos 170. Madrid: Gredos, 1972.
Anderson, Graham. *Ancient Fiction: The Novel in the Graeco-Roman World*. Totowa, N.J.: Barnes, 1984.
Arnold, Margaret, ed. *Pastor Fidus. Parthenia. Clytophon*. New York: Olms, 1990.
Arnold, Matthew. "George Sand." In *Mixed Essays*. New York: Macmillan, 1883. 238–60.
Austin, Mary Hunter. *Isidro*. Boston: Houghton, 1905.
Bakhtin, M. M. *The Dialogic Imagination: Four Essays*. Ed. Michael Holquist. Trans. Caryl Emerson and Michael Holquist. Austin: U of Texas P, 1981.
Baquero Goyanes, Mariano. *La novela naturalista Española: Emilia Pardo Bazán*. Murcia, Spain: Universidad de Murcia, 1986.
Barber, Giles. *"Daphnis and Chloe": The Markets and Metamorphoses of an Unknown Bestseller*. Panizzi Lectures. London: British Library, 1989.
Barnes, Julian. Rev. of *Flaubert-Sand: The Correspondence*, trans. Francis Steegmuller and Barbara Brayby. *New York Review of Books* 10 (June 1993): 5–12.
Bayle, Pierre. *The Dictionary Historical and Critical of Mr. Peter Bayle*. 1734–38. Intro. Burton Feldman. Vol. 3. New York: Garland, 1984. 5 vols.
Beaton, Roderick. *The Medieval Greek Romance*. Cambridge: Cambridge UP, 1989.
Beecher, Charles. *Harriet Beecher Stowe in Europe: The Journal of Charles Beecher*. Ed. Joseph S. Van Why and Earl French. Hartford, Conn.: Stowe-Day Foundation, 1986.
Belleau, Remy. *La Bergerie*. In *Oeuvres poétiques*. Ed. Charles Marty-Laveaux. 2 vols. Geneva: Slatkine [1965]. 1:177–316.

Berger, Harry. "A Secret Discipline." In *Revisionary Play: Studies in the Spenserian Dynamics*. Berkeley: U of California P, 1988. 215–42.

Bernardin de Saint-Pierre, Jacques-Henri. *Paul et Virginie*. Ed. Pierre Trahard. Paris: Garnier, 1964.

Bieder, Maryellen. "The Female Voice: Gender and Genre in *La madre naturaleza*." *Anales Galdosianos* 22 (1987): 103–16.

Billaut, Alain. "Les Amants dans l'île." *Bulletin de l'association Guillaume Budé* 1 (1985): 73–86.

Blanck, Jacob, ed. "Sarah Orne Jewett." In *Bibliography of American Literature*. Vol. 5. New Haven: Yale UP, 1955–91. 9 vols.

Blount, Paul G. *George Sand and the Victorian World*. Athens: U of Georgia P, 1979.

Bonnet, Henri. "Idyllique *Sylvie* ou l'astre trompeur d'Aldébaran." *Cahiers Gerard de Nerval* 6 (1983): 2–7.

Bowie, Ewen. "The Readership of Greek Novels in the Ancient World." In Tatum 435–59.

Brontë, Emily. *Wuthering Heights*. Ed. Hilda Marsden and Ian Jack. Oxford: Clarendon, 1976.

Burridge, Kenelm. *Someone, No One: An Essay on Individuality*. Princeton: Princeton UP, 1979.

Cafritz, Robert, Lawrence Gowing, and David Rosand. *Places of Delight: The Pastoral Landscape*. Washington, D.C.: Phillips Collection and National Gallery of Art, 1988.

Capote, Truman. *The Grass Harp* and *A Tree of Night*. New York: New American Library, 1951.

Caro, Annibal, trans. *Gli amori pastorali di Dafni e Cloe*. By Longus. Paris: Renouard, 1800.

Cary, Richard. "Jewett on Writing Short Stories." *Colby Library Quarterly* 6 (1964): 425–40.

Cate, Curtis. *George Sand: A Biography*. Boston: Houghton, 1975.

Cather, Willa. *O Pioneers!* Ed. Susan J. Rosowski and Charles W. Mignon. Lincoln: U of Nebraska P, 1992.

———. "The Treasure of Far Island." In *Collected Short Fiction, 1892–1912*. Ed. Virginia Faulkner. Rev. ed. Lincoln: U of Nebraska P, 1970. 265–82.

Cavaliero, Glen. *The Rural Tradition in the English Novel 1900–1939*. London: Macmillan, 1977.

Charlton, D. G. *New Images of the Natural in France: A Study in European Cultural History 1750–1800*. Cambridge: Cambridge UP, 1984.

Chase, Evelyn. *Feminist Convert: A Portrait of Mary Ellen Chase*. Santa Barbara, Cal.: Daniel, 1988.

Chase, Mary Ellen. "Five Literary Portraits." *Massachusetts Review* 3 (1962): 511–16.
———. "My Novels about Maine." *Colby Library Quarterly* 6 (1962): 14–20.
———. *Uplands*. New York: Grosset and Dunlap, 1927.
Chateaubriand, François-René. *Génie du christianisme*. Paris: Garnier, 1861. Vol. 2 of *Oeuvres complètes*. Ed. M. Sainte-Beuve. 18 vols.
Chatwin, Bruce. *On the Black Hill*. London: Cape, 1982.
Cherpack, Clifton. "*Paul et Virginie* and the Myths of Death." *Publication of the Modern Language Association* 90 (1975): 247–55.
Chodorow, Nancy. *The Reproduction of Mothering: Psychoanalysis and the Sociology of Gender*. Berkeley: U of California P, 1978.
Clémessy, Nelly. *Emilia Pardo Bazán como novelista*. 2 vols. Madrid: Fundación Universitaria Española, 1981.
Coleridge, Samuel Taylor. "Lectures on Milton and the *Paradise Lost*." In *The Romantics on Milton: Formal Essays and Critical Asides*. Ed. Joseph Anthony Wittreich. Cleveland, Ohio: P of Case Western Reserve U, 1970. 155–291.
Colette. *Le Blé en herbe*. Ed. Claude Pichois. Paris: Flammarion, 1969.
Collins, Jan Clanton, and Thomas Gregor. "Boundaries of Love." In Jankowiak 72–92.
Cox, R. G., ed. *Thomas Hardy: The Critical Heritage*. London: Routledge, 1970.
Crawford, Thomas. *Society and the Lyric: A Study of the Song Culture of Eighteenth-Century Scotland*. Edinburgh: Scottish Academic Press, 1979.
Cymerman, Claude. "L'Univers sexualisé de *María*." In *Le Roman romantique Latino-Américain et ses prolongements*. Intro. Oliver Gilberto DeLeon. Paris: L'Harmattan, 1984. 159–74.
Davidson, Cathy N., ed. *The Book of Love: Writers and Their Love Letters*. New York: Pocket Books, 1992.
Davis, Walter R., and Richard Lanham. *Sidney's "Arcadia."* New Haven: Yale UP, 1965.
Day, Angel, trans. *Daphnis and Chloe*. By Longus. Ed. Joseph Jacobs. London: Nutt, 1890.
DeCoster, Cyrus. *Juan Valera*. Twayne's World Authors Ser. 316. New York: Twayne, [1974].
Deschamps, Nicole, Raymonde Héroux, and Normand Villeneuve. *Le Mythe de Maria Chapdelaine*. Montreal: PUM, 1980.
Devine, Maureen. *Woman and Nature: Literary Reconceptualizations* Metuchen, N.J.: Scarecrow, 1992.
Dickenson, Donna. *George Sand*. Oxford: Berg, 1988.
Didier, Beatrice. "*Indiana* et Bernardin de Saint-Pierre." In *Etudes sur "Paul et Virginie."* Ed. Jean-Michel Racault. Paris: Didier, 1986. 215–24.

Donno, Elizabeth. "The Unhoopable Marvell." In *Tercentenary Essays in Honor of Andrew Marvell*. Ed. Kenneth Friedenriech. Hamden, Conn.: Archon, 1977. 21–45.

Donovan, John. Introduction. *Paul and Virginia*. By Jacques-Henri Bernardin de Saint-Pierre. Harmondsworth: Penguin, 1983.

Doody, Margaret Anne. *The True Story of the Novel*. New Brunswick, N.J.: Rutgers UP, 1996.

Dormann, Geneviève. *Le Bal du dodo*. Paris: Albion Michel, 1989.

Doyle, Charles Clay. "*Daphnis and Chloe* and the Faunus Episode in Spenser's *Mutability*." *Neuphilologische Mitteilungen* 74 (1973): 163–68.

Dryden, John, and William Davenant. *The Tempest, or The Enchanted Island*. Ed. Maximiliam Novak. Berkeley: U of California P, 1970. Vol. 10 of *The Works of John Dryden*. Gen. ed. Edward Niles Hooker and H. T. Swedenberg, Jr. 20 vols. 1956–.

Duchet, M. "Cinq lettres inédits de Juan Valera à William Dean Howells." *Revue de Littérature Comparée* 72 (1968): 76–102.

Duffy, Jean. *Colette, "Le Blé en herbe."* Glasgow: University of Glasgow French and German Publications, 1989.

Dunlop, John Colin. *The History of Fiction: Being A Critical Account of the Most Celebrated Prose Works of Fiction, from the Earliest Greek Romances to the Novels of the Present Age*. 2nd ed. Vol. 1. Edinburgh: Ballantyne, 1816. 3 vols.

Ebbatson, Roger. *Lawrence and the Nature Tradition: A Theme in English Fiction 1859–1914*. Brighton, Sussex: Harvester, 1980.

Edwards, P. D. *Idyllic Realism from Mary Russell Mitford to Hardy*. New York: St. Martin's, 1988.

Eliade, Mircea. *The Two and the One*. Trans. J. M. Cohen. New York: Harper, 1969.

Eliot, George. "George Sand." *Monthly Magazine* June 1842: 579–91.

El Saffar, Ruth. "Mother Nature's Nature." *Anales Galdosianos* 22 (1987): 91–102.

Evans, Robert. "Ben Jonson Reads *Daphnis and Chloe*." *English Language Notes* 27.4 (1990): 28–32.

Fabre, Jean. "Paul et Virginie, pastorale." In *Lumières et romantisme: énergie et nostalgie de Rousseau à Mickiewicz*. Rev. ed.; Paris: Klincksieck, 1980. 225–57.

Ferré, John P. *A Social Gospel for Millions: The Religious Bestsellers of Charles Sheldon, Charles Gordon, and Harold Bell Wright*. Bowling Green, Ohio: Bowling Green U Popular P, 1988.

Ferrini, Maria Fernanda. *Bibliografia di Longo, "Dafni e Cloe": Edizioni e traduzioni*. Macerata, Italy: Università degli studi di Macerata, 1991.

Fields, Annie, and C. E. Stowe. *The Life and Letters of Harriet Beecher Stowe*. Boston: Houghton, 1898.

Fletcher, John. *The Faithful Shepherdess*. In *Select Plays, [by Francis] Beaumont and

[John] Fletcher. Intro. M. C. Bradbrook. Everyman's Library. New York: Dutton, 1962. 239–313.

Florian, Jean-Pierre. "Essai sur la pastorale." In *Fables de Florian*. Paris: Didot, 1865. 277–85.

———. Estelle. In *Fables de Florian*. Paris: Didot, 1865. 287–361.

Freeman, Derek. *Margaret Mead and Samoa: The Making and Unmaking of an Anthropological Myth*. Cambridge: Harvard UP, 1983.

French, Marilyn. *Shakespeare's Division of Experience*. New York: Summit, 1981.

Frye, Northrop. *The Secular Scripture: A Study of the Structure of Romance*. Cambridge: Harvard UP, 1976.

Garber, Marjorie. "*Cymbeline* and the Languages of Myth." *Mosaic* 10.3 (1977): 105–15.

García Gual, Carlos. *Los orígenes de la novela*. Colección Fundamentos 16. Madrid: ISTMO, 1972.

Garnett, Edward, ed. *Letters from W. H. Hudson to Edward Garnett*. London: Dent, 1925.

Gerber, Helmut. *George Moore on Parnassus*. Newark: U of Delaware P, 1988.

Gesner, Carol. *Shakespeare and the Greek Romance: A Study of Origins*. Lexington: UP of Kentucky, 1970.

Gessner, Salomon. *Sämtliche Schriften*. Facsimile ed. 3 vols. Zurich: Orell Füssli, 1972.

Gittings, Robert. *Young Thomas Hardy*. London: Heinemann, 1975.

Glacken, Clarence J. *Traces on the Rhodian Shore: Nature and Culture in Western Thought from Ancient Times to the End of the Eighteenth Century*. Berkeley and Los Angeles: U of California P, 1967.

Goethe, Johann Wolfgang von. *Conversations of Goethe with [Johann Peter] Eckermann*. Trans. John Oxenford. Ed. J. K. Moorhead. New York: Dutton, 1930.

Goodden, Angelica. "Tradition and Innovation in 'Paul et Virginie': A Thematic Study." *Modern Language Review* 77 (1982): 558–67.

Gornick, Vivian. *The End of the Novel of Love*. Boston: Beacon, 1997.

Grant, Richard. "George Sand's *La Mare au diable*: A Study in Male Passivity." *Nineteenth-Century French Studies* 13 (1985): 211–23.

Greene, Robert. *Menaphon*. Ed. Edward Arber. Westminster, Eng.: Constable, 1895.

———. *Pandosto, or the Triumph of Time*. In *The Descent of Euphues*. Ed. James Winny. Cambridge: Cambridge UP, 1957. 67–121.

Grimm, Friedrich-Melchior. *Correspondance littéraire*. Ed. Maurice Tourneux. 16 vols. Paris: Garnier, 1877.

Guarini, Battista. *The Faithful Shepherd*. Trans. Thomas Sheridan. Ed. Robert Hogan and Edward A. Nickerson. Newark: U of Delaware P, 1989.

Guyard, Marius-François. "Lamartine et 'Paul et Virginie.'" *Revue d'histoire littéraire de la France* 89.5 (1989): 891–99.

Hagstrum, Jean. *Esteem Enlivened by Desire: The Couple from Homer to Shakespeare.* Chicago: U of Chicago P, 1993.

Hardy, Thomas. *Under the Greenwood Tree.* Ed. David Wright. London: Penguin, 1978.

Harris, Helen. "Rethinking Polynesian Heterosexual Relationships: A Case Study on Mangaia, Cook Islands." In Jankowiak 95–127.

Harrison, Elizabeth Jane. *Female Pastoral: Women Writers Re-visioning the American South.* Knoxville: U of Tennessee P, 1991.

Hassan, Ihab. *Radical Innocence: Studies in the Contemporary American Novel.* Princeton: Princeton UP, 1967.

Haymaker, Richard E. *From Pampas to Hedgerows and Downs: A Study of W. H. Hudson.* New York: Bookman, 1954.

Heilbrun, Carolyn G. *Toward a Recognition of Androgyny.* New York: Knopf, 1973.

Hemingway, Maurice. "Naturalism and Decadence in Zola's *La Faute de l'Abbé Mouret* and Pardo Bazán's *La madre Naturaleza.*" *Revue de littérature comparée* 61 (1987): 31–46.

Hémon, Louis. *Maria Chapdelaine.* Montreal: Fides, 1953.

Hibberd, John. *Salomon Gessner: His Creative Achievement and Influence.* Cambridge: Cambridge UP, 1976.

Hone, Joseph. *The Life of George Moore.* New York: Macmillan, 1936.

Howe, Irving. *Thomas Hardy.* 1967. London: Macmillan, 1985.

Howells, William Dean. "Lyof Tolstoy." In *Selected Literary Criticism*, vol. 3 (1898–1920). Vol. 30 of *A Selected Edition of William Dean Howells.* Bloomington: Indiana UP, 1979. 118–31.

———. "Thomas Hardy and Juan Valera." In *Selected Literary Criticism*, vol. 2 (1886–97). Vol. 21 of *A Selected Edition of William Dean Howells.* Bloomington: Indiana UP, 1993. 38–42.

Hudson, W. H. *The Book of a Naturalist.* London: Dent, 1923. Vol. 13 of *Collected Works.* 24 vols.

———. *Far Away and Long Ago.* London: Dent, 1923. Vol. 1 of *Collected Works.*

———. *Green Mansions.* London: Dent, 1923. Vol. 19 of *Collected Works.*

———. *The Purple Land.* London: Dent, 1923. Vol. 12 of *Collected Works.*

———. *A Shepherd's Life.* London: Dent, 1923. Vol. 11 of *Collected Works.*

Huet, Pierre Daniel. *Traité de l'origine des romans.* Facsimile ed. Paris, 1670. Stuttgart: Metzlerische, 1966.

Hunter, R. L. *A Study of "Daphnis and Chloe."* Cambridge: Cambridge UP, 1983.

Hunter, Shelagh. *Victorian Idyllic Fiction: Pastoral Strategies.* Atlantic Highlands, N.J.: Humanities, 1984.

Huxley, Francis. *The Way of the Sacred*. 1974. New York: Dell, 1976.
Ingamells, John. *The Wallace Collection: Catalogue of Pictures*. Vol. 1. London: Trustees of the Wallace Collection, 1985. 3 vols. 1985–89.
Isaacs, Jorge. *María*. Ed. Donald McGrady. Madrid: Cátedra, 1986.
Jankowiak, William, ed. *Romantic Passion: A Universal Experience?*. New York: Columbia UP, 1995.
Jeanclos, Jean-Pierre. " 'Maria Chapdelaine': Adaptations cinematographiques." In *Colloque Louis Hémon, Quimper*. Quimper, France: Calligrammes, 1986. 125–29.
Jeffers, Robinson. *The Loving Shepherdess*. In *Dear Judas, and Other Poems*. New York: Liveright, 1977. 50–114.
Jewett, Sarah Orne. *The Country of the Pointed Firs and Other Stories*. Ed. Mary Ellen Chase. Intro. Marjorie Pryse. New York: Norton, 1981.
———. *Letters*. Ed. Richard Cary. Rev. ed. Waterville, Maine: Colby College P, 1967.
———. *Letters of Sarah Orne Jewett*. Ed. Annie Fields. Boston: Houghton, 1911.
———. *A Marsh Island*. Boston: Houghton, 1885.
Jonson, Ben. *The Sad Shepherd*. In *Ben Jonson's Plays*. Intro. Felix E. Schelling. 2 vols. Everyman's Library. New York: Dutton, 1910. 2:635–64.
Jordanova, L. J. "Natural Facts: A Historical Perspective on Science and Sexuality." In *Nature, Culture and Gender*. Ed. Carol P. MacCormack and Marilyn Strathern. Cambridge: Cambridge UP, 1980. 42–69.
Karénine, Wladimir [Varvara Komarova]. *George Sand: sa vie et ses oeuvres, 1804–1876*. Vol. 3. Paris: Ollendorff, 1912. 4 vols. 1899–1926.
Keith, W. J. *Regions of the Imagination: The Development of British Rural Fiction*. Toronto: U of Toronto P, 1988.
Kermode, Frank. "Adam Unparadised." In *The Living Milton: Essays by Various Hands*. Ed. Frank Kermode. London: Routledge, 1960. 85–123.
———, ed. *English Pastoral Poetry from the Beginnings to Marvell*. London: Harrap, 1952.
Kern, Stephen. *The Culture of Love: Victorians to Moderns*. Cambridge: Harvard UP, 1992.
Kirkham, E. Bruce. "The Writing of Harriet Beecher Stowe's *The Pearl of Orr's Island*." *Colby Library Quarterly* 16 (1980): 158–65.
Knopf, Alfred A. Foreword. *W. H. Hudson: A Bibliography*. By John R. Payne. Hamden, Conn.: Archon, 1977.
Konstan, David. *Sexual Symmetry: Love in the Ancient Novel and Related Genres*. Princeton: Princeton UP, 1994.
Lackner, Stephan. *Peaceable Nature: An Optimistic View of Life on Earth*. San Francisco: Harper, 1984.
Lawrence, D. H. "England, My England." In *England, My England*. Harmondsworth: Penguin, 1982. 7–40.

Lebègue, Raymond. "Une source de la Bergerie de Remy Belleau." *Revue du seizième siècle* 4 (1916): 166–94.
Le Clézio, J.-M. G. *Le Chercheur d'or*. Paris: Gallimard, 1985.
Legouis, Pierre. *Andrew Marvell: Poet, Puritan, Patriot*. Oxford: Clarendon, 1965.
Le Guin, Ursula K. *The Beginning Place*. New York: Harper, 1980.
Leishman, J. B. *The Art of Marvell's Poetry*. London: Hutchinson, 1968.
Léonard, Nicolas. *Idylles et poëmes champêtres*. Ed. Emile Heuriot. Paris: Sansot, 1910.
Lestringant, Frank. "Les amours pastorales de Daphnis et Chloé: Fortunes d'une traduction de Jacques Amyot." In *Fortunes de Jacques Amyot*. Ed. Michel Balard. Paris: Nizet, 1986. 237–57.
Lindholm, Charles. "Love as an Experience of Transcendence." In Jankowiak 57–71.
Loewenstein, Joseph. *Responsive Readings: Versions of Echo in Pastoral, Epic, and the Jonsonian Masque*. Yale Studies in English 192. New Haven: Yale UP, 1984.
Logé, Tanguy. "Chateaubriand et Bernardin de Saint-Pierre." *Revue d'histoire littéraire de la France* 89.5 (1989): 879–90.
Longus. *Daphnis et Chloe*. Bibliotheque universelle des dames. Ser. ed. F.-V. Mullot. Paris: [Cazin], 1785.
———. *Daphnis et Chloé*. Trans. Jacques Amyot. Pref. Alexandre Dumas *fils*. London: Louys Glady, 1878.
———. *Daphnis and Chloe*. Ed. J. M. Edmonds. Loeb Classical Library. London: Heinemann, 1916.
———. *Daphnis and Chloe*. Trans. Paul Turner. Harmondsworth: Penguin, 1968.
———. *Daphnis et Chloe*. Ed. Michael D. Reeve. Leipzig: Teubner, 1982.
———. *Daphnis and Chloe: A Pastoral Novel*. [Trans. Charles V. Le Grice.] Penzance: [Vigurs], 1803.
———. *Les Amours pastorales de Daphnis et Chloé*. Trans. Jacques Amyot. Lille: Lehoucq, 1792.
———. *Longi Pastoralium de Daphnide et Chloe*. Ed. Jean-Baptiste Villoison. Paris: Didot, 1778.
———. *Longou Poimenikôn*. Ed. Raphael Columbanius. Florence, 1598.
———. *Longou Sophistou Poimenikôn*. Ed. Gottfried Jungermann. Hanau, 1605.
———. *The Pastoral Amours of Daphnis and Chloe: A Novel*. Trans. James Craggs. "Fourth ed." London, 1764.
Lott, Robert E. *Language and Psychology in "Pepita Jiménez."* Urbana: U of Illinois P, 1970.
Macowan, Norman, and Charlton Mann. *The Blue Lagoon: A Play in Four Acts*. London: Unwin, 1920.
MacQueen, Bruce D. *Myth, Rhetoric and Fiction: A Reading of Longus's "Daphnis and Chloe."* Lincoln: U of Nebraska P, 1990.

Magendie, Maurice. *Le Roman français au XVIIe siècle*. Paris: Droz, 1932.
Magowan, Robin. *Narcissus and Orpheus: Pastoral in Sand, Fromentin, Jewett, Alain Fournier, and Dinesen*. New York: Garland, 1988.
Mapson, Jo-Ann. *Hank & Chloe*. New York: Harper, 1993.
Marmontel, Jean François. *Oeuvres complètes*. 19 vols. Paris: A Costes, 1818–20.
Marvell, Andrew. *Complete Poetry*. Ed. George de F. Lord. New York: Modern Library, 1968.
Maury, Fernand. *Etude sur la vie et les oeuvres de Bernardin de Saint-Pierre*. Paris: Hachette, 1892.
Mauzi, Robert. Introduction. *Paul et Virginie*. By Jacques-Henri Bernardin de Saint-Pierre. Paris: Flammarion, 1966.
McDermott, Hubert. *Novel and Romance: "The Odyssey" to "Tom Jones."* Totowa, N.J.: Barnes, 1989.
McGuane, Thomas. Interview. *Washington Post Book World* 25 Oct. 1992: 15.
McPherson, David. *Ben Jonson's Library and Marginalia*. Chapel Hill: U of North Carolina P, 1974.
McQuilland, Louis J. "H. DeVere Stacpoole." *Bookman* (London) 60 (1921): 126–28.
Meeker, Joseph. *The Comedy of Survival: Studies in Literary Ecology*. New York: Scribner's, 1974.
Miller, Arthur. *After the Fall*. New York: Viking, 1964.
Miller, David. *W. H. Hudson and the Elusive Paradise*. New York: St. Martin's, 1990.
Millgate, Michael. *Thomas Hardy: A Biography*. New York: Oxford UP, 1982.
———. *Thomas Hardy: His Career as a Novelist*. New York: Random, 1971.
Milton, John. *Complete Poems and Major Prose*. Ed. Merritt Y. Hughes. New York: Odyssey, 1957.
Mishima, Yukio. *The Sound of Waves*. Trans. Meredith Weatherby. 1956. New York: Putnam, [1980].
Mistral, Frédéric. *Mirèio*. Trans. H. W. Preston. London: Unwin, 1890.
Monaco, Marion. *Shakespeare on the French Stage in the Eighteenth Century*. Paris: Didier, 1974.
Montague, Holly. "Sweet and Pleasant Passion: Female and Male Fantasy in Ancient Romance Novels." In *Pornography and Representation in Greece and Rome*. Ed. Amy Racklin. New York: Oxford UP, 1992. 231–49.
Moulin, Monique. "Daphnis et Chloé dans l'oeuvre de Gérard." *Revue du Louvre* 33.2 (April 1983): 100–09.
Munro, James. "On the Frontiers of Myth: *Daphnis and Chloe*, the Romance Tradition, the Théâtre Italien, and Marivaux." In *Myth and Legend in French Literature*. Ed. Keith Aspley, David Bellos, and Peter Sharratt. London: Modern Humanities Research, 1982. 117–36.
Murray, Nicholas. *Bruce Chatwin*. Bridgend, Wales: Seren, 1993.

Mylne, Vivienne. *The Eighteenth-Century French Novel: Techniques of Illusion*. 2nd ed. Cambridge: Cambridge UP, 1981.

Nathan, John. *Mishima: A Biography*. Boston: Little, 1974.

Nerval, Gérard de. *Sylvie; Aurélia; Lettres à Aurélia*. Ed. Raymond Jean. Paris: Corti, 1964.

Neumann, Erich. *Amor and Psyche: The Psychic Development of the Feminine; A Commentary on the Tale by Apuleius*. Trans. Ralph Manheim. Princeton: Princeton UP, 1971.

Nicetas Eugenianos. *Drosilla and Charicles*. In *Erotici Scriptores Graeci*. Ed. Rudolph Hercher. 2 vols. Leipzig: Teubner, 1859. 2:435–552.

Nyquist, Mary. "The Genesis of Gendered Subjectivity in the Divorce Tracts and in *Paradise Lost*." In *Re-membering Milton: Essays on the Texts and Traditions*. Ed. Mary Nyquist and Margaret W. Ferguson. London: Methuen, 1988. 99–127.

O'Brien, Sharon. "The Unity of Willa Cather's 'Two-Part Pastoral': Passion in *O Pioneers!*." *Studies in American Fiction* 6 (1978): 157–71.

Ogilvie, Elisabeth. *Waters on a Starry Night*. New York: McGraw, 1968.

Pardo Bazán, Emilia. *La literatura francesa moderna*. 2 vols. Madrid: Administración, n.d. Vols. 37 and 39 of *Obras Completas*. 44 vols. 1886–1926.

———. *La madre Naturaleza*. In *Cuentos y novelas de la tierra*. Ed. Marina Mayoral. 2 vols. Santiago de Compostela: Sálvora, 1984. 2: 391–645.

———. *Los poetas épicos cristianos*. Madrid: Administración, n.d. Vol. 12 of *Obras Completas*. 44 vols. 1886–1926.

Pattison, Walter. *Emilia Pardo Bazán*. Twayne's World Authors Ser. 134. New York: Twayne, 1971.

Pérez de Ayala, Ramón. *Divagaciones literarias*. In *Obras completas*. 4 vols. Madrid: Aguilar, 1964. 4:803–1042.

———. *Luna de miel, luna de hiel* [*Las Novelas de Urbano y Simona*]. Madrid: Alianza, 1969.

Polhemus, Robert. *Erotic Faith: Being in Love from Jane Austen to D. H. Lawrence*. Chicago: U of Chicago P, 1990.

Pope, Alexander. *Correspondence*. Ed. George Sherburn. Vol. 4 (1736–44). Oxford: Clarendon, 1956. 5 vols.

Pruvost, René. "Le *Daphnis et Chloe* d'Angel Day 1587." *Revue Anglo-Americaine* 10 (1932–33): 481–89.

Racault, Jean-Michel. "Pastorale et roman dans *Paul et Virginie*." In *Etudes sur "Paul et Virginie" et l'ouvre de Bernardin de Saint-Pierre*. Ed. Jean-Michel Racault. Paris: Didier, 1986. 177–200.

Radford, Jean. "A Certain Latitude: Romance as Genre." In *Gender, Language, Myth:*

Essays on Popular Narrative. Ed. Glenwood Irons. Buffalo, N.Y.: U of Toronto P, 1992. 3–19.

Ramsay, Allan. *The Gentle Shepherd: A Pastoral Comedy*. In *Poems by Allan Ramsay and Robert Fergusson*. Ed. Alexander Manson Kinghorn and Alexander Law. Association for Scottish Literary Studies 4. Totowa, N.J.: Rowman and Littlefield, 1974. 42–104.

Reed, T. J. *Schiller*. New York: Oxford UP, 1991.

Riggs, Lynn. *Green Grow the Lilacs: A Play*. New York: French, 1931.

Robinson, Philip. *Bernardin de Saint-Pierre, "Paul et Virginie."* London: Grant and Cutler, 1986.

——. "Traduction ou trahison de 'Paul et Virginie'? L'exemple de Helen Maria Williams." *Revue de l'histoire littéraire de France* 89 (1989): 843–55.

Rohde, Erwin. *Der Griechische Roman und seine Vorlaüfer*. Leipzig: Breitkopf and Härtel, 1876.

Rohde, Georg. "Longus und die Bukolik." *Rheinisches Museum* 86 (1937): 23–49.

Rougemont, Denis de. *Love in the Western World*. Trans. Montgomery Belgion. Rev. ed. New York: Harper, 1974.

Ruano de la Haza, José. "La identidad del narrador de los Paralipomenos de *Pepita Jimenez*." *Revista canadiense de estudios hispánicos* 8 (1984): 335–50.

Sackville-West, Victoria. *Grey Wethers: A Romantic Novel*. London: Heinemann, 1923.

Sand, George. *Correspondance de George Sand*. Ed. Georges Lubin. 26 vols. Paris: Garnier, 1964–.

——. *Les Maîtres mosaïstes*. Ed. Henri Lavagne. Paris: Nouvelles Editions du Chêne, 1993.

——. *La Mare au diable; François le Champi*. Ed. Pierre Salomon and Jean Mallion. Paris: Garnier, 1962.

——. *La Petite Fadette*. Ed. Pierre Salomon and Jean Mallion. Rev. ed. Paris: Garnier, 1958.

Saunders, Corinne. *The Forest of Medieval Romance*. Cambridge, Eng.: Brewer, 1993.

Schiller, Friedrich von. *"Naive and Sentimental Poetry" and "On the Sublime": Two Essays*. Trans. and intro. Julias A. Elias. New York: Ungar, 1967.

Schönberger, Otto, ed. *Hirtengeschichten von Daphnis und Chloe*. By Longus. 2nd ed. Berlin: Akademie, 1973.

Schor, Naomi. *George Sand and Idealism*. New York: Columbia UP, 1993.

Seaton, Beverly. " 'Beautiful, Entire, and Clean': The Maine Farm Novels of Margaret Flint and Gladys Hasty Carroll." *Colby Quarterly* 17 (1981): 39–45.

Shakespeare, William. *The Complete Works*. Gen. ed. Alfred Harbage. Rev. ed. New York: Viking, 1977.

Sharpe, Lesley. *Friedrich Schiller: Drama, Thought, and Politics*. Cambridge: Cambridge UP, 1991.

Sherman, Sarah Way. *Sarah Orne Jewett, an American Persephone*. Hanover, N.H.: UP of New England, 1989.

Sidney, Philip, Sir. *The Old Arcadia*. Ed. Katherine Duncan-Jones. Oxford: Oxford UP, 1985.

———. *An Apology for Poetry*. Ed. Forrest G. Robinson. Library of Liberal Arts 74. Indianapolis: Bobbs-Merrill, 1970.

Singer, Armand. "The Influence of *Paul et Virginie* on *La madre Naturaleza*." *West Virginia University Philological Studies* 4 (1943): 31–43.

Smith, Rowland, "trans." *Daphnis and Chloe*. By Longus. In *The Greek Romances of Heliodorus, Longus, and Achilles Tatius*. Bohn's Classical Library. London: Bohn, 1855.

Spender, Stephen. *Love-Hate Relations: A Study of Anglo-American Sensibilities*. New York: Random, 1974.

Spenser, Edmund. *The Faerie Queene*. In *Spenser: Poetical Works*. Ed. J. C. Smith and E. De Selincourt. Oxford: Oxford UP, 1910. 1–406.

Stacpoole, H[enry] De Vere. *The Blue Lagoon: A Romance*. London: Unwin, 1908.

———. "Correspondence." Additional MS 56818. Society of Authors Manuscript Archive. British Library. London.

———. *The Garden of God*. London: Hutchinson, [1923].

———. *Men and Mice*. London: Hutchinson, [1942].

———. *More Men and Mice*. London: Hutchinson, [1945].

———. *Poems and Ballads*. London: John Murray, 1910.

———. *Sappho: A New Rendering*. 2nd ed. London: Hutchinson, n.d.

Steiner, Wendy. *Pictures of Romance: Form against Context in Painting and Literature*. Chicago: U of Chicago P, 1988.

Steinmetz, Jean-Luc. "Du sarcasme à l'emerveillement: Un carré de lecteurs: Baudelaire, Ducasse, Jammes, Breton." In *Etudes sur "Paul et Virginie."* Ed. Jean-Michel Racault. Paris: Didier, 1986. 910–22.

Stevens, Michael. *Victoria Sackville-West*. London: Joseph, 1973.

Stowe, Harriet Beecher. *Dred: A Tale of the Great Dismal Swamp*. Vol. 1. Boston: Houghton, 1896. Vol. 3 of *The Writings of Harriet Beecher Stowe*. 16 vols.

———. *The Pearl of Orr's Island*. Boston: Houghton, 1900. Vol. 6 of *The Writings of Harriet Beecher Stowe*. 16 vols.

Sutton, Max Keith. *R. D. Blackmore*. Twayne's English Authors Ser. 265. Boston: Twayne, 1979.

Tasso, Torquato. *Aminta*. Trans. Henry Reynolds. Ed. Clifford Davidson. North American Mentor Texts and Studies 1. Fennimore, Wis.: Westburg, 1972.

Tatum, James, ed. *The Search for the Ancient Novel*. Baltimore: Johns Hopkins UP, 1994.
Thomas, Keith. *Man and the Natural World: Changing Attitudes in England 1500–1800*. London: Allen Lane, 1983.
Thomson, James. *The Complete Poetical Works of James Thomson*. Ed. J. Logie Robertson. New York: Oxford UP, 1963.
Thomson, Patricia. *George Sand and the Victorians: Her Influence and Reputation in Nineteenth-Century England*. London: Macmillan, 1977.
Thornley, George, trans. *Daphnis and Chloe*. By Longus. Illus. John Austen. New York: Rarity, 1931.
Thorslev, Peter L. "Incest as Romantic Symbol." *Comparative Literature Studies* 2 (1965): 41–58.
Thurin, Erik Ingvar. *The Humanization of Willa Cather: Classicism in an American Classic*. Lund Studies in English 81. Lund, Sweden: Lund UP, 1990.
Tilney, Edmund. *The Flower of Friendship: A Renaissance Dialogue Contesting Marriage*. Ed. Valerie Wayne. Ithaca, N.Y.: Cornell UP, 1992.
Todorov, Tzvetan. *The Fantastic: A Structural Approach to a Literary Genre*. Trans. Richard Howard. Ithaca, N.Y.: Cornell UP, 1975.
Toinet, Paul. *"Paul et Virginie": Repértoire bibliographique et iconographique*. Paris: Maisonneuve and Larose, 1963.
Toliver, Harold E. "The Dance under the Greenwood Tree: Hardy's Bucolics." *Nineteenth Century Fiction* 17 (1962): 57–68.
———. *Pastoral Forms and Attitudes*. Berkeley and Los Angeles: U of California P, 1971.
Tomalin, Ruth. *W. H. Hudson: A Biography*. London: Faber, 1982.
Turner, James Grantham. *One Flesh: Paradisal Marriage and Sexual Relations in the Age of Milton*. Oxford: Clarendon, 1987.
Turner, Paul. Introduction. *Daphnis and Chloe*. By Longus. Harmondsworth: Penguin, 1968.
Valera, Juan, trans. and intro. *Dafnis y Cloe*. Madrid: Biblioteca nueva, 1925. Vol. 10 of *Obras escogidas de Juan Valera*. 15 vols. 1925–29.
———. "Florilego de cuentos, leyendas y tradiciones vulgares." In *Obras Desconocidas de Juan Valera*. Ed. Cyrus Cole DeCoster. Madrid: Castalia, 1965. 81–88.
———. "Literatura extranjera contemporánea." In *Obras Desconocidas de Juan Valera*. Ed. Cyrus Cole DeCoster. Madrid: Castalia, 1965. 223–53.
———. *Pepita Jiménez*. Ed. Leonardo Romero. Madrid: Catedra, 1989.
Villemain, Abel-François. "Essai sur les romans grecs." In *Etudes de littérature ancienne et étrangère*. Paris, 1877. 161–96.
Webb, Mary. *Seven for a Secret*. 1922. London: Cape, 1929.
Weinstein, Arnold. *The Fiction of Relationship*. Princeton: Princeton UP, 1988.

Whitman, Cedric Hubbell. *Homer and the Heroic Tradition.* Cambridge: Harvard UP, 1958.

Wilson, Christopher. "Tempests and Teapots: Harriet Beecher Stowe's *The Minister's Wooing.*" *New England Quarterly* 58 (1985): 554–77.

Wilson, Forrest. *Crusader in Crinoline: The Life of Harriet Beecher Stowe.* Philadelphia: Lippincott, 1941.

Wilson, Jason. *W. H. Hudson: The Colonial's Revenge.* Working Papers 5. London: University of London, Institute of Latin American Studies, [1981].

Winkler, John J. *The Constraints of Desire: The Anthropology of Sex and Gender in Ancient Greece.* London: Routledge, 1990.

———. "The Invention of Romance." In Tatum 23–38.

Wolfe, Peter. *Yukio Mishima.* New York: Continuum, 1989.

Wolff, Samuel Lee. *The Greek Romances in Elizabethan Prose Fiction.* New York: Columbia UP, 1912.

Wright, Harold Bell. *The Shepherd of the Hills.* 1907. New York: Grossett, 1976.

———. *To My Sons.* New York: Harper, 1934.

Yourcenar, Marguerite. *Mishima: A Vision of the Void.* New York: Farrar, 1986.

Zazzo, René. *Les Jumeaux: le couple et la personne.* Vol. 2. Paris: PUF, 1960. 2 vols.

Ziff, Larzer. *The American 1890s: Life and Times of a Lost Generation.* New York: Viking, 1966.

Zola, Emile. *La Joie de vivre.* Ed. Henri Mitterand. Paris: Gallimard, 1985.

INDEX

Authors of idyllic romances appear in bold type.

Achilles Tatius, 30, 166
Alamanni, Luigi, 27
Amyot, Jacques. See *Daphnis and Chloe*: Translations
aristocracy, and idyllic romance, 10, 32, 41, 50–51, 69, 86, 120, 140, 164, 199, 256 n.1
Arnold, Matthew, and George Sand, 4, 122
Austin, Mary Hunter, *Isidro*, 197–98, 202–03, 257 n.1
Autreau, Jacques, *Les Amans ignorans*, 74

Bakhtin, M. M., 32, 227, 260 n.9
Bayard, Katherine, 139, 254 n.4
Bayle, Pierre, on *Daphnis and Chloe*, 66–67
Belleau, Remy, *La Bergerie*, 32–34
Bernardin de St. Pierre, Jacques-Henri: *Arcadie*, 90; *Paul et Virginie*, 1, 8, 23–24, 76, 84–93, 103, 107, 112, 114–15, 137, 154, 157, 213–14, 227–29, 250 n.4, 251 n.13, 252 n.26
Bertucci, Giovanni Battista, painting by, 28–29
Bianchi Ferrari, Francesco, 28
Blackmore, R. D., *Lorna Doone*, 76, 161
Bodsworth, Fred, *The Sparrow's Fall*, 229–30
Boismortier, Joseph, 31, 74
Bordone, Paris, 81
The Bridges of Madison County (Waller), 9
Brontë, Emily, *Wuthering Heights*, 153, 164–65
Brown, T. E., *Betsy Lee*, 161

Capote, Truman, *The Grass Harp*, 230–33
Caro, Annibale. See *Daphnis and Chloe*: Translations
Carroll, Gladys Hasty, *As the Earth Turns*, 133
Cather, Willa: *Death Comes for the Archbishop*, 162; and Jewett, 122; *My Ántonia*, 106; *O Pioneers!*, 1–2, 106, 126–28; and Sand, 125; *Song of the Lark*, 128; "The Treasure of Far Island," 105, 125–26
caves, in idyllic romance, 21, 28–29, 47–48, 52, 152, 177, 200, 225
Cervantes, Miguel de: *Don Quixote*, 66; *La Galatea*, 32, 77
Chagall, Marc, 81, 204
character types, in idyllic romance, 12–16, 19–20, 101, 109, 113, 165–66, 192–93, 199
Chase, Mary Ellen: and Hardy, 129; and Jewett, 122, 128–29, 132; and Spenser, 130–31; *Uplands*, 7, 19, 129–32, 253 n.6 n.7
Chateaubriand, François-René, 85, 88, 93, 213–14
Chatwin, Bruce, *On the Black Hill*, 103, 237–39, 260 n.11
Colette, Sidonie Gabrielle, *Le Blé en herbe*, 18, 106, 215–16
Columbianus, Raphael, 26–27
comedy, and idyllic romance, 14, 59, 75, 78, 92, 138–39, 169–70, 217, 244 n.7
Conrad, Joseph, 106, 173
couples, in idyllic romance, 8–9, 15–18, 23, 40, 64, 155, 197, 226, 236
Courier, Paul-Louis, discovery of manuscript by, 80
Craggs, James. See *Daphnis and Chloe*: Translations
Cuff, Henry, 27
Cunninghame Graham, R. B., 173

Daphnis and Chloe, 1–2, 4–6, 8, 10–23, 74–75, 77–78, 144–45, 234, 243–44, 246 n.4; in art, 28–29, 58, 81–84, 249 n.2 n.3; Bernardin and, 88–91; Colette and, 215; in France, 79–84;

Daphnis and Chloe (*continued*)
Hardy and, 165–66; Jeffers and, 194–95; Jonson and, 42–43, 247 n.13 n.14; Mapson and, 239–40; Mishima and, 222–25; modern editions of, 222; moral criticism of, 57–58, 65, 77, 79, 163, 203, 223; in music, 31, 74, 248 n.10; and mystery religion, 11, 243 n.4; Pardo Bazán and, 154; Pérez de Ayala and, 216–21, 260 n.6; rediscovery of text of, 26–34, 43, 80, 235; Sand and, 95, 97; Shakespeare and, 45–51, 247 n.15; "Sophist" reception of, 43, 53, 66, 216; Spenser and, 42–43, 247 n.12; Stacpoole and, 189; Villoison edition of, 79
—Translations: Amyot, 31–32, 43, 57–58, 79, 89; Caro, 31–32, 80, 246 n.5 n.6; Craggs, 67–68, 78; Day, 34–37; Jungermann, 43; LeGrice-Smith, 163–64; Manzini (of Caro), 57, 246 n.5; Marcassus (of Amyot), 58; Moore, 203–04; Mullot, 79; Thornley, 57–60, 78, 247 n.1; Turner, x, 57; Valera, 136–38

Davenant, William, and John Dryden, *The Tempest*, 52–53, 59, 78
Day, Angel. See *Daphnis and Chloe*: Translations
Dickey, James, *Deliverance*, 230
Diderot, Jacques, 72–73
Dormann, Geneviève: *Le Bal du dodo*, 227–29, *La Fanfaronne*, 229
Drayton, Michael: "Dowsabel," 30–31; sonnets of, 55, 57
Dreiser, Helen, 258 n.4
Dryden, John, and William Davenant, *The Tempest*, 52–53, 59, 78
Dumas, Alexandre, 89
"Dumuzi's Dream" (Sumerian tale), 11
Dunlop, John, 68, 163
d'Urfé, Honoré, 66–67
Dürrenmatt, Friedrich, *Grieche sucht Griechin*, 234–35

Eckermann, Johann, 80
ecofeminism, 260 n.13
ecphrasis, 21–22, 89, 181, 200, 244 n.10
Eggleston, Edward, *The Hoosier Schoolmaster*, 192
Ehle, John: *The Land Breakers*, 6, 233–34; *Winter People*, 234
Eliot, George, 122, 162, 164, 168
Epicureanism, 250 n.8 n.9
Estienne, Henri, 29

father figure, in idyllic romance, 33, 166, 212–14, 240
Fields, Annie, 116
Flaubert, Gustave, 147
Fletcher, John, *The Faithful Shepherdess*, 31, 44–45
Florian, J. P.: "Essai sur la pastorale," 77; *Estelle*, 76–78, 143
Forbidden Games (film), 233
Forbidden Planet (Hume; screenplay), 10
forest, as a setting in idyllic romance, 26
foundling motif, 19–20, 41, 46–47, 72, 97–98, 111–12, 175, 233, 241
Fouqué, Frederick de la Motte, 177
France, Anatole, 89, 252 n.26

gardens, in idyllic romance, 21, 47, 89–90, 143, 151, 157, 208, 219
Garnett, Edward, 172, 173
Genesis, Book of, 11, 17, 91, 151, 177, 219–20, 241. *See also* Milton: *Paradise Lost*
georgic fiction, 6, 125, 233–34
Gérard, Baron François, 81
Gessner, Salomon: *Evander und Alcimna*, 72–72; and Florian, 76; *Idylls*, 3, 10, 23, 71–72; and Milton, 71–72; and Thomson, 71
Gibbons, Stella, *Cold Comfort Farm*, 206
Gide, André, *La Symphonie pastorale*, 230
Godden, Rumer, *A Breath of Air*, 10
Goethe, Johann Wolfgang von: *Faust*, 80–81; *Hermann und Dorothea*, 137; praise of Longus by, 80
Greek romances, 10–11, 14, 163, 227; and Shakespeare, 45
Green, Paul, "The Humble Ones," 193
Greene, Robert: *Menaphon*, 37–39, 41; *Pandosto*, 36–37, 45–46, 51
Guarini, Battista, *Il pastor fido*, 31
gypsies, 206–07, 218

Hamsun, Knut, *Growth of the Soil*, 6
Hardin, Jennifer, 249 n.2
Hardy, Thomas, 76, 190–91, 205–06, 208, 252 n.29; and Cather, 162; *Far from the Madding Crowd*, 5–6, 21; *Jude the Obscure*, 85; *Mayor of Casterbridge*, 135; and Sand, 168, 256 n.2; *Under the Greenwood Tree*, 5, 13, 24, 161–62, 165–70
"Harpalus's Complaint," 30
Hawthorne, Nathaniel, 176

Heliodorus, 10, 29, 32, 66
Hémon, Louis, *Maria Chapdelaine*, 1, 8, 10, 209–12, 258 n.8–9
Henryson, Robert, "Robyn and Makyne," 30
Howells, William Dean, 135–36
Hudson, W. H.: *A Crystal Age*, 176; *Far Away and Long Ago*, 171, 178; *Green Mansions*, 5, 7, 21, 92, 170–81, 191, 257 n.4 n.6; *A Hind in Richmond Park*, 175; *Idle Days in Patagonia*, 176; *The Purple Land*, 5, 179; and Shakespeare, 174–75; *A Shepherd's Life*, 5, 171–72, 206
Huet, Pierre Daniel, 58, 65–66, 75, 77

idyllic romance, 1–24; character types of, 12–16, 19–20, 101, 109, 113, 165–66, 192–93, 199; as a counter to violence, 3, 24, 99, 108, 207, 222; couples in (mutuality, "sexual symmetry"), 8–9, 15–18, 23, 40, 64, 155, 197, 226, 236; discovery of identity in (initiation, second birth), 1, 47, 87, 104, 175, 178, 221, 224, 242; familial closeness of lovers in, 18, 93, 95, 98–99, 113, 148–49, 183, 213, 220, 238; fathers in, 33, 166, 212–14, 240; and the feminine, 15, 43, 48–49, 90, 102, 115, 175, 187, 219, 226; history of, 23; inarticulateness in, 178, 185–87, 201, 207, 210; intertextuality of, 18–23, 139, 154, 167, 200, 210, 236–37; lapse of childhood in, 22, 47, 89, 108 164, 183; narrator in, 18, 23, 56–57, 86, 95, 139, 168, 216, 223; pathetic fallacy in, 22, 90, 119, 128, 212, 224–25; as a picture, 12, 122, 137, 155–56, 166–67, 238; popularity of, 1, 10, 68, 84, 105, 173, 182, 198, 213, 222; seasonal structure of, 12–13, 22–23, 46, 126, 167, 194, 206, 210, 220, 227. *See also* aristocracy; comedy; ecphrasis; foundling motif; gardens; innocence; islands; regionalism; storms
initiation, 1, 47, 87, 104, 175, 178, 221, 224, 242
innocence, and idyllic romance, 18, 59, 63, 78, 92, 178, 196–97, 204, 209, 216, 231–35
Isaacs, Jorge, *María*, 93, 213–14
islands, as a setting in idyllic romance, 20, 89, 107, 117, 134, 181–89, 222, 252 n.26

Jeffers, Robinson, *The Loving Shepherdess*, 193–97
Jeux interdits (film), 233
Jewett, Sarah Orne: *Country of the Pointed Firs*, 19, 117, 122–25; *Deephaven*, 121; *A Marsh Island*, 1, 10, 117–22; and Sand, 121–22;

253 n.4; and Stowe, 116–19, 121, 123–24; *Tales of New England*, 253 n.5
Jonson, Ben, 43–44, 247 n.13; *Cynthia's Revels*, 247 n.14; *Pan's Anniversary*, 247 n.14
Jungermann. See *Daphnis and Chloe*: Translations

Kahn, Gus, "Chloe," 248 n.10
Knopf, Alfred, 172–73

Lamartine, Alphonse de, 93
Lawrence, D. H., 162, 190–91, 204–05; "England, My England," 207–08, Meynell family and, 258 n.5
Le Clézio, J.–M. G., *Le Chercheur d'or*, 227–28
LeGrice, Charles. See *Daphnis and Chloe*: Translations (LeGrice-Smith)
Le Guin, Ursula, *The Beginning Place*, 9, 240–42, 260 n.13
Léonard, Nicolas, *Idylles*, 71
Longfellow, Henry Wadsworth, *Evangeline*, 137
Longus. See *Daphnis and Chloe*
Louÿs, Pierre, *Chansons de Bilitis*, 227
love, 8–9, 18, 98–99, 101–02, 113, 121–22, 162, 243, n.3; homoerotic, 99, 230–31, 238
Lucretius, 250 n.8
Luis de León, Fray, 158

Maillol, Aristide, 17, 81, *82–83*
Mallock, William, *The New Paul and Virginia*, 85
Manzini, G. B. See *Daphnis and Chloe*: Translations
Mapson, Jo-Ann, *Hank and Chloe*, 239–40
Marie Antoinette, the "Hameau" of, 74, 95
Marie de France, "La Fresne," 25–27
Marivaux, Pierre de, *La Double inconstance*, 75
Marmontel, Jean François: "Annette et Lubin," 75; "La Bergère des Alpes," 6, 75, 248 n.11; *Essai sur les romans*, 75
marriage, 17, 22, 40
Marvell, Andrew, "Daphnis and Chloe" (poem), 53–57, 78
Melville, Herman, *Typee*, 10
Milton, John: *Comus*, 44, 60–62; and Gessner, 72; and Hardy, 169; *Paradise Lost*, 4, 59–65, 67, 78, 219; and Pardo Bazán, 156–57; and sex, 248 n.2
Mishima, Yukio: *The Sound of Waves*, 10, 24, 216, 222–26, 260 n.7; *Sun and Steel*, 225

Mistral, Frédéric, *Mirèio*, 104, 203
Montemayor, Jorge de, *Diana*, 29
Moore, George, 203–04, 258 n.3–4
mutuality, 8–9, 15–18, 23, 40, 64, 155, 197, 226, 236

narrator, of idyllic romance, 18, 23, 56–57, 86, 95, 139, 168, 216, 223
naturalism, literary, 7, 147, 151–52, 183; and British naturism, 161–62, 190, 202
nature: attitude toward, 23, 48–51, 67, 204, 241–42; imitation of, 13, 16–17, 21; and "nurture," 49, 144, 151–52, 164–65; peacefulness of, 7, 33, 123, 259 n.10
Nerval, Gérard de, *Sylvie*, 104, 106
Nicetas Eugenianos (Nikítas Evyenianós), *Drosilla and Charicles*, 27–28

Offenbach, Jacques, 74
Ogilvie, Elisabeth, *Waters on a Starry Night*, 133–34
Oklahoma! (musical), 192–93
Orleans, (Phillipe) Duke of, 67, 78
Orsini, Fulvio, 27

Pan, and Pan-figures, 12, 16–17, 46, 60, 97, 189, 193, 224
Pardo Bazán, Emilia, 135–36; *Apuntes sobre la nueva arte de escribir novelas*, 147; and Bernardin, 255 n.18; *La cuestión palpitante*, 147, 152; *La literatura francesa moderna*, 154, 158; *La madre Naturaleza*, 6–7, 10, 24, 99, 147–60, 252 n.29, 255 n.14, 255 n.17; and Milton, 63, 156–57; *Los pazos de Ulloa*, 24, 148; *Los poetas épicos cristianos*, 156; and Sand, 159; and Valera, 147, 153–54, 158
pastoral fiction, 42, 60, 92, 94, 120, 230, 247 n.11. See also idyllic romance; Theocritus; Virgil
Pastor Fidus (play), 31
pastourelle, 9–10, 31, 37, 40–41, 63, 148, 199, 236, 244 n.1
pathetic fallacy, in idyllic romance, 22, 90, 119, 128, 212, 224–25
Pérez de Ayala, Ramón: *A.M.D.G.*, 216; *Luna de miel, luna de hiel*, 13, 24, 143, 216–22, 259 n.1; and Valera, 259 n.2
Persephone, 209, 240
Phillipe, Duke of Orleans, 67, 78
Phillips, Katherine, 66

Plautus, *Rudens*, 12
Poliziano, Angelo, 28
Pope, Alexander, on Milton and Longus, 61, 66
primitivism, 201

Ramsay, Allan, *The Gentle Shepherd*, 10, 68–70, 73
Ravel, Maurice, 74
regionalism, and idyllic romance, 77, 94, 96, 104, 124–25, 133, 160, 167, 193–94, 197, 202, 207, 209, 213
Riggs, Lynn, *Green Grow the Lilacs*, 192–93, 208
romance, 22, 236, 244 n.7; and marriage, 8; medieval and Renaissance, 32, 53, 105, 216, 221, 242; in novels, 6–7, 66, 68, 103, 127, 145–47, 153, 168, 218, 223. See also Greek romances
romans champêtres, 93–105
Rousseau, Jean-Jacques, 31, 72, 74, 87

Sackville-West, Victoria, *Grey Wethers: A Romantic Novel*, 206–07
Saint Pierre. See Bernardin de St. Pierre
Sand, George, 93–103, 107, 165, 168, 233, 235, 251 n.14, 251 n.18; *François le champi*, 3, 96, 98–99; and Hardy, 168–69, 256 n.2; *Indiana*, 93–95; and Jewett, 122; *Les Maîtres mosaïstes*, 8; *Les Maîtres sonneurs*, 167; *La Mare au diable*, 96–97; *La Petite Fadette*, 3, 6, 9, 21, 24, 76, 93–105, 104–05, 237–38; *Promenades autour de mon village*, 122, 167; and Stowe, 109–10, 252 n.2
Sannazaro, J.: *Arcadia*, 29; piscatory eclogues of, 223
Sappho, 120, 189
Schiller, Friedrich, *Naive and Sentimental Poetry*, 4–5, 63–65, 73, 78, 153, 243 n.2
Scott, Sir Walter, *The Heart of Midlothian*, 194
second birth, 1, 47, 87, 104, 175, 178, 221, 224, 242
sexual knowledge, innate, 61, 248 n.2
"sexual symmetry," 8–9, 15–18, 23, 40, 64, 155, 197, 226, 236
Shakespeare, William: *As You Like It*, 1, 49–50, 118, 167; *Cymbeline*, 45–51, 99; *King Lear*, 195; *A Midsummer Night's Dream*, 44; *The Tempest*, 1, 10–11, 18–19, 45–51, 52–53, 107–09, 124, 174–75, 189, 199; *The Winter's Tale*, 10, 13, 21, 35, 45–51, 68–69, 260 n.8

Sidney, Sir Philip: *Apology for Poetry*, 45; *Arcadia*, 39–40, 66
Smith, Rev. Rowland. See *Daphnis and Chloe*: Translations (LeGrice-Smith)
Spenser, Edmund: and Chase, 130–31; *The Faerie Queene*, 19, 40–43, 56
Stacpoole, H. De Vere, 181–91, 257 n.7–10; *The Blue Lagoon*, 1, 162, 181–85, 227, 257 n.8; *The Garden of God*, 185–90; *Pools of Silence*, 190; *Street of the Flute Player*, 189; translation of *Sappho* by, 189
storms, in idyllic romance, 19–20, 47–48, 89–90, 92, 133, 176, 188, 224
Stowe, Harriet Beecher: *Dred: A Tale of the Great Dismal Swamp*, 2–3; and "idyllic," 2–3, 108; and Jewett, 116–19, 121, 123–24; *The Minister's Wooing*, 114; *The Pearl of Orr's Island*, 3, 18–19, 108–16, 122; and Sand, 3, 109–10; and *The Tempest*, 107–09

Tasso, Torquato, *Aminta*, 29–31, 42
Tchaikowski, P. I., 74
Theocritus, 1, 11–12, 19, 92, 125, 189–90, 199, 253 n.5
Thomson, James: and Gessner, 71; *The Seasons*, 67–71, 207
Thornley, George. See *Daphnis and Chloe*: Translations

Tilney, Edmund, *The Flower of Friendship*, 40
Trianon. *See* Marie Antoinette
Turner, Paul. See *Daphnis and Chloe*: Translations

Updike, John, *Brazil*, 9

Valera, Juan, *Pepita Jiménez*, 24, 135, 137–47. See also *Daphnis and Chloe*: Translations
Vian, Boris, *L'Ecume des jours*, 234
Villoison, J. B., 79
Virgil, 1, 29, 60, 92, 125, 199, 207

Wayne, John, 202
Webb, Mary, *Seven for a Secret*, 205–06
White, Patrick, *The Tree of Man*, 6
Wister, Owen, *The Virginian*, 192
wit, 52–78, 217–18, 220
Wordsworth, William, 77, 122, 159, 161, 204
Wright, Harold Bell: *Shepherd of the Hills*, 1, 6, 10, 198–203, 212, 257 n.2; *The Winning of Barbara Worth*, 199
Wroth, Mary, "Love's Victorie," 31

Zola, Emile, 147, 183; *La Faute de l'abbé Mouret*, 6, 106, 153, 252 n.29, 255 n.17; *La Joie de vivre*, 6, 103, 105